The Boundaries of the

The Boundaries of the Republic

Migrant Rights and the Limits of Universalism in France, 1918–1940

Mary Dewhurst Lewis

STANFORD UNIVERSITY PRESS

STANFORD, CALIFORNIA 2007

Stanford University Press
Stanford, California
© 2007 by Mary Dewhurst Lewis.

Printed in the United States of America on acid-free,
archival-quality paper.

Library of Congress Cataloging-in-Publication Data

Lewis, Mary Dewhurst.
The boundaries of the republic : migrant rights and the limits of universalism in
France, 1918–1940 / Mary Dewhurst Lewis.
p. cm.
Includes bibliographical references and index.
ISBN-13: 978-0-8047-5582-5 (cloth : alk. paper)
ISBN-13: 978-0-8047-5722-5 (pbk. : alk. paper)
1. France—Emigration and immigration—Government policy—History—20th
century. 2. Alien labor—Government policy—France—History—20th century.
3. Immigrants—Government policy—France—History—20th century. I. Title.

JV7933.L49 2007
325.4409'041—dc22   2006100236

Typeset by Westchester Book Group in 10/12 Sabon
Original Printing 2007
Publication assistance for this book was provided by
Harvard University.

In Memory of My Parents
Frederic Dewhurst Lewis, 1922–1989
Jane Spencer Lewis, 1927–1996

Contents

List of Illustrations

List of Tables

Preface

In 1928, my grandfather inscribed a copy of *America, Nation or Confusion*—his defense of racial quotas on individuals migrating to the United States—to my father, then a mere six years old: "To Freddy, who already knows that the flag must never touch the ground."[1] It was a fitting metaphor for his argument: America, like its flag, should not be "sullied." For him, our very democracy depended on it.

However distasteful I find my grandfather's reasoning, it exemplifies a problem inherent to democracies. All democracies face a "liberal paradox"—that fragile balance between their promotion of free movement and their constituencies' desires to limit who can move freely.[2] If no democracy is immune from the liberal paradox, none confronts it in exactly the same way. Unlike the United States, France never passed immigration quotas. To this day, French leaders suggest that discriminating between immigrants is anathema to the values of the one and indivisible republic. And yet, France faced some of the same tensions that rent American society at the time my grandfather wrote his book. As in the United States, these questions cut straight to the heart of France's political culture.

This book is about how French citizens and migrants dealt with those conflicts as they negotiated the latter's rights—and the limits to those rights—in the country that, in the 1930s, surpassed the United States in its rate of immigration. Because I am interested in the dynamics of inclusion and exclusion in democracies, this book focuses on the Third Republic, not on the authoritarian regime that followed it. If the republic's migration policies did in some ways lay the groundwork for exclusionary laws under the Vichy regime, this book insists on the historical contingency, rather than the inevitability, of these developments. This unpredictability should not give us less pause. Indeed, understanding the fragility of liberalism seems, today, to be an ever-more important task.

Cambridge, Massachusetts
April 2006

Sources and Acknowledgments

Whenever one conducts research in a foreign language, one comes across terms that simply cannot be translated. In this book, there are two words in particular that I have chosen to leave in the original French. The first is *refoulement*, a technical term literally meaning "pushing back" but in practice meaning an order to leave the country, short of formal expulsion. Because *refoulement* has such a precise meaning, I have left it, and related terms like the verb *refouler*, in French. International organizations concerned with refugees have done the same, as in when they refer to the "non-*refoulement*" clauses of the 1951 Geneva Convention on the Status of Refugees.[1] Similarly, I have found *sursis* (a suspension, or a stay, as in a suspended expulsion order) more precise than the available English translations. All translations throughout the text are my own, unless otherwise indicated. I have used underlining in the text to convey comments made on the original documents themselves. Readers should refer to the endnotes to see whether said markings were in the original typescript, or, as was more often the case, added in bluegrease pencil by an official reading the document. I am grateful to Stanford University Press for being willing to bring the archive to life in this way, which better conveys the back and forth negotiations over rights than would the standard italics. Throughout the book, names of migrants have been changed to protect their privacy, except in cases where the migrant was publicly active and well known.

Since I began this project, the conservator of the "contemporary" (post-1789) section of the Rhône departmental archives, Florence Beaume, has done a phenomenal job of cataloging previously uninventoried documents and of rationalizing the classifications of others. The work of Mme Beaume and her staff should be applauded as making research on immigration in the Lyon area much easier. As a result of their efforts, the "uninventoried expulsion files" (silo 1, travée 154 et suivantes, boxes 1–46) and the "uninventoried naturalization files" (silo 2, travée 285 et suivantes) I examined in the Archives Départementales du Rhône have since been reclassified under the Versement 829 W for the expulsions and 6 Mp 1047-1055 for the naturalizations. It would have been unwieldy, however, to verify how every file I examined had been reclassified. For this reason, I have left the original references in the notes. Similarly, the Rhône labor files (10 Mp) have also undergone considerable reclassification, which has involved splitting up documents formerly filed together. In the process, the filing system has become much more rational, but once again, for accuracy's sake, I have left the original references in the notes. The Archives Départementales des Bouches-du-Rhône also have been recataloging their collection for several years. This makes for frequently changing classifications. I have cited the classifications that were in use when I was there. However, many changes were in process, particularly between the 4 M series (Police) and the 1 M series (Cabinet du Préfet). Also, I looked at one set of dossiers, "Événements politiques étrangers Afrique du Nord 1927–39" (dossiers 1–3), that had not yet been cataloged. This collection, rather disturbingly, showed signs of pages having been cut out from reports. Special thanks to Mme Marie-Paule Blasini for helping me locate what of these documents remain.

The stories told in the following pages depend to a great extent on the special permission I obtained to look at closed files. For assistance in acquiring this permission, I would like to thank, at the French National Archives, its former director M. Alain Erlande-Brandenburg, as well as the archivists Mme Paule René-Bazin and Mme Claude Jullien. In departmental archives, thanks to Mme Arlette Playoust of the Bouches-du-Rhône archives and Mme Florence Beaume of the Rhône archives. The library at the Ministry of Social Affairs, Labor, and Solidarity includes a collection of uninventoried circulars issued during the interwar period. I would like to extend special thanks to Mme Martine Leblanc-Sauze for her extraordinary assistance in locating a particular circular in this collection after I had returned to the United States.

This book would not have been possible without financial assistance from many sources. I thank them all: the Graduate School of Arts and Sciences at New York University, the Remarque Institute for Advanced European Studies, the Fulbright Commission, the International Center for Advanced Studies at New York University, the American Historical Association, the Woodrow Wilson Post-Doctoral Fellowship Program (now, sadly, defunct), Smith College's Dean of Faculty, the Harvard University Faculty of Arts and Sciences Dean's Fund and Clark/Cooke Funds, the National Endowment for the Humanities, the American Council of Learned Societies, and the Institute for Advanced Study in Princeton. At Harvard, in addition to colleagues and the staff in the History Department, I would particularly like to thank Peter A. Hall and Jorge Domínguez, the former directors of the Center for European Studies and the Weatherhead Center for International Affairs, for supporting this project. Over the years I have spent on this book, I have greatly benefited from the reading and wisdom of friends and colleagues. I would like especially to thank Sandrine Bertaux, David Blackbourn, Vicki Caron, Herrick Chapman, Tita Chico, Alice Conklin, Frederick Cooper, Laura Lee Downs, Kirsten Fermaglich, Laura Levine Frader, Andy Gordon, Nancy Green, Patrice Higonnet, Paul Jankowski, Eric Jennings, Tony Judt, Michael Kimball, Michèle Lamont, Yves Lequin, Peggy Levitt, Amelia Lyons, Erez Manela, Gregory Mann, Terry Martin, Michael B. Miller, Leslie Page Moch, Gérard Noiriel, Molly Nolan, Clifford Rosenberg, Philippe Rygiel, Marty Schain, Jerrold Seigel, Dan Smail, Judith Surkis, and Patrick Weil. Thanks also go to David A.L. Levy for forwarding me one of the rare extant copies of his Oxford doctoral thesis. A few passages of Chapters 1 and 7 contain material also appearing in "The Strangeness of Foreigners: Policing Migration and Nation in Interwar Marseille," in *Race in France: Interdisciplinary Perspectives on the Politics of Difference,* eds. Herrick Chapman and Laura L. Frader (New York and London: Berghahn Books, 2004). Thanks to Marion Berghahn for granting permission to use this material.

Finally, my family has been an extraordinary source of inspiration and support throughout this project. To my brother, Griff, my parents-in-law, Ann and John, and especially to my husband, Peter Dizikes, I extend my deepest gratitude and love.

The Boundaries of the Republic

Introduction

Boris M. and Bruno G. were among the nearly quarter of a million foreign migrants who legally entered France with work contracts in 1923.[1] Boris came from Russia and had been evacuated from Sebastopol by French authorities after the Bolsheviks established their rule following several years of civil war. Bruno, an Italian, left his wife behind in Rome and departed for France to seek a more reliable source of income.

France had relied on foreigners to supplement its native workforce since the middle of the nineteenth century. But the tide of migration that brought Bruno and Boris to France was unprecedented in size. In 20 years, the country's foreign population almost tripled, from just over a million to nearly three million, surpassing the United States' rate of foreign population growth in 1931, a demographic shift unknown in other European nations before the Second World War.[2] Indeed, no modern European democracy has faced the challenges posed by mass immigration earlier or more persistently than has France. This book is about how French citizens and migrants confronted the conflicts arising from this encounter as they negotiated migrants' rights and their limits. It uncovers the hidden history of inequality that lay behind the official egalitarianism of the French Third Republic. In so doing, it exposes the origins of France's contemporary immigration policy.

Admitted legally in 1923, Boris M. and Bruno G. also figured among the more than 93,000 foreigners who were expelled by order of the Interior Ministry between 1919 and 1933.[3] Bruno was expelled in 1924, Boris in 1932—both for the same reason: vagrancy. However, by the spring of 1936, neither had left. Authorities recognized Bruno G.'s continued residence in France, suspending his expulsion order several times before finally rescinding it for good in July 1936. In September of that same year, Boris M. was imprisoned for failing to honor his expulsion order; this was at least the seventh time since 1932 that he had been incarcerated for that reason. In 1941, Boris began a year long sentence for this infraction; finally, later that same year, officials instead placed him under a form of house arrest, ordering him to live in the rural district outside of Arles. While Bruno G. remained in France through at least the 1950s, we have no trace of Boris M. after 1941.

These cases and thousands like them raise unaddressed historical questions. How could expelled migrants remain in France? Why, given that the two men were expelled for identical infractions of the French penal code, was Boris M. condemned to a life of insecurity and illegality while Bruno G. repeatedly earned legal recognition of his residency? What accounted for changes in their rights over time? How could such inequalities in treatment develop in a nation that officially eschewed discrimination as anathema to the values of its one and indivisible republic? Discovering the answers to such questions requires probing beneath the formal structure of immigration law to reconstruct how rights were put into practice. Doing so reveals that the republic was never monolithic in its incorporation of immigrants. It was neither wholly inclusive nor entirely exclusive, and it was certainly not egalitarian.

My purpose in entitling this book *The Boundaries of the Republic* is threefold. First, I wish to emphasize the ways in which the universalism of the republic was bounded. Second, the term "boundaries" calls attention to the many other divisions—diplomatic, political, administrative, or social—that helped to draw the borderline between inclusion and exclusion at any one time and for any particular migrant. Migrant rights turned not only on legal boundaries but also on a whole array of relationships that erected or broke down obstacles to exercising them. Together these factors could mean the difference between social security and destitution, personal freedom and imprisonment, or sustaining a life in France and being forced to leave. Third, in choosing to use the plural— "boundaries," not "boundary"—I suggest that the republic's limits were not fixed or stable but fungible. Migrants' rights were not uniform; they expanded and contracted, fluctuating from person to person, migrant group to migrant group, city to city, and year to year. Indeed, drawing on Charles Tilly, one might say that migrants' "citizenship" ranged from thin, "when it entail[ed] few transactions, rights and obligations," to thick, "where it occupie[d] a significant share of all transactions, rights, and obligations sustained by state agents and between people living under their jurisdiction."[4] Moreover, the arrangements forming the bases of rights changed over time. Rights once regarded as thick could seem to disappear into thin air.

No single word in French captures the set of rights organized around the assumption of temporary migration the way that "guest worker" or "*gastarbeiter*" does in English or German. Nonetheless, in the wake of the First World War, France established Europe's first "guest-worker" regime in all but name. In the 1920s, France's guest-worker system, like all subsequent ones, linked residency rights to labor contracts. During the depression, however, this rights regime was inverted, and the right to work came increasingly to depend on residency rights. A temporary migration policy had led to an immigration regime, premised on the selective incorporation of permanent settlers. Throughout this book, the terms "migration" or "migrant" and "immigration" or "immigrant" denote this change in status.

Because the shift from migration to immigration regime occurred in practice before it was recognized by policy, it has been disregarded by most historians. This book redresses that neglect. Although policy remained outwardly committed to the guest-worker model, in practice, France jettisoned its labor migration regime in the 1930s for a politics of population building. Instead of continuing to favor the temporary residency of single male migrants, authorities now gave special privileges to immigrants who had established families in France and could prove long-term ties there. As important as this transformation was, it was uneven and impermanent. Even those who emerged as the most protected of France's immigrants discovered this to their dismay, as hysteria over national security once again transformed migrant rights on the eve of the Second World War. By reconstructing this history, I shed new light on the promise of the French Third Republic in its final two decades, the inequalities it engendered, and the legacies left by its uneven rights arrangements.

FRANCE, THE LIBERAL PARADOX, AND AN ILLIBERAL ERA

Among European countries, France was the first to experience a paradox most democratic capitalist societies now confront. If democratic culture and free-enterprise economies oblige liberal societies to maintain relatively open borders, states pursue openness only to the extent consistent with maintaining domestic political and economic stability.[5] This generally requires a greater degree of what Max Weber called "social closure" than that allowed in a purely free market economy.[6] France precociously developed forms of policing aimed to enforce that closure.[7]

France's liberal paradox presented a particularly acute problem in the two decades following the First World War because it was precisely at this time that the question of migrant rights posed its greatest challenge yet to

French society. Although France survived the war with its political system intact, in many respects its victory was a Pyrrhic one. Fought to a great extent on French soil, the war devastated huge portions of the Northeast and dramatically reduced agricultural and industrial production. Proportionately, France lost more men than any of the other Western-front belligerents. As migrants flowed into France to fill the jobs left by some 1.5 million dead and at least another million disabled soldiers, they alternately served as unwelcome reminders of France's weaknesses as a nation and as beacons of hope for its future. How permanent a place they would occupy in that future, however, was a matter of great debate.

At a minimum, migrants proved essential to France's punctual postwar reconstruction needs. But other factors also encouraged immigration. The war and its settlements triggered the twentieth century's first refugee crisis, and France emerged from the war as the Western democracy with the fewest barriers to immigration.[8] In continental Europe, France stood out as one of the few countries where immigration was more significant than emigration.

Even so, France's openness to migration was hardly unconditional. In the 1920s, the union movement aimed to prevent employers from using migrants to undercut domestic wages. During the depression, citizens placed new pressures on their democratic representatives to constrain migrant rights. Quotas reduced the percentage of foreigners allowed to work in most industries, restrictions were placed on foreigners practicing medicine and law, and eventually merchants and artisans also demanded protection of their professions from competition by migrants. As French citizens' demands engendered new constraints on economic liberalism, the dimming of political liberalism's prospects in Europe sent new waves of refugees toward France.[9] As xenophobia in France mounted, authorities faced the dilemma of limiting immigration while defending a political culture based on liberal principles.

Two aspects of French political life rendered this task especially confounding. First, France had plenty of homegrown antiliberals. Fascist-style leagues questioned the legitimacy of parliamentary democracy and, in 1934, came as close as they ever would to bringing down the republic. Along with the emergence of the Communist Party on the Left, the advent of rightist leagues contributed to the polarization of politics. Migrants were often caught in their crossfire. Second was the question of whether or how colonialism and liberal democracy could be squared with each other. Although these two forces had always been in tension, the advent of migration from the empire brought these issues "home" in new ways.

The France that welcomed tens of thousands of foreign migrants each year after the war was in need of total reconstruction—physical, demographic, and moral. It was a republic whose liberalism was contested from within and without and a nation that clung desperately to its colonies even as it faced mounting resistance inside them. Immigration cut to the heart of each of the problems facing France: Reconstruction was impossible without importing labor; the use of police power vis-à-vis migrants often challenged liberal principles; and if rights were extended to migrants from the empire, the very basis of imperialism might be threatened. State officials, from the petty bureaucrats responsible for issuing identification cards in municipal offices to the heads of all the major ministries in Paris, juggled, in one way or another, these often conflicting interests, an endeavor rendered all the more difficult by the frequent shuffling of governments.[10] Migrants, in turn, had to respond to—and find ways to exploit—these tensions in order to make lives for themselves in France.

BETWEEN POLICY AND PRACTICE

Invented piecemeal during and immediately following the First World War, French guest-worker regulations were crafted to ensure that migrants would work only where the labor market most needed them and that they would return home once their services were no longer required. If all had operated as planned, Bruno G. would have returned to Italy in 1924 rather than wander around Greater Lyon until he was arrested. And Boris M. would have returned home as well, even though he regarded himself as a political refugee. Should he have wanted to leave France, there were few if any countries, including the Soviet Union, that would have accepted him as a legal migrant.[11]

In fact, however, very little in the lives of Bruno G. and Boris M. followed the bureaucratic plan for regulating immigration that had been drawn up by French authorities since the conclusion of the war. Official Labor Ministry policy held that foreign workers were "more easily ready for changes in region, and even in profession," than were the French, who were "constrained by their families, their homes, or who, even if they are single, have a harder time leaving the environment where they have often lived for many years."[12] Authorities prized foreign workers precisely because the former believed that they could "place them in other regions or professions or, if necessary, favor repatriation" when work became scarce.[13] Yet the fact that neither Bruno nor Boris left the country after losing his job suggests that both men were incorporated, however imperfectly, into the society beyond the walls of the factories that employed them. Labor officials had called for workers, but, to invoke an oft-quoted aphorism, human beings had come instead.[14]

The trajectories of Bruno G. and Boris M. do not merely prove that the French state had imperfect control over immigration. They also illustrate the degree to which the impact of state control was felt differently across space, over time, and between migrants of different origins. To be sure, France developed the "largest, most sophisticated immigration service anywhere in the world"—in Paris.[15] But in the provinces, police personnel numbered in the hundreds rather than the tens of thousands.[16] Moreover, provincial archives offer a wealth of information not available in the capital. Thanks to the special access I was granted to look at closed records, I have been able to reconstruct, as well as compare, the quotidian decisions of individual migrants and state agents. This approach allows for a more nuanced understanding of France's immigration history.

At first glance, nothing suggests that Bruno and Boris would encounter such different fates. They were about the same age upon arrival (31 and 34), were accompanied by no family, and had been legally admitted to work in France; the only feature distinguishing them was nationality. Officially, migrants of all nationalities faced identical controls: Even refugees were required to have valid labor contracts if they intended to work in France, and they were no more exempt from French laws on foreign-resident identification cards than were other foreigners. The fact that both men lost their jobs also first appears to explain little, since neither left the country as a result. If anything, one might think that Bruno G., who lost his job rather quickly, would have faced more troubles than did Boris M., who did not confront sustained unemployment until the depression. Already by mid-1924, Bruno was looking for work when he was stopped in Oullins, a suburb of Lyon, for vagrancy. He was expelled on 23 July 1924, barely seven months after his admission to the country had first been approved.

Upon closer examination, however, it becomes clear that losing a job in Lyon's booming industrial suburbs in 1924 did not impinge on the residency rights of migrants in the same way that losing regular work on Marseille's docks did in the 1930s. In the 1920s, as Chapter 1 shows, Lyon police were not particularly concerned by unemployment; instead, they were preoccupied with foreigners' militancy in the workplace. Perhaps this was why they made little effort to find Bruno until the spring of 1926, when they first notified him of his expulsion, almost two years after it was ordered. By that time, however, Bruno had been working at the Union Mutuelle des Propriétaires Lyonnais (UM), most likely in construction, for a year and a half. Upon learning of Bruno's expulsion, UM offered him an official contract for a year, and Bruno employed a lawyer, Jean Kreher, to intervene on his behalf to secure legal residency. Following the recommendation of Lyon's chief of police, the Interior Ministry approved a three-month suspension (*sursis*) of his expulsion; subsequently, Bruno succeeded in repeatedly renewing his *sursis*. Here, guest-worker regulations proved malleable. UM initially had disregarded them altogether by hiring Bruno without a contract, and then, at precisely the moment that Bruno's illegal residency in the country was discovered, it drew on guest-worker arrangements to help legalize Bruno's situation, offering him a valid contract.

Bruno was fortunate in his timing. He lost his job before the depression hit France and before the related attack on foreign employment. Later, when dramatic unemployment plagued Lyon's industries, Rhône officials spearheaded a crackdown on foreigners, and Bruno's case exemplified their shifting priorities. Authorities complained that he was still working at UM "while the number of French who are unemployed is still very high in Greater Lyon." Recommending reexpulsion, the prefect placed Bruno within the guest-worker model, calling attention to his lack of ties in France, exemplified by the fact that "his wife still resides in Italy." For the central government, however, Bruno's temporary status was not in itself a problem as long as he remained employed.[17] Thanks in part to turf wars between the central ministry and its local representatives, Bruno continued to receive *sursis,* which placed him in the position to request the annulment of his expulsion order two years later.

By contrast, Boris M.'s timing was less propitious, since he lost his job as thousands of others did. Arrested between stints as a stevedore in Marseille in 1932, Boris was notified of his expulsion on 10 August, the very day the French parliament passed a new law establishing quotas on foreign employment. What was more, Boris' arrest had come on Marseille's docks, where police were particularly uncompromising toward foreigners they regarded as transients. Had he worked in a different profession, or lived in a different neighborhood, or even had an official address, he might have found police more accommodating, as they so often were to foreigners who could show that they were respected in their community or had set down lasting roots. Chapter 1 explains the stratification of rights between Marseille's seemingly settled immigrants and its more unsettled migrants. Boris fell into this latter category. He had no regular residence in Marseille, even though he had worked there on and off since 1931, when he had been laid off from an industrial job in nearby Salins-de-Giraud. Like many others down on their luck, he worked on the docks; this meant that he circulated in the city center, where police surveillance was intense. Unable to extricate himself from this precarious existence, Boris was repeatedly incarcerated for failing to obey the expulsion order.

Having few ties in Marseille, Boris had not established many elsewhere in France either. When Bruno G. lost his first job, he stayed in the Lyon area and, apparently, was well-enough connected to know that Jean Kreher took on migrants' cases.[18] When his expulsion was rescinded, he had been working at the same company for 12 years. Boris' work history, by contrast, had been much more varied. One account had him changing jobs five times in six years and living in four different parts of France, including Corsica, before returning to mainland France. What the French had once prized in migrants—mobility—was now a liability.

Not only social associations but also international relations affected Boris' plight. After serving several prison sentences for failing to leave the country, he wrote to the Bouches-du-Rhône prefect, pointing out that as a refugee without papers, he was welcome in no other country. Boris' status as a refugee had other important effects on his welfare. Until 1937, Russians were barred from receiving unemployment assistance in Marseille, on the basis that only foreigners whose countries had signed reciprocity treaties with France were eligible. Policies such as these were commonplace in France's decentralized welfare state and became increasingly so as the depression took its toll on local budgets. Because of this, a class of what I call most-favored foreigners—those whose countries of origin signed guest-worker arrangements with France—often gained access to social rights. It was only after 1936, when the Popular Front ratified the 1933 Geneva Convention, that Marseille and other cities reluctantly began including Russians and Armenians on their unemployment rolls. Still others continued to lack most-favored-nation status and thereby fell outside the boundaries of social rights.

The election of the Center-Left Popular Front coalition seemed at first to change Boris' fortune, as it relaxed enforcement of hard-line immigration policies put into place by the Center-Right governments that preceded it. Like Bruno G. had years earlier, Boris now benefited from a three-month suspension of his expulsion order. For almost two years, he managed to get the suspension renewed. By the time the Popular Front coalition collapsed in 1938, however, his unemployment was not just occasional but chronic, and he resorted to living in shelters and eking out a living as a ragpicker. Temporary approvals of his residency in France could neither guarantee him work nor find him a place to live. His administrative grace ran out, the prison sentences resumed, and the time he spent incarcerated grew longer, as the decree laws of May 1938 mandated a minimum sentence of six months to three years for any infraction of expulsion.

Bruno G. and Boris M. had arrived in France the same year, but thereafter their trajectories diverged. Where the two men lived and how often they moved, where they had come from and whom they knew, what companies they worked for and when they lost their jobs—all these factors contributed to making Boris more of a stranger in France by the late 1930s than was Bruno. Except for a brief reprieve under the Popular Front, Boris became less—rather than more—secure over time. Bruno's trajectory was quite the opposite: He almost immediately lost his job and was expelled, but he then earned formal recognition of his residence after several years. This outcome, however, was not preordained: Police officials in Lyon clearly thought that Bruno did not belong in 1934, and Marseille officials were willing to give Boris a chance to prove he did in 1936, albeit after first incarcerating him at least seven times. Bruno and Boris encountered shifting boundaries to inclusion in the republic. Their rights ebbed and flowed.

Accounting for such divergences demands a different way of studying immigration. If some scholars of immigration have focused on the processes of "assimilation," "integration," or "adaptation" that migrants allegedly go through, others have turned their attention to cultural retention or even culture clashes.[19] Still others have centered their inquiries on identification and control, using immigration as a lens into the nature of the modern state, the distinction between democracy and totalitarianism, and, more specifically, the connections between the Third Republic and Vichy France.[20] By focusing on rights, this book exposes a realm of experience and historical contingency left largely obscure by previous scholarship.

BETWEEN PARIS AND THE PROVINCES

Because immigration policy and everyday experience heretofore have been analyzed independently of each other, our understanding of the place that immigration occupies in French history remains incomplete. Scholars focusing on regulatory regimes have assumed a generally straightforward relationship between legal prescriptions and the functioning of society, albeit often reaching vastly different conclusions in so doing. These scholars sometimes acknowledge but rarely analyze the uneven application of immigration policy.[21] Meanwhile, most work that considers the human drama of migration tends to focus either on a particular ethnic group or on a single region.[22] Rather than isolate a single place or a particular national or ethnic group, or assume that Paris can stand in for France, I reconstruct the divergent life trajectories of diverse migrants in the two largest cities outside Paris, adopting an approach that is both locally focused and comparative in perspective.

Focusing on Marseille and Lyon provides illuminating detail on the everyday lives of migrants. Readers are transported to the very places where migrants confronted and contested the limits of their rights, where employers hired and fired them, and where local officials struggled to maintain authority and social peace. Already large cosmopolitan cities before the First World War, Lyon and Marseille became urban metropolises during the period under study here. Home to many industries and commercial interests, cities such as Lyon and Marseille attracted migrants "like moths to light."[23] Compared to their counterparts living in France's agricultural regions, company towns, or mono-industrial areas, migrants in Lyon and Marseille encountered a wide range of employment opportunities. Each city also attracted similar groups of migrants: Italians, Spanish, Armenians, Russians, and North Africans in the 1920s, as well as Jewish migrants from Germany and other Central European countries in the 1930s.[24] These similarities make for a compelling comparison between the cities.

Yet the differences between the two cities also allow us to better discern the bases on which migrants claimed rights, as well as how these shifted across space and over time. Marseille and Lyon were two of only a handful of cities whose police forces fell under central state authority, but police centralization turned out to mean very different things in each place. Differences in urban geography and infrastructure also are brought into relief by virtue of comparison, as are contrasting patterns in labor, economic, and political relations. The postwar guest-worker system meant one thing in Lyon, where migrants staffed large-scale around-the-clock production floors in capital-intensive firms, and quite another in Marseille, where migrants facilitated the labor flexibility favored by the seasonal nature of the city's commercial shipping and manufacturing cycle. In turn, the cities experienced economic crises at different times and in distinct ways.

Combining this local focus with a comparative approach illuminates two dimensions of the stratification of migrant rights. First, comparison demonstrates how national policies were modified locally in two cities of critical importance to French economic and political life. Second, it identifies the uneven effects of policy on three different types of migrants—labor migrants, stateless refugees, and colonial subjects—whose histories are often studied separately.

Moreover, the comparative approach reveals the relationship of the local to the national in the foundation of migrant rights. Indeed, France's immigration policy was not simply implemented locally but in important respects constructed locally—through the interplay of national expectations and conditions on the ground. Often, migrant rights developed dialectically, as central authorities placed limits on migrants' civil liberties and social rights, migrants tested these limits, local officials responded, and national authorities in turn reacted to decisions made at the local level. Migrants' abilities to exploit this dynamic were uneven, not to mention ephemeral, as the late 1930s proved. The same factors that opened the doors of the republic in some circumstances helped close them in others.

Complementing the book's local focus and comparative approach is a broader perspective that places local communities within patterns of regional, national, and transnational exchange. After all, immigration history is never merely about where migrants arrive; it is also about the places from which they come. And while immigration policy is an expression of national sovereignty, state sovereignty is not exercised in a vacuum. This was especially the case in Europe in the aftermath of the Great War, when borders shifted, populations were displaced, new democracies and novel forms of dictatorship emerged, relations between metropoles and colonies were realigned, and alliances were brokered and broken. This book shows the effects of Europe's changing political landscape by situating local-level negotiations over migrant rights within these broader developments. Even the most locally based policy decisions regarding social rights often drew on inequalities engendered by the postwar world order. In this sense, as well, rights were contingent. As international and imperial relations shifted over the course of the interwar period, so too did their impact on migrant rights at the local level.

To show that migrant rights depended on local, national, imperial, and international relationships, I have drawn on a broad array of primary and secondary materials, ranging from local police, employment, and welfare records to parliamentary debates, central government memoranda, diplomatic correspondence, and more. Exploiting sources of such depth and breadth, I show that rights did not exist as stable abstractions; rather, they depended on the way economic conditions, social connections, political pressures, bureaucratic disputes, international affairs, and imperial relations combined to shape, and eventually alter, their form both within and beyond the law.

The materials contained in these archives were highly mediated. Migrants' letters to authorities, for instance, told stories, and sometimes their narratives were rather formulaic. Yet migrants were not the only ones crafting stories about their lives as they negotiated the extent or limit of their rights. State officials, too, shaped the way they told a migrant's life story in accordance with their own expectations—of what their job was, how their superiors might respond, or how they understood the "national interest." In drawing on such sources, I have not seen my role as deciding which version is "true," although I sometimes point out contradictions or differences in emphasis, and there are some matters that are less open to interpretation than others. Rather, I am more interested in understanding the interactions that are revealed through such exchanges, since these produced, or in turn curtailed, migrant rights.[25]

By demonstrating that migrant rights depended on contingent relationships, this book mounts a double challenge to existing scholarship. First, historicizing the practice of migrant rights casts doubt on the French myth of republican citizenship and offers an alternative understanding of immigration's importance in twentieth-century French life. Second, it suggests the limits of more general social-scientific arguments regarding the relationship between immigration policy and national sovereignty.

Proponents of the French myth of republican citizenship generally contrast an "assimilationist" and "universalist" French system of immigrant integration to one of two alternative approaches characterized either as "Anglo-American" (or, sometimes, "Anglo-Saxon") pluralism or "restrictive" German "differentialism."[26] These contrasts often are more prescriptive than descriptive.

Frequently depicted as timeless, the republican model of citizenship in fact developed in response to recent historical events, especially the rising popularity in the 1980s of Jean-Marie Le Pen, the leader of France's extreme-Right anti-immigrant party, the National Front.[27] In this context, French scholars and public officials tried to best Le Pen at his own game—defending French identity. Casting Le Pen's rhetoric as fundamentally un-French, they defined France as a "universal nation of equal and free citizens."[28] This rhetorical move not only emphasized citizens' equality before the law; it also insisted on the equal opportunity of immigrants to become French. If the French republic excludes foreigners, the argument goes, it does so by treating them uniformly.

As a powerful ideal, the republican model should not be discounted. It dates to the very foundations of French republicanism and concerns many aspects of life in France beyond the question of immigration. As the French sought to remake their polity following violent revolutionary upheaval in 1789, they set about eliminating the Old Regime's system of unequal rights and privileges. Provinces of enormous range in size were cut up and replaced by departments, uniform in dimension, each with equal standing vis-à-vis the capital. Feudal privileges were abolished, as were exemptions from taxation for the nobility. Jews were granted citizenship, in order that they might not constitute "an Order in the state."[29] Efforts were made to root out provincial languages, so that no barriers to understanding would come between the nation's citizens. Eventually, under the First Republic, the Jacobins instituted a new form of measurement—metrics—hoping to forge a citizenry with a common understanding of space. Even slavery in the colonies was, briefly, abolished. Of course, efforts to make the republic one and indivisible sometimes became excessive, as under the Terror, when differences between citizens fed accusations of treason and "enemies of the republic" were exiled or executed.

Still, Jacobinism, as this centralizing and homogenizing tendency has since been known, has had a powerful impact on relations between the capital and the periphery, and between the nation and its citizens. It is the legacy of Jacobinism that best explains why a plan to devolve certain legislative rights to Corsica was declared unconstitutional in January 2002 by France's constitutional council. The same penchant for eschewing legal boundaries between citizens explains the furor that ensued when the demographer Michèle Tribalat suggested in the 1990s that some form of ethnicity be traced in the French census.[30] Traditions of universalism were also invoked repeatedly in parliamentary debates leading to the legislature's overwhelming support for a 2004 ban on the wearing of religious symbols in French public schools; their authorization, legislators argued, would be tantamount to officially recognizing ethnic or religious difference.[31] And the Jacobin heritage also helps explain why the suggestion made by Nicolas Sarkozy, as leader of the majority party in parliament, that France consider reopening its borders to legal labor migration through a system of "quotas" for certain professions and nationalities, has raised hackles, including within his own party: The president of the National Assembly, Jean-Louis Debré, condemned quotas for foreigners as "divisive" in January 2005 and even suggested that the proposition risked provoking a "regime crisis." Sarkozy has since ceased using the word "quota," but his continued advocacy for selection remains controversial.[32]

The Jacobin legacy also has had an enormous impact on scholarship. Ever since Aléxis de Tocqueville observed that administrative centralization, absent in America but entrenched in France, "accustoms people to ignore their own wills completely and constantly and to obey, not a single order on a single occasion, but always and in every way," scholars have analyzed French society through the operations of its central state.[33] In focusing on the ways state centralization has "blocked" French society, however, scholars have underestimated both the ability of society to influence policy and the extent to which society and the state have changed over time.[34]

Scholarship in other domains of French history offers fruitful ways of rethinking state-society relations. Peter Sahlins argues that state and nation alike were built on France's periphery as much as from its center. Caroline Ford examines the new forms of political mobilization that resulted from backlash against state-sponsored secularization efforts. Isser Woloch's study of the postrevolutionary civic order confirms the importance of administrative centralization to French political culture and social life, while showing that centralization emerged from improvisation and had unintended consequences. Philip Nord argues that civil society in mid-nineteenth-century France was republicanized before the state, and this explained how republicanism mounted a viable challenge to Napoléon III's empire, resulting in modern Europe's longest-lived republic.[35] A burgeoning field of scholarship also tests the republic's claims to universalism by examining the varying degrees of exception that prevailed in France's empire.[36] For all the centrality of immigration to contemporary republican rhetoric, its historical study remains oddly cut off from such insights regarding the nature and contradictions of French civic and political life.

I share with these historians a refusal to reify the state or the republic and an attention to the sources of incremental change. In so doing, I avoid the rather top-down outlook of the prevailing scholarship on immigration and argue for an important shift that cannot be discerned, let alone explained, in the standard state-centered approaches to immigration. Regulations developed by central state authorities to manage France's immigrant populations were altered in the face of local realities that differed considerably from expectations. As a result, through improvisation and negotiation, local authorities and immigrants established boundaries of inclusion and exclusion along quite different lines than those intended by state policy. Over time, this cycle of confrontation and accommodation led to policy changes at the center.

This dialectic brings me to the second challenge mounted by this book. Scholars now generally agree that controlling immigration is an exercise of sovereignty.[37] However, social scientists tend to reach one of two flawed conclusions by proceeding from this assumption. Either they assume that states largely succeed in exercising sovereignty by implementing immigration regulations, or they take the expansion of migrant rights to reflect the limits of state sovereignty in a globalizing world. In fact, policing migration never has amounted to a straightforward assertion of sovereignty directed evenly at all foreigners by authorities protecting a clearly identifiable national interest. Rather, that interest was defined and redefined in part through negotiations at many levels of social exchange—in diplomatic affairs, through the legislative process, within the state bureaucracy, at the workplace or union hall, and on the street.

Nor does the expansion of migrant rights mean, ipso facto, that state sovereignty is compromised. Recent work on immigration to and within

Europe has highlighted the way suprastate integration, globalization, and the development of international human rights law have allowed foreign residents of many Western European countries to acquire substantial civil, social, and sometimes even political rights despite their lack of formal citizenship.[38] Historically, migrant rights have not followed the linear progression suggested by these scholars. Furthermore, negotiations for transnational rights have just as often confirmed as they have called into question the power of the nation-state system.

THE INTERWAR ORIGINS OF MIGRANT RIGHTS

The Boundaries of the Republic is organized both chronologically and thematically. Chronologically, it follows migrant life from the immediate aftermath of the First World War, through the depression and the rise of the Popular Front government in 1936, to the domestic and international crises of the late 1930s. Thematically, it discusses the development of four "rights regimes": the foundation of France's guest-worker system, the challenge presented to it by claims made on social rights during the depression, its reconfiguration in the mid-1930s as family connections and rootedness in France formed new bases of rights, and finally the unraveling of this new rights regime in the face of a national security crisis.

Chapter 1 focuses on the arrival after the First World War of migrants from regions as varied as Italy, Spain, Armenia, Russia, and North Africa and explains their subsequently uneven success in securing labor rights, social entitlements, and civil liberties during the 1920s. Chapters 2 and 3 follow the lives of the same migrants as full employment gave way to mass unemployment in the 1930s, leading migrants to seek social security outside of work, thereby challenging the premises of the guest-worker system. Chapter 4 explains how the guest-worker model, strained by uneven implementation in the 1920s and early 1930s, collapsed in the mid-1930s as central authorities' efforts to enforce it more strictly encountered practical impediments. Although guest-worker policy remained officially intact, authorities now recognized a growing number of exceptions to it, indirectly establishing new policies that selectively incorporated some migrants based on a new calculus of privilege and prejudice. Chapters 5 and 6 bring these developments into relief by considering the special cases of refugees and colonial subjects. The final chapter shows how this ever-changing balance between inclusion and exclusion contributed to the confusion that prevailed on the eve of war about what role immigrants should play in France, and therefore what rights they should have. As state agents desperately tried to balance xenophobic pressures against migrants' utility as soldiers, French immigration policy reached new levels of incoherence. Within these broad trends, migrants' rights remained contingent on a host of factors ranging from local social relations to national politics to international affairs, and dependent on the choices made by both state agents and migrants under the constraint of these shifting relationships.

Then as now, incorporation into French public life did not turn on the blind application of republican principles that abstracted individuals from their social particularities. Rather, it depended very much on social relationships that were mobilized to claim or defend rights. Interwar France was more inclusive of migrants than a simple glance at legal constructs would suggest. Migrants were not merely "guests" who could be asked to leave: Despite their legal vulnerability, they often succeeded in invoking rights that gave them some staying power. Yet at the same time, the rights migrants acquired were not only unevenly distributed but also fragile, for a combination of social and legal factors made them more difficult to acquire and sustain for some migrants than for others. Migrant rights were stratified in practice, if not always in the letter of the law. For some migrants, this fragility had always been obvious. For others, their very success in negotiating rights had given them a confidence that was rudely shaken only as the threat of war loomed. To understand this stratification in time and change over time, let us begin where Boris and Bruno did—at work.

CHAPTER ONE

Workers of the World Claim Rights

The Origins and Limitations
of France's Guest-Worker Regime

The rightless illegal migrant is the dream-worker for many
employers, and the nightmare of the labor movement.[1]

During the same years that working-class Europeans arrived en masse on
the shores of the United States, many also made the shorter trip to
France's mines, factories, and farms. Migration's impact on labor conditions was disputed almost from the beginning. The arrival of Belgian
strikebreakers in the mythical French mining village of Montsou served
as the turning point in Émile Zola's epic novel *Germinal,* set during the
Second Empire.[2] In the South, anti-immigrant violence erupted several
times in the 1880s and 1890s, the worst of which, at Aigues Mortes
(1893), caused at least eight deaths and some 50 injuries.[3] The conflicts
were not always about wages. Labor organizations also complained that
employers favored foreign workers because their work would not be interrupted by military service. Since lawmakers were gravely concerned
about the size of the military, less than two decades after the disastrous
end to the Franco-Prussian War, organized labor's concerns dovetailed
with their own agenda. A liberalized nationality law, passed in 1889, established the legal principles that serve as the foundation of citizenship
rights in today's France.[4]

At the same time that the republic eased access to citizenship, it invested nationality with new meaning, creating a legal opposition between
citizens and foreigners through various forms of social legislation.[5] This
trend was already well developed when the First World War intensified
both demand for migrant workers and state involvement in the economy.

For the first time in French history, the government became actively involved in labor recruitment, bringing in nearly 440,000 workers for the war economy.[6]

As they had been for the war economy, migrant workers also became vital to postwar rebuilding. Thus, war and reconstruction were the dual catalysts for new policies and practices of labor recruitment, control of migrants, and adjudication of rights. These policies and practices involved state bureaucrats, employers, unions, police, and migrants in negotiations that simultaneously engaged international, national, and local relationships. Of course, all these actors experienced such overlapping relationships as intertwined. Nonetheless, by way of introduction, I have unraveled the fabric of migrant life and will proceed thread by thread. I begin at the war's end, with utopian efforts to establish equal rights among all "workers of the world." These objectives were quickly undermined in practice, as some migrants acquired most-favored status in the newly established guest-worker system. While most-favored foreigners gained facilitated access to residency and social rights, others were comparatively disadvantaged by this new politics of protection. Already distinguished by their origins, migrants also enjoyed different rights according to their destinations, since variations in economic cycles, urban geography, and social life, as well as policing practices, affected the manner in which rights were put into practice. The final section of this chapter shows the effect that curtailed civil liberties had upon migrants' participation in public life, and the chapter concludes by considering how migrants weighed their various rights against the risks of exercising them.

WORKERS OF THE WORLD

Perhaps paradoxically, the total war between nations helped to produce a new form of labor internationalism. Under Léon Jouhaux's leadership, the Conféderation Générale du Travail (CGT) put aside anarcho-syndicalism for a coordinated effort among employers, labor, and the state in the interest of production. According to the CGT's vision for the postwar world, this "tripartism" would prevail throughout Europe, ensuring that high wages and equal working conditions could be maintained, even as migrant workers filled in gaps in the French labor force.

The same sort of optimism had spawned calls for universal labor laws to be written into the peace treaties. If disputes between nations would henceforth be settled through arbitration, not war, perhaps arbitration could end acrimonious industrial relations as well.[7] The CGT and labor leaders across Europe who embraced what John Horne has called "international labour reformism" believed in good faith that the war had permanently changed industrial relations.[8] Immigration, as long as it was organized, would be crucial to this agenda, for without it, labor shortages would hurt production. Through organization, workers of the world would be assured the same rights, guaranteed by states in consultation with organized labor.[9]

Despite an extraordinary growth in union membership after the war, the optimism with which labor had greeted the peace did not endure.[10] Demobilization quickly challenged the notion of equal rights for all migrant workers. Only a month after the armistice, for instance, government officials polled local port authorities on which "race would be most desirable to employ" while awaiting the return of demobilized soldiers.[11] Despite enormous regional variation in the response, only Algerians were repatriated en masse.[12] Failed strikes over the summer of 1919 also exposed fault lines in the international reformist movement, while elections in November returned the most right-wing parliament since 1875. These developments, coupled with the new government's crushing of strike movements the following spring, led the unified postwar labor movement to collapse. The CGT majority's hold on the direction of the union rapidly weakened, and the minority defected in December 1921. The emergent Confédération Générale du Travail Unitaire (CGTU) became closely tied to the Communist Party, while the CGT pursued its nonaligned, reformist course. Soon, France's union movement became highly fractured, as the CGT and the CGTU pursued conflicting strategies and other factions—ranging in orientation from Christian to anarchist—emerged.

Portions of labor's postwar internationalist vision survived in bilateral treaties that were negotiated between France and a number of nations of emigration, but in distorted form. Ironically, then, these treaties served to create new inequalities among migrants in France in the years that followed. Immigration had already begun to test the postwar settlement even before other developments exposed the limits of the "Wilsonian moment."[13]

Postwar migrant rights reflected the uneven power relations that reemerged between nations in Europe after the war and that persisted between European countries and their colonies. Wartime allies and new states earned special status, while colonial territories remained subject to exceptional forms of discrimination. Labor's pledge that "workers of color" would be recruited "under the same conditions as is European labor and will benefit from the same guarantees" was never realized.[14] Instead of the uniform international labor laws that unions had envisioned, bilateral treaties guaranteed equal work conditions, salaries, and social rights for nationals from each contracting state.[15] These agreements diverged from the CGT's plans for the postwar international labor order in three respects: They provided organized labor little oversight; they did not offer foreigners exactly the same union rights as nationals; and, most crucially, they were bilateral rather than universal. Not only were important countries of emigration, such as Spain, initially excluded from equal treatment provisions, but foreign nationals from treaty countries also acquired, in some respects, more substantive rights than did migrants from within the French Empire. I call this privileged class of migrants "most-favored foreigners." Not only had organized labor's plans to guarantee equal rights to "workers of color" not materialized, but even European workers emerged from the war with stratified rights.

Nonetheless, the treaties provided leaders of some nations the assurance they needed that facilitating emigration would not undermine their own economic interests. On paper, the agreements meant that recruiters could draw workers only from regions and economic sectors approved by the sending country for placement in regions and professions authorized by the host country. They had clauses allowing either the sending or host country to agree, via their diplomatic envoys, on measures to take in the event of a change in the labor market. Most-favored foreigners would be guaranteed equal salaries for equal work, identical compensation in the event of a workplace accident, equal access to pensions, mutual aid, and other forms of social assistance including unemployment indemnities in cities where those were offered, medical care for aged or indigent persons having lived in the host country five years or more, and the right to representation on collective bargaining committees. In addition, no special tax could be levied on the employment of workers from treaty states.[16]

These guarantees were important because while foreign governments often considered emigration necessary for social peace in periods of economic stagnation, their leaders worried about its impact on economic development in the long run. During times of job scarcity, emigration could substantially benefit a sender country by removing unemployed persons and the attendant social and political problems they engendered. But while state officials had to take weaknesses in their economies seriously, none could afford to proclaim that insufficient jobs were a permanent aspect of economic life in their nation. Foreign leaders who successfully negotiated labor agreements with France saw emigrants, as Gary Cross has noted, as "economic assets, capital exports, vital for their potential repatriation of wages and skills."[17] Those who did not, such as Spanish leaders before the advent of the republic in 1931, drew little distinction between economic and political migration, viewing both as an insult to the nation. Emigration, as the Primo de Rivera regime's emigration office director put it, was not a "necessary evil"; rather, he thought, "our country can amply insure its inhabitants' existence." The future of Spanish workers, he argued, "is in Spain itself, which is in full and expanding growth."[18] Incongruously, Miguel Primo de Rivera finished his days in exile—where else but Paris?

THE POLITICS OF PROTECTION

Although originally aimed at securing equal work conditions and salaries, reciprocity treaties proved especially important when it came to social rights, which were monitored closely by the state. T. H. Marshall had these sorts of rights in mind when he coined the term "social citizenship" in 1949. For Marshall, social citizenship encompassed "the whole range from the right to a modicum of economic welfare and security to the right to share to the full in the social heritage and to live the life of a civilized being according to the standards prevailing in the society."[19] Scholars since Marshall have shown how social rights not only produce new common identities but also serve as "system[s] of stratification."[20] Largely concerned with class stratification, however, scholars have often missed how social rights vary over time, between and within cities, and between and within national groups.

The case of an injured Moroccan is illuminating. When Lahcen A. tried to claim lifetime worker's compensation following a 1922 accident that led to the amputation of his left hand, he was refused. His lawyer, P. Hémery, initially was stunned to learn that his client had been informed that "as a Moroccan, you are a foreign worker; returning to Morocco which is not a colony but a protectorate, you cease to live in French territory." Even more galling was the fact that most-favored foreigners, upon returning home, "continue to receive their allowances as if they were French or resided in France." If Lahcen had died, his wife and family in Morocco would have no rights, whereas the survivors of most-favored foreigners benefited from payments "as if they were French." Meanwhile, Lahcen had served in the army for two years, "in theory no doubt for the Moroccan army, in reality in the service of France." How could he be treated worse than were "real foreigners"? Inequitable treatment of this kind could, according to Hémery, have deleterious effects on Franco-Moroccan relations. A reciprocity treaty with Morocco was in order.[21]

Hémery's pleas fell on deaf ears. Franco-Moroccan relations were premised on unequal power relations, whereas the basis of bilateral treaties was equal protection. According "reciprocity" to the French in Morocco would have amounted to reducing, not improving, their status. Conversely, granting Moroccans rights equal to those of the metropolitan

French might have called into question France's authority over Morocco. Lahcen's case, however extreme, illustrated the degree to which international and imperial relations affected migrants' access to social rights.

Even for treaty beneficiaries, protectionist pressures did not disappear overnight, since it took time for treaty guidelines to penetrate local practices. When the mayor of Port-de-Bouc, a shipbuilding center near Marseille, proposed in 1923 to deny residency authorization to the Livornese workers who swooped into the town "like vultures on carrion," the Bouches-du-Rhône prefect admonished him that he had no right to turn away Italians who arrived with valid contracts in hand. By virtue of international treaties, the prefect reminded him, these foreigners had "public rights" and could not be denied identification papers.[22] Similarly, when Municipal Council members in Lyon contemplated levying a special tax on foreign residents of the city, the treaties were invoked and the proposal was dropped.[23]

Once acknowledged locally, the treaties formed a basis for including most-favored foreigners in social citizenship. Lyon's unemployment regulations explicitly included most-favored foreigners from 1926, even specifying that this meant "that only Belgians, Italians, Poles and Czechoslovaks can be admitted for assistance," provided they met the other requirements of such aid.[24] In Marseille, it meant that Italians—"almost exclusively" among foreigners—benefited from medical assistance, aid to the aged and indigent, assistance for new mothers and needy children, and hospitalization of the mentally ill.[25] Indeed, Marseille explicitly did not include stateless persons in such benefits, for mayoral officials contended that the law on obligatory medical assistance "is not applicable to Armenian subjects and, what is more, since Marseille's nursing home is insufficient for those who do benefit from the law, we do not accept Armenians in these nursing homes." Both Armenians and Russians found that their special refugee passports did not remove the impediments posed by their statelessness.[26]

Armenians posed a unique problem not only because they were stateless but also because many of them were unable to work. The plight facing Armenians and other refugees is examined in greater detail in Chapter 5. For now, suffice it to say that local administrators accustomed to linking residency rights to work permits for the able-bodied were overwhelmed by the arrival of widowed, orphaned, sickly, or emaciated Armenians.[27] Moreover, since refugees did not—unlike many most-favored foreigners—arrive with labor contracts in hand, they became stuck in a vicious cycle: Employers reportedly told them that they needed to see identification papers in order to hire them, while public agencies insisted on seeing labor contracts prior to issuing identification papers.[28] While the truth of this first accusation is difficult to ascertain, it is incontrovertible that local authorities received instructions not to issue identification cards to Armenians in order to encourage them to leave France.[29] The difference between these directives and the instructions given to Port-de-Bouc's mayor obliging him to honor the "public rights" of Italian workers was glaring.

By the mid-1920s, business and labor organizations alike criticized the treaties' effects. Predictably, business leaders thought the treaties were not laissez-faire enough, while union leaders condemned the nonenforcement of treaty-mandated controls, which they attributed to the minimal oversight role granted to organized labor. As one union put it in 1924, France's "international magnanimity" should not exceed its "good sense." The only solution was to place recruitment under the "constant control of labor organizations."[30] Employers, meanwhile, decried the "significant burden" that payroll taxes placed on their budgets.[31] On balance, however, labor was less successful at imposing its prerogatives than were employers. Even representatives of the CGTU, whose mantra upon splitting from the CGT had been that "workers have no fatherland," acknowledged at its September 1924 meeting that foreign workers were in "oversupply."[32] A CGTU representative from the Bouches-du-Rhône alleged at the same meeting that union members from Marseille had "chased the *bicots* from the boiler rooms and had given a number of foreigners a taste of Joliette Basin's depths."[33] The following spring, another CGTU affiliate, the masonry union of Lyon and its suburbs, began placing construction companies on its blacklist if they employed foreign workers; the union then tried to incite French masons to refuse to work on these sites.[34] Although the union's central office still condemned immigration regulations as the product of "bourgeois governments," its local secretary, Gustave Eysséris, called for the government's help after strike leaders were fired, asserting that the foreign masons were "intended for other enterprises outside of Lyon, while our comrades are out of work."[35] The incident, and others like it, demonstrated not only labor's minimal success in controlling immigration but also the state's limited involvement in the day-to-day functioning of the labor market. Construction companies were reputed to hire workers through local drinking establishments rather than through the public placement office. As long as valid contracts were produced through this process, however, public officials had little recourse: Migrants from reciprocity nations had the right to enter France without a contract and to then "regularize" their situation by finding legal employment once in the country. In practice, regularizations often applied to other foreigners as well.

While the treaties contained provisions designed to ensure that workers migrated from only those regions in emigrant nations where they were in abundance and arrived in only those parts of France where there were labor shortages, such provisions proved difficult to enforce. The state, while nominally responsible for guaranteeing the treaties, allowed employer interests to influence treaty enforcement for several years. The most spectacular example of this was the free rein given to a private recruitment company, the Société Générale de l'Immigration, which turned a huge profit as it recruited nearly 30% of all France's migrant workers in the peak years of postwar immigration.[36] But even small-time employers recruited with little oversight and were infamous for skirting the salary provisions in the treaties. Classifying foreign labor as less skilled, they avoided the equal-pay-for-equal-work clauses. Unions and Labor Ministry officials complained about such practices, but to little avail: Labor inspection reports contain no indications of salary enforcement.[37] Local placement offices did not fare much better. When Marseille officials tried to enforce prevailing salaries in 1926, they ended by concluding that their efforts were "doomed in advance."[38]

REGIONS AND RELATIONS

If officials concluded that efforts to regulate Marseille's labor market were doomed in advance, it was in part due to seasonal fluctuations endemic to port economies. Marseille's economy was structured around commercial trade and the transformation of imported raw materials for reexportation in such forms as refined sugar, soap, vegetable oil, and pasta. Thus the extent to which Marseille employers' profit margin depended on the continued influx of cheap, mostly migrant, labor may have signaled its imminent decline, as it lost ground to rivals such as Rotterdam and Genoa.[39] By contrast, postwar Lyon was undergoing rapid economic expansion. The First World War had ushered in Lyon's "second industrialization," and the city emerged from it with an economy based on concentrated, capital-intensive firms specializing in automobile and machine construction, synthetic fiber, and chemical production. Employers in both cities depended heavily on migrant labor, but for different reasons. In Lyon, they recruited migrants to staff the new large-scale, around-the-clock production floors; in Marseille, migrants facilitated the labor flexibility favored by the seasonal nature of its trade and production cycle.

Lyon and Marseille have long been rivals for the status of France's second-largest city. Because officials were driven by this rivalry to falsify censuses between the wars, the cities' population shifts are impossible to determine with precision. Nonetheless, the legally recorded foreign populations of both cities grew, exceeding 74,000 in the Lyon agglomeration and topping 206,000 in Marseille by 1932.[40] In Lyon, such mass migration was an utterly new phenomenon; in Marseille, it was part of a pattern that stretched back at least a century.[41] In both cities, as new migrants arrived, industries and working-class settlements expanded into new districts and suburbs. At the same time that local officials were newly charged with regulating the place of foreigners in their communities, migrants themselves helped to shape the contours of those communities in important and lasting ways.

Although both cities underwent rapid changes after the war, the character and cadence of these changes varied from one to the other. Not surprisingly, local officials in each city responded differently to the administrative challenges such changes posed. In particular, their understandings of where migrants fit into each city's social geography affected their approach to regulating them. To appreciate the degree to which everyday social relations shaped the contours of migrant rights in interwar France, it is necessary to understand the cities in which they lived.

Marseille

With dramatic fluctuations in production and export cycles, Marseille's companies had little incentive to invest in modern technology;[42] instead, they became increasingly dependent on cheap, dispensable, and often migrant labor, whose employment fluctuated with the season, the supply of raw materials, international prices, and the demand for finished products.[43] In this "Marseille system,"[44] employers used "day workers" (*journaliers*)—whom they hired by the week, day, or half day—to complement a core of more permanent employees.

More than any other industry, the dock companies exemplified the Marseille system. Twice a day, the following scene was repeated:

6:30 a.m., in winter, Joliette plaza: the labor market or the market for men, as you will. All along the cafés and the sidewalk, the dockers wait. It's still dark out. Every once in a while, a group forms. It's the team captain or foreman who has come to hire his personnel. In the group surrounding him, some just pass through: these are the reliable regulars who are sure to be hired and just show up for good measure. A signal, and they go back into the café to await the start of work. But the others continue to squeeze around the foreman, these are those without work, and each is trying to get to the front.[45]

Stevedores, or "dockers" as the French called them, were hired for four hours of labor. When there was enough work for a second shift, another set of dockers would be hired to work in the afternoon. By the time a

stevedore had stood in line to collect his payment for the morning, however, he had often missed the afternoon roundup. Each day, dockers were
unsure of being hired for the afternoon, much less for the next day. Little
wonder, then, that this often was a job of last resort. Who were dockers?
The prominent journalist Albert Londres tells us who they were not:

One learns to be a mechanic, a boiler-maker or a mason. One becomes a docker.
To be a miner, a forger, a cabinet-maker, is to have a profession. A docker is not
a profession. If one is a docker he is not a worker. . . . One finds workers among
the dockers, but they are workers who, precisely, are out of work.[46]

The dockers unions, which labored tirelessly throughout the 1930s to secure recognition of their members' work as a profession and to protect
"professional" dockers from being displaced by the itinerant unemployed,
might have begged to differ.[47] Even for a long-term docker, though, "insecurity rule[d] his life," as the priest and social reformer M.-R. Loew put
it.[48] Perhaps because of this insecurity, neither Londres nor Loew nor any
of the local officials observing the situation were surprised that dockers
were often made up predominantly of migrants: "They are French transients, Arabs, Syrians, Spanish, Belgians, Italians," wrote Londres.[49]
"The best and most regular labor is without a doubt Armenian," added
Loew; "North Africans are the quickest to accept with indifference the
worst work (coal, phosphates, bulk minerals)." If Italians and Spanish
came next in Loew's order, only the "shiftiest, most unstable, out of luck"
French persons would be desperate enough to be dockers.[50] Marseille's
economy depended on a steady supply of "out of luck" people.

    Marseille's urban geography reflected its social and employment struc-
ture. The configuration of the city limits to allow for municipal control of
23 kilometers of docks and 57 kilometers of coastline meant that some
22,800 hectares, more than twice the size of Paris intra muros, fell within
city limits. Until the last third of the twentieth century Marseille was a
"deformed body," a succession of disconnected villages, each with its
own name: St Henri, St Louis, Les Aygalades, Le Canet, La Capelette, En-
doume, and so on (see Figure 1.1).[51] These villages were separated from
one another and isolated from the center by *terrains vagues* of semirural
space. As the port grew, the imbalance of urban development in Marseille
was exacerbated: Members of the working class who could afford it built
maisonnettes of two to six rooms in the villages that followed the expansion of the port and its related industries to the north and east.[52] Marseille's bourgeois, meanwhile, tended to settle along the southern hills of
the city. In between, the central port districts were left primarily to floating
populations. There one found the thousands of casual laborers upon whom
the Marseille economy depended: stevedores, sailors, migrants for whom

FIGURE I.I *Map of Marseille*

SOURCE: *Pinol, ed.,* Atlas historique des villes de France, *193.*

Marseille was simply a way station en route to a final destination, or anyone whose earnings were uncertain enough to make staying in a "furnished room"[53]—where one paid rent by the day, week, or month—preferable to acquiring furniture of one's own and paying the trimestrial or annual rent that prevailed in the rest of the city. A plethora of rooming houses filled the narrow streets of the port district, in close proximity to the city's bars, music halls, and brothels. These precarious lodgings often served as the first stop for many of those transients who became, by virtue of staying, immigrants.

Although the port district had few streets where foreigners in fact outnumbered the French, journalists often wrote about central Marseille as they might have about some exotic land in a travelogue. Yet even in the most densely populated sector of the city, foreigners comprised just over a quarter of the population.[54] French or foreign, residents of the central port area seemed to correspond to every available stereotype of patholog-ical behavior: They were disproportionately male, with uncertain or un-stable residence, an irregular means of existence, and no apparent family connections—all of which were particularly worrisome in a country with a declining birth rate and a deficit of young men.[55] The fact that colonial migrants were also overwhelmingly male, detached from their families, living in overcrowded and unstable housing conditions, and extremely vulnerable to the vicissitudes of Marseille's labor market further colored these districts as unstable even though colonials never made up more than 4% of the population of even the most densely populated districts.[56]

The city center attracted not only migrants but also, disproportion-ately to its population size, the police. Marseille's reputation as a city where armed thugs ruled the Old Port neighborhood while ineffectual po-lice failed to pursue cases had prompted the nationalization of the city's police in 1908. This placed Marseille among only a handful of cities with nationalized police forces, where authority was removed from municipal control. Under such *police d'état* systems, the local police answered directly, via the prefect, to the Ministry of the Interior's Direction de la Sûreté Générale. As a result, they were forced to compete with other Sûreté services for their share of the ministry's national budget.[57] Despite this central government oversight, Marseille's *police d'état* was continu-ally plagued by insufficient personnel, overlapping administrations, which lacked a clear hierarchy, as well as labor unrest and absenteeism.[58] This was the police force charged with securing France's largest port: It was responsible for counterespionage and passport control, abating drug and contraband traffic, and preventing theft of merchandise from its open-air docks—all of which was made more difficult by the city's constantly rotating population of sailors, dock workers, and passengers. When faced with chronically insufficient resources and expanding re-sponsibilities, "street-level bureaucracies" such as police forces inevitably ration decision making.[59] Some Marseille police responded to this stress through illegal "mechanisms of accommodation,"[60] others by profiling their clientele. As we shall see, casually employed migrants, especially those living in the city center, bore the brunt of police power.

Police officials might have recognized the connection between the res-idential instability of central-district dwellers and the flexible structure of the Marseille labor market; instead they evaluated irregular work, im-permanent housing, and (presumed) bachelorhood as indelible markers of a person's antisocial constitution.[61] This perspective was not, how-ever, a simple oversight; rather, its source lay in the difference between police work and labor regulation. Police are charged with ensuring order and stability, whereas guest-worker policy, in privileging mobility and

FIGURE 1.2 *Street in Marseille's central district*
SOURCE: *Personal collection of author.*

impermanence, rests on a different logic. Ironically, the way Marseille police approached the city-center dwellers helped maintain their provisional status by making them legally vulnerable. This legal vulnerability, in turn, contributed to their subordinate status on the labor market.[62]

The social map of Marseille followed a decidedly different pattern than that of many other cities, where marginals lived quite literally on the city's margins.[63] Marseille's peripheral districts, where a majority of the population lived by the end of the First World War, emerged as semirural, family-oriented villages together with populations that, at a glance, appeared more rooted, stable, and "integrated" than were central-district residents.[64] Once away from the city center, migrants tended to live in the same place, or at least in the same neighborhood, for the rest of their years in Marseille. If they were able to find work away from the docks, they gladly ceased coming into the center. The French entertainer Robert Ripa claims, for example, that it was only to register his birth that his father

FIGURE 1.3   *Village in Marseille's outer districts*
SOURCE: *Personal collection of author.*

finally went, in 1920, "to the city, I mean to the center of Marseille" for the first time since he had arrived from Italy in 1911.[65] Ripa's slip—referring to the center as the "city," as if his own neighborhood were outside it—provides a glimpse into Marseille residents' mental maps, maps that authorities shared and helped to reproduce.

Although social stigma was not a simple effect of Marseille's geography, there were nonetheless important correlations between where one lived in Marseille's urban landscape and the resources one could mobilize based on social relationships. Such differences in "social capital"[66] meant that a foreigner living in Marseille's central districts, or one who was deemed to be "without a fixed domicile," was almost five times more likely to be expelled from the country than one who was living in the peripheral districts. In this way, local social relations affected who was included in or excluded from the nation.

If every arrest of a foreigner could potentially lead to expulsion, not all did. Local police had wide discretion in such matters, especially in border departments such as the Bouches-du-Rhône, where the prefect had the option of expelling without consulting the Interior Ministry. Unless a foreigner's crime was heinous, it rarely served as the sole motivation for an expulsion. Rather, expulsion offered a way for authorities to solve local social problems by way of national exclusion.

Arrested for his first known offense in 1919, Larbi Z., a Moroccan, was sentenced to a 25-franc fine for illegal weapons possession; the arm in question was a razor.[67] This fairly ordinary punishment for a very common infraction led to a more extraordinary measure: expulsion. Police reports gave conflicting accounts of how long Larbi had been in France and how regularly he had worked, finally concluding, despite Larbi's contention that he had lived in Marseille for two years, that he had resided there a mere three days and had, during that time, worked for more than one employer. "Without work and without a regular means of existence," according to the prefect, Larbi had no justification for remaining in Marseille.[68] Larbi may well have lived in Marseille longer than three days. The trouble was that he could not prove it. He claimed to rent a room over a Moroccan restaurant at 7, rue des Chapeliers, but then, so did dozens of others.[69] This street in the Pressentines neighborhood, "named for its prison but known for its Arabs,"[70] was already known, several years before Albert Londres likened it to the medinas of Sfax, Rabat, Oran, and Algiers, for its unattached, presumed to be transient, male population coming from France's overseas possessions.[71] No doubt it was this relatively new population that led Ludovic Naudeau to comment in *L'Illustration* that no one wore a *chapeau* anymore in the street named for them; fezzes had replaced hats on Hatmakers' Street.[72]

The social dynamics that informed Larbi's treatment become all the more apparent when one compares him to migrants living elsewhere in Marseille. Hector W., a Spaniard, was convicted for an identical offense. But whereas the prefect had stressed Larbi's instability and transience, Hector's file, by contrast, noted that he was married, had two children, and lived with his family in a working-class village north of the port known as La Madrague. Yves Montand, then known as Ivo Livi, grew up a stone's throw from there, and while his family often had trouble making ends meet, the stability that their home on a small dead-end street off the Chemin de la Madrague-Ville provided them was vital.[73] As was common among residents of the periphery, Hector's arrest led to a warning rather than to an expulsion.[74]

Social factors stratified rights within as well as between national groups. While Garabed G., a single Armenian man of 24 who lived in a rented room and worked irregularly, was first *refoulé* and then expelled, police preferred to recommend a warning for Hagop Z., a married Armenian father of four who lived on the Chemin de St Loup in the Campagne Ripert sector of Ste Marguerite, a village in southeastern Marseille. That recommendation was honored, and several years later, Hagop requested naturalization.[75]

While the social relations of migrants living in the periphery allowed them to provide affidavits testifying, for example, that they had been "settled in the community for approximately 12 years," or that they had "never given rise to any complaints from the population,"[76] population turnover was so frequent in central Marseille that the migrants living there had little means for establishing a reputation. Indeed, when in doubt, police emphasized the lack of verifiable information they could collect on such foreigners. Corrections to oral testimony recorded in police files reflect this problem. Assertions such as "in France for five years" were crossed out and replaced with "unknown"; addresses such as "17 rue St Lazare" were replaced with "no fixed domicile."[77] In contrast to inhabitants of the periphery, where a person's domicile could be verified with relative ease, the presumed or real transience of central-district residents made it difficult for police not only to account for them but to hold them accountable. Operating on the assumption that any equivocation would allow transient foreigners to slip from their grasp, police and local officials meted out harsher punishments to those who lived in social surroundings that did not correspond to those of the presumed norm. Consequently, police only exacerbated the marginality of the persons in question by turning them into illegal aliens overnight.

The norms informing police behavior were not clear-cut, nor did they reflect any explicit racial hierarchy. Racial ideologies only made sense inasmuch as they corresponded to an equally profound social division between the center of town and the periphery, "two distinct worlds, foreign to one another," as Ludovic Naudeau put it.[78] Thus a peculiar alchemy of class, marital status, gender, and social deviance marked the port-area population as quintessential outsiders.

Expulsion patterns between 1919 and 1932 reflected the association of central Marseille with transience, criminality, and social instability. All but five among a sampling of 166 summary expulsions ordered unilaterally by the Bouches-du-Rhône prefect between 1919 and 1932 concerned persons who were deemed not to have a fixed residence. Even taking into account the much higher number of cases referred to the Interior Ministry, a bifurcation of rights and opportunities emerges between foreigners who circulated in the infamous city center and those who lived on the periphery. Despite the fact that a majority of Marseille's population lived in the periphery, fewer than 16% of expulsions sampled concerned persons living in the city's outer districts. Indeed, in more than 66% of the cases regarding residents of the periphery, the individuals concerned were spared expulsion. Meanwhile, almost 74% of the cases involving residents of the center and persons deemed to have no fixed domicile triggered an immediate recommendation for expulsion.[79] Naturalization cases often exhibited a similar constellation of values.[80] In short, local authorities drew on existing social divisions as they made legal distinctions among the foreigners who lived in Marseille. Together, social and cultural factors functioned to create national, if not entirely racial, boundaries between people living in the same city.[81]

Lyon

In the decade following the First World War, Lyon—then one-fifth Marseille's geographic area—became metropolitan Lyon as new industries and suburbs mushroomed (see Figure 1.4). War production helped initiate this trend. After the war, capital-intensive industry continued to grow, and the region became known for automobile and machine-tool construction, synthetic fiber, and chemical production. As in Marseille, Lyon employers relied on migrant workers. Yet by contrast to Marseille, where employment of migrants helped business owners avoid capitalization, Lyon's industrialists hired migrants to staff huge factory floors where, at least in the 1920s, production continued 24 hours a day. Due to the size of the factories, few of these industries were located in Lyon itself. Lyon's changing economic base thus altered its urban space.[82] Once, Lyon's most famous industries were located in its hills, where even today loft-style buildings bear witness to the city's long history of silk weaving. From the First World War on, however, its industry has been concentrated in the river plain that extends from the banks of the Rhône toward the Alps.

The location of the new industries in former rural villages away from the city center, along with the disagreeable and often dangerous work these industries entailed, posed challenges for labor recruitment. Work in the acetate and rayon industry was divided into three eight-hour shifts. Quantity and quality control were rigorous, and those not able to keep up were promptly dismissed. As a result,when Gillet built its plant in Vaulx-en-Velin, "it was difficult to find 3,000 workers in Lyon."[83] With the establishment of the eight-hour day, and the stimulus that the war gave new industry, not to mention the "unhealthy work at what were initially relatively mediocre salaries, it was almost impossible to convince French people to sign on."[84] As former villages gave way to industrial suburbs, farmers in the area kept to themselves, preferring not to engage with the "working-class population that arrived from countries throughout Europe."[85] By 1930, foreigners comprised an estimated 64% of employees in Lyon-area synthetic fabric factories.[86] Not surprisingly, a population explosion accompanied the expansion of these advanced industries into the Lyon suburbs. Between 1911 and 1936, the number of inhabitants in Lyon proper grew only 9%, while that of St-Fons grew 74%, Villeurbanne

FIGURE 1.4 *Map of Lyon and major suburbs*
SOURCE: *Pinol, ed.,* Atlas historique des villes de France, *163.*

91%, Bron 216%, Vénissieux 234%, Décines 438%, and Vaulx-en-Velin 462%.[87] By 1936, foreigners made up an impressive 17% of the population within Villeurbanne city limits. But they made up an even more stunning 89% of the residents of the "Cité de la Soie," the housing compound for employees of the Société de Soie Artificielle du Sud-Est, located on the far edge of Villeurbanne, in the commune of Vaulx-en-Velin.[88] The city of Vaulx-en-Velin as a whole, which had no foreigners in 1901, boasted a foreign population of 48% in 1931.[89] That same year, foreigners comprised over 40% of the inhabitants of Vénissieux, the industrial suburb southeast of Lyon that was home most notably to the Berliet automobile-manufacturing plant.[90] In next-door St-Fons, they comprised 28% of the populace. East of Villeurbanne, the synthetic fiber town of Décines was 55% foreign.[91] In fact, as migrant populations in the suburbs grew, the numbers of foreigners living in Lyon also dropped, perhaps indicating that the appeal of jobs with these new industries not only drew new migrants but also encouraged earlier arrivals to leave the city for the industrial periphery.[92] Thanks to this unprecedented growth, construction jobs were also abundant. Migrants worked in, inhabited, and literally built Lyon's suburbs.[93]

Administrative and police files on foreigners provide an additional clue to what distinguished life in Greater Lyon from that in Marseille. In Lyon, files on foreigners listed the profession of the person in question: mason, tailor, mechanic, metal cutter, boilermaker, cabinetmaker, stoker, electrician, plasterer, and so on. In Marseille, this detail was extremely rare. This difference in precision may have come in part from the conditions under which Lyon's police operated. Compared to Marseille, Lyon's *police d'état* had a higher police-to-population ratio, a simpler chain of command, a smaller territory to cover, and, judging from the fact that its reports were usually typed while those in Marseille ordinarily were handwritten, a better infrastructure and secretarial support.[94] Even so, the difference in how police filled out forms in the two cities also expressed something very real about what distinguished the Lyon and Marseille economies: While Marseille's fluctuating labor market drew transient workers, these were precisely the kind of workers that Lyon employers were trying to avoid. Turnover, although crucial to the functioning of the Marseille economy, was a problem for Lyon-area industries, which operated on mass-production scales and around-the-clock schedules.

To recruit and retain a workforce for which their rivals also competed, many of the area's larger chemical and manufacturing industries built company housing complexes in the first few years after the war.[95] Among the many firms responding to this challenge, the Société Lyonnaise de Textiles built a massive "Silk City" (*Cité de la Soie*) in Décines; Gillet built a housing complex to address the "urgency of the labor situation" at its acetate factory in Vaulx-en-Velin;[96] and Berliet Automobiles built worker lodgings in Vénissieux. Company housing varied in size and amenities but usually offered two to three clean, well-ventilated rooms plus a small kitchen area in a space totaling anywhere from 40 to 70 square meters. Some offered indoor toilets; others housed sanitary facilities separately. Many complexes included churches, stores, and even privately run schools. Although company housing invariably meant employer paternalism, in the context of a major postwar housing crisis in French cities, this was a price many migrants were willing to pay.

Unlike in classic company towns, even the largest firms in the Lyon suburbs never provided enough housing for all their employees.[97] Migrants who did not meet company housing criteria, who worked for smaller firms, or who arrived in France with no contract hoping to regularize their situation, initially crowded into *garnis* and *meublés*. This kind of housing stock was prevalent in the industrial districts of the left bank of the Rhône River and was especially concentrated in the Guillotière neighborhood.[98] The account of a Frenchman, Georges Navel, who spent the latter part of his youth during and after the war in the neighborhood, provides some idea of how migrants, too, may have lived: "Families like ours squeezed into one- or two-room apartments." Access from the street was through a "dark corridor," and to reach the apartment, one had to "climb an open-air wooden staircase on which laundry was always hanging from lines. Stray dogs and cats, garbage, and the latrine stunk up the corridor." Nonetheless, Navel "forgot quickly that we were in a *garni*" and characterized his block of the rue de la Part-Dieu as an "honest street bordering an infamous quarter."[99]

With the postwar housing crisis rendering neighborhoods like Navel's even more crowded, migrants sometimes set up camp on vacant lots, where they constructed their own housing from crates, wood, and discarded

FIGURE 1.5 Cité *SASE—Typical housing for skilled foreign workers*
SOURCE: *AML 1120 WP 001-2. Courtesy of Archives Municipales de Lyon.*

metal. Shantytowns were hastily built, often had little or no running water, no toilets and inadequate means for sewage disposal, insufficient shelter from rain and mud, and no safe means of heating. Overcrowded even by the standards of the day, their inhabitants were reportedly "piled on top of one another," sometimes more than one large family per shack.[100]

Lyon's migrants thus lived in glaringly different circumstances. Some lived in the relative comfort of company housing (see Figure 1.5). Others were more likely to face difficulties in Lyon's tight housing market. It should come as no surprise that many of the illegal, but tolerated, shanty-towns that migrants built in industrial districts were inhabited by those who came to Lyon without prearranged contracts (see Figure 1.6). These included Armenians and Spanish, but also antifascist Italians who avoided official emigration channels for political reasons. Armenians arriving in Décines who did not qualify as "skilled" workers, for example, proceeded to build their own housing next to the Silk City. Recently arrived Italians and Spaniards were prevalent in the shacks that stretched along the avenue Débourg in Lyon's Gerland district. The Chateau Gaillard encampment in Villeurbanne was home almost exclusively to Spanish

FIGURE 1.6 *Lyon, Gerland—"A corner of the Spanish colony"*
SOURCE: *AML 1120 WP 001-2. Courtesy of Archives Municipales de Lyon.*

migrants. Other shantytowns were scattered throughout Greater Lyon, particularly in the suburbs to the east and south.

Often thrown up overnight before officials could intervene to impose health and safety standards, these homes were tolerated "reluctantly" because condemning them would have meant "throwing the inhabitants of these shacks into the streets" only to have them face the housing crisis in Lyon and the impossibility of finding affordable shelter.[101] Some attempts were made, at least, to educate inhabitants of the growing shantytowns about construction standards: The public health office enlisted the help of consulates to translate its regulations.[102] This proved ineffective, and as the shantytowns "popped up overnight like mushrooms," so did the public health problems they posed.[103]

Conditions in the shantytowns also sparked complaints, usually from neighboring residents and businesses. Representatives of a housing cooperative near a newly forming shantytown on the Chemin des Buers in Villeurbanne, for example, complained in September 1923 that makeshift homes of wood and sheet metal had "neither latrines nor water closets." The fact that the shacks were occupied mostly by Spaniards merely added to the concerns of the cooperative's members, as its president claimed that they brought with them "illnesses heretofore unknown in France." This complainant acknowledged the housing crisis but remained firm that it was no excuse for letting "a crowd of foreigners come to poison the community, causing additional medical expenses for it."[104] Others objected to residents, and again especially to foreigners, who raised chickens, rabbits, pigs, goats, and fowl in the shantytowns. Still others reported overcrowding, nauseating odors, and standing water.[105]

With complaints growing, the shantytowns and their foreign inhabitants became targets of social commentary. Gnafron, the nom de plume of a columnist for Lyon's satirical newspaper *Le guignol*, reported in 1926 on the growing practice of subletting the homemade shacks. In trademark Lyonnese slang, so colorful that it must be cited in the original, Gnafron connected Lyon's recent census score as the second-largest city in France to the numbers of foreigners packed into shantytowns:

Quand on pense au nombre d'Espagnols que viennent s'implanter chez nous, que trouvent le moillien de prendre en location de grandes baraques et pis d'y entasser en garnis leurs concitoilliens en les entassant comme des z'harengs dans une caque . . . et que si l'Hygiène existait comme on le pretend à l'Hôtel de Ville, on devrait ben nous débarrasser de tous ces empoisons. . . .

Mossieu Édouard, je m'en fous d'être la second ville de France, mais je préfèrerais vous du travail pour tous mes concittolliens que de voir augmentasser tout le temps cette foute d'étrangers que finira par nous manger un jour si on n'y prend pas garde.[106]

FIGURE 1.7 Le guignol's *rendition of the 1926 census, 10 April 1926,
exaggerating the results. The cartoon shows North Africans,
derisively called "Sidis," as the largest group when in fact they
never numbered more than a few thousand and should have been
counted as "French nationals" in the census. French and "Lyonnese"
are depicted as minuscule. The captions reads, "All right, pals,
behold, look at this chart!!! If ever all these folks who are not from
here start to have children in proportion to their share in the city
[population], there will surely hardly be a crumb left for the French.
And to think they don't even pay taxes!"*
SOURCE: *ADR, Pér. 415. Courtesy of Archives Départementales du Rhône.*

Calling the encampments a "shambles," Gnafron likely drew a deliberate contrast to the newly completed, state-of-the-art slaughterhouse designed by the hygienist architect Tony Garnier, which was located in the same neighborhood as one of the larger shantytowns.

In Marseille, the inhabitants of such *bidonvilles-avant-la-lettre* no doubt would have been labeled in any police report as "lacking a fixed domicile." And this label, in turn, would have increased their vulnerability vis-à-vis laws on foreigners. Yet as long as near-full employment prevailed in the Lyon region, as it did for most of the 1920s, distinctions in foreigners' social experience did not translate into differential rights in the same way that differences between settled and transient migrants did in Marseille.

Makeshift houses in Lyon, however ramshackle, precarious, and in some cases unsanitary, were, in effect, fixed domiciles. Indeed, they were ascribed legal addresses: 10 avenue Débourg, 73 avenue Débourg, 228 chemin des Culattes, 119 chemin du Chateau Gaillard, 281 rue de Gerland, and so forth. They housed masons, welders, stokers, ironsmiths, metalworkers, and manual workers of all types. An important feature of these neighborhoods was the commercial and social life they became home to as well. A number of migrants, mostly wives of industrial workers, opened groceries, fruit and vegetable markets, hair salons, second-hand shops, bars (*débits de boissons*), even restaurants.[107] Like the shacks, not all of these businesses were legal, but many were officially registered with authorities—often under the husband's name even when operated by the wife—and some were quite profitable. Lorenzo R.'s grocery on the rue Favier in Vaulx-en-Velin, for instance, brought in 250 francs a day in receipts, which was considerable given that his rent on the land was only 150 francs a month.[108] Ignacio N.'s family had a legally registered restaurant and grocery business in a Villeurbanne shantytown that authorities recognized as "very successful [*bien achalandé*]."[109] Filomena C.'s grocery in the Gerland section of Lyon was regarded by authorities as having "many clients."[110] Businesses in the shantytowns not only provided an important supplement to industrial workers' wages; they also became an important center of migrant social life. Perhaps this explains why, despite the living conditions, some migrants remained in these makeshift developments for many years, sometimes going on to naturalize.

High levels of employment in Lyon through most of the 1920s helped to mask social differences among migrants, but it did not erase them. As in Marseille, Lyon police often prized stability over mobility. As in Marseille, family ties served as one measure of social stability. The fact that Saverio L. lived at 228 chemin des Culattes—a shantytown address—did not detract police from noticing that he was "married and the father of 4 children aged, respectively, 8, 6, 5 and 3."[111] By contrast, in recommending against Bartolomeo R., Lyon's general secretary for police rested his case with the final line "In addition, [R.] is unmarried."[112] Authorities admired migrants who opened businesses. By favoring the sedentary, these decisions pointed to the limits of the guest-worker model of migration.

Although patterns of migrant inclusion and exclusion in Lyon did not follow the clearly bifurcated geographic pattern that became apparent in 1920s Marseille, migrant life in both cities suggested a growing disconnection between policy formulas and lived experience. National policy makers envisioned guest workers with a near perfectly elastic response to changes in the job market. Already in the early 1920s, however, local authorities confronted situations that did not correspond neatly to laws of supply and demand. Treaties forced local police to grant residency

FIGURE 1.8 *Small business created by a foreigner selling
products from Spain*
SOURCE: *AML 1120 WP 001-2. Courtesy of Archives Municipales de Lyon.*

authorizations to persons even if their work was not needed. The labor
movement lobbied for restrictions on migrant employment that, if implemented, would decrease foreign workers' flexibility and mobility within
France. Regional and neighborhood differences influenced relationships
between migrants and authorities, and, as the next section illustrates, so
did the tenor of political debate.

PROTEST AND POLICING

It was one thing to guarantee migrants from reciprocity nations the right
to work and quite another to protect their right to organize at work. In
this domain, too, postwar developments dashed organized labor's hopes.
When the treaty between France and Italy was first under negotiation, the
CGT's Léon Jouhaux had expressed his satisfaction that the treaty would
abolish all labor-organizing restrictions that French law imposed on foreigners. "Never again will an administrative expulsion be ordered for acts

that are exclusively syndicalist or corporative," he added confidently.[113] In their final, ratified versions, however, the Italian treaty and its brethren provided few assurances in this regard. In particular, treaties were powerless to prevent employers from firing workers who organized to enforce such provisions. As guest workers, migrants constantly lived with the threat of being asked to go home.

Migrants' legal vulnerability made labor organizing difficult, as did the protectionism of some sectors of the labor movement. On the one hand, labor leaders decried immigration policies that threatened to displace French workers, especially the skilled. Inadequately regulated immigration, they held, created labor surpluses or "organized unemployment."[114] On the other hand, it was important to organize those foreign workers who did come. At best, organizing migrants meant working around legal limits on their labor rights: Foreigners were allowed to be union delegates but could not form their own unions and could not hold elected union office.[115] At worst, it meant exposing them to reprisals, not only from employers, but also from the police.

Police records suggest that expulsions for labor militancy were not uncommon. According to some reports, they rose after the onset of labor unrest in 1919 and 1920. "Never has the government of the republic resorted, as much as in the past few months, to the dirty trick [*coup de Jarnac*] of expulsion," opined *L'Humanité* in November 1920. "In a *real* Republic, expulsions would only be issued by a competent court, after an investigation of both sides [*instruction contradictoire*]. But in our bourgeois antirepublican republic, expulsion is by fiat, it is a police measure. And they expel with all their might."[116] Assessing such claims is difficult, since records report expulsions issued but not necessarily enforced. Nonetheless, Interior Ministry files for November 1920 did record an escalation of more than 165% in new expulsion orders over the previous month; at least a few of these had come on the heels of a massive strike in an aluminum-processing plant north of Marseille, which led to the dismissals of some 200 workers, "practically all" of whom were Italian.[117] Rising expulsion rates may have been due to a philosophy increasingly held by police that expulsions not only served to punish the individual in question but also to set an example to the larger migrant community. Thus, when an Italian communist working as a Marseille docker publicly declared that he would sooner kill himself than cede the eight-hour day, Marseille's special police commissioner responded by expelling him so that "numerous foreigners, Spanish and Italian, who might likely get involved in the movement will remain reserved and avoid speaking at meetings."[118]

French Interior Ministry authorities were already concerned about migrants' participation in labor disputes when the Fascist Party's ascension to power in Italy and Miguel Primo de Rivera's coup in Spain posed new challenges for policing Italian and Spanish nationals, as well as new potential for international discord. Antifascists' political jockeying both in Italy and in France following the assassination of the Socialist deputy Giacomo Matteotti in Rome by *squadristi* only heightened these concerns. That this occurred early in the Cartel des Gauches government, and as Dawes Plan negotiations were in their final stages in London, presented additional difficulties for the new Center-Left coalition, which, having defeated the Right in May 1924 after the controversial effects of the latter's Ruhr policy, now sought to stabilize intra-European relations. Already in June, the Foreign Ministry under Radical Party leader Herriot's leadership began expressing concern about the impact of political organizing by foreign nationals. While internally the Ministry of Foreign Affairs was careful to distinguish "political rights, whose benefits foreigners living in France do not enjoy," from "public rights, regarding which there are merely some special restrictions applying to foreigners," within a week the Interior and Foreign Affairs ministries took aim at public rights as well, having agreed that "necessary sanctions" would be taken against "all foreigners who abuse French hospitality" by engaging in "reprehensible" provocations.[119]

Deteriorating international relations and the polarization of domestic politics both played roles in restricting migrants' civil liberties in France. Indeed, migrants frequently found themselves caught in the crossfire of domestic political conflicts not of their own making. After Marseille's Committee for Anti-fascist Action assembled thousands of people to demonstrate against a rally called by General Édouard Curières de Castelnau, the leader of the National Catholic Federation (Fédération Nationale Catholique, FNC), the city's *police d'état* sought to limit foreign residents' political expression.[120]

De Castelnau's rally and the counterdemonstration it triggered constituted one incident in what Henry Rousso has called the "Franco-French" civil war.[121] As leader of the FNC, de Castelnau opposed the Cartel des Gauches' anticlericalism and its attempt to bring the highly religious Alsace-Lorraine region into line with the secularist policy that prevailed in the rest of the country.[122] Meanwhile, Pierre Taittinger, whose Jeunesses Patriotes (JP) served as bodyguards at FNC events and who owed much of his financing to de Castelnau, had founded the JP in deliberate reaction to the formation of the Cartel.[123] Debates in the chamber two days after the violence in Marseille echoed the Franco-French character of the dispute.

Shifting between the Left on the one hand, and the centrists and Right on the other, with loud interruptions from either side as well as exceptionally

FIGURE 1.9 *Cartoon depicting a figure clearly meant to be Premier Édouard Herriot, in a revolutionary bonnet and pushing a man toward Italy or Spain. The caption reads: "Yell all you want: 'Long live Mussolini! Long live Primo!' But 'Long live Communism!' Never that!" The communist daily called into question Herriot's dedication to the traditions of "liberty, equality, fraternity" by featuring variations on the bonneted Herriot theme throughout the Cartel government.*

partisan exclamations and applause from the assembly, the debate replayed the conflicts that had set in motion the street violence in Marseille. Each side was relentless in accusing the other. The Right charged the Socialist senator-mayor of Marseille, Siméon Flaissières, with having provoked the counterdemonstration by displaying posters throughout Marseille that disingenuously "appealed for calm" while inciting conflict. The Left countered that, as the Socialist Louis Cluzel put it, "it wasn't the Marseillais who went looking for General de Castelnau but de Castelnau who sought them out." De Castelnau's own posters "call[ed] for a civil war," added another Socialist, Jean Bouveri. When Camille Blaisot (Union Républicaine, Calvados) read a depiction of the incident from the *Petit Provençal* newspaper, St-Etienne's Socialist mayor Simon Reynaud retorted that the paper (which was known for its Radical Party leanings) amounted to the same thing as the royalist daily *L'Action Française*! Marseille Socialist Jean-Baptiste Canavelli was repeatedly interrupted by violent shouting from the Right of the assembly, and when Canavelli accused de Castelnau of using the JP as enforcers, Taittinger did nothing to disabuse him of this impression when he promised that the JP stood ready to respond to "violence with violence."[124]

Deputies made a few scattered references to migrants: Taittinger sarcastically remarked that the person responsible for one of the deaths "just happened to be an Italian." The centrist Bouches-du-Rhône deputy Louis Régis chastised, to applause from the Center and Right, "all manner of metics who poison our ports." And Jean Ybarnégaray (Union Nationale Républicaine, Basses-Pyrénées) called for foreign agitators to be "barred access to France." At the heart of the debate, however, was not so much the political engagement of foreigners but rather recurring domestic conflicts that pitted church against state, royalists against republicans, and the nationalist Right against the internationalist Left. As with the Marseille street battle, the chamber debate proved how polarized French politics was becoming. What was more, the deputies quite literally perpetuated the dispute by voting to pick up the discussion another day.[125]

Despite the domestic origins of these political disputes, it was especially foreigners' civil liberties that were curtailed in the incident's aftermath. Following the rally and counterdemonstration, police targeted a number of militants, including Italian communists and two Armenians, whose expulsions were intended to give "foreign extremists the impression that they are closely watched," the Bouches-du-Rhône prefect Louis Thibon reported to Interior Minister Camille Chautemps after the incident. "None of the eight foreigners expelled," with the exception of one who had been indicted for homicide, Thibon added, had taken part in the violent exchanges ensuing from the demonstration. At most, the prefect conceded, they had been guilty of "singing the 'Internationale' and the 'Bandiera Rossa' anthem." Instead, his report continued, the expulsions had been ordered in an effort to "reassure the population," which tended to blame foreigners for Marseille's troubles.[126] Presumably, a two-day series of nocturnal police sweeps that same month, in which a few thousand foreigners were interrogated, also aimed as much to restrain political expression in migrant communities as to uncover violent agitators.[127] Given how rancorous political debate had become, the repression might have been intended to stifle accusations from the Cartel's adversaries that it was soft on crime. Regardless of its true targets, the impact on migrant politics was profound.

With both the Interior Ministry and the Quai-d'Orsay closely surveying their performance, local police trumpeted the success of their tactics. In March, Marseille's special police commissioner Antoine Borelli claimed that thanks to the measures police had taken, "foreign communists abstained from participating in the meeting organized . . . by the Committee for anti-fascist action." Many militants, he asserted, had even turned in their party cards.[128] Similar results have been cited by the historian Pierre Milza, who claims that police records nationwide indicate a minimum of 3,000 Italian militants abandoning communist organizations in the following year.[129] At least as revealing of the effect that political policing had on migrants, however, are the records of communist organizations themselves.

A change in strategy by communist-influenced organizations suggests that intimidating tactics employed by local police successfully curtailed the civil liberties of foreigners. In both Lyon and Marseille, the CGTU—which had hitherto placed foreign militants in its vanguard—shifted course early in 1925 and initiated efforts to protect its foreign members from public exposure. Even before the crackdown following the de Castelnau incident, CGTU leaders in Marseille announced that union delegates "unanimously recognized that foreign militants are currently susceptible [*exposés*] to expulsion" and that, as a result, the CGTU should take measures to avoid making its foreign members vulnerable. Although the CGTU would continue its organizing efforts among foreign workers, it would endeavor to do this without relying on foreign militants themselves; instead, French militants should attend classes in foreign languages to facilitate their communication with foreign workers.[130] While this change in strategy was mainly a response to the repressive measures used against foreign militants, it also emerged from the CGTU's new recognition that immigration was "permanent."[131]

Similarly, at a March 1925 meeting of the Rhône conglomerate of CGTU affiliates, a local leader declared that "we must change our tactics" regarding foreign labor. Up until that point, he noted, the CGTU had placed foreigners in the forefront of its movement. But "following governmental repression and expulsions, we have decided to adapt our way of doing things." Because foreigners could no longer militate for the CGTU "in broad daylight," it would have to be done more "slyly."[132] These "sly" new propaganda methods included separate "language sections" and foreign-language newspapers for the principal migrant groups working in France. By 1926, 16% of the CGTU's budget was allocated to propaganda among migrant groups, principally through newspapers such as *La Ricossa, El Proletario, Trybuna Robotnika,* and others.[133] Rhetorically and programmatically the CGTU remained internationalist; only its methods embraced national differences among workers.

Most migrants were not active members of political organizations, but all migrants experienced the impact of political policing. Joining the Communist Party "took a lot of courage for the worker who valued [keeping] his job," the historian Janine Ponty points out.[134] Even joining unions came with risks, especially since police often blurred the ideological distinctions among various forms of syndicalism. A remarkable percentage of migrants were willing to run those risks: Unionization rates among Italian migrants, for instance, were often considerably higher than those among their French counterparts, as was membership in antifascist organizations.[135] But many others "just wanted to work; and they didn't want to unionize."[136] Guilt by association was also a concern. In Lyon, nine Italian antifascists were expelled in 1923 because they had been "pointed out" as responsible for attacking compatriots who had come to work in the Lyon suburbs and who were reputed to be fascists. In at least one case the expulsion was ordered despite what police acknowledged as a "lack of evidence."[137] Instead, the expulsion was based on "information gathered indicating that this individual engaged in communist propaganda in the commune of St-Fons, where he lived."[138] In another Lyon incident, a Spanish construction worker was recommended for expulsion after trying to warn the notorious anarchist Francisco Ascaso that police were looking for him and had arrested his fellow anarchist Buenaventura Durruti.[139] In other parts of France, militants claimed that coworkers were expelled for simply "defending their union and association rights" or even "for having been seen with the union secretary."[140]

Although the majority of expulsions followed convictions for violations of civil or criminal law, police records confirm some of migrants' fears regarding guilt by association. A "special observations" column on police forms allowed officers to provide a political motivation for initiating an expulsion procedure, instead of the usual indications of arrest date and court record. Foreigners with no arrest record could thus be expelled for such offenses as being "a member of the anarchist group 'Sacco and Vanzetti,'" "a union delegate for the *syndicat autonome,*" "an extremely dangerous revolutionary," "a convinced anarchist," "a violent anarchist," "an antifascist," "a militant communist," "a notorious communist," "a militant antifascist communist," "suspicious from a national point of view," or "unobjectionable, outside of his *opinions,*" among other political labels.[141] Of course, as Claire Auzias has pointed out, many of these appellations had nothing to do with one another, "libertarian thought on syndicalism [being] in complete disagreement with Bolshevik theory and its party-union hierarchy." However, "police reports did not acknowledge this difference."[142] Reviews of naturalization applications showed a similar approach to politics, as requests were more likely to be granted to those whose politics could be characterized as "reserved" [*éffacée*].[143]

The politics of policing thus profoundly affected migrants' civil liberties. Their rights in 1920's France depended on the impact of the postwar settlement on their legal status, the nature of local social and economic life in the cities to which they migrated, and the intersection of domestic and international politics. In the face of these overlapping concerns, whether and how migrants chose to exercise civil liberties emerged from individual calculations of claiming rights against the risks of exercising them.

RIGHTS VERSUS RISKS

In an obscure footnote to his 1932 thesis, the self-styled immigration expert Georges Mauco penned a comment that scholars have since cited repeatedly as the central insight of his work. The foreign worker, he wrote, loses "a large part of his individual liberties" because he is under "permanent control" and the administration "dictates his salary, as well as the location and nature of his work. He can change neither place nor profession without authorization."[144] Mauco was only half right. Migrants did face limits to their liberties, but these limits could not be attributed solely to the impact of administrative regulations. As we have seen, the ability of the French administration to control the labor market was limited.[145] Moreover, even when regulations were effective, they not only constrained migrants but also created opportunities for them. Arguably, it was precisely the lack of regulations applying to nonreciprocity migrants that most threatened their civil liberties. The array of choices facing them was unquestionably more circumscribed. This is not to say that most-favored foreigners faced no obstacles to exercising civil rights—far from it. But individual liberties were not "lost" as an object is; rather, migrants made decisions about how much and in what ways to express themselves given what limited information they had about political and economic developments in their home countries and in France, what they had seen happen to their neighbors, and what they had witnessed police do.

Migrants' tolerance of risk depended on a host of factors, including the circumstances of their migration, their legal status, and their family situation. Perhaps it was his statelessness that encouraged an Armenian electrician to cross a Lyon picket line in 1928. He may have decided to show support for the boss to avoid being fired, a strategy that Gérard Noiriel found among some migrants in the Lorraine.[146] Perhaps he shared the view of a compatriot living in Décines who later recalled "at the time anyone who refrained from working on the first of May, even if ill, was fired without recourse, as was anyone suspected of being—or denounced as—a communist. The good will of the boss was law."[147] Or he may have remembered, from a few years before, warnings by Armenian leaders to avoid politicized conflicts.[148]

If the Armenian strikebreaker was so cautious, what made Gasparo G., the Italian union militant who threatened violence to him, less fearful—at least initially? Could he have predicted that even though he would be arrested for "disrupting the freedom to work," his union would win its wage demands and then join his employer in pressuring local authorities to refrain from expelling him? Did the subsequent expulsion with an immediate three-month renewable *sursis* lead him to moderate his labor organizing? Was it fear that authorities might let his suspension expire that encouraged him, in the ensuing years, to ensure that five of his children born in France were officially declared French nationals?[149] Certainly others like him found that an expulsion, even when suspended, "marked [one's] whole life."[150]

Even the most ardent revolutionaries often took care to protect themselves from retribution for their political activities, sometimes victimizing others in the process. Innocenzo C., a manual laborer at a Marseille oil producer, was expelled in July 1929 after coworkers "malevolently" made him carry communist newspapers under his arm "without his understanding their nature."[151] Living under *sursis* for the next eight years until his expulsion order was rescinded in 1938, Innocenzo likely showed less "naïveté" and greater care in choosing his associates from then on.[152] Still, a political past was often hard to shake. Natale M., active in Lyon's antifascist movement after the murder of Giacomo Matteotti, had to put up with police watching his every move even several years later. An acknowledged lack of solid evidence against him—police reports indicated that he "frequents communist meetings, but doesn't speak"—did not deter the general secretary for police from advocating his expulsion on the grounds of past participation in antifascist organizing and the "almost certain" evidence that he retained contact with notorious antifascists.[153] Although the director of the Sûreté in Paris granted the general secretary's request and expelled Natale, his admonition that Natale "should be free to choose the border by which he leaves our territory" suggests that he too wondered whether an expulsion was really warranted.[154]

Militants who managed to avoid enforcement of their expulsions still were often marked for life by the measure. Matteo C., expelled after alleged violence toward police officers during an anarchist demonstration, went from holding long-term jobs at Marseille refineries to working on the docks after he was expelled. This changed only once he began receiving regular *sursis* to his expulsion.[155] The expulsion also appears to have influenced decisions he made about his family's legal status. Having already declared his then-five-year-old son French shortly following his arrest, Matteo did the same when a second child was born. Beginning in 1934, he lobbied to have his expulsion repealed. If Matteo did hold anarchist views, he put them aside long enough to solicit the state's protection through naturalization, which he requested in 1937.[156] Those who were less careful sometimes paid the price. No amount of maternal insistence that a son's attack on members of the JP three years earlier "were nothing more than the indiscretions [*espiegléries*] of adolescence" could outweigh the utter foolishness of Ignazio C. painting "Soldiers, fraternize with the Soviets" on the St Nicolas Fortress in Marseille's harbor while already under an expulsion order.[157] Ignazio's case showed that youthful behavior engaged in with little forethought could have long-term and serious consequences. His mother understood this better than he.

Scholars have sometimes suggested that the generation of migrants who came to France before the Second World War integrated into French life by way of their engagement in working-class politics. According to Pierre Guillen, for instance, the most important motor to Italian integration was "the many antifascist demonstrations organized jointly by exile groups and the French left: after stirring to the same speeches, marching side by side behind the same banners, yelling the same slogans, how could they retain doubts and suspicions about one another?"[158] But, as Pierre Milza acknowledges, it is easy to exaggerate or romanticize this cross-national solidarity. Prior to the Second World War, "the French syndicalist movement aimed as much to use foreign workers' dynamism as to facilitate their fusion with natives."[159] Certainly, as the clash over the de Castelnau counterdemonstration had proved in Marseille, French left-wing organizations enlisted the support of international antifascist movements to build alliances against what were in many ways long-standing domestic enemies. It is possible that the same migrants who felt solidarity when demonstrating on 9 February 1925 felt exploited 13 days later when police swept their neighborhood trying to smoke out militants and intimidate the general population.

Then too there were regional and sectoral differences in the labor and antifascist movements. In the Lorraine steel-producing town of Longwy, the confrontation of employer paternalism and foreign militancy was a volatile one that drove a wedge between foreign and French workers, with the latter internalizing the bosses' paternalism.[160] It was perhaps due to these divisions that the Longwy steelworks went 15 years with no strikes.

Meanwhile, mines in the same region hardly had a single year without a strike, a fact that Gérard Noiriel attributes to the important presence of second-generation Italian militants in the mining unions. In any case, antifascism did not forge "solidarity" between nationalities in Longwy, because the only antifascists, according to Noiriel, were Italian.[161] Nor did the labor movement successfully bridge gaps between metropolitan French workers and colonial migrants. As a result of the weak integration of colonial workers into the French labor movement, Stéphane Sirot has explained, strike movements by colonial workers more often ended in violence.[162]

Scholars looking back at the 1920s from the vantage point of the post–World War II era, when the Communist Party emerged as the largest French party and briefly participated in government, may forget the degree to which communists, French and foreign alike, were perceived as a threat in the 1920s. The right-wing Bloc National had been elected in 1919 not only thanks to changes in election rules but also because anti-Bolshevism had been the principal campaign issue during the parliamentary elections. This government brutally put down the waves of legal strikes launched in 1920 by railroad workers. Because strikers and Bolshevik sympathizers were construed as "enemies of the nation," anticommunism became not just a majority opinion but also a government practice.[163] Government repression of communism intensified once the French Communist Party was established at the December 1920 Congress of Tours and began taking direct orders from the Comintern. The arrival of the Left in power in 1924 did little to quiet fears of communism as the Cartel des Gauches distanced itself from the communists, and the Right deliberately used anticommunism to polarize parliament in order to impede the Cartel's effectiveness. Changes in police practices also demonstrated a new peacetime preoccupation with sedition, which meant that "surveillance officials came increasingly to devote more attention to foreigners likely to endanger internal order than to French nationals."[164]

The fears driving surveillance of foreigners' political activities ebbed and flowed throughout the interwar period, but never disappeared entirely. Indeed, of the foreigners who were arrested for political behavior in the 1920s who acquired the right to stay in the country through *sursis,* many were subsequently sent to the Vernet concentration camp as "dangerous foreign nationals" at the onset of the Second World War. After the war, many migrants who had been labeled "notorious communists" in the 1920s finally saw the repeal of their expulsions and earned "privileged resident" cards.[165] This was evidence not so much of immigrant assimilation as of the integration of communism into mainstream French politics.

However incorporated into certain milieus within working-class political life migrants were, they faced increased surveillance of their mail, press, and associations, as well as other obstacles to political expression. While intimidation of foreigners was undoubtedly more diffuse in large, diverse cities such as Marseille and Lyon than it was in highly controlled paternalist environments, authorities in France's second and third cities did not shy away from using expulsion or the threat of it to try to control migrant behavior. Ironically, as Maud Mandel has demonstrated, this sometimes had the effect of making migrant communities all the more insular as they retreated from engaging in French public life.[166]

In the wake of war, "workers of the world" arrived in France at an unprecedented rate. Then, as now, workers' rights became central to debates that raged about the effects of a globalizing economy. Today, in the case of both illegal labor migrants and "outsourced" labor, differentials in labor and social rights pose a dilemma to policy makers in advanced nations. Keenly aware of the potential for such a dilemma to present itself, the crafters of France's guest-worker migration regime in the aftermath of the First World War made labor and social rights central to its organization.

By design, the French guest-worker program was to have privileged the migration of single, mobile men who would work the length of their contracts, then return home. Labor and social rights, granted to migrants from a select group of countries, were intended, first, to ensure that employers did not use the availability of migrant labor to undercut wages and disadvantage French workers and, second, to prevent migrants from permanently settling in the host country. However, from the outset, inequalities between and within nations affected both the formal standards that delimited migrant rights in France and the informal relationships that made rights meaningful. The theory and practice of rights often diverged, with profound implications both for migrants and for nationals of mainland France.

By the end of the 1920s, the limits of the postwar vision had become manifest. Spontaneous labor migration from nontreaty states continued. Tens of thousands of refugees arrived from Russia and Armenia, and their lack of labor and social rights contributed to the creation of a formally segmented labor market. The fact that migrants from France's empire also often fell outside the realm of treaty-conferred rights contributed to this development as well. Today, within the European Union, we might call this a "third-country national" problem, but the conundrum it presents is hardly new.[167]

While the vicissitudes of international and imperial relations had a profound impact on the outline of migrant rights in the post-Versailles era, the content of rights depended on much more than the formal relations between states or within an empire. First of all, guaranteeing labor rights required employment regulation, and employment regulation was difficult: Not all industries were suited to long-term contracts, and even in those that were, employers frequently found ways to avoid the equal-salary clauses of the treaties. At the same time, employers often succeeded in intimidating migrants from defending their labor rights. French government authorities, themselves worried about political radicalism, did little to prevent such intimidation by employers and often engaged in some of their own, using expulsion and the threat of it in an effort to control the political expression of migrant communities. As this occurred, migrants faced tough decisions about how to balance labor, social, and civil rights.

These decisions were rendered especially difficult by inconsistencies in how rights were enforced. Throughout France, local police were the gatekeepers of migrant rights, since police inspectors' opinions were solicited on everything from identification card renewals to naturalization requests to expulsion orders. All localities received the same instructions from the central government on these matters. And yet, throughout France, police practices differed. A foreigner who was considered to have a fixed residence in Lyon might instead be labeled a transient in Marseille. A migrant in one part of Marseille might be expelled for a crime that, if committed by another migrant living in a different neighborhood, led only to a warning. In short, the remarkable variety of circumstances in which migrants lived and worked, the structure of the local economy, the tenor of local and national political conflicts, urban infrastructure and social life, and long-standing police practices all contributed to the substance of migrant rights.

Migrant rights not only differed across space; they changed over time. The depression, to which we now turn, was one catalyst of change. Yet, as with the boom, the bust was felt unevenly.

CHAPTER TWO

From Labor Contract
to Social Contract

The Impact of the Depression on Migrant Rights in Lyon

To be an immigrant and be unemployed . . . is a paradox and a scandal.[1]

Lyon mayor Édouard Herriot had begun worrying about the growing number of migrants arriving "in our cities which are already over-crowded" as early as 1928.[2] When the depression hit France, he was among those leading the charge for more stringent immigration policies. "According to the latest statistics, there are 5,000 unemployed in Lyon and 20,000 foreigners," he declared to commotion in the Chamber of Deputies on 11 December 1931.[3] Four days later, when the labor minister Adolphe Landry claimed that "in general . . . French employers . . . have taken great pains to lay off foreign workers prior to the French," Herriot interrupted him, crying, "It's completely the opposite. You are being mis-led, Mister Minister."[4] A 1926 law had tightened identification card controls and fines on noncompliant employers. Yet policy and practice had diverged, and as the French began to feel the effects of the worldwide economic crisis, local leaders demanded accountability from the central government.

Within a few months, parliament passed more restrictive labor legislation. Although some deputies, including Herriot, advocated establishing a fixed 10% maximum on foreign employment in all industries, the emergent law "for the protection of national labor" (10 August 1932) allowed local parity commissions housed at the public placement offices to phase in thresholds that made sense for each region and its industries, subject to

Labor Ministry approval. Employment legislation finally recognized that labor markets differed by sector and region. But legislators still assumed that local officials could control employment practices in their departments. As Gary Cross has suggested, this was impractical. Still, even if the law itself was, as Cross has argued, "scarcely more than a public relations measure," in some parts of France it helped set in motion a logic whose effect was far from merely rhetorical.[5]

Because the growth of the advanced industrial sector had been so stunning in the Lyon metropolitan area, the impact of the economic downturn in the 1930s was especially dramatic. Although police personnel in Lyon and its inner suburbs fell under the authority of the department (and thus the Interior Ministry)—and not Herriot's municipality—they drew the same statistical inferences as Herriot had: The more foreigners they could encourage to leave Lyon, the more jobs that would be opened up for French men and women. To pursue these ends, they did not wait for employers to reduce their foreign personnel or for foreigners to voluntarily head home; instead they used their police powers proactively, increasingly using economic protectionism as a rationale for *refoulement* and expulsion.

As Lyon police aggressively aimed to exclude migrants they regarded as superfluous to the local economy, migrants who had arrived in the 1920s without any initial intention of settling had since become invested in staying for all manner of reasons: because political developments in their home countries made them wary of returning, because the unemployment crisis at home was even more grave than it was in France, because they had brought their families or had formed new ones. Yet now, the future seemed uncertain. Migrants were used to balancing rights against risks, but the latter seemed to be mounting. With unemployment or job insecurity threatening the very source of their residency authorizations, on what basis could immigrants assert the right to stay?

The strategies migrants deployed in response to the Lyon crackdown once again shed light on the uneven relationships they developed with agents of the French state. Some newly recognized the importance of treaty rights that at times had seemed hollow in the 1920s, when equal wage provisions often went unenforced and the freedom to protest working conditions unprotected. Now they invoked those same treaties in order to claim unemployment insurance. For others, living in the rare municipality that made no distinction between treaty beneficiaries and other foreigners became their saving grace. When these migrants lost their labor contracts, they often successfully invoked a social contract.

Making a direct claim on France's burgeoning but still highly localized welfare state was not the only way that migrants sought social security.

Some creatively overturned the assumptions that informed immigration policy. Rather than base their claims on jobs that were increasingly regarded as rightfully French, many migrants instead went into private enterprise and sought "nonworker" identification cards. Nor were all coping mechanisms licit. Out-of-work migrants—especially those who could not invoke social rights—sometimes turned to petty crime to survive. Since an arrest for any infraction of French law could trigger an expulsion, this was a particularly risky survival strategy.

The relationships that emerged between migrants and state authorities in depression-era Lyon were hardly uniform. Invariably, as in 1920s Marseille, some migrants bore the brunt of police power more heavily, while others were better able to establish enforceable claims on state services. This dialectics of inclusion and exclusion did not rely solely, of course, on direct relations between migrants and the state. Countless individual and familial decisions—some strategic, others made with little forethought—came into play. These often made the difference between retaining a job and losing it, eating and going hungry, or remaining in France and leaving. Nonetheless, migrants' interactions with state officials—from the employment office to the police precinct and beyond—provide an exceptional vantage point from which to evaluate the interplay of personal strategies, state power, and interstate relations at a time when migrant rights were undergoing realignment. This chapter examines four domains in which migrants' encounters with officials in Lyon garnered special attention: social criminality, economic flexibility, social entitlement, and naturalization. In time, each of these also captured national attention.

FROM BOOM TO BUST

Although France resisted the initial shock in 1929 better than its European neighbors did, when the international crisis did hit, it hit hard. It also hurt the advanced industries driving Lyon's economy first.[6] By early 1931, companies that had run around the clock in the 1920s were lucky if they could offer a fraction of their regular workforce a reduced workweek. Metallurgy and synthetic fiber, two of the leaders of the Lyon industrial boom, were among those suffering the most.

In February 1931, Lyon's special police commissioner reported 2,000 lost jobs in metallurgy and 1,500 fewer jobs in textiles than the year before.[7] Worse, it soon became obvious that these reductions marked only the beginning. Just over a month later, textile industries reported 4,000 unemployed and partially unemployed. By the end of 1931, an estimated

20,000 people were unemployed in the Lyon area, and the main textile employer's federation took the extreme measure of halting all production between mid-December and the New Year. By January 1932, metallurgy opted for a similar solution, with the automobile giant Berliet closing for a week.[8] Although there were brief periods of recovery, overall the outlook remained grim in the advanced industrial sector for several years. As late as the fall of 1934, the surviving synthetic fiber, automobile, and heavy machinery companies were still making new cuts in personnel.[9] Textiles exemplified these economic trends. Dye industry revenue declined 75% between 1929 and 1937, while the number of companies devoted to dying cloth plummeted from 110 to 69 during that same time. Employment in textile dying, similarly, dropped from 16,800 to 6,450.[10]

The impact of the downward economic spiral on migrants in metropolitan Lyon was enormous. Dramatic unemployment replaced the spectacular growth that had helped to draw foreign migrants to the region in the first place. Like the boom, the bust had an uneven impact on the region's social map. Writing on Lyon's foreign workers in his 1935 thesis, Henri Baroin highlighted the geography of unemployment. Whereas foreigners comprised 20% of those receiving unemployment compensation in Lyon proper, in Villeurbanne this figure rose to 28%, and in the newer working-class suburbs of Bron, St-Fons, Vénissieux, and Vaulx-en-Velin, foreigners comprised, respectively, 55%, 63%, 67%, and 72% of those receiving unemployment compensation.[11]

Census and Rhône department figures also point to the effect of the depression on migrants—especially in Lyon's suburbs. The biggest reductions in foreign population were recorded in suburbs that were home to large firms, often with company housing, where losing one's job frequently meant losing the roof over one's head as well. According to Baroin, the suburbs of Vénissieux, Oullins, Givors, and Vaulx-en-Velin together experienced nearly a 41% drop in foreign population between December 1931 and December 1934.[12] Special censuses taken of foreigners show even more dramatic declines in some industrial towns: over 67% in both Vénissieux (between 1929 and January 1932) and Vaulx-en-Velin (between January 1931 and 1935), although the latter's foreign population was still reportedly growing between 1929 and 1931, while the former showed a slight resurgence between 1932 and 1935 (see Figure 2.1). Some of these differences might be attributable to naturalizations or to the acquisition of citizenship at the age of adulthood by foreigners' children born in France, errors in census figures, or an increase in illegal status invisible to the historical record. Whatever the explanation, it is significant that the most dramatic shifts in foreign population occurred in the areas that were most heavily populated by the industrial working

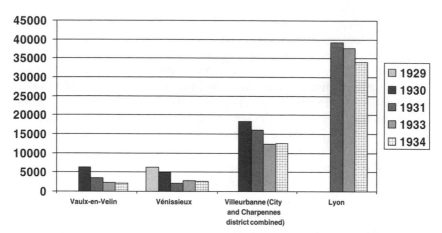

FIGURE 2.1 *Impact of the depression on Lyon-area population*
SOURCE: *ADR 4 M 416; 4 M 417.*

class. These demographic indicators provide one glimpse into the depression's impact on foreigners' rights. The strategies of those who stayed on provide another. It is to these strategies, and to their consequences, that we now turn.

SOCIAL CRIMINALITY

In theory, Rhône department policy held that any foreigner who "was not able to produce the work contract that had been requested from him for the completion of his identification card" would be ordered "to leave our Territory . . . under threat of expulsion."[13] In practice, foreigners who were entitled to social rights such as unemployment compensation often were able to base residency claims on those rights. By contrast, migrants who lacked social rights and sustained themselves through marginal (and sometimes illegal) social behavior generally earned less sympathy from Rhône authorities.

Beginning in the early 1930s, migrants living in Greater Lyon suddenly became more vulnerable to exclusion, as the police began arresting foreigners for petty infractions of the civil code, infractions one might call "social crimes": failure to pay one's fare on the tram, sitting in a higher class of service than that for which one had paid, stealing coal residue from train tracks for fuel, fishing or hunting illegally, or simply, unemployed, not meeting authorities' idea of sufficient resources to live on.

Not only did prosecution of foreigners for social crimes rise during the depression but so too did arrests and expulsions for misdemeanors related directly to foreign status: for expired identification cards, for bogus contracts, for working with identification cards that were not appropriate for the employee's labor category, or for failure to honor an injunction to leave (*refoulement*). These infractions were intimately linked to the effect of the economic downturn on foreign populations in the Lyon area, as migrants changed jobs, took jobs without contracts, and were unable to renew previously legitimate identification cards. Like social crimes, the intensified prosecution of these offenses pointed to new policing priorities.

Poaching, petty theft, and the like were hardly unusual coping mechanisms in poor communities. George Orwell, for example, vividly depicted women sifting through slag heaps in search of usable coal in 1930's England.[14] In their acclaimed analysis of depression-era unemployment in the Austrian town of Marienthal, the sociologists Marie Jahoda, Paul Lazarsfeld, and Hans Zeisel reported that townspeople resorted to stealing pet dogs and cats for consumption, violating fishing laws, swiping neighbors' home-grown vegetables, and other economically motivated crimes. "I sometimes go to the railway yard to swipe some coal," a woman told them. Most of these offenses were largely "ignored by the authorities" in Marienthal. In Lyon, however, police and prefectural officials became newly interested in such infractions, particularly when their perpetrators were foreign.[15]

I have labeled this behavior "social crime" even though I am aware that other scholars have used this term to refer to politicized resistance or banditry. My use of the term is closer to Stephen Humphries' characterization of social crime as "a short-term family solution rather than part of a long-term political solution to their problems."[16] In a sense, of course, all crimes are "social." As Michelle Perrot has argued, "There are no 'facts of crime' as such, only a judgmental process that institutes crimes by designating as criminal both certain acts and their perpetrators. In other words, there is a discourse of crime that reveals the obsessions of a society."[17] That Perrot made this observation in an article on delinquency is significant: It is perhaps especially in the prosecution of petty offenses that the reordering of social relations and societal expectations is made most apparent. These expectations changed in depression-era Lyon and engendered novel predicaments for the city's migrants. Of course, the peak in French hysteria over petty subsistence crimes came in the nineteenth century.[18] Victor Hugo captured this nineteenth-century sensibility in *Les misérables* with the protagonist Jean Valjean, who was sentenced to 19 years in prison for stealing a loaf of bread.[19] Since petty crimes had long ceased to preoccupy authorities to the degree that they had in the nineteenth century, one must ask: Why did forms of delinquency that had faded from view suddenly recapture, at least in Lyon, the attention of police agents?

It was not as if police officials had never paid attention to delinquency. Certainly they were aware, as we have seen, of glaring differences in living conditions among migrants. In the 1920s, however, Rhône authorities had not connected social marginality to the migrant condition as such. Convictions for vagrancy and begging in the 1920s, for instance, concerned largely French nationals. The case of Bruno G., whose story opened this book, was a rare exception. In the early 1930s, this pattern began to change, as the proportion of French persons charged with vagrancy in Lyon began to drop, while that of foreigners rose.[20] Perhaps more significantly, convictions of foreigners for violating laws pertaining to their residency more than doubled.[21] Another, more subtle, change had also taken place. Whereas police reports had always mentioned individuals' addresses, places of employment, and family status for identification purposes, this once ancillary information now became a crucial element in police decision making. Unlike their Marseille counterparts, who already drew on social information as they adjudicated the boundaries of belonging in the 1920s, prior to the depression Lyon officials had generally judged crimes (excepting some cases involving political militants), not criminals.[22] This now changed.

The expulsion of complete families signaled this shift. When Police Inspector Bonnand cited the Spanish national Carlos G. for illegal fishing, Carlos, his wife, and their five French-born children were all recommended for expulsion. Although the Ministry of the Interior's response recommended giving Carlos a chance to find work, the local employment placement office repatriated Carlos and his family at Ministry of Labor expense at the end of January 1933. No doubt the economic situation was no better in Spain, because the family returned in December, only to have their apparent impoverishment trigger a new cycle of expulsion recommendations.[23]

Carlos G.'s family was hardly the only Spanish family whose poverty attracted the attention of Lyon-area administrators. Particularly before a reciprocity treaty guaranteed Spanish nationals equal access to unemployment assistance in France, they were hit hard by the decline in jobs. Nationwide, they disproportionately accepted repatriation.[24] Their difficulties surviving largely without state assistance were compounded by the fact that they often tended to have large families. Spanish strategies for coping with poverty, moreover, often met with considerable disapproval from local authorities. Citing animal codes, police targeted Spanish families who raised chickens, rabbits, and pigeons for their own consumption and for sport. Foreigners hardly had a monopoly on this lifestyle.[25] Still, French nationals could not be expelled for violating social norms. Meanwhile, this behavior, characterized by the deputy chief of police Henri Teyssier as "very common in this neighborhood [the Chateau-Gaillard section of Villeurbanne] in which only foreigners live" led authorities to threaten one family with expulsion for "keeping a clandestine dove under a net."[26]

Lyon officials had known about migrant poverty for years, but, as we have seen, the action taken to address it involved such measures as trying to get migrants who built their own shacks to learn building codes and apply for construction licenses. In the 1920s, authorities had concluded that however much migrant shantytowns violated health and building regulations, the one obvious remedy—eviction—did nothing to treat the cause of the problem, which they identified as Lyon's housing shortage. Since migrants were necessary for the smooth functioning of Lyon's economy, authorities were interested in encouraging them to stay. In the early 1930s, that changed. With unemployment growing, officials wanted not only to evict but also to expel migrants. Increasingly, Rhône department authorities identified migrants' lifestyles as a cause, not only a consequence, of Lyon's social ills. From that point forward, few domains of migrant life escaped the scrutiny of authorities. Many years later, officials approached similarly makeshift housing developments (newly baptized "*bidonvilles*") in much the same way: mostly with neglect until this became politically unacceptable.[27]

As police personnel took on the role of social psychologists, the trick for the administration became distinguishing destitution as a way of life from destitution as a wave of bad luck. Nowhere did they face this problem more than in the numerous cases of foreigners stopped for stealing coal residue from train tracks, presumably because the economic situation made acquiring fuel for heating and cooking more difficult. The fact that officials rarely pursued expulsion for coal theft in cases of people who worked regularly, or who could rely on family support, suggests that police paid less attention to the precise infractions committed than to the way of life of the foreigners committing them.[28] For one Italian woman whose expulsion was recommended by the general secretary for police, clemency by way of renewable *sursis* was ultimately granted when her husband wrote insisting on the exceptional and frivolous nature of her error: "For the last ten years I have lived in France," he wrote in impeccable, and very formal, French, "and had never been reproached until my wife was overtaken by an unfortunate impulse that I cannot myself explain."[29] The fact that her husband—also an Italian migrant—had a regular job working for Jangot Bonneton et Cie and earned 42 francs a day probably also entered into how authorities weighed the case. Certainly police officials were less accommodating to those who had no family upon which to fall back.

Having lost her husband, Roberta G. learned how true this was. Authorities ordered Roberta's expulsion when she failed to obtain the proper license prior to opening a new bar. Unlike her compatriot who had stolen coal residue, Roberta had no one to assure Rhône authorities that she would not become a public charge. This alleged inability to support herself, not the licensing infraction, motivated her expulsion.[30] Roberta's lawyer, Jacques Locquin, evidently failed to recognize this, as he repeatedly mentioned Roberta's hardship as a rationale for leniency in her case. Since her husband had been brutally killed by a Frenchman who "decapitated" him after he had defended Arab clients in his café, Locquin explained, a loss of clientele had forced her to close. Since then, she "had difficulty supporting her two minor children," despite aid from her grown daughter and son-in-law. "This difficulty, the settlement of part of her family in France, and especially the misfortune that the crazy rage of one of our compatriots inflicted upon [Roberta G.] are sufficient, I believe, to justify the favor of clemency I request."[31] Locquin had miscalculated. When the prefect followed up with his report to the Interior, he refrained from including the lawyer's story and wrote simply that Roberta had no means of existence in France.[32]

Widows were not alone in being presumed incapable of supporting themselves. Belinda W. was expelled following the enforcement of an expulsion order against her husband, for she was deemed unable to support herself and her family without his assistance, having lost her own job in 1931. The assumption grounded in the civil code that family members should live together probably also affected her case.[33] Among women, only the young and single were regarded as viable economic actors. When Bedros T. sought authorization for his 15-year-old sister, Takouhi, to join him in the Rhône department in 1931, the request was rejected because the general secretary for police deemed that Bedros and his wife "were not in a position to house and provide for [Takouhi], who will seek work."[34] Takouhi came anyway, paying a compatriot to secure her a "nonworker" card. Violating the conditions of her card, she began working as a seamstress, triggering her expulsion. The prefect suspended her expulsion only when the family claimed she would marry, at which point he conceded to a *sursis* on the condition that "she marry as soon as possible and agree not to work." After her marriage to an Armenian barber, Takouhi earned regular *sursis* to her expulsion order; at least officially, she ceased sewing for a living upon marrying.[35]

Other single women also elicited suspicions among authorities. Police refused to authorize residency for Bianca N., whose French aunt and uncle, bar owners in Villeurbanne, had promised to support her. Convinced that "it seems likely, if not certain, that sooner or later [Bianca] will occupy salaried employment or will work at the . . . bar without authorization," Rhône officials recommended Bianca's expulsion when she failed to procure a legal work contract.[36] Similarly, Bettina M. was enjoined to leave, then officially expelled, in 1933 for working without compensation at her aunt's bar. "Whether she is remunerated or not," the prefect explained, Bettina M. "must obtain authorization from the Ministry of Labor in order to hold this job."[37]

The ideas that authorities held regarding single women were not just stereotypes: Takouhi, Bianca, and Bettina had all worked, albeit to varying degrees, precisely as authorities had predicted they would. All had violated the law. At the same time, however, the decisions that police officials made regarding women betrayed a deeply gendered understanding of the household economy. Although police assumed that unmarried young women would inevitably work and thereby compete with French nationals for jobs, they also believed that a woman who once had benefited from a man's economic "protection" would be helpless once that protection was removed. Even though French women had one of the highest rates of economic activity within Europe, authorities assumed that once migrant women married, they would cease to participate substantially in the labor market. Foreign women did work outside the home at lower rates than their French counterparts did; still, it was nonetheless a leap to conclude that no widowed or abandoned female migrant could support herself.

Not all authorities made this leap. When Jacques Locquin's appeal for clemency on Roberta's behalf failed, she left Lyon for the Jura, where her daughter and son-in-law lived. There, in a town that still only counts about 3,000 inhabitants, officials evidently harbored few concerns that she would become a "public charge." While Lyon officials evaluated Roberta's case with reference to the growing crisis facing their social services, their Jura counterparts focused on the nature of the infraction she had committed, which they called "not very serious."[38] Despite continued opposition from the Rhône prefect, Roberta G. earned a *sursis* in the Jura, then transferred it to Lyon, where she supported herself through the end of the 1930s as a cleaning woman. In the end, Roberta proved capable of supporting herself and her minor children despite being a widow. Because authorities in Lyon had doubted this, however, it was not enough to prove this to herself; she also had to prove it to police over and over again to maintain her *sursis*. Finally, her expulsion was rescinded in 1944.[39]

Whereas evaluations of foreign women hinged on whether or not they were dependents, Rhône police judged foreign men by whether or not they were providers. Men whose claims they deemed suspicious were susceptible to expulsion. Boghos H., for instance, first encountered police when a train conductor reported him for riding in a second-class train car with a third-class ticket; he was expelled for this offense on 29 December 1931. As a refugee from Armenia, Boghos sought the assistance of the French representative to the International Nansen Refugee Office, who requested leniency from the director of the Sûreté Générale in Paris. In making his appeal, not only did the Nansen representative underscore the "minor" nature of Boghos' infraction, but, perhaps cognizant that the infraction was not all that police were judging, he also claimed that Boghos was one of the only supports for a family of 12.[40] When confronted by his superior at the Sûreté with this new development, the Rhône prefect replied defensively:

This foreigner is not in the least the support for his family. In fact, his father, brother and two of his sisters occupy salaried employment. Moreover, the person in question has never been authorized to work in France and he cannot, because of current economic circumstances, obtain this authorization.[41]

In the end, Boghos apparently did not have the same standards of male economic independence as did the prefect, since the record demonstrates that he managed to stay on clandestinely, presumably thanks to family support, through at least 1935.[42]

Disagreements between Rhône authorities and Interior Ministry officials regarding the appropriate punishment for social crimes and misdemeanors committed by foreigners highlight the exceptional approach of the former in this regard. The disputes demonstrate that Rhône officials chose punishments not so much to fit the crime but to control the criminal, and especially his or her place in society and the economy. The example of Xavier M. makes this abundantly clear. Xavier arrived from Italy in 1926 and worked regularly for the Rhodiaceta synthetic fiber factory on a legal contract. One day in 1931, however, he made the error of evading payment of his tram fare. Perhaps the fact that he was newly married had stretched his 20-franc daily wage further than he could handle.[43] Or perhaps he was deviously trying to save a few centimes. In any case, citing the "current economic situation," Lyon's police chief called for his expulsion on 24 February 1932. Unlike their local representatives, officials in the central Interior Ministry focused more on the infraction itself than on the employment status of the accused. Responding to the recommendation from the Rhône department, they wrote that "the facts imputed against" Xavier M. "do not seem of sufficient gravity to warrant an expulsion order against him, particularly considering that this individual enjoys, by the way, a good reputation." Notes penciled angrily, then subsequently erased, on the ministerial decision showed how committed Rhône officials were to their approach: "And there are 15,000 unemployed in the Rhône department, of whom 12,000 are in Lyon! Should we insist on our point of view?"[44]

Although Rhône police officials' intransigence sometimes earned them reprimands, it usually produced the results that they desired. They had taken seriously Interior Minister Albert Mahieu's instructions of 2 June 1932, which had insisted that "it goes without saying that even a single conviction will lead to the rejection of [identity card renewal] . . . and to transmission of an expulsion proposal to the appropriate division."[45] No doubt Mahieu had violent criminals in mind when he issued these instructions less than a month after President Paul Doumer was assassinated by a Russian, an event that ignited concerns about immigration regulation, and the control of refugees in particular, throughout the country.[46] New instructions sanctioned expelling any person who failed to obtain a valid identification card or who, having obtained the card, "had it taken away . . . if circumstances demonstrated that he no longer presents the necessary assurances indispensable for being authorized to live in our country." The vague language left much room for interpretation.[47] For Rhône officials, the new directive fit well with the approach they had already adopted for foreign lawbreakers both large and small, and they continued to hew to this principle even though Camille Chautemps replaced Mahieu as interior minister the day after the latter had issued the circular. When, for instance, Chautemps' office proposed to warn rather than expel Quirino R. (found guilty of hitting his brother), the Rhône prefect greeted the order with consternation, reminding the ministry that Quirino was "out of work and finds himself unable to find an occupation because of the current economic crisis, the vacant jobs being reserved for nationals. . . . There is no reason, in my opinion, to retain in our territory this foreigner, condemned by common law, who constitutes a public charge for a duration which is unforeseeable but no doubt long given the likely prolonging of unemployment."[48] The Interior Ministry answered this letter with an order of expulsion.[49]

If expulsion was intended as a "central, even centrifugal, institution of the policing of foreigners in France,"[50] the process for ordering expulsions was, by contrast, centripetal. Expulsion practices revealed and often reinforced local policing priorities more than they implemented any centralized plan for regulating migrant activity in France.[51] Local police had the upper hand in negotiations with Sûreté officials because only they could claim intimate knowledge of a foreigner's situation. It was hard for Interior Ministry officials to question local knowledge, since the ministry depended on petty bureaucrats to enforce residency regulations. The fact that local police officers tended to hold their posts considerably longer than interior ministers—there were 23 changes in cabinet and 13 different interior ministers between 1930 and 1938 alone—also reinforced the power of local police.[52]

The dynamics of police bureaucracy gave Lyon officials the leeway to use expulsion—and equally important, the threat of expulsion—to try to force migrants from jobs or from living in the area. Slowly and almost imperceptibly, Rhône authorities were modifying the objective behind expulsion. Whereas officials in the central government generally used expulsion to remove foreigners who posed a security threat, Rhône officials redeployed expulsion for another purpose: to engineer the local population. Whether or not the foreigner in question left France was less a concern to Rhône authorities than whether he or she left the Lyon area. In the cases cited above, Xavier's record ended after the exchange between Rhône police and the Interior Ministry, a fact suggesting that he chose to move before a decision could be reached in his case. Quirino left Lyon in May 1933.[53] Among the women, Roberta left the Rhône department temporarily; Bianca's family convinced Rhône police that she "appears to have gone back to Italy"; Belinda went undiscovered until 1939; and Bettina resurfaced in 1940, in the interim having lived in the Saône-et-Loire department and Italy before returning to Villeurbanne.[54] While the strategy of Rhône police often impinged upon individual migrants' rights for years to come, it accomplished with reasonable effectiveness what departmental authorities wanted: It removed problems from their jurisdiction. Those foreign expellees who did not leave the Lyon area proceeded to exercise extreme caution and, in this way, also ceased to perturb local authorities.

Just as important as these sticks were the carrots authorities offered. That is, police used their expulsion powers not only to exclude but also to grant reprieves. Often the beneficiaries of such reprieves were migrants who defied the expectations of the guest-worker system and risked going into business for themselves. These migrants' survival strategies, although not always legal, paid off in a way that social crime did not.

ECONOMIC FLEXIBILITY

With the advent of mass redundancies in Lyon's advanced industries, increasing numbers of migrants adopted the strategy of shifting from one job or economic sector to another. In many respects, there was nothing particularly new about this. During the war, fears that foreign agricultural workers might displace demobilized French soldiers working in war industries had led to the creation of color-coded identification cards intended to distinguish agricultural from industrial workers. In 1926, in response to allegations that the greater flexibility of foreign workers constituted unfair competition, parliament had passed a law aimed at limiting the ability of foreigners to change jobs rapidly. Although the Napoleonic *livret ouvrier*, or worker passport, had been abandoned as impractical in the late nineteenth century before finally being abolished in 1890, parliament now instituted similar restrictions on foreign migrants, even though they initially had been invited to France largely because they were willing to follow the labor market. While not as reliant on labor turnover as Marseille, Lyon's labor market nonetheless defied these new restrictions.

Even before the advent of mass international migration to France, Lyon's economy had challenged rigid labor market regulations, serving as a pole of attraction for regional migrants who sought temporary work as an "intermission" between the seasons of "agricultural life."[55] Files on foreigners in the Rhône confirm that the city attracted migrants seeking a change in profession; they are replete with examples of individuals whose work histories show them migrating first to mono-industrial areas such as the company towns of the Lorraine, then to Lyon after a few years. For both regional and international migrants, Lyon's diverse economy was attractive because it meant that if one job failed, there would probably be another.[56]

With the depression, switching economic sectors became a common strategy for Lyon's migrants. Already in 1931, Lyon's special police commissioner reported that unemployed metal workers were flooding the manual labor trades such as construction and, he claimed, driving wages below contract levels.[57] Because the new labor laws were designed to prevent this kind of behavior, however, working without a contract or in a labor category other than that indicated on one's identification card was hazardous. When Taddeo G., once a skilled mechanic, tried to replace the word "mechanic" on his identification card with "manual laborer," he was expelled.[58] As much as a year before national policy sanctioned the practice, Rhône police ordered the *refoulement* and sometimes expulsion of foreigners whose applications for identification cards were late, incomplete, falsified, or otherwise inadequate.[59] By changing job categories, foreigners risked becoming illegal aliens.

One alternative to changing labor categories was to open a legal business and apply for a "nonworker" identification card instead, a practice that became increasingly common as the depression took its toll on salaried labor. Authorities were sometimes skeptical of this strategy and often sought proof that a given migrant was indeed independent and not secretly working for others. Of course, even without the extra scrutiny that being foreign brought, independent contracting was no magic bullet. In a deflationary environment, striking out on one's own was risky business and often brought in less revenue than a steady job. As Jean-Charles Bonnet demonstrates, commercial registrations by foreigners were often a sign of distress rather than success. Proof of this came in the modifications to commercial registers made by foreigners in Greater Lyon during the depression: A Spanish grocer added "sale of vegetables in the public market" to the list of his business activities in 1934, then, presumably to reduce his overhead costs, abandoned the storefront altogether in 1936 and sold exclusively at the public market. An Italian hairdresser added "traveling ice-cream sales" to her activities in 1933, while a bistro owner added haircutting to his![60] Identification card applications also testify to similar fluctuations: One man went from being employed as a painter in 1929 to working independently as a fruit merchant the following year, to opening his own painting business in 1931, only to return to waged labor as a painter-plasterer again in 1934.[61] Although turning independent came with risks, it became a common practice among foreigners who faced employment quotas or increased difficulty in procuring valid worker identification cards. Nationally, while the number of foreign workers declined by more than 390,000 between 1931 and 1936, the number of foreign "heads of business" increased by nearly 24,000.[62] Locally, registrations for commercial licenses among foreigners spiked upward in 1931, even as they declined among French nationals.[63]

One of those new heads of business was Yuri H., a Russian metalworker who became an independent mechanic after losing his job at Établissements Wenger. Although expelled following a fraud conviction, Yuri earned an immediate and renewable *sursis* in part because authorities concluded that his business "generates work [for others] outside his workshop." Working as an independent mechanic allowed Yuri to avoid enforcement of the expulsion; he then quietly returned to salaried employment in 1936. As of 1937, he was back working for his original employer as a turner.[64] Without articulating it explicitly, the police inspector had advanced what might be called a Keynesian argument, since it considered the problem of how migrant economic activity contributed to aggregate demand.[65] In effect, the police inspector saw Yuri as part of an integrated economic system. Keeping Yuri in business was itself, in this way, a "protectionist" measure. This same rationale was applied to the tinsmith Donato U. because he turned profits of up to 12,000 francs per year and because four of his five employees were "of French nationality."[66] Similarly, a Spanish masonry contractor employing 29 French, four Italian, and seven Spanish nationals was warned, rather than expelled, following his arrest for accidentally causing injury (*blessures involontaires*), and Tomasi I. was granted a reprieve because "he employs twelve French nationals who would be rendered unemployed by his departure." The gamble paid off; within a year, Tomasi's personnel had doubled in size. Perhaps that, or the fact that 18 of the workers were French, is why a new infraction of the labor code in 1937 for employing an unauthorized foreign worker went unreproached.[67]

Rhône authorities' attention to small-scale industries run by foreigners speaks to the degree to which the depression had transformed Lyon's economy: Every job mattered. While this outlook often produced intransigence toward foreigners, it also sometimes led officials to make exceptions to rigid formulas, if they concluded that doing so would benefit French workers in Lyon. Once again, then, the rights of migrants, albeit framed by national policy guidelines and international agreements, drew their substance from complex negotiations that took place both between migrants and local officials and within the state bureaucracy.

SOCIAL ENTITLEMENT

As Rhône officials considered which residency authorizations to extend or discontinue, ever present in their minds was not only the state of the labor market but also the ballooning cost of social assistance that had accompanied the deepening of the depression. This concern led them to focus on how (or whether) migrants supported themselves. This was hardly a novel concern for societies hosting migrants. From 1882, immigrants arriving in the United States could be refused entry if they were "likely to become a public charge."[68] Unlike the United States, France had never adopted specific policies aimed at eliminating destitute migrants. The closest it came was when it required Muslim Algerians, as of August 1926, to possess a minimum amount of money in order to disembark on the French mainland, and, from 1928, proof of a paid repatriation deposit.[69] Meanwhile, the bilateral treaties that had facilitated the migration of some Europeans in the 1920s had only vague references to the possibility of fluctuations in the job market, which would be addressed through "common agreement" between the contracting governments "regarding the appropriate measures" to take.[70] The treaties explicitly addressed repatriation only for those who had long-term illnesses or infirmities. This reflected not so much an oversight as the assumption that able-bodied workers would naturally follow the labor market and leave when there was no more work; only the non-able-bodied would have to be sent home. Such assumptions did not prevent mass repatriations of unemployed

Europeans from taking place on the basis of local initiatives, especially in mono-industrial areas.[71]

Evaluating migrants' place in the social welfare system became, like public assistance itself, an intensely local affair in interwar France. In Lyon, as authorities simultaneously tried to protect French jobs and prevent skyrocketing social service expenditures, contradictory priorities sometimes emerged. On the one hand, officials made clear that they valued economic independence. On the other hand, enforced self-sufficiency presented a number of problems. First, if foreign wage laborers were forced off unemployment rolls and back into the labor market, the potential for wage depression only grew. This was especially true because, despite regulations requiring that foreigners receive equal pay for equal work, migrants frequently felt pressure to work below their skill level or to accept substandard wages, particularly when their residency authorizations were about to expire and new labor contracts were required for renewal. Second, since the depressed labor market would never be able to absorb all those who were not entitled to social protections, destitution was likely to increase. Forcing self-sufficiency by limiting migrants' access to social assistance thus had the potential to exacerbate, rather than alleviate, social tensions. Throughout the 1930s, departmental and municipal leaders in the Rhône department struggled with how to balance these interests. Once again, the impact of their practices was felt unevenly.

Before the advent of a national welfare system after the Second World War, local assistance to the unemployed and indigent in France was paid through a combination of municipal revenue and state subsidies, with the largest share of the burden often falling on the municipalities themselves.[72] Within scholarship on social welfare, a great deal more attention has paid to France's mandatory pensions and, after 1932, family allocations. However, these social insurance programs, funded by contributions from both employers and employees, with some provisions for state subsidy, were structured around employment during one's productive years. Outside of sickness insurance, these initiatives made almost no provision for the temporary unemployment of able-bodied persons.[73] Until it was reformed after the Second World War, unemployment insurance thus remained the optional responsibility of local-level government. As such, access to unemployment indemnities was subject to considerable local manipulation.

In the Rhône department, rising unemployment costs combined with bills for ambitious urban projects in the 1920s to create major budget deficits in the 1930s. In early 1932, Villeurbanne's Socialist mayor Dr. Lazare Goujon reported that the city had spent more than two million francs on assistance during the previous year. After state and department subsidies were accounted for, the city's unemployment insurance expenditures would be 600,000 francs over budget. To make matters worse, Goujon predicted even larger shortfalls for the coming year—in the neighborhood of 1.5 million francs.[74] Lyon faced even more serious challenges. By 1933, the city was reportedly a billion francs in debt. While not all of this could be attributed to the rising costs of unemployment assistance, welfare programs surely put a significant dent in the city's budget.[75]

It did not take long for authorities to seize on the fragile rights of foreigners as a way to address their budget crises. As early as 1931, Goujon called upon Villeurbanne employers to give preference to French nationals, "who ask for nothing more than to work." Recognizing "the rights of all individuals, of whatever nationality, to a livelihood," Goujon nonetheless distinguished French workers, "who have contributed since childhood to the prosperity of the country," from foreigners, "especially those who have resided in France only a few years" and who can "return to their country of origin." Actually, French nationals did not only ask for work; they also asked for unemployment compensation. Mounting debt, due as much to Goujon's ambitious urban-planning programs of the past few years as to "the high number of beneficiaries and the limited resources of the Commune," motivated the mayor's request more than any ideological commitment to economic protectionism.[76] He hoped that he could simultaneously get French nationals off his unemployment rolls and encourage foreign nationals to leave France. When Goujon's efforts failed to have the desired effect on Villeurbanne's municipal coffers, the Municipal Council first raised the city residency requirements for unemployment compensation from three to six months then excluded, albeit temporarily, foreigners from nonreciprocity states.[77] Even so, Goujon left a deficit for his successor.

In Lyon, too, mounting social expenditures led to belt-tightening at the expense of some foreigners and, as we will see in Chapter 6, French nationals from North Africa. After briefly allowing foreigners from nontreaty states to receive an unemployment indemnity at two-thirds the standard rate, Lyon returned in mid-1931 to its 1926 policy of excluding foreigners who did not fall under reciprocity agreements.[78] In July, Jean Perret, the director of the municipal and regional placement office, called on disbursement centers to "strike" from their rolls all foreigners who had been receiving either cash indemnities or meal vouchers, unless they were Belgian, Italian, Polish, or Czech. Perret also asked officials to discontinue aid to Russian and Armenian refugees "if they do not accept, even in other regions, jobs that might be offered them" by the placement office.[79] Lyon authorities may have been precocious in adopting this strategy, but they were probably not alone in encouraging foreigners to seek work elsewhere.[80] Asked how he responded to foreign workers who refused transfers to other regions, one placement director allegedly replied, "It's very simple. I cancel their unemployment cards and their allocations."[81]

Jean Perret drew new distinctions, as well, among long-term unemployed persons who were no longer eligible for cash indemnities but who could receive meal vouchers: Among persons unemployed longer than six months, refugees and most-favored foreigners were accorded different rights from one another and from French nationals.[82] Even so, within months Mayor Herriot, citing "rising unemployment and increased distribution of meal vouchers," which "results in very high expenditures for the city," took additional steps to rein in expenses, replacing meal vouchers with soup kitchens, where rising costs could be better controlled.[83] A month after that, in December 1931, the mayor's deputy announced that district offices should direct Armenians (who evidently had not heeded Perret's injunction to find work outside the department) to a special "soup kitchen reserved especially for Armenians."[84] The new canteen would be called "municipal," but it appeared to finally fulfill the wish Herriot had expressed in 1928 that "large cities [should] appeal to the rich families" of Armenians to provide for their compatriots: The kitchen was, at a minimum, subsidized by an Armenian restaurateur, Mr. Katcha-Dourian.[85] Still excluded at this date from cash indemnities and never mentioned as rightful beneficiaries of food assistance, Spanish, Portuguese, and Swiss unemployed persons also were explicitly barred from receiving the food aid as of May 1932.[86] Ironically, the same Herriot who actively sought to reduce his unemployment budget also came to negotiate in November of that year, as premier and foreign minister, the treaty that would entitle Spanish nationals to social rights in France following ratification in late December 1933.

Austerity measures targeted foreigners first, but not exclusively. Fearing that unemployed persons "with no domicile" could use their homelessness to claim assistance in more than one municipal district, the municipality required homeless persons, from November 1932, to report to a central facility, where they would be fed.[87] This was still not enough to control escalating social costs, and by 1933, the city was spending an "unprecedented" two million francs per month on unemployment relief. That same year, it was revealed that Lyon was one billion francs in debt.[88] And so the cutting continued: As of August 1933, single unemployed persons who received cash assistance could not also receive food.[89] Herriot and his deputy mayor also tried to crack down on unemployed persons—especially women—whose leisure activities they found repugnant. Complaining that the unemployed spent their days at dance halls or movie theaters where they could easily meet "idlers and exploiters inciting them to bad behavior," they demanded that district offices summon citizens for verification of their unemployed status at inconvenient hours, especially in the late afternoon or very early on Monday mornings.[90]

Such cost-cutting and repressive measures place Lyon's status as "one of the most advanced urban welfare states in France" in perspective.[91] Lyon did have an extensive public health-care system, including the state-of-the-art hospital at Grange Blanche, built between 1914 and 1933 (today bearing Herriot's name), municipally funded moderate-income housing, a municipal slaughterhouse that sold meat at reduced rates, and other socially progressive initiatives that made it the envy of many other French cities at the time. Yet these ambitious urban development plans, of uneven benefit to foreigners, were in part responsible for Lyon's budget shortfalls in the 1930s.[92] The fact that neighboring Villeurbanne, which had also pursued extensive urban infrastructure and housing developments in the 1920s and early 1930s, also began cutting social services suggests that both cities, like the industries they housed, had become the inadvertent victims of their postwar prosperity.[93] Smaller, less well-endowed municipalities with fewer spectacular urban projects, although also facing declining revenues, had fewer conflicts over social services. Perhaps the fact that plans for municipally funded moderate-income housing never got off the ground in Vénissieux, for instance, helped it to continue providing equal access to unemployment compensation to all persons, regardless of nationality or ethnic origin throughout the 1930s.[94]

Once Lyon had restricted unemployment insurance to treaty beneficiaries, its leaders set about trying to purge long-term foreign beneficiaries from the rolls as well. These tactics, however short-lived, appear to have succeeded in intimidating some migrants. Leandro N., a Spanish man who had been receiving unemployment compensation for 16 months, or almost exactly the amount of time that had transpired since France had ratified the bilateral treaty with Spain, promised to "ask nothing of the Unemployment and assistance office" in exchange for the continued right to reside in France.[95] Others pointed out, however, that most-favored foreigners could not be forced to leave the country merely because they received public assistance. If the archival record is any indication, police acknowledged the legitimacy of this reproach, since they appear to have ceased this form of intimidation rather quickly. Indeed, there is little trace of such tactics being pursued after the victory of the socially progressive Popular Front government in national elections.[96]

Despite limits placed on beneficiaries, and sporadic attempts to intimidate foreign recipients of unemployment insurance, expenditures of two million francs per month for Lyon alone meant that many people, both

French and foreign, did receive assistance. Access to unemployment insurance became not only a means of survival but also a basis for claiming continued residency rights. Remarkably, even expelled foreigners hoping to gain reprieves emerged, in their negotiations with state officials, less as vulnerable supplicants than as participants in a social contract that allowed them to make powerful claims on the state.

The case of an Italian man, expelled with an immediate *sursis* for taking some fabric from the factory where he was working, demonstrates the degree to which persons living under suspended expulsion orders developed dependent relationships with agents of the Interior Ministry. In broken French, this foreigner wrote on *papier timbré* (paper stamped with a filing fee), explaining that

for 10 years, I have lived in Lyon, married and father of three young children. For a simple mistake, working at the Factory and having found a little scarf . . . , I had to have inflicted upon myself a 15 day suspended [sentence], and ultimately, my card was taken from me *and I am obliged every three months to request a provisional card,* believe, Mr. Prefect, and as the father of a family, that I did not commit a theft. Now I come . . . for my three children and my wife, to have my card given to me, with the hope that you will take my request into consideration, [I] beg of you to accept, Mr. Prefect, my most profound respect. Your devoted servant, [Savio X.].[97]

Yet the same case also reveals Savio's entitlement to a social safety net whose basis was independent of the police. Out of work, Savio received unemployment insurance from the Villeurbanne municipality first in his own name, then in his wife's. To the question scribbled at the bottom of each inquiry conducted for Savio's *sursis* renewals, "Can we renew . . . ? Unemployed, three [or, later, four] children," the response was always "yes."[98]

Despite Savio's fragile legal situation, he took advantage of his family's social entitlement. When their insurance was canceled in the spring of 1936, he lobbied local officials to reinstate the insurance payments. First, he addressed himself to the mayor of Villeurbanne, then to Deputy Georges Lévy of the National Assembly, and finally he requested a meeting with the prefect.[99] Motivated perhaps by desperation, these pleas nonetheless demonstrated Savio's conviction that he was entitled to a share of the French social contract. Although the police chief recommended that Savio's future *sursis* be contingent upon his looking for work, the prefectorial administration, in fact, had no way to prevent him from receiving the unemployment insurance that he was qualified to receive as an Italian national living in France. All they could do was threaten to remove his right to residency. By 1937, their threats proving empty, the question police scribbled at the bottom of their report was no longer

"Can we renew?" but rather, "After the 6th year of *sursis,* what proposal to make to the Interior?" The response finally followed the police chief's advice: "Grant only 3 months, advising him that the [expulsion] order . . . will be reactivated if he doesn't succeed."[100] Although the administration had given Savio few reasons to believe in its willingness to enforce his expulsion order, Savio did manage to find work two months after being informed, in September 1937, "that if he has not found a job between now and 31 October of this year he will be instructed to leave the territory." In a similar case involving an unemployed Italian man living in Vénissieux, *sursis* were granted for eight consecutive years while Gaetano W. received unemployment payments for himself and his family, until "Finally!," he secured employment in 1939, after having been "unemployed since 16 March 1931."[101] Although these two families and the others like them probably relied on multiple forms of income, it was of all things the unemployment insurance they received that legitimized their residency in France, for it provided a legal source of income at a time when they were unable to procure legitimate labor contracts as foreigners.

NATURALIZATION

When the bilateral treaties that benefited migrants such as Savio and Gaetano were first negotiated, social rights were written into the agreements for two reasons. First, it was important that labor costs be, at least nominally, the same for French and foreign labor, for if foreign workers were exempt from payroll taxes, employers might be disinclined to hire French nationals. The second reason was to assure leaders in sending countries that migrants would not need to change their citizenship status in order to secure basic protections of their labor rights. The idea was not to give migrants an incentive to stay in France but rather to maintain their ties with their home countries on the assumption that they would return. No one expected these provisions of the treaties to form the basis of more permanent claims on the French social contract. Although the treaties did come to provide a real social safety net for most-favored foreigners in cities such as Lyon and its suburbs, where extensive social welfare programs were developed, naturalization remained the most secure form of residency authorization for migrants. As such, however, it was also harder to acquire. At the very time when practical considerations increased migrants' interest in applying for naturalization, Lyon officials tried to raise new obstacles to granting it, deploying many of the same arguments they used to justify *refoulements* and expulsions.

With the downturn in the economy, and especially after the promulgation of the 10 August 1932 law to protect national labor, foreigners who had long resided in France suddenly requested naturalization. Naturalization statistics bear witness to this strategy: Among foreigners who became naturalized there was an increase of 31,036 in the number classified as "workers" on the census between 1931 and 1936.[102] In the long and involved process that led to naturalization, each request went through several layers of review. At each step, different administrative priorities came into play. While the police chief sometimes exhibited sympathy toward the applicants, the general secretary for police and the prefect took a broader and often more detached approach, fitting the individual attributes highlighted by the police chief into the larger social and political context of the Lyon area. Their disagreements have left visible traces in the historical record, as they crossed out the chief's recommendations and penned in corrections while preparing their own reports.[103]

Naturalization requests in the Rhône were screened by police personnel before being forwarded to the prefecture and then to the keeper of the seals (minister of justice). The fact that police officials were involved in assessing naturalization candidates at the earliest stages is significant, for it meant that the applications were likely to be evaluated in much the way that expulsion cases were.[104] As had been the case with expulsions, Rhône authorities proved themselves extremely focused on protecting the economy. Rising numbers of naturalization requests drew criticism from local officials—sometimes warranted—that foreigners filed for naturalization only because they felt their employment threatened. In this climate, proof of long residency in France incongruously may have delayed or undermined the applications of some foreigners, since it raised suspicions about the timing of their requests. Paradoxically, this concern became more prevalent as the liberalization of naturalization requirements under the 1927 nationality law took effect, reducing the residency requirement from ten to three years.[105]

Ironically, the liberalization of the nationality code had occurred in large part thanks to the tireless lobbying of a deputy from Lyon, Charles Lambert (Radical). Lambert's argument in favor of liberalizing naturalization in the 1920s was grounded primarily on the notion that migrants were vital not only to French production but also to reproduction. The requirement of ten years' residency prior to naturalization was, according to Lambert, crippling the country's efforts to rebuild its population and, crucially, its army. Naturalization therefore should be made easier for "assimilable" migrants. This "grafting" onto the "old tree of France would allow it to flourish again with splendor."[106]

Lambert extended his grafting metaphor further. As was true in arboriculture, he claimed, not all grafts would take.

A judicious selection is thus imperative. One must avoid mixing races that cannot meld together. Without having, in principle, any objection to the assimilation of Asians or Africans, and without adopting toward them the severe hostility of the United States, we conclude that, in fact, this is not a desirable mix. The objective of a politics of renewing the French race must first and foremost be to encourage the assimilation of similar individuals.[107]

For Lambert, the most similar were Italians, Spanish, and Belgians. But he thought it was also important to "counterbalance" these groups with the assimilation of "Slavs, Nordics, Czechoslovaks, Poles, Russians, Swedes, Dutch and Swiss," who were "strong and prolific."[108] Interestingly, some of the very groups whose naturalization Lambert wished to encourage figured among those whom American quota laws sought to exclude. His first preference was for Catholics, especially southern Europeans, and he also saw Slavs as compatible. These groups figured among those whom American nativists vilified.[109] While American laws precluded some ethnic groups from naturalizing, nothing similar occurred in France, despite the evident biases in Lambert's rhetoric and that of the powerful populationist lobby, the Alliance Nationale pour l'Accroissement de la Population Française. In addition to reducing from 10 to three years the length of residence required prior to naturalization, the new nationality code aimed to increase the French population by making it more difficult for children born in France to opt out of French nationality upon reaching legal adulthood. It made no distinction between populations; naturalization, at least in theory, was open to anyone.[110]

Lambert had shepherded the nationality reforms through parliament during Lyon's boom. Less than four years later, perhaps concluding that selection had not worked, he joined Herriot in advocating a fixed 10% quota on foreign employment in all industries, a measure that, at least in theory, affected all foreigners regardless of where they fit on Lambert's scale. Whatever motivated Lambert's newfound economic protectionism, the decisions made by local authorities with respect to naturalization flew in the face of his original objectives in lobbying for the 1927 law, for Rhône officials often tried to turn down the very people Lambert had wanted to recruit as procreators of the French "race." This occurred largely because Rhône authorities, unlike Lambert, saw naturalization as a legal fiction.[111]

Over and over again, the general secretary and the prefect evaluated naturalization applications through a protectionist lens, arguing, "He is only asking for nationality because he is afraid of being laid off due to unemployment";[112] "Once he became French he would find work more easily which would therefore be deprived to one of our nationals in the same situation";[113] "The petitioner only requested our nationality because he is afraid of being laid off due to unemployment";[114] "It appears, at least to a degree, that [Mr. L.] requests our nationality because he is afraid of losing his salaried employment as a result of the measures taken to protect national labor;" and so on.[115] Of 271 naturalization files sampled for the period 1927–38, the general secretary for police or the prefect cited economic concerns as a reason to reject or postpone naturalization in a minimum of 48 cases, and there was hardly a report from 1932 or 1933 that did not make this argument.[116] This was a departure, as requests filed before 1931 made no mention of the economy and were almost invariably approved quickly. When in 1932 the general secretary responded to a request from a "rentier" with 160,000 francs in assets who lived solely from investment income by rejecting it on the basis of "current economic circumstances," he showed how unthinking and automatic this response had become.[117]

As Rhône officials went on the offensive, even marriage to a French native ceased to be evaluated as evidence of a clear connection to France and, indeed, was often taken as exhibiting quite the opposite. A Spanish man on a reduced workweek was criticized for having "waited 22 years to request our nationality even though he has been married for 14 years to a French woman. He appears to only be doing so because he fears losing his salaried employment completely."[118] His 14-year marriage to a French-born woman, the prefect later explained to the keeper of the seals, "proves this—since he did not try earlier to obtain the nationality of his wife—not only has she obviously not exercised enough influence over his mind-set [*mentalité*] but also he does not have any real sentiment of attachment to our Country."[119] Unconvinced by the prefect's reasoning, the minister granted the naturalization.[120] The Justice Ministry, in fact, quite readily overrode local-level recommendations. Unlike his counterpart at the Interior, the keeper of the seals could grant naturalizations against the wishes of local police without undermining a chain of command upon which his authority and efficacy ultimately depended.[121]

The prefect and the general secretary for police may well have been right that these foreigners' requests to naturalize had little to do with their attachment to France. Certainly the isolated admissions by foreigners filing for naturalization in order to "benefit from the advantages" enjoyed by nationals did little to persuade them otherwise.[122] But these decisions neglected the possibility that, isolated cases aside, foreigners' previous failure to request naturalization also may have said equally little about the degree of their attachment to France. Surely the fact that the

Spaniard's wife had not asked to be "reintegrated" into her birthright nationality prior to 1932 had little to say about her attachment to her native country.[123] If anything, the timing of their dual request for naturalization and reintegration indicated that their obvious attachment to France—which they had exhibited by making it their home and by raising their children there—was no longer enough to guarantee their continued right to residency.

Indeed, the new vulnerability faced by foreigners was exemplified by the fact that naturalization requests could occasionally backfire, rendering migrants' situations even less secure. Noë C.'s story is a case in point. Noë had never bothered to request an identification card prior to 1932. Because he was born in Morocco and married to an Algerian, he had always assumed that he did not need one.[124] In a letter he dictated (himself illiterate), Noë stated, "I never renewed my card, I thought that I was French." How Noë went from thinking he was French to applying to become French we do not know. Perhaps he was being disingenuous, or perhaps his employers had hitherto been unconcerned by (or unaware of) his foreign status. Regardless, the timing cannot be accidental: It was only as employers in the area began to reduce their personnel that Noë discovered the importance of his nationality. Ironically, Noë's naturalization request brought his illegal status to the attention of authorities and led to his expulsion.[125] While ultimately unsuccessful, Noë's petition for naturalization demonstrated his keen understanding, despite being illiterate in French, of a new connection between nationality and the right to a continued livelihood in Greater Lyon.

The fact that individuals who had requested naturalization before the depression received favorable recommendations from the local administration, while their family members who waited until 1932 faced recommendations for postponement or rejection, suggests that foreigners were probably justified in concluding that "feeling" French was no longer sufficient. Bartolomeo F. probably thought his naturalization would be routine, after seeing his brothers sail through the process in the late 1920s. But when he applied in the early 1930s, local authorities opposed his application on the grounds that he had "waited to be almost to the point of being unable to render any services before he requested our nationality. One cannot find in this the proof of a sincere attachment to France. . . . It seems that it is only in order to have a greater chance of retaining his employment that [Bartolomeo F.] currently requests our nationality."[126]

No doubt the young foreign men who had lived in France most of their lives and who suddenly felt compelled to prove their attachment by requesting naturalization so that they could "serve in the French army" were equally if not more calculating. Their declaration of loyalty to France in fact may have had little to say about their attachment to the country, but since it served the interests of state authorities, these cases often served as the exceptions that proved the general rule of preliminary rejection.[127] Perhaps, too, the construction foremen who had "one after the other, requested naturalization" did so cynically.[128] The fact that countless other migrants who had lived untroubled in France for 10, 20, 30, or more years filed requests to naturalize in 1932 and 1933 was a sign of the times.[129] In the context of depression-era Lyon, the protectionist activism of the police and the prefectural administration made clear to many migrants that juridical belonging threatened to trump membership established through any other means.

Except for the occasional misfiled case, the Rhône archives retain the naturalization records only of applicants who were eventually successful, sometimes after many years of waiting and several postponements. We have no record, for instance, of Noë's naturalization request, probably because there is no evidence that it was ever granted; Noë shows up only in expulsion files. Without access to all applications, successful or otherwise, it is impossible to fully evaluate naturalization trends in the Rhône department. What does it mean that more than 60% of the eventually successful cases retained in the archives concern Italians? Did Italians, at approximately 40% of the foreign population in the Rhône, simply apply for naturalization more readily than others? Or rather were their applications more likely to be approved? Why did fewer than 10% of the records pertain to Spanish nationals and only 2% concern Armenians, when Spanish and Armenians comprised, respectively, at least 20% and 4% of the Rhône's foreign population? It seems unlikely that Spaniards would have refrained from filing requests, especially given, as the French-born wife of one applicant put it, "I no longer know where to turn and everywhere one hears these words, 'you are Spanish there is nothing for you.'"[130] If indeed migrants had instrumentalist motivations for naturalizing, as police suspected, then one would have expected to see a disproportionately high number of applications from foreigners who had few other means by which to claim labor and social rights, which would have meant high application numbers from both stateless refugees and Spanish nationals prior to the ratification of the bilateral treaty between France and Spain in late December 1933. The question becomes all the more pertinent when one compares the Rhône records to national statistics, which show that while Italian naturalizations increased by a remarkable 189% between 1926 and 1936, Spanish and Armenian naturalizations, lower in absolute terms, increased 230% and 278% during the same time.[131]

Whatever the reasons for these disparities, one thing is clear: Lyon authorities came to believe that naturalization undermined the spirit of protectionist regulations by simply masking migrants' foreignness. Given their preoccupation with solving the local unemployment problem, Lyon authorities almost never responded favorably to naturalization requests in the early 1930s. In fact, rejections on the grounds of the "current economic situation" were so frequent that they became a reflex. Where once Lyon's healthy economic life had led officials to encourage migrants to stay, even if it meant looking the other way as they built unsafe and unsanitary shantytowns, now they tried to use migrants' limited rights to encourage them to leave. If they did not leave France, perhaps they would leave the Rhône department. Decisions regarding naturalization reflected this desire to maintain migrants' legal vulnerability. In this sense, the logic that authorities drew upon as they weighed naturalization cases was not so different from that which informed their approach to expulsion. Both reflected a power play by police and departmental authorities, one deployed much more broadly and mercilessly since Lyon's economy had gone from boom to bust in the course of little more than 10 years.

As France rebuilt its economy after the First World War, Lyon emerged as an important center of advanced industry. So pressing were labor needs in the expanding urban agglomeration that many of the Lyon area's largest industries built housing facilities for the thousands of migrants who arrived to work in the automobile, artificial fiber, and chemical industries to which Lyon owed its resurgence after the war. The Rhône department's foreign population, hardly noticeable before the war, doubled in size between 1921 and 1931. By late 1931, however, the same industries that had attracted migrants started to founder, replacing three shifts of workers and around-the-clock production with shortened workweeks, mass layoffs, and plant closures. The resulting wave of unemployment was both disproportionately foreign and geographically concentrated in Lyon's suburbs.

The dramatic shift in fortunes in Lyon presented a formidable test to the regulation of migration in interwar France. The economy, Rhône officials quickly realized, did not follow the "laws of equilibrium" in the manner postwar planners had envisioned it would.[132] Instead, migration's so-called laws of nature confronted human nature. This being the case, Rhône authorities tried to engineer the response they desired. By aggressively policing migrants' economic activity, they hoped to achieve the results that policy had promised but had not delivered.

In some respects they succeeded. Some migrants were sufficiently threatened that they moved on, if not to their home countries, then perhaps to a nearby department, where they became someone else's administrative problem. However, the crackdown on migrants by police and prefectural officials in Lyon also forced adaptive behavior by both migrants and state officials. In response to Rhône authorities' turning of the vise, many migrants actually expanded the realm of their claims on rights, no longer limiting them to the workplace as they often had in the 1920s. As they were laid off, they claimed social rights; as expiring labor contracts jeopardized their residency authorizations, they became business owners; as protectionist measures went into effect, they sought to naturalize and join the protected class. All these adaptive responses revealed that immigrants who had invested in French society now expected something from it in return. This was no longer, if ever it had been, a reserve army of labor. Over time, Lyon and Rhône officials also adapted, acknowledging through their practices that foreigners were more rooted in the Lyon community than they had assumed. Even so, authorities' responses were not evenhanded: Considerations of gender, age, nationality, and family life all affected the nature of relations between migrants and the gatekeepers of their rights in the administration. The same subjective process that protected some migrants made others increasingly vulnerable.

Indeed, not all migrants succeeded in broadening the scope of their claims-making beyond the narrow confines of employment rights. Some migrants showed their investment in staying not by making legal claims but rather by violating the law, eking out a living by resorting to social crime. Then, too, some 166,447 foreigners nationwide officially accepted repatriation from France between the beginning of 1930 and the end of 1934, comprising nearly half of the 334,269 recorded departures from the country during that time.[133] According to some estimates, real departures were as much as three times higher.[134] Scores of others were incarcerated for failing to leave when ordered to do so. Even the relative success stories often came with a price: the resignation to becoming a one-salary family, being forced to move to another region of France, quarterly checkups from the police, and many other compromises of civil liberties. These were different trade-offs than those of the 1920s. Then police surveillance had largely concerned politics, not whether one's spouse worked or how one put food on the table.

The depression years had profoundly transformed migrant rights, and thus the life choices migrants made, in metropolitan Lyon. This transformation resulted neither from impersonal laws of the market nor from the disinterested application of new legal standards. Rather, it emerged through a cycle of confrontation and accommodation among migrants, local officials, and policy makers in the capital. The effect of the depression on migrants in Marseille, by contrast, was less pronounced. While Lyon officials viewed the depression as a social crisis, Marseille authorities continued to approach a certain part of town as permanently crisis ridden, and while the changes in migrant rights in Lyon turned on local responses to the downturn in the economy, in Marseille it would take political turmoil, not economic crisis, to transform the port city's migrant rights regime. The depression fundamentally altered Lyon's economic and social life, stimulating adaptive behavior on the part of both migrants and officials, which worked to reshape the boundaries of belonging in the river city. In Marseille, by contrast, it exacerbated certain tendencies that were already in place.

CHAPTER THREE

Working the "Marseille System"

The Politics of Survival in the Port City

> You see very well that I am the mayor of Naples.
> —Attributed to Marseille mayor Siméon Flaissières[1]

On 15 December 1931, the same day Édouard Herriot complained in parliamentary debates about the ineffective enforcement of immigration regulations, members of Marseille's chamber of commerce came to a rather different conclusion at their meeting. While Herriot wanted greater limits placed on migrant labor, Marseille's business leaders felt that regulations pertaining to foreign workers were, if anything, already excessive. "It would be first of all an injustice" to place quotas on foreign workers, they wrote in a resolution, "because this labor is indispensable in a large number of industries, and particularly in border areas as well as ports. Second, the measure would have the immediate effect of increasing the cost of production at the same time that, by all possible means, it behooves [us] to decrease costs so as to lower prices and balance them with consumer purchasing power."[2]

Marseille employers greeted the idea of a fixed threshold of 10% on foreign labor with alarm, since, as their resolution pointed out, foreigners constituted 60% to 80% of the city's masons, 80% of the soap and glycerine workers, 75% of workers in the oil refineries, and more than 67% of the sugar refinery workers, to name only the city's largest industries. They also rejected the proposal to let local parity commissions establish quotas, for this would create "a period of uncertainty and trial and error, during precisely which time a factory ought to be able to resume its normal rhythm without hesitating."[3]

As business leaders met in the Marseille Bourse, the worldwide depression had not yet hurt Marseille to the degree it had many other industrial cities. The export market had been aided by the undervaluation of the franc, and the years 1928 to 1932 were Marseille's most prosperous of the interwar period. But the tide was turning. Britain abandoned the gold standard in September 1931, the United States quickly followed suit, and this struck "a brutal blow to the French economy and its gold-standard partners."[4] Marseille-based business owners knew that it was only a matter of time before a higher-value franc would hurt their exports. The last thing they wanted to hear in December 1931 was that they might also be forced to increase their labor costs.

In truth, it was not just that Marseille's employers did not want new controls on foreign labor; they would have preferred no controls at all. Contracts were anathema to the "Marseille system." Legal vulnerability was its lifeblood. For this reason, the depression did not fundamentally alter the nature of migrant rights in Marseille. By making people more insecure, it instead fed into the logic of the port economy. Indeed, migrant employment, at least initially, increased in depression-era Marseille. Whereas Lyon's dramatic shift from near-full employment to glaring unemployment led to a reordering of state-society relations in the Rhône capital, the depression confirmed, rather than called into question, the Marseille system.

Employers in Marseille were not the only beneficiaries of migrants' legal vulnerability; so too were municipal and departmental officials in a city known for clientelism. The legal protections offered through Marseille's notorious patron-client political system, however, followed a different logic than that of the liberal labor market. Whereas those controlling labor markets treated their "clients" as birds of passage, political and bureaucratic patrons presumed that their clients would stay, and expected to extract some advantage from ongoing relations with them. Clientelism is a form of protection, but Marseille and Bouches-du-Rhône authorities never warmed to labor-market protectionism in the conventional sense. Rather, they, like the people they served, embraced a culture of getting by and circumventing rules. As Marseille's economic system exacerbated social insecurity, the city's system of political patronage thrived on it. It promised protection to vulnerable migrants in exchange for their loyalty. Both systems worked to reinforce the divisions between the city's transient and more settled populations. This chapter illustrates what made this possible by first examining the impact of the worldwide economic crisis on Marseille's labor market and then considering how migrants and local officials responded.

On the surface, the coping mechanisms of Marseille's migrants looked similar to those adopted by their Lyon-based counterparts: Naturalization applications rose, claims on unemployment insurance increased, and new forms of social crime also emerged. Beneath these surface similarities, however, one finds rather different relationships between migrants and state authorities. The adjudication of migrant rights in these domains highlighted not only migrants' own survival strategies but also those of the officials charged with regulating their rights. If naturalization applications exposed migrants' increasing desire for legal security, they also revealed the dependence of Marseille politicians on patronage politics. Then, too, where migrants encountered numerous obstacles to claiming social welfare, city officials relied on these obstacles to stem Marseille's growing debt. And if new forms of social crime bore witness to the broadening impact of the depression on the city's population, the adjudication of these crimes showed police authorities carefully trying to manage the image of criminality they presented to their superiors in the capital.

Paris called Marseille's bluff when the king of Yugoslavia and France's foreign minister, Louis Barthou, were killed in broad daylight on a Marseille street by an undocumented alien in the fall of 1934. Critics quickly blamed the 9 October assassination on ineffectual policing of migrants in the port city. Just when migrants were at their most socially vulnerable, they once again found themselves embroiled in violent political battles not entirely of their own making. Many of them already had scaled back their political expression in the wake of the crackdown on foreign "communists" following the de Castelnau incident in 1925. Now they surely wondered what was in store for them next.

Reforms to migration regulations that ensued from the assassination had a long-term impact on the policing of foreigners in France. Ironically, however, they served in the short term to reinforce existing police practices in Marseille. Police redoubled their surveillance of the port, already long the disproportionate focus of their attention. Reviews of identification cards ordered in the wake of the assassination, meanwhile, rewarded long-term residents and rebuked the itinerant. Marseille remained a city divided by neighborhood, lifestyle, and class, even as the effects of the depression began to blur such distinctions.

THE MARSEILLE SYSTEM REINFORCED

Marseille's unemployment rates began to climb in 1931 and spiked upward beginning in 1932. Despite this, the structure of employment relations in the city remained unchanged. Employers continued to maintain a core workforce, which they complemented with temporary workers according to the fluctuations of their business cycles. The Marseille Gas and Electricity

Company, for instance, noted in December 1932 that only 43% of the for-eigners under its employ had labor contracts; the others had been hired without contracts to respond to "seasonal peaks in production."[5] Other in-dustries from sulfur to sugar to oil refinement hired seasonal workers, often the same ones each year, to meet the demands of short-term production cycles.[6]

Over the long term, Marseille's artisanal production methods posed serious problems for economies of scale and competitiveness, and con-tributed to Marseille's long decline relative to its rivals. In the short term, however, the flexibility of these industries allowed them to remain in business while companies that had modernized in the 1920s faced great difficulties.[7]

Marseille looked to be immune from the worldwide crisis until 1933, a "year of mourning" for the oil and soap trade.[8] Each subsequent year was worse. Trade with colonies, protectorates, and mandates, which initially had helped to insulate Marseille against the effects of the worldwide de-cline, eventually collapsed as well.[9] By the time war was declared in 1939, the Marseille economy was, as Olivier Lambert cleverly puts it, "out of gas."[10] As advanced industries throughout France cut back production, so too, eventually, did Marseille's industries of transformation. These, in turn, dismissed all but their core, often native French, workforce. As this happened, more and more migrants sought work on the docks. But the de-mand for dockworkers, too, contracted as export markets dwindled. It was as if workers' trajectories followed in reverse the chain of connections between French industry and the world economy: As it unraveled, so did their prospects. Employment in Marseille industries began dropping and never recovered the level of the early 1930s, not even at the peak of the "glorious years" of economic expansion after the Second World War.[11]

Marseille's worsening economy made the city's industries increasingly reliant on the flexibility provided by migrant workers—a position that flew in the face of pending protectionist legislation aimed at reducing French employers' dependence on foreign labor. Work certificates enclosed with naturalization applications confirm the perpetuation into the 1930s of the "Marseille system": What had been noncontract casual labor in the 1920s simply became all the more casual (see Table 3-1). Active and inactive peri-ods ranged from as short as a week or two to as long as several months. The slacker the labor market, the cheaper foreign labor would be and the easier it would be to find workers willing to put up with the dangerous and unpleasant work conditions that prevailed in most Marseille industries.

The flexibility that was built in to the Marseille labor market also made the city particularly attractive to migrants whose contracts had run out elsewhere. Boris M., whose story opened this book, headed for

TABLE 3-1
The Marseille system as seen through sample employment trajectories

Spanish worker employed at multiple companies

Employer	Dates
Jean Mavel	20 May – 4 July 1930
Société Méridionale de Travaux	19 – 29 September 1930
Société Générale des Tuileries de Marseille	24 June – 27 August 1931
M. Caillol et Cie	25 September 1931–30 January 1932
Chagnaud et Fils	23 March – 13 November 1932
Marius Barbier	14 November – 19 December 1932
Louis Jean Entreprise	3 – 20 July 1933
Ancienne Cie du Canal de Beaucaire	4 – 18 September 1933
Maconnerie Ferdinand Rabezzana	20 April – 1 May 1934
Maconnerie Ferdinand Rabezzana	20 November – 8 December 1934
Entreprise Felix Bondil et Fils	18 December 1934 – 4 January 1935
Cie Générale d'Entreprises Electriques	29 April – 12 June 1935
Chagnaud et Fils	6 July – 11 August 1936

Italian worker employed at a single company

Employer	Dates
Société des Chantiers et Ateliers de Provence	22 October 1928 – 27 May 1929
	7 August – 11 October 1930
	17 September – 3 November 1931
	11 December 1931 – 4 Feb 1932
	1 July – 1 August 1932
	27 October – 3 November 1932
	14 November – 12 December 1932
	8 July – 13 July 1933
	27 – 31 October 1933
	18 – 30 December 1933
	8 January – 18 August 1934
	24 August – 14 September 1934
	5 November – 13 December 1934
	25 February – 24 May 1935
	31 May – 8 June 1935

SOURCE: ADBR 6 M 1243 and 6 M 1306: Work certificates in naturalization files.

Marseille's docks in 1931 when his job at the Compagnie des Produits Chimiques et Électrométallurgiques in Salins-de-Giraud ended. Similarly, a Czech who had been working legally in the Eure department in 1930 arrived in Marseille the following year seeking employment as a day worker, and a Serbian who had once worked in the Decazeville (Aveyron) mines became a ragpicker in Marseille.[12] Many migrants arrived from mono-industrial areas such as the Lorraine, where repatriation efforts had been intense. An Italian who had been working in Briey, in the heart of the Lorraine iron-ore basin, was found vagrant in Marseille four days after arriving there to look for work in 1932.[13] Another Italian who had been working in the Lorraine industrial city of Villerupt

(Meurthe-et-Moselle) also made his way south, first stopping in the Haute-Savoie, where he obtained an identification card in 1931, and then moving on to Marseille in 1932.[14] And a Russian man who had worked in Audin-le-Tiche (Moselle) arrived in Marseille in May 1932 after first trying his luck in Nice in 1931.[15] Once in Marseille, these workers often became the "out of work" workers described by Albert Londres, those who turned to dock work as a last resort.[16]

Statistics collected by the Labor Ministry confirm both the reduction of new contracts in the North's mono-industrial areas and the attempt by many foreigners to enter Marseille's labor market after first working elsewhere. New cases of foreign workers processed by the Lorraine regional placement office in Toul fell by more than 24% from 1929 to 1930 and, even more dramatically, by more than 96% from 1930 to 1931. Official placement statistics such as these undoubtedly underestimate the numbers of workers who headed to Marseille after losing jobs elsewhere, since many of them may not have sought placement through government channels. Nonetheless, as Figure 3.1 shows, while introductions in Toul continued to drop (another 63% from 1931 to 1932), the Marseille office's record of reassigned workers (*placements de travailleurs étrangers antérieurement introduits*) began to rise. From 1931 to 1932,

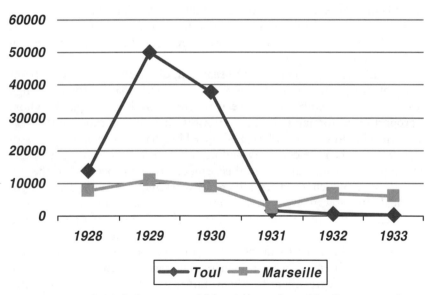

FIGURE 3.1 *Initial placements of foreign workers (Toul) compared to reassignments of already admitted foreigners (Marseille), 1923–33*
SOURCE: BMT.

such reassignments rose by more than 248%.[17] Of all the regional placement offices (Toul, Marseille, Hendaye, Perpignan, Menton, Metz, Strasbourg, Lille, Lyon, Nantes, Toulouse, Bordeaux, and Paris), only Marseille
saw growth in this category.

Employers' desire to hire foreigners at will meant that even after protectionist legislation passed in parliament, Marseille businesses continued
to oppose the quotas' enforcement. In early 1935, an organized letter-
writing campaign and questionnaire prompted by the Society for the Defense of Marseille Commerce and Industry reminded Bouches-du-Rhône
authorities that, despite reductions in foreign employment agreed to by
parity commissions, employers still persisted in defending high levels of
foreign workers. Among the diverse industries responding, margarine
producers wrote that they needed to be able to retain foreign employment levels as high as 40% to maintain the flexibility required for an industry dealing with perishables.[18] The Marseille branch of Établissements
Kuhlmann, a chemical fertilizer company, wrote that more than 51% of
its workers were foreign and that it had been "difficult to modify the percentage of foreign workers much" because of the "hard work which
French workers reject" and its remote location in the city's periphery. Its
Port-de-Bouc branch had even higher levels of foreign employees: as much
as 80%. Another producer of chemicals for agriculture wrote that 60%
to 75% of its personnel were foreign, in large part because French workers
were not interested in working with sulfuric acid and superphosphates.
Similarly, two sulfur refineries reported levels of foreign employment at
50% and 60%.[19]

Repeatedly, employers cited the seasonal, disagreeable, and sometimes
outright dangerous nature of the work as an explanation for their high
levels of foreign employees. One manager of a chemical plant, whose
"proportion of foreign labor . . . surpasses 80% during times of the year
when production is active," even admitted in a letter to an employer association that when the company had used higher levels of French workers
in the past, they had encountered enormous problems because of the frequency with which workers afflicted by arsenic poisoning had sought
medical attention, increasing their insurance costs.[20] Although the manager claimed that foreign workers were preferable because they followed
the health and safety procedures that Frenchmen ignored (allegedly reducing poisoning cases to almost none), one wonders whether that reduction may have been aided by foreigners' reluctance to report their medical
problems or seek treatment for them. Either way, the manager stood firm
that if the government forced him to hire more French nationals, "we
would still find ourselves in the same position as in the past with respect
to work-related illnesses."[21]

Bouches-du-Rhône employment authorities appear to have been sympathetic to this line of argument. Although employers submitted decreasing numbers of requests for contract approval from 1930, the rate of authorization increased until 1933, dipped in 1934, and then reached nearly 91% in 1935 before dropping again (see Table 3-2). Rates of regularization—or the approval of worker identification cards for foreigners having arrived in the country without labor contracts—told a somewhat different story: They declined, then steadily increased, both relatively and absolutely. This suggests the growing importance, in the later 1930s, of legalizing one's status.[22] For the early depression, by contrast, it indicates that migrants may have refrained from seeking approval of their contracts and identification cards, figuring that it was safer to risk being caught illegally residing in Marseille sometime in the future than it was to be issued an immediate *refoulement*—a risky strategy, to be sure, especially since migrants could not have known the perfunctory nature of the weekly reports the prefecture sent the Interior Ministry. Every week, in response to inquiries regarding the "detection and *refoulement* of irregular foreigners," the Bouches-du-Rhône employment office reported that "rigorous controls" were ensured. Departmental officials never elaborated on such comments with details on enforcement, details their Rhône counterparts were only too happy to provide.[23]

TABLE 3–2

Marseille and Bouches-du-Rhône placement office, approvals
and rejections of identification cards

	New Contracts Approved	New Contracts Rejected	"Regularizations" Approved	"Regularizations" Rejected
1930	1,349 (75.15%)	446 (24.85%)	2,086 (64.22%)	1,162 (35.78%)
1931	581 (84.57%)	106 (15.43%)	980 (66.8%)	487 (33.2%)
1932	273 (86.12%)	44 (13.88%)	873 (67.67%)	417 (32.33%)
1933	336 (90.32%)	36 (9.68%)	888 (48.23%)	953 (51.77%)
1934	230 (79.31%)	60 (20.69%)	1,297 (47.72%)	1,421 (52.28%)
1935	171 (90.9%)	17 (9.1%)	1,959 (58.96%)	1,417 (41.04%)
1936	156 (82.11%)	34 (17.89%)	1,964 (61.96%)	1,206 (38.04%)
1937	332 (78.49%)	91 (21.51%)	6,567 (70.07%)	2,805 (29.93%)
1938	307 (77.53%)	89 (22.47%)	5,147 (82.51%)	1,091 (17.49%)

SOURCE: ADBR 14 M 23_5: Rapports sur le fonctionnement des services de l'office de la main d'oeuvre au cours des années 1930–1938.

NOTE: The Bouches-du-Rhône Placement Office, in theory, ruled on all new labor contracts issued to foreigners for employment in the Bouches-du-Rhône department. It also approved "regularizations"; that is, it granted contract approval to foreigners who had entered the country without it or whose contracts had expired. As indicated by the data in Table 3-2, approvals for "regularization" exceeded rejections in all but two years, 1933 and 1934. "Regularization" is not the same thing as renewal. "Renewal" rates were available in this data record only for 1936: 12,771 "renewal dossiers" approved in 1936, a rate of 93.45%.

Lyon officials drew most of their conclusions regarding migrants from having witnessed, in less than a generation, the city's rapid shift from full employment to mass unemployment. By contrast, Marseille's longer history of immigration may have led its leaders to develop views that were less closely tied to the short-term vicissitudes of the economy. Perhaps this was an admission on the part of the Marseille authorities that they really had no control over the labor market, which was dictated by the city's powerful business interests. In any case, the stance of the Marseille and Bouches-du-Rhône officials toward migrant employment was quite different from that of their counterparts in Lyon. If employment office records hinted at this difference, naturalization practices exemplified it.

NATURALIZATION, POPULATIONISM, AND PATRONAGE

In Marseille as in Lyon, the depression triggered an upsurge in naturalization requests among foreign migrant workers. With mass redundancies in Lyon, French nationality became increasingly important to maintaining or getting a job, particularly after the 1932 quota law was instituted. Wage laborers also figured heavily among naturalization applicants in Marseille, albeit for different reasons. Marseille industries tended to hire a core of permanent workers, often French nationals, and complement them with day workers, who could be hired and dismissed as needed. Even among day workers, as hiring practices on the docks exemplified, in-group status mattered. This tendency probably became only more pronounced as new outsiders flooded into Marseille after losing their industrial jobs elsewhere in France. Naturalization, in this context, did not so much guarantee access to a labor contract as increase the consistency with which one might be employed casually.

Unlike their Lyon counterparts, Marseille authorities appeared ready to naturalize workers, apparently with little regard to any competition they might pose for jobs held by the native-born French. Indeed, as labor-protectionist measures were instituted at the national level, naturalization rates of wage laborers increased in Marseille (see Figure 3.2).[24] Marseille's naturalizations rose from 1,508 in 1930 to 1,756 in 1931, and from 1,973 in 1932 to 2,333 in 1934.[25] In the department as a whole, they increased by more than 10,000 between 1931 and 1936.[26] Whereas Rhône authorities tried to block the naturalization of workers on the grounds that foreigners requested the favor only in order to keep their jobs, Bouches-du-Rhône officials recommended worker after worker for naturalization throughout

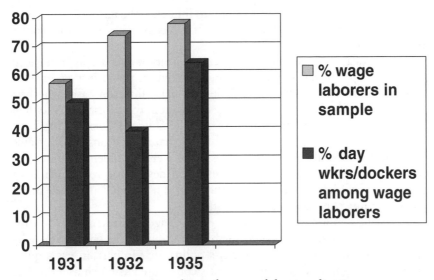

FIGURE 3.2 *Sampling of successful naturalizations*
in Marseille, 1931–35
SOURCE: *ADBR 6 M.*

the 1930s, almost never making an overtly protectionist argument—
sometimes quite the contrary.

It would be tempting to see the willingness of Marseille authorities to
naturalize foreign workers as evidence of an effort to thwart government
interference in the local labor market. Marseille businesses, after all, ve-
hemently opposed the institution of the quota laws. Moreover, as we have
seen, the prefecture often replied to queries from the Labor Ministry regarding implementation of controls with disinterest or even consternation.[27] If the central government insisted on a certain threshold of French
workers in all industries, why not make foreign workers French? Such
ideas may indeed have served as a backdrop for naturalization decisions
in Marseille. At the same time, however, Marseille's industries depended
on the vulnerability of foreigners. Employers surely must have been
pleased by the fact that Marseille authorities did not recommend naturalizing just any worker; most of the successful applicants had been in
France for years, many since before the First World War, something Lyon
authorities rarely if ever encountered. Even though day workers were
prevalent among the successful applicants, these were very likely the day
workers who were consistently rehired by the same companies, not the
ones that police picked up for vagrancy on the docks. Although there is

no direct evidence of employers trying to influence the naturalization process, Marseille's business climate likely affected the naturalization process in these intangible ways.

By contrast, there is evidence that naturalization was deeply influenced by the city's political system. Unlike in Lyon, where police inspectors were responsible for the first level of review in naturalization cases, the first evaluation in Marseille was ordinarily conducted by an official in city hall and then forwarded to the prefecture, not the police. This procedural difference meant that the persons evaluating naturalizations in Marseille were elected officials or persons whose jobs were beholden to elected officials. In an electoral culture that relied on developing relationships of patronage, politicians depended on the newly naturalized almost as much as immigrants depended on elected officials.

Marseille had long been known for patronage politics, and at no time was this reputation better deserved than in the interwar period. Yet why were foreigners important to the city's politicians? In part, it was a question of demographics. Foreign nationals constituted as much as a third of the city's population and a growing number of the residents of its peripheral districts. The same dynamics of social geography that led Marseille police to treat the city center's transient populations more harshly than established residents of the periphery also drew the attention of elected officials. Peripheral neighborhoods had developed with the expansion of industry north from the Old Port and in reaction to overcrowded housing conditions in the center. This had fostered Marseille's distinctive urban geography, giving it the "rare characteristic of a city whose suburbs are within the limits of the city."[28] These various "suburbs" were not integrated by urban infrastructure, however. Tram lines linked most of the outer villages to the city center, but roads, sewage and access to clean water, and other amenities still left much to be desired. As a result, an "increasingly large portion of the working population," as David Levy notes, "was badly integrated into the local political system."[29] The high proportion of foreigners living in these neighborhoods may have contributed to the relative disregard city officials paid the periphery, but eventually this stance became politically untenable. City leaders could not afford to have whole sections of the town escaping their influence. This was one of many factors that encouraged the inclusion of migrants in Marseille's clientelist networks.

Compared to their Lyon-based counterparts, Marseille officials evaluated naturalization requests in terms of what migrants contributed, rather than, as had often seemed to be true in Lyon, what they threatened to take away. More than anything else, it seemed, they contributed children. In emphasizing this, the arguments of Marseille and Bouches-du-Rhône authorities in favor of naturalizations appeared populationist rather than protectionist.[30] Populationists had been an important lobby group in France since the early Third Republic; largely concerned with trying to increase the French birthrate, they initially saw immigration as a temporary palliative. Best known for opposing contraception and abortion as well as for advocating a "family vote" (whereby men with large families would have more electoral power), populationist organizations also weighed in on debates regarding immigration. Deeply conservative and patriarchal, they were also ardent nationalists. Neomercantilists of a sort, populationists believed that size mattered, and they were particularly concerned about the size of France's army. It was the military aspect of population politics that had led them to cautiously advocate immigration, much as Lyon deputy Charles Lambert had, as long as it was based on a careful selection of migrants for their reproductive potential. The largest and most powerful populationist group, the Alliance Nationale pour l'Accroissement de la Population Française, even went so far as to suggest that the assimilation of adults worked only if they had children.[31] Marseille authorities' approach to naturalization recommendations frequently appeared to reflect this logic: Childless families often were rejected, while large families, even those barely able to support themselves, were more likely to be approved.

In fact, under the guise of populationism, Marseille officials displayed protectionism of a different sort. Instead of protecting French labor against competition from foreign workers, as their Lyon counterparts had endeavored to do, they often were protecting their own political careers. In a climate where ballot-box stuffing, falsified electoral lists, and electoral "enforcers" linked to organized crime were common, Marseille officials saw immigrants as easily manipulable potential members of their constituency.[32] The procedural differences between Marseille and Lyon naturalization practices help explain why files in Marseille contained considerably more inquiries or letters of support from the city's elected officials than did comparable files in the Rhône department. If the "favour was the currency of clientelism," as Paul Jankowski has noted, naturalization was one of many favors politicians offered their clients.

The elected officials, deputies in particular, prevailed on judges to reduce fines, lift expulsion orders, delete prostitutes from the registers of *filles soumises,* reprieve criminals, grant naturalizations—between June and September 1939, [Senator-Mayor Henri] Tasso intervened 70 times on behalf of protégés, 31 times to request naturalisation.[33]

Tasso—a Marseille-born son of Italian immigrants who was a Socialist municipal councillor from 1919 to 1926, deputy to the National Assembly from 1924 to 1938, councillor and vice president of the Departmental Council, mayor from 1935 until his powers were suspended by decree in 1939, and senator from 1938—was hardly the first Marseille elected official to hand out such favors. The art had been perfected earlier by Simon Sabiani.

Sabiani had won Marseille's fourth canton seat to the National Assembly in 1928 by a narrow margin over the Socialist Jean-Baptiste Canavelli in part thanks to patronage politics. The following year, he also became Socialist mayor Siméon Flaissière's principal deputy (*premier adjoint au maire*), a position he held from 1929 to 1931; after Flaissière's death in 1931, Sabiani again served as deputy mayor under Georges Ribot until 1935. As deputy mayor, he condemned fiscal irresponsibility while at the same time adding to it by hiring his clients en masse. A native Corsican and colorful opportunist who moved from leaning communist to fascist during the course of his political career, Sabiani became infamous for patronage politics and for protecting members of the Corsican mob who served as his "electoral agents."[34]

Naturalization files from these years do not indicate which of the mayor's deputies was responsible for vetting applications. Nonetheless, it seems clear that Sabiani tried to exert some influence over the outcome, as did deputies Tasso, Joseph Vidal (Gauche Républicaine), and Toussaint Ambrosini (Socialist).[35] While these interventions were not always successful, neither can their influence be completely discounted. At a minimum, they appear to have accelerated the long review process.

If naturalization aimed in part to expand local leaders' political bases, it made sense that they should start with the oldest and largest foreign population in the city. Across the department, Italians represented 74% of the successful naturalizations in the 1930s. Although Italians were the largest migrant group in the department, the naturalization figure was about 20% higher than their share of the foreign population.[36] While Armenians comprised about 10% of the department's foreign population, not quite 4% of the successful naturalizations concerned Armenians. The rate at which Armenian requests were postponed was also skewed: Almost 19% of the postponements sampled affected Armenian applicants, whereas postponement of Italian requests, at almost 51%, came closer to their representation in the foreign population. Statistics on Spanish naturalizations are particularly puzzling. Their representation among the successful naturalization applicants, at nearly 12%, was not too far off from their concentration in the department, which hovered around 13% of the foreign population. But their representation among the postponements was much lower: just over 8%.[37] Did this figure mean that Spanish nationals applied for naturalization at lower rates? Why would so much greater a percentage of Armenian requests be postponed rather than approved? Without records of outright rejections as opposed to indefinite postponements, we remain at the level of conjecture. Nonetheless, these figures are not surprising politically: Longer-term immigrants fared better than recent arrivals. This pattern, however, did not always follow clear neighborhood lines, as it often had with regard to expulsions. Rather, some 40% of successful naturalizations sampled for the period between 1928 and 1939 concerned residents of Marseille's central districts, strongholds of both Sabiani's and Tasso's political bases.[38]

Irrespective of neighborhood or nationality, social characteristics that contributed to negative evaluations by police inspectors did not lead to the same conclusions among municipal officials. Destitution, for example, often elicited pathos rather than condemnation. The deputy mayor recommended the naturalization of one man even though he was "certified indigent."[39] Municipal officials sometimes even cited a candidate's unemployment as a valid rationale for reducing the processing fees associated with naturalization: "Currently unemployed, the sum offered corresponds to his means."[40] In this respect, reports contained in Marseille naturalization files struck a very different tone from those in Lyon. Among 377 postponed or rejected cases sampled for the Bouches-du-Rhône department, only once did the phrase "the applicant has a non-worker identification card, he appears to be requesting naturalization only in order to be authorized to work," or anything resembling it, emerge as a reason for rejection.[41] Only once did a municipal official suggest that a candidate might become a charge on the system, and even then the issue was not unemployment but the candidate's advanced age.[42] These were the exceptions. In many more cases, the most instrumentalist motivations for naturalizing hardly raised objections. Marseille's deputy mayor even favored the naturalization of a mason whose stated purpose in naturalizing was "to benefit from the advantages conferred by French nationality."[43]

As in Lyon, however, such recommendations sometimes produced tension between local and national officials. Umberto D.'s case, in favor of which Henri Tasso intervened on more than one occasion, at once exemplifies the indulgence of municipal officials and the difference between their outlook and that of the Justice Ministry. Umberto was an Italian father of six who, the deputy mayor wrote, "does not work regularly . . . does not pay his rent . . . and is facing eviction." His children dressed "in rags and don't go to school." Yet whereas police had recommended Umberto's *refoulement,* the deputy mayor recommended naturalization, "by humanitarianism, taking account of the desperate situation of this large family which eventually may improve." After all, he concluded, Umberto's naturalization would render six children French.[44]

The deputy mayor's pleas for compassion did not convince the Justice Ministry right away. Rather, the ministry wanted some guarantee that Umberto "works regularly," has "good conduct," "doesn't waste his income on games or the cabaret," and owes his financial troubles uniquely to the "burden of numerous children."[45] In reply, the deputy mayor remained positive about Umberto's naturalization while being honest about his shortcomings. He noted that the number of Umberto's children had risen to eight and that the applicant had no police record. Although he did not waste his money on gambling or entertainment, he worked as a mason only until he acquired a bit of money, then slacked off until the money was gone. Nonetheless, the deputy mayor concluded, "public opinion will not object to the applicant's naturalization." The family was naturalized on 1 July 1930.[46] In a similar case from 1931, both the deputy mayor and the prefecture's naturalization division recommended Nicolo U., an Italian father of seven who "worked on various construction sites in our city and is currently unemployed." Once again, officials did not hold unemployment against the candidate and instead cited his "family situation" as a "valuable asset to the country."[47] After some hesitation on the part of the keeper of the seals (*garde des sceaux*), Nicolo and family were naturalized on 4 September 1932.[48] Even after the depression finally hit Marseille more significantly, local officials did not regard unemployment as an obstruction to naturalization. Although Gaetano N. had been unemployed for a year and was receiving 14 francs a day in assistance, the deputy mayor recommended in late 1933 that he and his wife be naturalized since their eight children had been born in France; the family was naturalized in August 1935.[49] Although not all those who were unemployed or who risked unemployment earned the approbation of local officials, objections were usually made on some other basis.

Local authorities were most likely to get their way on naturalization decisions if they were able to present the case in terms officials in the Justice Ministry cared about, such as utility for military service or the number of children a candidate had. Mentioning that a family was childless virtually condemned an applicant's chances. When either the deputy mayor or the prefectural official was in favor of a candidate, however, authorities tried to emphasize mitigating factors, often in vain. In the case of a childless Italian couple, ages 47 and 49, the prefecture emphasized that the man had "served faithfully and honorably" during the war, but to little avail—the Justice Ministry issued a postponement.[50] Similarly, despite the recommendations by the deputy mayor and the prefecture of Giovanni D., an unmarried Italian man living with his sister and working in the Marseille soap industry, the justice minister issued a postponement "until establishment of a hearth" (*jusqu'à fondation d'un foyer*). When Giovanni reapplied after marrying, the Justice Ministry requested medical certificates, which, among other things, reported a "large varicocele on the left side," a common cause of male infertility. Despite continued support from the deputy mayor and the prefecture, Giovanni's application for naturalization was rejected, definitively this time.[51] Foreigners quickly learned of these priorities. After two failed attempts to naturalize in 1933 and 1936, Filippo Z. wrote the prefect, "<u>I have one more child and I know that must count.</u>"[52]

Even when a foreign applicant had children, it was important that at least some of them be boys. Badrig B. and his wife, Armenian refugees, had already failed to impress the deputy mayor in their command of the French language. But the naturalization division's report probably told the real story:

47 years old, married to one of his compatriots and father of two female minor children. The applicant has lived in France for about ten years and resides in Marseille. This foreigner has worked assiduously in the same factory since 1924; he enjoys the esteem of his entourage and has not been the object of any negative reports. Nonetheless, his request not presenting any immediate interest for the country, I propose postponement.[53]

The Justice Ministry concurred. Another request, this time from a successful Italian businessman who had been the object of a complaint regarding his commercial probity, was rejected on the grounds that "the applicant has already been rejected two times and is currently fifty years old. He only has daughters."[54] In a related vein, fitness for military service was often at issue in deliberations over naturalization requests. Exceeding the age of military service was one of the most prevalent reasons cited by Marseille officials for "postponing" naturalization requests, an act which for all intents and purposes meant rejection, since the candidate would only be older the next time around.[55]

Local authorities appear to have learned from their encounters with the Justice Ministry and tailored their future recommendations accordingly. In the case of a young Italian who first applied in 1929, for instance, both the deputy mayor and the third division official approved the naturalization of Dario O., who was "single, works regularly and enjoys the esteem of his entourage."[56] After the naturalization was postponed by the Justice Ministry, however, a new deputy mayor, though still in favor of naturalizing, responded to the question "Will the naturalization of the applicants have the effect of creating a truly French family?" with a resounding "No! It would seem, since [he is] single."[57] Probably wary of attaching a recommendation to such a report, the naturalization division forwarded it to the Justice Ministry and suggested postponement "until the candidate marries and a child arrives."[58]

Yet military fitness or having a large family was not always a sufficient condition for naturalization. Often candidates with many children encountered rejection because they were deemed to be lacking in "assimilation." No precise measurement of assimilation was possible, but it seems that authorities considered applicants' fluency in French as well as the migrants' desire to return to their homelands—their *"esprit de retour."* The fact that assimilation came up at all suggests that there were limits to the instrumentalist approach authorities brought to bear on many naturalization cases. If children, or, rather, future soldiers, were all that mattered, then the parents' linguistic abilities in French would be immaterial. That not all families were approved suggests that authorities still harbored a deep ambivalence about naturalizing adults.

Tobiah T.'s case exemplifies this ambivalence. A Turkish merchant living in France since 1921 and the father of three, Tobiah first applied for naturalization in 1931 when he was still of military age. Although his application was supported by both Joseph Vidal and Henri Tasso, the justice minister rejected the request without offering any explanation. In response to Tobiah's later applications, the mayor's office was more circumspect, noting among other things that he now exceeded the age for military service. For its part, the naturalization division proved how short institutional memory was by asserting that "he appears to have waited to request naturalization until he was no longer required to perform active duty in our army." Not only is the aphasia regarding Tobiah's previous request striking, but so too is the fact that in this second round of reports, his three children were not mentioned. By the time of his third application, he was the father of four, including two boys. This made no impression on the deputy mayor, though it did meet with the third division's approval. The minister, however, rejected Tobiah's request definitively.[59]

What explains these repeated rejections and the local authorities' contribution to them after having first recommended Tobiah? Were geopolitical concerns at play here, given the side taken by Turks in the First World War? This might have been a factor when Tobiah first applied in 1931, but by 1934, Turkey was a member of the Balkan Entente, with Romania, Greece, and Yugoslavia—an alliance that largely served French interests. Perhaps cultural prejudice was at play? Would the Jewish consonance of the names Tobiah and Sarah, his wife, have entered into officials' calculations, at a time of rising anti-Semitism in France, particularly given that this was often directed at merchants? Did the justice minister have such public opinion in mind when he often asked local authorities how the naturalization would be "received" by the local population? Another case involving a Turk of probable Jewish background suggests that Tobiah's experience may not have been exceptional. Ira T.'s naturalization was denied despite his marriage to a Frenchwoman, despite having a son, and despite being "perfectly assimilated to our customs and fluently speaks our language."[60]

Rhône officials, too, had demonstrated ambivalence about naturalizing adults, but of a different sort. There, authorities seemed to regard naturalization as a legal fiction, a juridical label that did not remove the essential characteristic of the foreigner as a factor of production, and a dispensable one at that. Marseille authorities regarded transients as dispensable but felt differently about longer-term migrants. Curiously, in a city overflowing with migrant workers, immigrants had a utility in Marseille that extended beyond their immediate employment. In return, select migrants gained some legal security. In countless other ways, however, local political priorities exacerbated migrants' insecurity. Nowhere was this more obvious than in welfare provision.

SOCIAL INSECURITY

However indulgent authorities were regarding identity cards or even naturalization, the same could not be said of unemployment indemnities. Officials wanted to facilitate employment of migrants; they had no interest in absorbing the social costs of an exacerbated turnover in labor. Marseille's unique economy in part explained this reticence. Social rights, by their very nature, are bounded; not only do they tend to be restricted to a certain population, but they also are triggered by particular events—the birth of a new child, arrival at the age of retirement, the onset of unemployment, and so on. In Marseille, it was unclear how to define unemployment in a city where employment itself was so ephemeral. Most employed workers in Marseille were forever partially unemployed or on the brink of becoming so. At what point did the casually employed cross the threshold into unemployment? By limiting casual workers' access to unemployment assistance, authorities helped perpetuate the Marseille system, forcing laborers to seek social security through temporary work rather than social welfare payments. This affected all workers in the city but hit migrants especially hard.

Unemployment compensation regulations from 1926, still in effect as Marseille entered the depression, excluded foreigners from nonreciprocity states. How rigidly this was applied in the early years of the depression is unclear. But in October 1934, the Bouches-du-Rhône departmental council formally voted to enforce this exclusion for budgetary reasons.[61] The new enforcement measures "affected Armenians in particular." From at least that point until the Popular Front government forced local authorities to revisit the issue, the only public monies for unemployment to which Armenians had access were emergency funds allocated to a private Armenian organization and distributed as it saw fit to the neediest families.[62] In many parts of France, barring nonreciprocity foreigners from unemployment assistance had a negligible impact; in Marseille, it affected a sizable portion of the migrant population. In December 1932, there were 22,780 Spanish, 20,275 Armenians, 5,011 Turks (some of whom may have been in fact Armenian), 3,286 Russians, and several thousand other foreigners from nonreciprocity states officially residing in Marseille. Among the recorded foreign populations living in the city, only Italians (a clear majority at 128,495 residents) and a few hundred each of Czechs, Belgians, and Poles were eligible for social assistance by virtue of reciprocity treaties.[63] A year later, the Spanish population also became eligible.

Unemployment indemnities peaked in 1936, when the Socialist municipality allocated 11 million francs from its "extraordinary expenditures" budget. This was a significant increase from the measly 121,326 francs allocated to unemployment assistance from its ordinary budget in 1929, the 3,338,000 francs allocated in 1932, and the nearly 5.6 million francs allocated in 1933. Yet it still fell far short of what Lyon was spending on unemployment and it still failed to incorporate foreigners on par with their participation in Marseille's labor force. In the first seven months of 1932 alone, Lyon's Municipal Council voted budget increases for the unemployment funds almost every month; allocations from January to July reached 15.8 million francs.[64] Even when one takes into account the separate dockers' fund in Marseille, the city of Lyon still drastically outspent Marseille on unemployment relief.

Moreover, unlike their Lyon counterparts, Marseille's most-favored foreigners did not necessarily secure social rights that were identical to those of French nationals. Under an arrangement concluded in the 1920s between Louis Thibon and Mr. Coletti at the Italian Royal Embassy's Migration Office in Paris, unemployed Italians living in Marseille would receive 1.5 francs rather than the ordinary 3 francs per day in indemnities and 50 centimes for each dependent up to a maximum of 3 francs per day, rather than the standard 6 francs. This was presumably intended to encourage unemployed Italians to receive the balance of their aid through the consulate, which sponsored many social programs.[65] When Thibon's successor reported on the arrangement in December 1926, he gave no indication that he intended to discontinue this policy. The Cartel de

Gauches government expressed concern about the use of consular services as a means for the Italian Fascist Party to engage in surveillance of Italian populations living abroad, but its right-wing successor was less preoccupied by this, particularly after Carlo Barduzzi, who "had many times demonstrated his friendly sentiments toward our country," was named consul general to Marseille.[66] Even if authorities at the Foreign Ministry had come to appreciate Barduzzi, however, not all Italian migrants in Marseille felt the same way. Assuming the shared funding scheme remained in place, unemployed Italians in Marseille balanced new political risks against social rights. Those with antifascist politics probably avoided going to the consulate.

On a less dramatic scale, other migrants also had to weigh the ramifications of making unemployment claims. With the advent of the depression, the unemployment office shifted its foreign caseload to the Foreign Workers Office (*dépot de travailleurs étrangers*). This meant that in order to claim unemployment, a foreigner had to report to the same bureau that was responsible for renewing—and denying—residency authorizations.[67] Surely this was intended to have a chilling effect on foreign applications for unemployment assistance. Since foreign claims on unemployment declined even as total unemployment increased, every indication is that the tactic worked.

In addition to policies that specifically excluded some groups of foreigners, other provisions of the Marseille regulations likely had an important impact on migrants. While the requirement of being able to prove three months' residency in the municipality was crucial to preventing abuse, it also meant that the portion of Marseille's working population having no permanent residence would be ineligible. Just as important, in order for a municipality to be eligible for state subsidies, it had to ensure that claimants had worked for at least six months prior to becoming unemployed. This provision, if applied strictly, had the potential to exclude persons who worked as day workers for periods shorter than six months.[68] Perhaps it was persons falling into this category who took to the Marseille streets, one thousand strong, in 1932, only to have the mayor inform them that he could not help them as the budget had made no provision for them. This prompted another, larger, demonstration several days later and may explain why that same year saw the institution of some food provision to unemployed persons who were ineligible for monetary aid.[69]

Despite these stopgap measures, additional policies instituted by the Bouches-du-Rhône employment office restricted access to unemployment insurance still further. Dockers, for whom a three-day workweek was common, were deemed ineligible for the standard assistance. Instead, the city helped to finance a separate docker fund administered by the union. To receive assistance from the union, dockers had to establish, first, that they worked "regularly" as dockers and, second, that they had been without work "more than one day during a week." Verification of unemployed status was quite onerous: Unemployed dockers had to register twice daily, at 9 A.M. and at 2 P.M. The docker fund's regulations also specifically eliminated "all those who do not really belong to the profession and whose casual presence on the docks only aggravates for the real professionals the difficulties of being hired."[70] This introduced considerable room for exclusion. It may explain why people like Boris M. ended up vagrant.

In addition to excluding dockers, Bouches-du-Rhône policy barred the following persons from the benefits of regular unemployment insurance:

Persons who have been unemployed for more than a month when they first come to register as a job seeker;

Persons "committed to only looking for reduced work and who have abandoned their habitual profession to seek a less taxing job";

Persons whose profession has annual off-seasons (fashion, entertainment, etc.);

Persons age 16 (or under), except in exceptional circumstances (orphaned, or the oldest in a large family);

Persons committed to habitual drinking or disreputable conduct.[71]

These restrictions help explain disparities between numbers of job seekers and those receiving unemployment aid (see Tables 3-3 and 3-4). While there were 13,683 French job seekers in 1933, on average each month only slightly more than 7,000 of them were eligible for indemnities. Similarly, of the almost 5,000 registered foreign job seekers that same year, hardly more than half that number received unemployment assistance in any given month.

TABLE 3-3

Registered job seekers, Bouches-du-Rhône department

	1933	1934	1935	1936
French	13,683	15,336	19,038	17,145
Foreign	4,905 (26.39%)	6,464 (29.65%)	4,517 (19.18%)	3,791 (18.11%)

SOURCE: ADBR 14 M 23_5: Rapport sur le fonctionnement des services de l'office de la main-d'oeuvre.

NOTE: These data represent a snapshot of the number of job seekers on a single day in each year, not the total for the whole year.

TABLE 3–4

Unemployment assistance data for the
Bouches-du-Rhône department, 1931–37

Year	Number of French Indemnities Paid (Monthly Average)	Number of Foreign Indemnities (Monthly Average)	% of Total Indemnities to Foreigners
1931	16,126 (1,344)	5,046 (420)	23.83
1932	61,699 (5,142)	25,104 (2,092)	28.92
1933	84,635 (7,053)	30,460 (2,538)	26.47
1934	126,609 (10,551)	44,429 (3,702)	25.98
1935	191,227 (15,936)	45,482 (3,790)	19.21
1936	215,618 (17,968)	47,883 (3,990)	18.17
1937	171,139 (14,262)	44,589 (3,716)	20.67

SOURCE: ADBR 14 M 23_5: Rapport sur le fonctionnement des services de l'Office de la Main-d'Oeuvre.

NOTE: Indemnities paid for full-time unemployment, excepting dockers.

The first figure likely exceeds the total number of unemployed, as it represents the sum total of each month's figures. A single claimant may be counted several times. For this reason, this table also lists the monthly average in parentheses.

Marseille's share of the unemployment expenditures in the department ranged from 82% to 96%. Exact proportions varied year to year, but in general, Marseille's share declined over time (as more towns added unemployment insurance programs during the 1930s).

Foreign job claimants, and rates of foreign indemnification, declined in number even as Marseille industries finally began implementing quota laws. This is hardly surprising. Although quota-law enforcement undoubtedly increased foreigners' unemployment more than these numbers suggest, foreigners who lost their jobs on this basis would have been unlikely to seek reassignment or compensation through the same state agency that was responsible for implementing the quota laws. This reluctance likely grew after the October 1934 assassination of King Alexander and Louis Barthou triggered increased scrutiny of Marseille's migrant populations under stiff new regulations instituted by two premiers intent on cracking down on illegal migration, Pierre-Étienne Flandin and Pierre Laval.[72] Perhaps this explains why the most dramatic decline in official foreign job seekers occurred from 1934 to 1935. In any case, even though Marseille officials were less zealous in enforcing protectionist measures than their Lyonnese counterparts, this fact did not confer on Marseille's foreigners the ability to make more powerful claims on the state in the domain of social rights.

In part because of the structure of Marseille's economy and in part due to conscious policies established by local officials, aid to the unemployed, although not insignificant, was far less comprehensive in Marseille than it was in Lyon. With formal social rights often eluding them, how then did migrants in the port city seek social security during the depression? As in Lyon, the prosecution of social crime provides some clues.

Much as in Lyon, the incidence of social crime in Marseille highlighted the effects that the depression had wrought on migrant populations. But, as if to confirm the "social" nature of social crime, prosecution of delinquents underscored the unique relationship in the port city between social and legal boundaries of belonging. Moreover, as police officials prosecuted some migrants' survival practices more stringently than others, their own strategy for administrative survival also took shape. By choosing which cases to enforce themselves and which to forward to the Interior Ministry, Bouches-du-Rhône police officials hoped to keep the intervention of their superiors to a minimum. Migrants were not the only ones who stood to benefit from keeping a low profile.

As had been the case in the 1920s, vagrants, beggars, and marauders were the most likely to come into contact with police. More novel was the number of long-term Marseille residents who found themselves in this situation. Luis N., a 67-year-old Spanish man and longtime resident of Marseille's St-Loup district, had worked for numerous employers over the years but had since become, along with his wife, a ragpicker. He was picked up by police, who found him taking fresh rabbit furs from the street.[73] The 73-year-old Italian Bonifacio B., similarly, "doesn't work at all but lives miserably from the sale of rags he picks up in the street." He was arrested for begging.[74] Benedetto D. had once worked regularly in the soap industry to support his wife and four children but, as of 1931, only worked irregularly "due to a lack of hiring" (*faute d'embauche*). Police found him asking for money while pretending to be blind.[75] Bedros B., a resident of the fifteenth arrondissement, had worked regularly at a shoe factory until January 1931, when he was stopped for alleged vagrancy.[76]

Petty theft also became more common among long-term residents. Haig L., a married father of two and a resident of the St-Jérome district for several years, had been unable to find work in his profession as a joiner and had thus worked as a day worker in the Gouin soap factory for six years. It was only in 1932, however, that he was found at fault for taking soap from work: Either Haig was trying to save on his grocery bill or Gouin was newly prosecuting its employees for what labor historians have sometimes called "gleaning."[77] Darius N., a Greek who had lived in Marseille since the middle of the war, was found with 600 grams of pears that he had gathered up from the docks, leading to a theft conviction on 16 March 1932. Teghtsanig P., a "Turkish" (possibly Armenian) sexagenarian widow living in Marseille's St-Antoine neighborhood, was found by police having swept up some 20 kilograms of dirty wheat from the ground, along with 300 grams of tobacco leaves. She too was convicted for theft.[78]

None of these instances of social crimes committed by immigrants having established residency in Marseille led to an expulsion order. By contrast, as in the 1920s, police recommended expulsions almost as a reflex for newly arrived migrants or migrants who had no fixed residence when they committed the same or similar infractions. Almost all the summary expulsions ordered by the prefect or the general secretary for police in 1932, for instance, concerned persons who were single and had no fixed or known domicile. Meanwhile, those circulating in the dock district whose only crime was a lack of proper identification tended to be recommended for *refoulement*. More so than their Lyon counterparts, Marseille police still distinguished between infractions of identity card regulations and other misdemeanors or crimes. Still, *refoulement* was not the same thing as the more innocuous warnings that were issued to long-term residents of the periphery. In theory, *refoulement* had no penal implications; in practice, it often led to expulsion. In effect, police and prefectural officials still drew a distinction between immigrants and transients, even as the differences between them became blurred.

Day workers were not alone in feeling the impact of the economic crisis. Merchants and market farmers who faced declining prices and revenues encountered new hardships as well. These migrants, often long-term residents, now sometimes engaged in a different kind of social crime. To be sure, they were rarely so desperate as to maraud on the docks or resort to ragpicking, but their circumstances were straitened enough to prompt some of them to engage in commercial fraud or tax evasion. In keeping with the distinction they had long drawn between immigrants and migrants, Marseille authorities approached small-business crimes with the expectation that their perpetrators would stay in France. Thus, while rising incidences of social crime among long-term residents showed the effects of the depression throughout Marseille, this shift did not translate to a leveling of migrant rights across the city.

Commercial fraud convictions testified to these difficulties. Milk dilution, an increasingly common practice among dairy farmers living in the Marseille periphery, was a case in point. Judging from the length of prison sentences associated with it, a conviction for commercial fraud was considered at least as serious an offense as was marauding on the docks. Nonetheless, Bouches-du-Rhône authorities usually recommended warnings rather than expulsions for first-time milk-dilution offenders. Only repeat offenders were systematically recommended for expulsion.[79] Other small-business owners also deployed new methods of saving money, economizing on labor costs through such means as employing apprentices after hours, an infraction of the labor code. Like the dairy farmers, small-business owners found skirting labor standards were invariably spared expulsion. Both business strategies exemplified the degree to which people from all walks of life now attempted to stretch each franc a bit further.

A number of factors combined to protect foreign businesspeople from immediate expulsion. First, although these foreigners derived at least a portion of their means of existence from illicit activity, they were not visibly delinquent, nor did the nature of their offenses make it likely that they would be apprehended by the police, whose focus continued to be diverted toward the center of town. While dairy farmers' fraudulent behavior and employers' violations of the labor code could be discovered only through inspections, central Marseille's delinquents committed their infractions in public spaces that fell under intense police scrutiny. Second, while summary expulsions by the prefect were common in cases concerning so-called transients inhabiting the center, they were almost unheard of for anyone else. The time allowed residents by this reprieve from summary judgment gave them a better chance to garner support for their cases, support that became crucial to arguments for warnings or, when the Interior Ministry refused a warning, for suspensions of expulsion orders.

Not all long-term residents were spared expulsion, but often police expelled long-term residents hoping that they would stay. Indeed, by the 1930s, Bouches-du-Rhône authorities had developed two distinct uses for their expulsion powers. On the one hand, they continued to use their power as administrators of a border department to summarily and expediently expel new arrivals and a highly mobile, often unattached, port-district population whom they wanted to force out of the country, or at least the city. In this sense, their use of summary expulsions was not so different from their Lyon counterparts' approach to migrants they wished to encourage to move on, though Bouches-du-Rhône authorities could adopt this strategy without involving the Interior Ministry, thanks to the department's location on the border. On the other hand, they invented new uses for ministerial expulsions; these were predicated on the assumption that their targets' interest in remaining in France would make them receptive to complying with the conditions that authorities placed on retaining their residency rights.

Expulsions for unpaid taxes exemplified this innovative use of police power. The idea was to scare delinquent taxpayers by expelling them, and then suspend the expulsion order so that they had the time and incentive to pay. Enforcing such an expulsion order would be self-defeating, because the Treasury would never be repaid.[80] Migrants often understood this. Demetrios D., an Asia Minor Greek with Turkish nationality who owed more than 13,000 francs in taxes from his export business, for instance, told authorities that he would do everything he could to pay his taxes—"it is a question of time and patience." This letter earned several exclamation points and an exasperated "Ah, no!" in the margin from its reader.[81] "On the other hand," Demetrios threatened, "by expelling me, inevitably the Treasury will receive nothing. Likewise my creditors will lose all hope of being paid, and, what is more, what would become of my family?"[82] The recommendations that local authorities forwarded to the Interior Ministry proved that on a certain level, Demetrios was right: Prefectural officials concluded that his expulsion would have the effect of "denying the Treasury an important sum which can be recovered if the aforementioned is kept in the territory."[83]

Despite the paradox of using expulsion to make immigrants better residents, usually authorities' threats quite literally paid off. Dadour Z., an Armenian cobbler living in the St-Jérome district of the Marseille periphery, paid the 950 francs he owed in commercial taxes less than two weeks after he was warned to pay under threat of expulsion.[84] Biagio M., a carter, initially paid only 200 of the nearly 400 francs he owed, but when authorities claimed that he had fabricated a "fake state of insolvability" and threatened his expulsion, he managed (despite claiming to work only two to three days a week) to pay all of it.[85] How did people on the verge of bankruptcy suddenly come up with the funds to pay their public debts in order to save their residency rights? Unless delinquent taxpayers had been deceiving authorities all along, they likely had to borrow from Peter to pay Paul. Buying legal security thus probably engendered other forms of insecurity. In a city known for its organized crime, the premiums undoubtedly were often high. Yet it was crucial to respond quickly to threats from the administration. Dadour Z., Biagio M., and others like them avoided expulsion, while dawdlers found out the hard way the high price of delaying.

Although Bouches-du-Rhône authorities actively pursued foreigners who cheated the state, they seemed less concerned with foreigners who defrauded the general public. As in Lyon, exchanges between local and ministerial authorities in response to migrant infractions of the law exposed the differences in their priorities. When, for instance, prefectural officials recommended a warning for one dairy farmer, "taking into account his long residency in France and his good record [*antécedents*]," the Interior Ministry's Direction de la Sûreté Générale responded:

I have the honor of informing you that I did not believe I should adopt your conclusions and that I have ordered the expulsion of this individual. I see no reason, in effect, to tolerate the presence in our territory of a foreigner who has no scruples and whose behavior poses a danger to the health of consumers. This measure is all the more appropriate in that, despite the serious penalties faced by them, the number of foreign swindlers seems to be growing, especially in your region.[86]

The same case also illustrated the authorities' divergent views on due process. While the Sûreté director wanted to know "the reasons that the conviction of this foreigner was brought to my attention more than 18 months after being issued by the Court," Bouches-du-Rhône prefectural officials had been waiting for the outcome of an appeal by the same defendant on a separate "involuntary injury" charge against him before forwarding the case to the Interior.[87] Immigrants, they seemed to be saying, should not face arbitrary or excessive punishment. This view resonated with a contemporaneous argument advanced by politicians on the Left for a *statut des immigrés*—a sort of immigrant bill of rights.[88] In Marseille, however, the stance reflected entrenched practices and a desire for immigrant loyalty more than any political commitment to migrant rights. After all, authorities raised no similar concerns for due process in cases regarding transients committing more visible social crimes in the city center. There, they pursued expedient punishment as a matter of course.

Lyon authorities also had engaged in bureaucratic competition, but of a rather different sort. Whereas power plays between local administrators in the Rhône department and ministerial officials often resulted in the former convincing the latter to mete out more severe punishments, in cases pertaining to social crimes committed by migrant residents of Marseille's periphery, such jockeying often worked in precisely the opposite fashion, with Bouches-du-Rhône authorities making minimum recommendations and the ministry insisting on greater severity.

Like their Lyon-based counterparts, Marseille and Bouches-du-Rhône officials also wished to exhibit independence and authority. However, they went about it in an entirely different fashion. First, by summarily expelling those thought to be most unstable, the Bouches-du-Rhône prefect avoided publicizing to the Interior Ministry the levels of lawlessness, petty or otherwise, that Marseille police encountered on a daily basis. By keeping this to himself, he quickly disposed of part of his caseload and simultaneously kept the ministry off his back. The decision to forward cases to the Interior Ministry appears to have been equally calculated. All the delinquent tax cases, for instance, were sent to the Interior Ministry, even though the main intention behind them—a powerful threat—hardly required ministerial approval. Not only did the strategy buy time, which helped the delinquent taxpayers to earn, borrow, or otherwise acquire the money to pay their debts; it also helped shape the image the prefect presented of Marseille to national authorities. Much of the criminal activity for which Marseille was notorious was handled within the prefecture; meanwhile, the cases forwarded to the capital often involved nonviolent crimes such as tax evasion, milk tampering, or labor-code infractions. This was a rosier picture of Marseille than that painted by the press, which regularly conjured up an image of the city's underworld by calling it the "Chicago of France." To be sure, the prefect had to report the names of expellees so that they could be entered in a national file for distribution to law enforcement officers nationwide, but this presented a fait accompli and provided no opportunity for judgment.

CRISIS ON THE CANEBIÈRE

Judgment day came in October 1934, when mayhem in Marseille exploded the prefect's carefully crafted picture of migrant life and law enforcement. On 9 October, Foreign Minister Louis Barthou greeted Yugoslavia's King Alexander as he disembarked in Marseille for a state visit. Minutes later, as their motorcade advanced up La Canebière, the main artery leading away from the port, an assassin who had blended into the crowd jumped onto the car's running board to shoot them, mortally wounding them both and injuring a few others. For a few days, the world watched in trepidation, wondering whether the murder of this Balkan king might precipitate another war just 20 years after the last.[89] No European war broke out, but this strike at the legitimacy of France's southern European ally did alter the balance of power in Europe away from France. For one thing, Barthou, a strong opponent of Germany, was replaced by Pierre Laval, later infamous as the architect of France's collaboration with the Nazis during the Second World War. Just as important, the assassination, while not conspired to directly by either Mussolini or Hitler, served Italian and German interests by weakening the Yugoslav autocracy and nourishing the country's existing divisions.

The assassination briefly drew attention away from the place that migrants occupied in Marseille's social geography to focus it instead on where they fit into international power politics. It was first reported that the assassin was a Croatian nationalist, working for the Croatia-based terrorist group the Ustashi. It was later learned that the assassin was from

Macedonia and had committed other assassinations under the leadership of Ivan Mihailov and the Macedonian Revolutionary Organization.[90] Regardless of the precise identity of the assassin, the notion that foreigners would use France as a staging ground for violent political battles was particularly alarming to public opinion, especially coming only two years after President Paul Doumer's assassination.

It also was not the first time that foreigners had been implicated in violent street clashes in Marseille. As with the de Castelnau rally and counterdemonstration in 1925, the Right quickly blamed the Left and the Left rebuked the Right.[91] Philippe Henriot, a militant Catholic supporter of General de Castelnau in 1925 and now a deputy from the Gironde, alluded to the earlier inefficacies of the Marseille police as he wrote in *France d'abord*:

Many were those who, before the tragedy, were surprised that Marseille would be chosen as the port of disembarkation. . . . Marseille, city of gangsters [*nervis*] and untrustworthy foreigners . . . The entire world knows that no police is less reliable [*sûre*] than that of this oriental port. Its floating population prevents any serious surveillance.[92]

Coincidentally, Maurice Thorez, the leader of the French Communist Party, met with Socialists on the very day of the assassination to organize a broadening of the tenuous unity pact between the parties. Taking advantage of Thorez's timing, *L'Action Française* associated the new front with the assassination when it wrote, "Down with the Common Front between thieves and assassins."[93] Taittinger's Jeunesses Patriotes called, on 10 October, for revenge: "*What are we waiting for? It is not enough to cry for the dead,* WE MUST AVENGE THEIR DEATHS!"[94] On the Left, Léon Blum argued that the international social democratic movement, "which had itself suffered so from political murders, had always condemned [assassination] as a means of struggle and liberation."[95]

Political anxieties quickly gave way to social profiling. The day after the assassination, the extreme Right paper *L'ami du peuple* quickly called for the "mass *refoulement* of these international dregs, of this refuse from all the world's nations who have chosen France as their promised land." Collapsing the political and social dangers it perceived immigration to pose, it continued, "How much longer will the government allow foreigners to . . . interfere with our internal politics and eat the bread of our unemployed workers?"[96] *Le matin* joined the fray as well, writing that, "more than ever, public opinion rises up against the invasion of France by foreign agitators, at the very moment when all is being done to prevent the unemployment of our national workers."[97] The following day, Colonel François de la Rocque, leader of the Croix de Feu league, began his condemnation of the attack with, "I won't insist today on the insufficient protection given to French labor," before moving on to blame the "Common Front" for "training" the world's "deracinated" peoples.[98]

While attacks on foreigners were often partisan, condemnations of the police were unanimous. *L'écho de Paris* called the incident "a serious sign of the disorganization of one of our most important public services."[99] The assassination had been captured on motion picture film, which circulated as newsreel before being banned in France and several other countries. The public saw for itself that the car carrying the king and Barthou had a running board, in violation of protocol for visiting dignitaries. They saw the police with their backs turned to the crowd at intervals of 20 or more feet, and the panic of officers after the assassin fired his first shots. One international observer called the police disorder "far greater even than [that of] the Bosnian police in June 1914."[100]

It was hardly surprising, then, that three weeks after the incident the same observer reported that "an acrimonious quarrel between the Sûreté and the local Marseilles police is still raging."[101] French public opinion was still smarting from the revelations of corruption and incompetence within the police and justice administrations that had emerged during the Stavisky affair earlier that year. Now, accusations flew that the Judicial Police had warned Marseille of the potential for an attempt on the king's life. Meanwhile, Albert Sarbach, the commissioner of Marseille's *police d'état*, insisted that he had taken the proper precautions but had been overruled by Commissioner Sisteron, whom the Sûreté had sent to Marseille to prepare for the event. Sarbach claimed that he had planned to deploy a motorcycle brigade to encircle the king's motorcade. "No, no," Sisteron allegedly replied, "the King must see the crowd who welcomes him and respond to their cheers."[102] Even the xenophobic *Je suis partout* paused from its usual generalized attack on foreigners to poke fun at the Marseille police:

Shortly after the attack, two Armenians, whose names sounded strange to Corsican police officers, were arrested. And the Sûreté spread the rumor that two accomplices were being held. "Armenians, Armenians, they claim to be Armenians! But everyone knows that Armenia is in Yugoslavia," declared a brigadier-chief. But despite some serious "roughing up" [*passage à tabac*], they couldn't get them to admit anything. . . . So they decided to proceed with verifying their identity, which is where they should have started.[103]

For *L'écho de Paris*, the police administration was "in full decomposition"; for the Radical-leaning *L'oeuvre*, it was "impotent." And the Radical Party paper *La république* condemned a member of its own party, Interior Minister Albert Sarraut, under whose watch the incident occurred.[104]

The policing of foreigners did not change overnight, but it nevertheless seemed clear that something had to be done to address fears that foreigners might try to drag a still-healing France into another war. Nor was anxiety limited to migrants from the Balkans. With northern Spain erupting in violence, authorities clamped down on political migration, barring Spanish refugees from residing in Marseille within days of the assassination.[105] In practice, it was of course difficult to distinguish a Spanish insurgent from a labor migrant, but this ruling announced the second categorical exclusion of refugees from certain border regions in a little over a year.[106]

The assassination shook up both the local and national administrations. Interior Minister Sarraut demanded the removal of the Bouches-du-Rhône prefect Pierre Jouhannaud as well as the director of the Sûreté Nationale, Jean Berthoin; Sarraut then handed in his own resignation. The justice minister Henri Chéron soon resigned as well, but not before the Marseille City Council adopted a resolution condemning the "campaign of calumny carried on against the city on the subject of responsibility for the assassination on October 9," as it voted to honor the outgoing prefect with the Grand Medal of the city.[107] The ardently republican journalist André Ulmann wondered whether the resignations were enough: "The rot within the police . . . its disorganization, its anarchy, all demonstrated by the attack, demand other remedies. More complete ones."[108] It was true that there long had been disagreements between Marseille's *police d'état* and the Sûreté Nationale regarding police administration in the port city. Jouhannaud had informed Berthoin in February that a lack of sufficient personnel in the special police force made it difficult for the Bouches-du-Rhône police to "insure the surveillance of suspicious foreigners who most often have entered our territory clandestinely"; he asked Berthoin for the means to tighten security, only to be told that revenues were insufficient for increases in personnel.[109] This was not the first of such exchanges, nor would it be the last.

The problem was one not only of funding but also of police culture. Poor working conditions led to high absenteeism rates, and although it was clear that the city's various police forces lacked coordination, the rank and file did not welcome the imposition of a general secretary for police in 1931. Remarks written in response to a report on police commissioned by Marseille merchants and industrialists in 1930 suggest the defensive posture of the police leadership: "It is not at all proven that crime rates are higher in Marseille than in other cities," an official wrote in response to one of the findings; "one mustn't compare the current situation to that which existed at the time that the *police d'état* was created in 1908. At that time, indeed, armed gangs battled one another in the middle of the Canebière."[110] Once again, crisis on La Canebière would call into question Marseille's approach to policing.

Although most diagnoses of the assassination cited organization and communication problems within and between various divisions of police administration, if anything, the remedies, by slapping new mandates on local services without addressing their infrastructural problems, widened the gulf between the Bouches-du-Rhône administration and the Ministry of the Interior. It was not until another crisis erupted, in the fall of 1938, that Premier Édouard Daladier deemed that gulf unbridgeable, replacing the prefect with a special administrator reporting directly to him.[111]

In the meantime, Marseille continued to defy policy makers' visions for the role that migrants would play in French society. The elegant, instrumental approach to the economy prescribed by policy had never held much promise in Marseille. In the 1920s, thousands of refugees arriving in Marseille had belied the expectation that all migrants were guest workers. Scores of others had proved that they were more than mere factors of production when they became involved in labor and antifascist politics. Moreover, police practices had highlighted the fact that not all migrants were young, single, interchangeable male workers. Indeed, persons who did meet these ideal criteria of the guest worker often were precisely those whom port-district police wanted to send home or keep legally vulnerable.

In the 1930s, the disjunction between the postwar framework for migrant rights and Marseille's social reality only became more glaring. First, the degree to which rights had been conceived with regard to the shop floor of factories dating to the second industrialization became all the more apparent. Pressure mounted to establish and enforce quotas on foreign employment nationwide. But quotas made little sense in industries that altered the size of their workforce by the month, week, or even day. The central government now expected local authorities to ensure that migrants without valid contracts were ordered to leave France. However, labor migrants in Marseille often had never had any contract— much less one approved by the Labor Ministry. Now that very fact contributed to new migrants arriving in Marseille once they lost their contracts elsewhere.

Only with respect to welfare provision did the Bouches-du-Rhône prefecture become overtly protectionist. Access to unemployment compensation was about as irregular as was employment in the port city. Labor and social rights simply did not mean the same thing in Marseille as they did in some other industrial cities. No wonder the prefect's replies to Paris inquiries on enforcement of labor legislation were often dismissive. He knew better than they.

Or at least his administration approached migrants' rights as if he did. He issued summary expulsions—his right as a border-department prefect—of those migrants he deemed dispensable. He consulted his superiors in the Interior Ministry only with regard to those migrants he thought perhaps were not. Migrants, in turn, drew on this assumption as they negotiated for rights. In the new context of the depression, these were not positive rights so much as negative ones: not a right to work so much as freedom from being expelled. Still, certain classes of migrants often bargained as if having concluded that not only they, but also France, would be better off in the long run if they stayed. This formed the essence of delinquent taxpayers' arguments; it also informed the logic of many requests for naturalization. This longer-term vision did not square easily with national immigration policy, even though access to naturalization had been eased in 1927.

In this sense, migrant rights in Marseille diverged not only from national expectations but also from patterns that had emerged in Lyon. International labor migration to Lyon was new, clearly linked to the expansion of the city's advanced economy. With mass immigration a recent phenomenon in Lyon, it is hardly surprising that authorities adjudicated rights with punctual economic goals in mind. It was only as migrants resisted such a utilitarian approach to their rights that Lyon officials began to recognize the longer-term investment of migrants in society. Marseille officials, by contrast, had always pursued both short- and longer-term goals as they adjudicated migrant rights.

Prefectural authorities, by definition, had to represent the central state and enforce employment quotas aimed at foreigners. But prefectural authorities used their other powers to knowingly recommend the naturalization of individuals who stood to be affected by that enforcement. They increased, until 1931, the number of new foreign labor contracts that they approved, while excluding many foreigners, or at a minimum discouraging them, from claiming social rights when those contracts expired. If Lyon authorities were systematic in evaluating foreigners largely as a threat to the economic well-being of French nationals, their Marseille counterparts were anything but.

Police practices in the city center remained relatively predictable. As migrants dismissed from jobs in other regions of France tried their luck in the port city, swelling the transient population of the city center, the patterns of inclusion and exclusion that had developed in the 1920s became, if anything, only more pronounced. Even as residents of the periphery, hurt by the depression, came increasingly to share the economic insecurities of the port-district population, they remained comparatively insulated from police power. These patterns emerged from long-standing assumptions about social and political insecurity, not from protectionist policies targeted to address a sudden downturn in the economy. The shake-up in local and national police administration that followed the assassination did little to alter these overall patterns. As we shall see in the next chapter, however, the change in government following the assassination did contribute to realigning migrant rights.

Then, too, police proved not to be the only gatekeepers of rights in 1930s Marseille. Elected city officials became involved in adjudicating migrant rights inasmuch as the mayor's office was responsible for the first review of all naturalization applications. Perhaps because elected officials viewed immigrants as future political actors, naturalization reports in Marseille did not treat foreigners as mere factors of production; their role in reproduction was just as significant. Although prefectural officials had to approve the recommendations of the city officials prior to forwarding an application to Paris, and although the Justice Ministry tried, as it had in Lyon, to provide something of a check against local priorities, the imprint of electoral politics on immigrant life in Marseille was undeniable.

It was undeniable, but not necessarily transparent. There seemed to be few rules, only entrenched practices and administrative competition. Certain patterns emerged: In encounters with the police and municipal officials alike, it paid to know people who could vouch for one's character and stability. That left a lot of people very vulnerable, and many others highly dependent on the goodwill of neighbors, employers, local police, or politicians. What would happen if these relationships changed?

CHAPTER FOUR

Privilege and Prejudice

The Invention of a New Immigration Regime in the Mid-1930s

You could judge that old rat. From time to time you will condemn
him to death. That way his life will depend on your justice. But you'll
pardon him each time for economy's sake.[1]

While other countries were beginning to rebound from the depression,
France's crisis was deepening. In response, more and more sectors of
French society demanded state protection of their economic interests. In
1933, medical students successfully lobbied parliament to pass a law limiting foreigners' access to practicing medicine; in 1934, law students followed suit. What group would be next to make such demands? Adding
fuel to the xenophobic fire were revelations that the massive municipal
bond fraud engineered by Alexandre Stavisky, a French national of
Russian-Ukrainian birth, had also implicated a number of elected officials.[2] Under this pretext, antiparliamentary leagues held violent demonstrations on 6 February 1934 to the cry of "France for the French!" forcing the premier, Édouard Daladier, to resign. The riots and subsequent
counterdemonstrations made clear that there was little middle ground
between the extreme poles of French politics. Another battle in the
"Franco-French civil war" had begun.[3]

With Daladier's resignation, Gaston Doumergue formed a "truce"
government in his stead. Threatening the inevitability of civil and international war if his reforms were not passed, Doumergue was forced to resign when they were not. As Pierre-Étienne Flandin formed the fifth government of 1934 in November, French and foreign observers alike had to
be wondering: Would Doumergue's threat prove true? The new premier

likely shared this fear. He had to find common ground, but where? Starting with immigration, Flandin made it his first act of government to create a new "interministerial commission to protect French labor." Perhaps he thought labor protectionism was one policy on which all political factions could agree.

Things did calm down. Violent street clashes subsided, with help from a new policy outlawing public political demonstrations and requiring that "nonpolitical" demonstrations be preapproved by prefectures.[4] Still, as oratory on the floor of parliament showed, the parties were as divided as ever. Among the issues they disagreed about was the role of migrants in France. The themes were not new; once again they turned on rights. For the extreme Left, equal rights were the issue. If French workers were being displaced by foreigners, this was because the latter had fewer rights, making them easy prey for employers. For many others, however, the problem was not that foreigners had too few rights but that they had too many. These rights, in their view, were bankrupting the state. In spite, or perhaps because, of the passions displayed in parliament and on the street with respect to the migrant question, the fate of foreigners was left to increasingly frequent extra-parliamentary decrees and circulars issued by the various ministries concerned with immigration. From Flandin forward, every government avoided bringing questions pertaining to migration to the floor of parliament. In place of parliamentary procedure, ministers tried to respond directly to public pressure. Inevitably, this increased the arbitrariness of migrant rights.

As Flandin tried to change the tone in domestic affairs, international discord grew. Anthony Eden later wrote that the shots fired in Marseille on 9 October 1934 had been "the first shots of the Second World War."[5] Others had worried as much at the time. Alexander I had been an autocrat, but he had unified the various ethnicities of Yugoslavia under one state and he had brokered regional alliances that allowed him to maintain independence from Italy and Germany. These alliances did not end with his murder, but they were severely compromised. Coming just months after Hitler's nonaggression pact with Poland, the assassination without question weakened France's alliances. Other events also destabilized the Versailles settlement. In October 1933, Hitler announced Germany's withdrawal from the League of Nations, thereby preparing the path for remilitarization. The summer of 1934 saw the assassination of Austrian chancellor Engelbert Dollfuss and an attempted Nazi putsch in Vienna. Meanwhile, on the day before the assassination of King Alexander and Louis Barthou, the Spanish army landed in the Asturian port cities of Avilés and Gijón in response to local uprisings. The Spanish republic was splintering. For some, a civil war already had begun. Within two months of the assassination, another blow to French security came when more than 90% of Saarlanders voted in a plebiscite to rejoin Germany. Days after the Saarland's incorporation into Germany, Hitler announced a return to military conscription, in violation of the Versailles treaty. The significance of these events was brought home to French citizens by the number of refugees that each triggered—refugees who, at the height of the depression, wished to make France their new home. For Frenchmen and -women, international and domestic affairs had become part of the same crisis, and no matter how one looked at it, migration was at its heart.

Perhaps because the causes of the crisis seemed intractable, government officials instead took aim at its symptoms. Circular after circular, first issuing new demands with respect to regulating migration, and then making new exceptions, testified to the contradictory pressures the government faced and the continuation of practices that eluded executive control. To be sure, treaties, statelessness, colonial politics, local budgets for social entitlements, economic differences across the country, divergent policing methods, and the relationship of politics to administration had long conspired to establish profoundly different migrant rights across or even within regions. But this latest round of bureaucratic competition over migrant regulation had produced a novel response: formal discrimination. Circulars now blatantly asked local authorities to distinguish unmarried migrants from those with "French attachments," families from the childless, and some nationalities from others.

These foreigners, whom I shall call "privileged," earned rights as "immigrants." Meanwhile, temporary or short-term "migrants"—those around whom French migration policy had been constructed—faced new prejudice. Even the Popular Front government, known for its support of refugees, was not entirely immune to this new calculus of privilege and prejudice. France had jettisoned its guest-worker regime for a politics of population building. The line between migrants and immigrants, however, was at best blurry and at worst subject to arbitrary manipulation. This chapter examines how that line was redrawn both nationally and locally.

WHAT TRUCE?

Doumergue's threats backfired when Édouard Herriot and the Radicals resigned from the cabinet on 5 November 1934. Doumergue's own resignation came two days later.[6] His successor, Flandin, in a conciliatory move, named Herriot to chair his new "interministerial commission to protect French labor." Within weeks, Herriot's commission made formal recommendations to the Council of Ministers. In typical Herriot style, the commission report began with some numbers: "350,000 assisted unemployed, 800,000 foreign workers." The statistical inference he meant to draw was unstated but obvious. He had adopted this approach before. In 1931, as he helped push through legislation placing quotas on foreign employment, he had made the same insinuation on a smaller scale.[7] Then his declaration had caused commotion in the chamber. Now, commotion was replaced with almost intractable division.

Opening the session of the Chamber of Deputies on 13 November, Flandin began, "The truce continues."[8] Yet the ensuing debate laid bare the country's divisions. The extreme Left erupted in applause when Flandin declared that order had been reestablished, despite "regrettable provocations." The Center and Right applauded when he paid homage to Gaston Doumergue, his predecessor. There was applause all around when he said that "the republican state will not capitulate to the factions." The Center and moderate Left liked it when he declared that "no one can object to priority being given to the French in the labor market." As he reminded the chamber, "Our first act of government addresses that."[9] Yet even his final appeal, "Let us unite," which earned prolonged applause, was not applauded on all sides. After several long speeches by deputies on the extreme Left, and contentious interruptions from the Right and extreme Right, Flandin spoke again, this time invoking the specter of civil war.

I know of countries—they are not far away from ours—where democracy gave way to groups confronting one another, first with words, then in the streets, creating a permanent state of riot and civil war. And in both cases, that ended in dictatorship. If that's what you want, do it. But I don't want that.

Deputies moved a vote-of-confidence resolution. The Socialists balked. They wanted dissolution and new elections. As Léon Blum explained, to heavy applause from the extreme Left, "Mister President of the Council, we consider that, with respect to fascism, its leagues, its organizations, its plots, its arms, there is no truce possible." Blum's protest notwithstanding, the vote of confidence passed easily, by 423 to 188. Yet the vote was telling. Virtually all the Socialists and Communists voted against the resolution. The 66 abstentions came from across the political spectrum.

In the ensuing weeks, the chamber moved on to budgetary discussions. These, too, showed the imprint of Flandin's first act of government, as well as Herriot's framing of the question. Within minutes of putting Alsace-Lorraine's budget on the table on 15 November, the Christian trade unionist Henri Meck (Union Populaire Républicaine, Bas Rhin) had turned the discussion to that area's unemployed, "who see their situation exacerbated by the influx of many foreign workers."[10] For the rest of the debate, this theme was sounded repeatedly; the budget as such was discussed relatively little. The following day, the expense of caring for foreigners was mentioned in the discussion of the health budget, as Henri Queuille (Radical, Corrèze), the health minister, questioned the wisdom of maintaining reciprocity treaties.[11] In discussions over the education budget, Pierre Amidieu du Clos (Indépendants d'Action Économique Sociale et Paysanne, Meurthe-et-Moselle) suggested limiting university scholarships to French nationals and protested what he regarded as financial advantages given to foreign students in French secondary schools.[12] Migrants came up again in discussions that afternoon of overcrowding in primary schools. On 22 November, it was the minister of agriculture who declared he found it "shocking" that foreign workers continued to be admitted to the country even as there were 350,000 unemployed. He promised to "remedy the situation, in such a way as to not leave French workers without work while there is a plethora of foreign workers."[13] This promise was greeted with cheers of "Well said! Well said!" Unemployment, and the role migrants had in exacerbating it, again took center stage in the Public Works Ministry budget discussions on 23 November.[14] Migrants were everywhere, it seemed, and everywhere they posed problems.

Unsurprisingly, deputies discussed the effect of immigration most extensively when they turned to the Labor Ministry budget on 27 November. Ludovic-Oscar Frossard (Haute-Saône), the former secretary-general of the SFIO (Section Française de l'Internationale Ouvrière [Socialist Party]) who had joined the Communist Party at Tours, becoming its secretary-general only to rejoin then drift away from the SFIO, first acknowledged that the foreign labor issue was "delicate and difficult" and could not be resolved "with the wave of a magic wand." He nonetheless concluded to cheers of "Well said!" that "French labor has, obviously, a right to priority."[15] Arthur Ramette (Communist, Nord) retorted, later that same day, "If you do not want foreign labor to compete with French labor, you must accept the principle of equal treatment between French and foreign workers. . . . Then management would no longer have a preference."[16] Ramette went on to accuse Herriot and the labor minister of reinforcing xenophobia, however unintentionally.[17] It was not foreign workers themselves, but their lack of rights, he argued, that caused their disproportionate employment in some industries. This brought Camille-Jean Fernand-Laurent (Indépendant, Seine) to reply that Herriot had been perfectly right when he argued that France is "no longer rich enough to nourish at one and the same time its own children and the foreign workers that it had to bring to its land in the painful hours after the war."[18]

Fernand-Laurent called it his "duty" to recommend the "discontinuation of unemployment [compensation] to foreign workers," even though he knew it would "provoke recriminations." Recriminations indeed came, in the form of interruptions from the extreme Left.[19] "As for me," chimed in Jacques Doriot (Seine), by then expelled from the Comintern but still a partisan of the Left, "I will take up an expression of Jaurès: 'The word "foreigner" does not mean anything to my mouth.' "[20]

This was the truce: no more street battles, just a war of words.

CIRCULAR REASONING

By the time budget discussions turned to the Labor Ministry, Herriot's commission had already announced new policy provisions, and police in the capital had begun enforcement raids significant enough to garner the attention of the *New York Times*.[21] The reforms entailed mostly procedural changes: Henceforth the Labor and Agricultural ministries' foreign worker offices would be united. No new foreign worker cards would be issued, and renewals of current cards would be subject to "meticulous scrutiny."[22] Current cards of a short-term validity would not be renewed, barring "exceptional cases which the labor minister will judge." Application of policy was also to be more uniform. Parity commissions, designed to take local labor market dynamics into account, were still in place, but now the central government ordered them to review "existing decrees, when they have provided for a percentage [of foreign labor] that exceeds 10%." Herriot had been an advocate of a uniform 10% cap on foreign employment in 1931, but debate in the chamber had led to a compromise. Now, as commission president, Herriot required local parity commissions to revisit the issue. Finally, sanctions would be stiffened. Border patrols would be reinforced, controls of identification cards within the country would be stepped up, and punishment for evading expulsion orders would be more severe.[23] All of this should be carried out immediately and dutifully, for it was "in the national interest."[24]

Herriot's mandate had been to protect national workers, but soon other forms of economic protectionism appeared on the agenda. During the debates that led to passage of the 1932 national labor protection law, some deputies had predicted the potential for popular demand to snowball. "Once you have resolved the question of foreign workers in France," Deputy Charles-Louis Coutel (Union Républicaine et Démocrate, Nord) had noted in December 1931, "nothing dictates that French merchants will not ask, in their turn, for legislation protecting them from the foreign merchants established here."[25] Coutel was on target, though the snowball effect was hardly limited to merchants. Responding to pressure from French medical students, parliament passed the Armbruster Law, promulgated 21 April 1933, which limited medical and dental practice in France to French nationals who had French doctoral degrees. Similarly, law students, citing the "plethora" of German refugees who were studying law in France, succeeded in having a bill passed on 19 July 1934 that precluded newly naturalized citizens from being members of the bar for ten years following their naturalization.[26] Two days after Herriot announced new restrictions on foreign labor, 45 deputies presented a bill to limit foreign artisans as well. Ironically, Coutel, the same deputy who had warned in 1931 of the potential for protectionist demands to snowball, now signed his name to those introducing the bill on artisans. Not coincidentally, 26 of the deputies were from Alsace-Lorraine, where complaints had grown of Jewish merchants and artisans flooding the market since Hitler's arrival in power.[27] The crafts cited by the deputies as most in danger of "tight competition" that could be characterized as "unfair" also not coincidentally included "furriers, tailors, shoemakers, dressmakers," and other trades frequently occupied by Jews.[28]

Artisans would have to wait until 1935, when Pierre Laval issued a decree to protect them from competition by foreigners. But small merchants quickly earned the attention of Marcel Régnier, Flandin's interior minister. According to Régnier, foreigners claiming to be "traveling salesmen" escaped control too easily. French law required them to have a "real domicile, a sure residence and not a hotel or a room rented in a rooming house." Their identification cards should be approved only in "truly exceptional cases which you must justify to me."[29] Interior Minister Régnier was not entirely unfounded in concluding that traveling salesmen were often unemployed workers seeking a legal means to stay in the country. As we have seen, many foreigners became self-employed in order to survive the ravages of the depression.[30]

But if fears over "invasions" of the merchant trades by foreigners stemmed in part from the overflow of unemployed industrial workers into commerce, they were also fed by assumptions about the new influx of migrants who had owned businesses in their home countries, namely, refugees from Germany. Here, economic fears mixed with stereotypes about Jews and added fuel to the merchants' growing fire. As one spokesperson at the International Conference of Traveling Salesmen noted, "Since the events in Germany, a large number of Jewish salespeople have come to France and, in agreement with their patented coreligionists sell door to door."[31] Had assumptions of this kind been limited to merchants' associations, the effect might have been slight. Yet the anti-Semitism exposed by such comments also found its way into the rationale of local officials making decisions to authorize or decline residency. Even before Régnier encouraged prefects to regard traveling salesmen with circumspection, Rhône authorities had concluded that a recently arrived Jewish family did not meet the requirement of traveling salesmen; rather, they had "most certainly come to France to exercise their profession more lucratively and to abuse the hospitality accorded by our country toward political refugees." On that note, the prefect recommended their expulsion from the country.[32]

A flood of circulars followed, each fine-tuning some aspect or other of immigration regulation. In some respects, this was hardly new. As Gary Cross has suggested, much of French immigration policy from the mid-1920s on "was ceded to the government ministries, each working within the limits of its own powers and serving different constituencies."[33] But something also had changed. From late 1934, ministerial circulars were often reactive rather than programmatic. Flandin had saved the republic from the factions, but now his ministers were currying favor with them by issuing memoranda responding to their concerns. I call this development "circular reasoning" because it relied on government memoranda—that is, circulars—instead of parliamentary lawmaking, and it developed in response to the circuit of information flowing between the central ministries and the departments.

Circular reasoning allowed ministries to react quickly and directly to public pressures rather than by calling for parliamentary debate on the matter. Circulars aimed to streamline policy and its enforcement. But, issued with little or no deliberation, they also sometimes made contradictory demands. As these became apparent, or as novel situations on the ground emerged, revised circulars flew out of the capital to the provinces. With local authorities left to interpret policies that changed by the month, or even week, implementation rarely met expectations. This fact, too, led to new circulars designed to clarify standards or ease the job of local administrations. At once an acknowledgment that policy and practice diverged, and an attempt to bring the two in line with each other by authorizing exceptional practices, circular reasoning led to a fundamental shift in priorities with respect to residency rights in France. Crucially, however, all this occurred behind closed doors, away from public debate, and outside the lawmaking authority of parliament. The turn to circulars was perhaps an understandable move, given the context. The Radicals' refusal to give Doumergue the authority to dissolve parliament had brought down his government. Almost every subject seemed to polarize the chamber. Administrative decision making was deemed necessary in these conditions. Moreover, the practice of circular reasoning was not always unequivocally bad for migrants. The Popular Front recognized this when, in the fall of 1936, it created a special status for refugees coming from Germany, something that might have led to acrimonious debate even in a Center-Left majority chamber. And even before the arrival of the Popular Front, circular reasoning allowed some migrants to earn special privileges. The question was: Which ones, and on what basis?

Calling for a review of all existing foreigner identification cards, Flandin's government instructed local officials to reject renewals of short-term cards for persons having lived in France less than two years, leaving the local officials to decide what constituted sufficient proof of residence. Aimed at excluding transient foreigners who had no intention of staying, the measures also targeted recent arrivals, seasonal migrants, and those whose very mobility made it difficult to prove how long they had lived in France. The 6 February 1935 decree required that foreign residents, whether they held "reduced validity" (temporary) or "normal" (two-year validity) cards, would be required to show proof of a valid labor contract, approved by central authorities, if they wished to renew their cards as workers. Those with temporary cards had the added burden of applying for renewal before their cards expired.[34] Both types of cardholders had to meet a new requirement of providing "the names and addresses of two French citizens who consent to serve as guarantors," a clause that proved more problematic for new arrivals than for long-term residents.[35] Even more worrisome to new arrivals were policy prescriptions that had been circulated in advance of the 6 February decree, whereby no short-term card would be renewed unless its bearer had lived in France for more than two years.[36]

The impact of circular reasoning was first apparent in Marseille, whose problems, after all, had triggered the sweeping new policies. No record remains of the precise decisions Bouches-du-Rhône officials made in the Flandin review, but if authorities in Marseille applied the expected standard—guarantee of two French citizens and, for all intents and purposes, two years' residency—then surely they would have rejected renewals for virtually all but the most stable of the foreigners living in central Marseille. In practice, the Flandin measures made day-to-day policing more difficult in a number of ways. Not only did the directives increase the volume of card renewals, but also they added other requirements to already overworked local bureaucracies. New cards were to be valid only for the department in which they were issued, so in addition to worrying about renewals, prefectures also had to approve changes in domicile. The bureaucracy was further burdened by a new requirement that lodgers and hoteliers report the arrival of new tenants within 24 hours.

In response to the Flandin directives, local authorities almost immediately reported backlog. In Marseille, only five employees were initially assigned to the task. Eventually this was increased to eight, and then 11, but the prefect nonetheless reported in September 1935 that it would take at least another six months to finish the review. By that time, there would be new renewals waiting in what was already a queue of 30,000 files.[37] The rejected foreigners, meanwhile, did not necessarily depart Marseille; instead, they often swelled the numbers of illegal aliens living in the city undetected. Increasing the work expected of local police, the Flandin reforms did not address the infrastructure problems that had so come under fire in the wake of the assassination. Between 1931 and 1936, the Marseille police force added 12 inspectors and 20 peace officers. As a per capita figure, however, their numbers still paled when compared to the force in Paris, or even Lyon.[38] In the end, the very measures that aimed to redress the inadequacies of Marseille policing actually reinforced long-standing police practices in the port city.

Judging from follow-up circulars, Marseille was not the only city where the review of cards had become bogged down. The Flandin identification card review had been intended to be comprehensive. All foreigners were to have their cards reviewed. All employment contracts were to be approved by the central Labor Ministry. And all persons without valid cards or who failed to renew their cards were expected to depart the country. In practice, such draconian policies proved unwieldy, and in circular after circular, new exceptions were decreed.

Scarcely more than two weeks after issuing guidance on procedures for renewing identification cards, Labor Minister Paul Jacquier told local authorities to consider his circular of 25 January abrogated and instead apply the principles contained in a new circular effective immediately.[39] This new circular, dated 12 February, laid down new restrictions, while it also created new exceptions, identifying several classes of foreigners who were to receive preferential treatment. Beneficiaries of the new exceptions included foreign men married to French-born women; French-born women who had lost their nationality through marriage; the fathers or mothers of French children; those having French siblings living in France; former legionnaires; and those having lived in France more than 10 years.[40] Although the new policies required, again in theory, categorical rejections of residency renewals for foreigners who worked in professions experiencing unemployment, migrants meeting certain criteria would receive "immediate approval regardless of the labor market situation in the profession concerned." Foreigners falling into the first four of the preferential categories, all of which were based on family ties to France, would automatically receive residency cards valid for two years. Other privileged persons received cards valid for six months. Refugees and the stateless were listed among those potentially eligible for exemptions and six-month cards, but the circular also stipulated that only the central government would be allowed to grant exceptions to refugees and stateless persons, on an exceptional rather than automatic basis.[41]

Despite these new exceptions, dossiers continued to pile up in prefectures, approved barely in time to come due again. This state of affairs had "drawbacks," as the ministry put it; it meant that some migrants' cards were perpetually under review.[42] Jacquier's solution was to ask local officials to add three months to any card that "seems to require a minimum of six months' validity."[43] Soon, however, saying that six months really meant nine proved equally confusing. With the local backlog growing, the Labor Ministry went back to the drawing board; a month later, it issued a new confidential circular. Although the circular maintained the objective of "eliminating superfluous foreign labor" regardless of migrants' origins, the remainder of the circular abandoned the pretense of universalism. Calling for renewals to be carried out "with the greatest speed possible" and acknowledging "the difficulties confronted by public placement services in accomplishing the task requested of them," Jacquier suggested that in the interests of speed, discrimination had become necessary.[44]

Jacquier already had created a class of foreigners eligible for automatic renewal of residency authorizations. The 12 February circular had stipulated that under no circumstances would foreigners, other than those with family connections to France, be authorized for more than six months' residency. Jacquier's new circular nevertheless extended these privileges to two years. That was not all. If a foreigner had resided in France longer than five years, and worked in a profession where there was no unemployment, his or her identity card could be renewed for as long as a year. Distinctions were to be drawn, as well, between foreigners who entered France with contracts already in hand and those who entered France to find work. This was a veiled way of distinguishing those who benefited from reciprocity treaties from those who, like refugees, had their status legalized after arriving in France. Finally, Jacquier announced that in light of a "recent protocol" between France and Italy, requests for renewals of identity cards presented by Italian workers living in France more than five years should be "examined with a particular benevolence, in order to avoid refusals of renewals as much as is possible."[45] Was this final provision what earned the circular its "confidential" label?

Like the identification card review, the Franco-Italian protocol was a consequence of the Marseille assassinations. With Louis Barthou dead, Pierre Laval became foreign minister. Almost immediately, Laval set about reestablishing what he regarded as France's neglected relationship with Italy. Most famously (or some might say infamously), he negotiated an agreement with Mussolini whereby Italy would lose some of the special concessions it had in the French protectorate of Tunisia in exchange for France's neutrality when Italy entered Abyssinia.[46] Similarly, the 23 February 1935 protocol calling for "benevolence" toward applications from Italians having lived in France more than five years probably had Laval's stamp on it. After Laval became premier in June, he extended further goodwill toward Italians, as illustrated by a new "confidential" circular issued in September by Laval's labor minister, Ludovic-Oscar Frossard, asking local officials to show "benevolence" toward Italians even if they had committed "anti-French" acts.

What were "anti-French" acts? Jacquier's 12 February circular specified that foreign nationals who declined, or who forced their French-born family members to decline, French nationality were not worthy of special consideration.[47] In other words, Jacquier regarded building France's population as a matter of national interest and perceived efforts to thwart it—including efforts by the descendants of one-time guest workers—as "anti-French." In this way, Jacquier acknowledged that France was not merely the host of guest workers but an immigrant nation. Regardless of how local authorities understood "anti-French" acts, the September 1935 circular presented a complete reversal from the Labor Ministry's earlier conception of the national interest. Probably this testified to the shift in France's relations with Mussolini: Henceforth nothing could be held against Italian applicants whose wives had deliberately returned to Italy in order to give birth and had thus deprived their children of the benefits of France's liberal 1927 nationality law. Similarly, although young Italian males whose parents lived in France and who were called to Italy for military service would have to reapply for entry into France, the "special situation" of such workers and their "previous residency in French territory" now would be taken into account.[48] This controverted another provision of the 12 February circular, which had granted special treatment to long-term migrants who could prove *uninterrupted* residency in France. Finally, the circular reminded placement offices that they were to refrain from "all pressure whose object is to bring [Italians] to change their nationality" and "in no case hold against [Italians] the anti-French acts targeted by the 12 February 1935 circular."[49] Mussolini's concern over Italian naturalizations was not new, but previously, French policy makers had been hesitant to appear to advocate his position.[50] Laval and his cabinet now shifted course on this issue. By allowing Italy to maintain as citizens young men who would otherwise become French at the age of adulthood, these concessions worked against future French military interests.

In granting special favors to Italians, Frossard opened a Pandora's box. At the bottom of his confidential September circular, he added, almost as an afterthought, that local offices should refrain from putting pressure on "Belgian and Swiss workers to whom I have decided to extend the favorable treatment accorded to Italians with respect to the nonapplication of those dispositions of my circular targeting anti-French acts."[51] Three days later, Frossard reminded the same offices that "requests from former legionnaires will receive immediate approval, regardless of their length of residence in France."[52]

What was originally intended to be a generalized elimination of "superfluous" foreigners therefore provided, in subsequent months, a rationale for new forms of discrimination. This discrimination had not been an intended consequence of the Flandin and Laval crackdown. Rather, it emerged from the divergence between policy prescription and what was achievable on the ground. Instead of allowing local authorities to work out their own accommodations to contradictory demands, as they had previously done, national leaders responded to local officials' inability to implement their reforms by dictating exceptions to the rule. This forced them to articulate priorities about who deserved exceptions and who did not. Long-term residents, certain nationalities, and those with family connections to France became privileged, while new arrivals, especially single men and refugees, faced new prejudice.

Those not benefiting from these special dispensations faced renewed repression. The length of sentences for failing to honor an expulsion order was increased, and, once a sentence was served, the foreigner was supposed to be escorted to the border. These measures were justified, Laval explained, because it was necessary to "reinforce sanctions that have lost their effect of intimidation." Revealing that expulsion was not, to his mind, a measure aimed solely at traditional criminals, Laval added that "these measures will prevent . . . foreigners, ever more numerous, from remaining in France where they burden public services or unemployment or assistance bureaus."[53] That same day, a separate decree prevented foreigners from exercising the profession of traveling salesmen unless they had lived in France for at least five years.[54]

Even with a new government on the horizon in the spring of 1936, circular reasoning continued. Two days after the Popular Front coalition scored significant gains in the first round of legislative elections, the director of the Sûreté Nationale, Charles Magny, reminded prefects that a refusal by the Labor Ministry to approve a foreigner's labor contract was not, on its own, "a sufficient reason" for a *refoulement*. The fact that Magny sent this circular at all suggests that local authorities often thought otherwise, which is hardly surprising given the tone that Laval set while serving as premier. "The situation of the interested parties must be examined objectively," Magny now wrote, and the following factors were to be taken into account: means of existence, family attachments, and the conditions in which immigrants lived. Some foreign workers "own property, whether it is an inexpensive house, or some other kind of building, a fact which implies, obviously, a desire to remain on our soil, and that demonstrates the investment of their savings in France." These foreigners were different from those who found themselves "permanently unemployed" or whose presence had long obstructed the labor market; such foreigners could be repatriated after careful consideration.[55]

Was this really a reminder of existing Interior Ministry policy, or an attempt by the Sarraut government (which replaced Laval's in January 1936, keeping Laval's cabinet partially intact) to tone down the excesses unleashed during the governments of Sarraut's two predecessors? If Labor Ministry policy is any indication, continued circular reasoning aimed to achieve better administrative control by allocating repressive resources selectively, but always from the perspective of making exceptions, not from the point of view of liberalizing the general rule. In this vein, even after the second round of legislative elections on 3 May 1936 had secured a victory for the Center-Left antifascist Popular Front coalition, Frossard issued a final circular, reiterating exceptions to the tight limits placed on foreign workers, which had been Flandin's rallying cry as he formed his government in the fall of 1934.

The exceptions prescribed by the May 1936 circular showed the results of a year and a half of circular reasoning. First, Frossard reminded local officials that renewals of worker cards required special approval from the central administration. Second, since policies had been modified by a series of circulars, Frossard reviewed the cases in which individuals should be granted identification cards "automatically regardless of the labor market situation."[56] These were the following:

1. Foreigners married to women who were French by birth (whether or not they have retained their original nationality after marriage);
2. Women who were French by birth but lost their nationality upon marriage;
3. Foreigners whose children all were born in France and hold French nationality;
4. Foreigners having brothers or sisters who hold French nationality (either by origin or naturalization);
5. Foreigners who are under 18 years old and who were born in France;

6. Former legionnaires who have honorable discharge notices;
7. Foreigners having lived in France more than 10 years, or five years in the case of Belgian, Italian, Swiss, Czech, Polish, and Yugoslavian workers.[57]

Migrants from the states with which France had concluded reciprocity treaties over the years—save for Spain—received special treatment. With this circular, Frossard recalled that policy now favored migrants with families over the unattached single men who, after all, were the ones whom policy makers and employers had originally aimed to attract in the immediate aftermath of the First World War. Thus, at precisely the moment when guest workers were supposed to go home, France's guest-worker system had metamorphosed into a populationist one, complete with the selectivity that populationism implied.

Jean-Baptiste Lebas, Léon Blum's labor minister, did nothing to reverse these exemptions. In fact, Lebas' general director of labor, Marcel Bernard, maintained a two-track approach when he announced that while the law protecting national labor "does not permit any discrimination between categories of foreigners," employers should nonetheless "reserve special treatment for foreigners whose situation is particularly worthy of interest (former combatants in allied armies, foreigners having French children) and to resort as much as possible to laying off other foreigners before them."[58] Even more surprising, given the connections between anti-Semitism and small-business protectionism, the second Popular Front cabinet issued circulars implementing Laval's policy on artisans.[59] Only in the domain of refugee treatment, as we shall see in Chapter 5, did the Popular Front seriously reverse course on migrant rights.

Decree by decree, circular by circular, labor and interior ministers under Flandin, Laval, and Sarraut destabilized the logic of the guest-worker system. Oddly, they did this in the guise of enforcing the guest-worker model. Faced with the impossibility—or at least the impracticality—of sending home each and every "superfluous" foreigner, the government improvised new policies that signaled a shift in priorities. France's guest-worker policy, however imperfectly implemented, had emerged from a tripartist outlook in which organized labor, employers, and the state, at least theoretically, were equal partners. Rights, in this system, belonged to individuals; the role of organized bodies was to enforce them. In the mid-1930s, however, enforcement of the guest-worker model took on a decidedly more corporatist and familialist character. Here, legal privilege accrued to groups: professions, families, the military, and even some nationalities. In some respects, of course, such treatment was hardly new: Reciprocity treaties had allowed for legal distinctions to be drawn between foreigners from different states. Crucially, however, such treaties had been intended to ensure that employers and social services did not discriminate between treaty beneficiaries and French nationals; only in the context of the depression had they been deployed by local governments as a means of discriminating one foreigner from another. What was new was the formal policy recognition given to constituted groups in society. Bowing to interest-group pressure from merchants and artisans, the government increasingly sanctioned the rights of professions to refuse entry to outsiders, reinvigorating the corporatist idiom that was said to have been abolished during the French Revolution. Similarly, it granted new privileges to persons by virtue of the place they occupied in a family, and, by extension, society. Foreigners without families were double outsiders, legal and social strangers. To be sure, familialist understandings of society had influenced the distribution of rights among migrants in practice, especially in Marseille, for some time. Still, where such exceptions had once been made on a case-by-case basis, increasingly, they were categorical. Migrants came to understand this, to their advantage or disquiet.

LYON'S FAMILY FORTUNES

In November 1934, Herriot promised his municipal council that he would "give priority to French workers."[60] Paradoxically, however, the practices that emerged from circular reasoning dampened the protectionist zeal of Lyon authorities and replaced it with a more selective exclusion. To be sure, the departmental placement office saw to it that its parity commissions followed the Herriot directives regarding quotas of foreigners, issuing 14 decrees in 1935 to limit foreign employment in Lyon-area industries.[61] Even so, however, labor protectionism ceased to be the automatic reflex of Lyon-based officials as it had in the early days of the depression when they coped with sudden and massive unemployment. It was not that officials stopped caring about the state of Lyon's labor market, but as concern over still-rising unemployment grew, new mitigating factors entered the decision-making process of Rhône officials. Whether motivated directly by the Flandin-Laval crackdown or not, the exceptions made by Rhône police closely paralleled many of the prescriptions decreed in the ministerial circulars of 1935.

One of the new policies under the Flandin decrees was that foreigner identification cards be valid for only one department. In a city such as Lyon, whose industrial hinterland stretched into the neighboring departments, this led to a multiplication of identification card reviews. Although the policy theoretically allowed a department to refuse entry to migrants in order to protect its local labor market, the outcome of these reviews suggests that Rhône police no longer substituted their own judgment for that of the central state. In meting out new privileges—and punishments—they now acted as the executive's agent rather than its competitor. This cooperation launched a new era in relations between the Rhône department police and the Sûreté; for the first time in years, they shared a similar outlook on the policing of migrants. Whereas Rhône authorities had previously adjudicated migrant rights largely in relation to the role they played in the economy, those rights now turned largely on family ties.

Lyon's foreign families came to realize the benefits of invoking family in their negotiations for residency rights. When Carmelita D., a Spanish widow, filed a request for herself and her daughters to transfer their identification cards from the nearby Ain department to the Rhône, where one of her daughters had found work at the Usines Gillet in Vaulx-en-Velin and the other as a domestic servant, she did not hide the fact that she saw this "as the only means of freeing from destitution and famine three miserable women who have no protection."[62] Less than a year earlier, the lawyer Jacques Locquin's attempt to elicit pathos for another "unprotected" widow, Roberta G., had backfired. In stark contrast, Rhône officials this time took pity: "Given the special situation of the family and the interest that members of the family have to group together," Jean Perret, the director of the departmental placement office, recommended approving Carmelita's request, and the general secretary for police agreed.[63] Now Roberta, too, gained the nerve to transfer her residence from the Jura back to the Rhône.[64]

Pasqualina U.'s case also reflected the new focus on immigration over migration. Rhône authorities approved her request to move with her family from a nearby department to Vénissieux, where she planned on running a grocery. Local authorities' remarks in Pasqualina's file suggest some hesitation: The Ain prefecture warned its Rhône counterpart that her move from his jurisdiction was "motivated in part by the persistent unemployment of her husband and son," and in the Lyon police chief's report, the remark "the husband and son are currently unemployed" was underlined. Nonetheless, authorities answered yes when asked, "Can one authorize these foreigners established in France for more than ten years to fix their domicile in the Rhône?"[65] The formula "for more than ten years" came directly from the new circulars. This—and perhaps the secret protocol with Italy—allowed Pasqualina's residency to be approved, even though her family's situation entirely contradicted the expectations of the guest-worker model.[66] Compared to decisions made by Rhône authorities in the early depression years, the change in outlook with respect to women was striking. In each of these cases, a woman served as the principal breadwinner for her family. Instead of regarding migrant women as incapable of supporting their families, Rhône authorities now gave legal recognition to those families, regardless of who sustained them.

Not only women but other vulnerable migrants appeared newly confident in calling for state protection in the Lyon area. Armenians, often the most cautious of foreign migrants due to their statelessness, risked bringing attention to themselves with new requests to change residency, but these risks paid off. Nareg L.'s request to move to the Rhône from Décines (then in the Isère department) to be closer to his work, for instance, drew the following response from the departmental placement office: "The labor market situation does not enter into account, because the applicant retains the same job that he has occupied since October 1930."[67] Rhône authorities issued a similar decision in the case of another Décines-based Armenian, Jivan J., who had been working at Rhodiaceta in Lyon since January 1934. Like Nareg, Jivan's work dated (albeit barely) to the period before the departmental limits on cards had been enacted, and, as in Nareg's case, the placement office determined that the labor market situation should not stand in the way of honoring Jivan's request.[68]

One wonders: Why were these men living so far from their workplaces? Had they worked in Décines, perhaps in the synthetic fabric factory there, and then found work closer to Lyon? Or had they moved to the Isère as a strategy for avoiding the Rhône police in the early 1930s? The trajectories of other foreigners suggest that this might have been the case. Guillermo B., for instance, a Spaniard who had been living in Vénissieux until he got into a vicious fight with a compatriot, continued to work at the Berliet auto plant in Vénissieux but moved to St Priest (then in the Isère department), about seven kilometers away.[69] Another Spanish man, Diego D., who had been considered for expulsion following his theft of coal residue from train tracks in 1933, had also moved to St Priest. He, too, continued to work in the Rhône, at Établissements Maréchal in Vénissieux. Only in the fall of 1936, with the lifting of the departmental limits on identity cards, did he request to move back to the Rhône, claiming that he wanted to allow his three children to be closer to a school.[70] Regardless of what motivated their settlement in the Isère department, these men seemed to have judged it safe to apply now for favors from the Rhône department; this in itself was perhaps a sign of a change in tone.

Another sign of change came in migrants' claims on the state, which now increasingly invoked family ties and other signs of investment in France. Migrants had long referred to family in their interactions with French officials. When facing expulsion, for instance, they often called attention to the misfortune this would bring upon their suffering families. The register in which they invoked information about their families, however, changed as they increasingly expressed a sense that the state had obligations to them because of their family situations.[71] For instance, Giovanni U., an Italian expellee whose last recorded *sursis* dated from 10 November 1934, officially declared all five of his children French on the same day in February 1936, then requested a renewal of his *sursis*. In response, Lyon's deputy chief of police wrote that he saw no objection.[72] Savio X., who repeatedly earned *sursis* despite spending years on the dole, was probably helped by the fact that he had lived in France for more than 10 years, was Italian, and had multiple children. Gaetano W., who received similar reprieves, may have been aided by the fact that his companion was French even though he never married her.[73]

Did the word spread? Benigna U., a Philadelphia-born woman of Italian background whose husband, Tullio, had been expelled in 1934, noted several times in a letter to Rhône department authorities requesting *sursis* for Tullio that they had four children, that all of them had been born in France, and that all had been declared French. The letter was not above supplication: "Please have the goodness to let him come back." More significantly, however, when the prefecture rejected her request in October 1936, Benigna must have believed herself in her rights to appeal to his superiors, for shortly thereafter, the Rhône prefect received an inquiry from the Ministry of the Interior attaching a letter he had received from Benigna. Forced to initiate a new inquiry into her case, the prefect responded by acknowledging her family situation. Benigna had "fixed all four children in French nationality as of 5 September 1936"; she had four married sisters, one of whom was married to a Frenchman, and four brothers; all her siblings lived in Lyon. The prefect therefore "saw no reason" why the husband could not return, on a trial *sursis*.[74]

Still, French family connections were not always a magic bullet. In a case involving a Portuguese expellee married to a Frenchwoman, for instance, local authorities ignored multiple pleas from his wife during the course of 1934 and 1935 until the Ministry of the Interior granted a *sursis* in December 1935 "given his family situation." Benedito E. had entered France in 1921 and had always worked regularly in St-Fons and Vénissieux until injured at work in 1933. He was expelled in October 1934 for hitting a man. Although his marriage to a Frenchwoman was something "he never ceases to repeat," this was not enough to endear him to the St-Fons police commissioner. Even so, the prefect's language in his October 1935 report to the Interior Ministry showed an awareness that family had become increasingly important to ministerial decisions, for he wrote that "*despite the fact that this foreigner is the father of two French*

FIGURE 4.1 *Immigrant families described as "prolific," Lyon*
SOURCE: *AML 1120 WP 001-2. Courtesy of Archives Municipales de Lyon.*

children, I have concluded, based on his bad reputation, that the measure against him should be enforced."[75]

Meanwhile, Benedito E.'s wife, Delphine, also was feeling her way through the process. Her letters, full of spelling and grammatical errors, showed a poorly educated woman appealing for help in all directions; they were addressed alternatively to the interior minister, prefect, and even, despite her residence in the suburbs, to Lyon's mayor Herriot. Each letter mentioned her French nationality and that of her children, but her tone often was one of victimization rather than entitlement, and her argument varied from letter to letter. Her first letter, to the interior minister, called the motive for her husband's expulsion "trivial." To the prefect, she wondered aloud, "how I am supposed to raise" two children and a third on the way without the aid of her husband. To Herriot, meanwhile, she bared all. She told him of the circumstances that had provoked the fight in which her husband had hit their neighbor with a cane. Benedito, still in a cast from his work accident, had gone for a walk after dinner. When Delphine went looking for him, she found their neighbors trying to provoke a fight. She intervened, at which point one of them "pushed me and threw me to the ground." Seeing this, Benedito hit the neighbor with his cane. Her next line was perhaps the most revealing: "and at that moment Mister Mayor I found myself in an 'interesting situation' after that." Euphemistically, Delphine implied that her neighbor had raped her—"interesting situation" being a reference to pregnancy—and that, to add insult to injury, her husband now paid for the neighbor's abuse with a fine and an expulsion. Delphine had confessed all to the one public official who had absolutely no jurisdiction in her case. Herriot's office forwarded her letter to the prefect, but to little avail.[76]

Delphine's first three letters were posted before circular reasoning had created new exemptions for migrants married to French nationals. It seems improbable that Delphine would later have learned of these, given the limitations in her understanding of administrative jurisdiction. Still, what Delphine lacked in sophistication she made up in persistence, for a fourth request—this time after the circulars of 12 February, 11 May, and 9 September 1935 had been issued—led the Interior Ministry to grant a *sursis* "given her family situation." We know that this decision responded to a new letter from Delphine to the interior minister, though we do not know what version of her story it contained.[77]

Had Delphine employed a familialist strategy consciously and deliberately, or was familialism simply in the air? If the latter, not all picked up its scent. Contrast, for instance, the sympathy given families to the treatment of Luis T., a Spanish national having worked and lived in Vénissieux for several years, albeit with a card issued for a different department. Luis had been living in Vénissieux since 1929 and working at its glassworks since August 1935. A quick reference to his parents-in-law in a police report suggests that he was married, but the file says nothing of his spouse, or whether he had any children. Perhaps Luis could have made more of the fact that his in-laws lived in Vénissieux—did their presence there suggest long-term connections to France? Was it that familialism sounded more credible when it was advanced by a woman? Perhaps the result might have been different if Luis' wife had written to the prefecture; we shall never know. Or perhaps the fact that his wife earned no mention was a sign that she resided in Spain? If so, his "transnational family" made him forever a temporary migrant in the eyes of state authorities.[78] In any case, the prefecture treated the information provided about the in-laws in the same manner as it had been given: inconsequentially. For all intents and purposes, prefectural officials treated Luis as a single man who had been living in France only six years. Therefore, Luis did not qualify for the special dispensations granted his compatriot Carmelita D. Nor did Spanish nationals figure among those for whom the length of residency required for special treatment was reduced from ten to five years. For Luis, the 6 February 1935 decree applied as it was written;

thus, unemployment in the glass industry provided a rationale for denying both his card renewal and his request for relocation to the Rhône department. A presumably childless man, in France only a few years, Luis had become an illegal alien by virtue of the new provisions of the 6 February decree.[79]

By the time the first Flandin decree was issued in the winter of 1935, authorities in Lyon had coped with the effects of the depression on the city's migrant population for almost four years. On their own, they had tried draconian measures, only to find themselves forced to recognize that many migrants had become immigrants. This led them, again largely on their own, to institute exceptions to the rule. These initially did not follow the rationale expressed in circular reasoning, but the experience prepared Rhône authorities to accept the idea of making exceptions. Migrants also had learned. Already by late 1935, migrants living in the Lyon area discovered the benefits of invoking their eligibility for the new and growing list of exemptions. These new policies and practices were well under way months before the Popular Front electoral victory. As draconian as the Flandin and Laval decrees were, their effects were not uniformly exclusionary. In fact, paradoxically, their "reign of terror" created an opening for a select number of migrants.[80] This opening widened under the Popular Front as police repression was toned down, but the bases for the exemptions remained the same. Administration, not just politics, thus proved crucial to how migrant rights developed.

NEGOTIATING POWER IN MARSEILLE

In Marseille, arbitrary police practices had divided migrants from immigrants long before circular reasoning had encouraged such practices nationwide. Nevertheless, Marseille authorities did not at first experience the Flandin and subsequent reforms as a ringing endorsement of their approach to managing the city's foreign population—far from it. Throughout the 1930s, Marseille and Bouches-du-Rhône officials negotiated and renegotiated their relationships to their superiors in Paris and to one another. This situation sometimes led to rapid reversals of fortune for Marseille's foreigners.

To begin with, in response to Herriot's demands, the departmental placement office grudgingly forced local parity commissions to review the percentages of foreign workers allowed in Marseille industries.[81] The same industries that previously insisted they could not reduce the percentage of foreigners employed now buckled under the pressure. Foreign employment levels remained high, but not as high as they had previously been. Although some of Marseille's parity commissions voted to "maintain the status quo" that had been established in 1933, others agreed to reductions in foreign employment: Chemical and fertilizer companies within Marseille city limits would henceforth reduce foreign employment to 25% of their personnel. Sugar refineries were limited to 20% and soap and oil producers to 30%. Levels of foreign employment in dock work and warehousing varied from 50% to 70%, depending on the weight and type of product being transferred.[82]

When Bouches-du-Rhône officials finally began to enforce the quota laws on employment, their efforts often were largely symbolic. A case in point: After fruitless exchanges between the labor inspectorate and the departmental placement office regarding whether the number of foreign musicians in a nightclub band could be "rounded up," the prefect was forced to get into the act. Acknowledging that he had "no knowledge of the difficulties of the 'bandoleom' and the technique of the 'marachas,'" he nonetheless wondered whether there were no Frenchmen who could play these instruments.[83] Six months later, when the matter still remained unresolved, the prefecture took a hard line, writing that 30% of 7 equals "2.1 and not 3!"[84]

Other sectors of the Bouches-du-Rhône administration acted as a partial counterweight to newly protectionist practices. As the labor placement director, Eugène Montagne, finally forced Marseille's parity commissions to lower the levels of foreigners whose employment they authorized in January and February 1935, the naturalization division continued to naturalize workers quite readily. The division had no qualms, for example, recommending Ippolito N. and his wife, Victoria, for naturalization on the grounds that Ippolito had been in France since 1925 and had always lived in Marseille, where he "works regularly as a day worker for the same company now a dozen or so years." Ippolito and Victoria were naturalized extraordinarily quickly, on 24 May 1935.[85] Then, too, just four months after parity commissions had agreed to reduce foreign levels of employment in the sugar and oil industries to 20% and 30%, respectively, the naturalization division recommended naturalizing Giuseppe N., who had worked in the same sugar refinery for 15 years, and his wife Bella, who worked in an oil refinery.[86] Giuseppe and Bella were naturalized in June 1935, and other employees of the Raffineries de Sucre de St Louis, the firm employing Giuseppe, also naturalized that year. In the same year that the parity commission for shoemaking lowered the percentage of foreigners allowed to work in the industry, both the deputy mayor and the official in the prefecture took at face value Ilkir R.'s claim that he worked "uncompensated" for his uncle, a shoemaker, who "provides for his needs."[87] Similar arrangements in the Lyon area had earlier led to the expulsion of the unremunerated workers. Here, while department officials felt compelled to assent to the new quotas, they also proved quite willing to work around them.

Although a number of Marseille's migrants probably benefited from such bureaucratic compartmentalization, we should assume that many more did not. Police attitudes toward migrants in this period are difficult to judge with precision because 9,801 expulsion files initiated between late 1933 and early 1938 are missing from the departmental archives.[88] While reports in each of these files presumably weighed whether to expel a foreigner who lived in or passed through Marseille, we shall probably never know how many of them led to actual expulsion orders, let alone how many of those were enforced or amnestied. If the missing expulsion files were evenly distributed over five years, they would represent an increase of 479 expulsion files per year when compared to the 1919–32 period.[89] It is more likely that the new expulsion files were not evenly distributed and spiked in the first year after the assassination. Indeed, evidence culled from already pending expulsion files suggests that in the wake of the Marseille murders, migrants, the police, and Bouches-du-Rhône prefectural officials all had difficulty negotiating power relations within the hierarchical structure of the French administration. Having lost credibility on account of the assassination, local authorities often proved wary of appearing too indulgent of foreigners.

It was no wonder. When Marseille police admitted in December 1934 that they had based the decision to grant Ilario D. a *sursis* on his neighbors' insistence that he "worked on the docks," only to find out that he had been in prison for defying an expulsion order at the very time that they had taken the neighbor's testimony, the interior minister was infuriated, both by the incompetence of the Marseille police and by their proposal to grant him the *sursis* upon his release from prison.[90] Ordering them to put the expulsion order back into effect, the general director of the Sûreté Nationale then fumed, "I am astonished that your administration lost sight of the repercussions" of Ilario's arrest and that "it summoned him to the prefecture, when it should have known that he was serving time for his first offense."[91]

The press had blamed the assassination largely on a lack of communication between the Sûreté Nationale and Marseille's *police d'état*. In the immediate aftermath of the assassination, however, it became clear that there were also differences of approach within the Marseille police force. Sarraut's replacement at the Interior, Paul Marchandeau, had quickly promised that political agitation by foreigners would be censured.[92] How to go about ensuring this repression was less obvious. Disputes over the question exposed the persistence of deep divisions within the prefecture.

When an Italian Socialist and known antifascist was reported to have stated publicly that the deaths of Barthou and the Yugoslav king were no loss for the proletariat, one local official argued that this former member of the Italian parliament ought to be expelled since he "seems singularly ignorant of the obligations incumbent upon him to respect the rules of French hospitality."[93] But the commissioner of special police, Jean Baptistin Dhubert, offered a different analysis. Probably remembering that on 12 February 1934, Marseille's strikes and demonstrations in opposition to the leagues had been the largest of any city in France outside Paris, Dhubert likely was concerned about exacerbating existing animosity between the Left and the Right.[94] Expulsion was ill-advised, he thought, since it would only grant the foreigner in question "an importance that he surely does not merit," from which he might not hesitate to garner a "moral advantage" in his political battles, making him more dangerous.[95] The rights of migrants seemed to depend on who won such arguments.

Advocates of erring on the side of repression often won, at least for a time. Rationally wishing to avoid the wrath of the Interior Ministry, Bouches-du-Rhône officials trod cautiously for a year or so after the assassination. When Fernand Maille of the department's General Council tried to intervene in favor of an Italian antifascist in the spring of 1935, Marseille's general secretary for police, François Jacquemart, sounded resigned and impotent. Maille pointed out that, as an antifascist, Mario D. would "obviously be relegated to an island if his expulsion is enforced." To this, Jacquemart responded, "All the requests he has presented so far have been rejected, and I cannot, given this situation, offer a positive response to the request that you have brought to my attention."[96] Jacquemart did not want to send this request on to the Interior Ministry; it simply was not worth it. Asked again, he replied in the same vein: "Impossible to reconsider decisions to reject."[97]

It was not until the head of the expulsions section at the Sûreté wrote to the prefect in August, noting that an appeal for clemency had been forwarded to him by the president of the republic, that Jacquemart reconsidered his decision to reject. The timing was significant. Marseille's chief of police still emphasized on 21 August that Mario had been sentenced to two months' prison for falsification of his identity card; authorities had given Mario 15 days after his release from prison to leave the country. A day after Labor Minister L.-O. Frossard reminded prefects that "anti-French" politics could not be held against Italian nationals, Jacquemart summoned Mario.[98] The ensuing letter to the Interior Ministry struck a new tone. Jacquemart started by noting that there was "no bad information" about Mario. Then Jacquemart described Mario's family, noting that he lived *"maritalement"* with the mother of his child, whom he had recognized.

He has always worked as a bakery employee in order to support his family. What is more, if he is authorized to live in France, he will acquire a bakery business and will work for himself. As far as I am concerned, I see no drawback to granting him a three-month trial *sursis,* under the reserve nevertheless that he not work as a salaried laborer in our territory.[99]

The irony, of course, was that the 9 September 1935 circular had resulted in part from pressure by the Italian government. Here, Jacquemart seemed to take advantage of its provisions to help one of Mussolini's detractors. Was this an indication that, three weeks shy of a year since the assassination, Bouches-du-Rhône authorities had regained their confidence and independence? Not entirely.

Perhaps rumors of the new provisions protecting certain classes of foreigners led Francine G., a French-born woman married to an Italian national living in Marseille, to admit in September 1935, for the first time in several years, that her expelled husband had never left France. Or perhaps she was simply at her wit's end. Francine had been sustaining an elaborate ruse ever since her husband Maurizio's expulsion had first been enforced in 1929.[100] She had first tried to invoke her French origins in her negotiations with authorities, arguing in 1929 that "when I married him, I kept my French nationality and the child is also French." When that failed, she began insisting that Maurizio was living in Italy. Local authorities had long suspected that Maurizio was merely in hiding, a suspicion lent credence by the fact that Francine gave birth to three additional children during his alleged absence. Perhaps because Marseille police had never been in favor of expelling Maurizio in the first place, they did not actively search for him, but neither did they recommend responding favorably to Francine's many pleas for *sursis* on his behalf.[101] By September 1935, Francine and Maurizio had had their fourth child. After carefully crafted attempts to "prove" Maurizio had left, which included showing police letters postmarked from Sardinia, Francine now admitted that her husband "had not left France and is currently on a farm in the Marseille area waiting for a decision in his favor."[102]

Still, the prefecture proceeded cautiously. What consternation Francine and Maurizio must have felt when, after six years of leading their family life in secret, having the courage to finally come clean still got them nowhere. With the knowledge that Maurizio had never left France, Marseille authorities apprehended him, and he was sentenced to a month in prison for evading expulsion. Even though Bouches-du-Rhône officials had more or less played along with Francine's ruse for some time, they had clearly become wary of appearing too lenient in regulating immigration, perhaps because the 6 February 1935 decrees had emerged directly from controversies surrounding how they handled the policing of foreigners. The police chief even acknowledged that Francine and Maurizio's "family situation is of great interest," but he still felt compelled to reject their request.[103] Foreign men married to Frenchwomen had new rights, but these were not systematically extended to expellees.

As in the cases of Mario D. and Delphine E., it took Francine's appeal to higher authorities in the Interior Ministry for Maurizio's status to be legalized.[104] The legalization of Maurizio's status made a world of difference. Not only did it allow him to cease hiding on a farm in outer Marseille, but it also enabled him to begin working legally in October 1936 at the Société Française des Glycérines, a Marseille vegetable oil plant. His regular work and good behavior, not to mention his French wife and growing family of French children, earned him renewed *sursis* until his expulsion finally was repealed in 1943. As of 1956, he and his wife had seven French children, and he was still (or again) employed by the Société Française des Glycérines. Receiving the official right to reside in France not only returned the civil liberties Maurizio had sacrificed while in hiding for seven years; it also helped to ensure his family what T. H. Marshall might have called a "modicum of economic welfare" by granting him access to a more stable form of income.[105]

Maurizio first came to France in search of work as a single man at the age of 18. It was 1920, and a treaty concluded the previous year, though still unratified, had aimed to encourage young and mobile Italian men like him to work temporarily in France. Sixteen years later, after seven years of evading an expulsion order, Maurizio claimed the right to work in France on the basis of the family ties he had made there. These claims became widespread. When the dockers' union protested *refoulements* and expulsions of its members following labor unrest in March 1936, it did not oppose the principle behind the measures so much as their application to "foreigners who are married to Frenchwomen or who are fathers of French children."[106] As Maurizio, the dockers' union, and others made these claims, France closed its doors to new labor migrants and issued regulations aiming to exclude foreigners who were single, had no family ties, or had arrived in the country only recently—in other words, the very sort of people its postwar migration policy had initially aimed to attract.

The changing bases of rights must have been profoundly confusing to migrants living in Marseille. Witness Francine's multiple strategies for protecting her husband from enforcement of his expulsion; she had tried invoking her French nationality, dissimulating, lying, and then finally returned to invoking her French nationality and her husband's ties through family to France. Her actions exhibited fear but also defiance. As her family grew, Francine G. became bolder, and Maurizio G. earned his first *sursis* and came out from his hiding place in the Marseille periphery just weeks before Léon Blum formed his first government on behalf of the Popular Front coalition. All over France, workers—many of whom had never dared before to join a labor union—emerged as if themselves from hiding to publicly claim new rights. In so doing, they helped usher in a new era of French labor relations. As to migrant rights, the impact made by this new mass movement was more ephemeral.

SPRINGTIME OF THE MIGRANTS?

It was a festival, some said; an explosion, said others. Following elections in April and May 1936, the Center-Left Popular Front government assumed power in June.[107] Even before the new government took over, the largest strike movement in the Third Republic's history was launched, seemingly spontaneously. En masse, workers made public their grievances. They took over the factories from the bosses and occupied them; they sang and danced. There was joy, but also fear—trepidation of the police who might have come to end the workers' sit-in strikes but never did.[108] Workers, even foreign ones, sensed a new power. Was this the dawn of a new day for workers' rights? For migrant rights?

On the first question, there is little debate, even if some of the gains were short-lived.[109] The strikes pushed Léon Blum's new government to accelerate reforms. The Matignon Accords raised wages, introduced compulsory arbitration, and included provisions for an outline law (*loi cadre*) to be voted by parliament in order to shorten the workweek to 40 hours and create mandatory paid annual vacations. Although the workweek was lengthened again in 1938, the other Matignon mandates have had a lasting impact on workers' rights, not to mention French popular culture. Forever memorialized in photos and film, the strikes of June 1936 became a *lieu de mémoire,* even if they are not included in Pierre Nora's collection of the same name.[110]

On the second question, the jury is still out. Few have doubted that the victory of the Popular Front helped usher in a better climate for migrant rights. As to how much better, there is considerable disagreement. For Jean-Charles Bonnet, one "looks in vain for a major text concerning immigration" in the first Popular Front government's "active" period from June to September 1936.[111] Granted, Blum's government created a new protected status for "refugees arriving from Germany," a development that is explored more thoroughly in the next chapter. However, not all migrants were refugees, and one could regard policies aimed specifically at them as additional stopgap measures substituting for overall reform. To be sure, the Popular Front discontinued the unpopular provision of the Flandin decrees that had limited foreign identification cards to a single department; in addition, Marius Moutet's *statut des immigrés* was reintroduced as a bill. Yet the *statut* was never brought to debate and never passed.[112] Considering how much the left wing of the Popular Front's partisans had criticized the Flandin and Laval governments for their treatment of foreigners, one might have expected more sweeping reforms.

The broader reforms proposed by Moutet's *statut des immigrés*—to equalize the rights of French and foreign nationals—went nowhere under the Popular Front. In December 1934, just a few weeks after Flandin had made labor protection the first item on his agenda, the Socialist Moutet proposed a comprehensive law that would address all aspects of foreigners' rights in France. Tellingly, it was not Blum's Socialists but rather the Communists who resurrected the bill and proposed it to the chamber on 31 July 1936, sponsored by the Villeurbanne deputy Georges Lévy and cosponsored by Maurice Thorez and Jean Cristofol, the newly elected Communist deputy from Marseille.[113] The proposed reform sought to redress what its drafters regarded as utter arbitrariness in the treatment of migrants. "For a year," they declared in their opening statement,

merciless rejections of identity cards of men who have, after all, contributed to the enhancement of France's riches, have greatly increased the general malaise. Here, a father of children born in France is refused renewal of his card on the pretext that he has not been in the country long enough; there, it's a young man or woman aged fifteen whose residency is rejected while that of the head of their household is approved. Elsewhere, political refugees and the stateless are the object of truly inhumane measures, even though it is impossible for them to leave France, since every border is closed to them.[114]

The proposal aimed to replace such arbitrary treatment with a comprehensive bill of rights for foreigners. It addressed foreigners' rights as workers, as well as their social, civil, and political rights. Employers would be allowed to hire foreigners only if they met conditions stipulated by the CGT (now reunited with the CGTU), including salary provisions; the quota laws would be abrogated. Identity cards would be valid for five years, and after three years, foreigners with clean police records would be naturalized upon filing a simple request. Foreign workers would have the right to change their professions and move between economic sectors at will; their contracts would last a minimum of a year; their right to participate in labor organizations or in any other form of political or cultural group would be protected; and they would be allowed to vote in labor arbitration board elections. No reciprocity-treaty requirement could be placed on the provision of unemployment assistance, and unemployment indemnities provided to foreigners could not be reduced in value. Foreigners leaving France before benefiting from mandatory pensions would be reimbursed their contributions to the pension system. Expulsion from France could occur for only two reasons: endangering state security or committing a serious infraction of common law. In the former case, the expulsion could be ordered by the Interior Ministry. In all other cases, the bill proposed that expulsions be subject to the judicial, rather than administrative, process. This would allow the foreigners to defend themselves before a court. An expelled foreigner would have a month to settle his or her affairs before leaving the country, by whatever border crossing he or she chose. The bill also proposed a broad definition of what constituted a political refugee.[115]

In many ways the bill recalled the idealism of plans made for the post–World War I era in its insistence on formal equality and the central place it accorded organized labor. In other respects, it testified to the disappointments that had been registered since then. It addressed not just employment but also unemployment—and at length. Even as it called for formal equality among workers it also insisted that naturalization would occur, quasi automatically, after three years, thus raising the question: Why would this be necessary or desirable in a world where formal rights were the same, regardless of nationality? And whereas the treaties that emerged from negotiations after the war made oblique references to "common agreements" regarding the "appropriate measures" to take in the event of labor market fluctuations,[116] the *statut* discussed punitive expulsions at length, placing limits on their use. It thus attested to how widespread such expulsions had become.

Despite its built-in cynicism, the *statut* would have been revolutionary had it passed. It did not. In fact, the bill's sponsor and committee *rapporteur,* Lévy, never brought the bill to the floor for debate. Rahma Harouni speculates that Lévy did not dare; he knew that the Communist Party's constituency was not opposed to protecting French labor first.[117] Another of the bill's sponsors, Arthur Ramette, also toned down his internationalist rhetoric. While opposing Flandin's government, Ramette had made forceful arguments before the chamber regarding the imperative of equalizing the rights of French and foreign workers. In November 1936, reporting for the Finance Commission on the Labor Ministry's budget, Ramette still condemned the "threat of expulsion suspended above the heads" of foreign workers and the "odious . . . xenophobic campaigns" undertaken against them, but he also acknowledged that "we do not deny the necessity of protecting French workers from the competition of foreign workers."[118]

Nor did Blum take up any of the *statut*'s principles in decree form. Perhaps this should hardly be surprising. Blum, whose coalition had won on a platform of defending democracy, bristled at the idea of using his powers as premier to legislate by fiat. Moreover, Blum was acutely aware that his party had not won the May elections; the coalition had. "We are socialists," he declared on 6 June,

but the country has not given a majority to the Socialist Party. It has not even given a majority to the parties of the proletariat. It has given the majority to the Popular Front. . . . Our objective is not to transform the social system, it is not even to apply the specific program of the Socialist Party, it is to execute the program of the Popular Front.[119]

The special recognition of refugees fit within that program, for the Popular Front was an antifascist coalition, and the refugees it sought to protect were fleeing fascism. An overhaul of migrant rights did not. Electoral politics do not necessarily endorse, and indeed frequently oppose, liberal policies toward migrants.[120] It was in the name of democratic accountability, of all things, that Blum honored the Flandin and Laval decrees.

The Popular Front government did make some changes that applied to migrants other than refugees. A new decree, issued in October 1936, discontinued the departmental limits placed on identification cards because it deemed them ineffective and cumbersome.[121] At the same time that it abolished this hated clause of the February 1935 decrees, Blum's government also slightly modified a different clause. Lodgers and hoteliers still had to report, within 24 hours, the arrival of a new foreign tenant. But now this provision no longer applied to landlords renting unfurnished residences; instead, it applied exclusively to transients who rented furnished rooms.[122] Still, a greater effort was made, as Charles Magny—now director of the Sûreté Nationale—instructed prefects to "soften the rules heretofore employed."[123] Similarly, Blum's labor minister told the chamber that "even if the policies applied since June 1936 are not fundamentally different from those which preceded, they have taken on a humane tone that had been a bit forgotten."[124] Since, as we have seen, policy depended on implementation, the importance of this change in tone cannot be underestimated.

With the extraordinary pressures the Popular Front government faced, its commitment to softening the impact of the hard-line policies of earlier administrations was increasingly tested. After the suicide of Interior Minister Roger Salengro in November 1936, and especially following Blum's own resignation in June 1937, the coalition, and migration policy along with it, lost some of its direction. For Blum, the death of his confidant

Salengro could not have come at a worse time. Not only was conflict esca-
lating in bordering Spain, but also Hitler was beginning to undermine the
Versailles treaty by remilitarizing the Rhineland. In October, the Rome-
Berlin Axis agreement was concluded. Then, days after Salengro's death,
Hitler held talks with the Japanese that formed the basis of the Anti-
Comintern Pact.[125] Faced with the reascension of their traditional enemy
and the defection of their Great War ally, the French, not surprisingly, began to feel encroached upon from all sides. The renewed possibility of
conflict with Germany, in turn, only added fuel to the fire of mounting domestic crises. As Germany founded the Anti-Comintern Pact, the Popular
Front government continued to depend on the support of the French Communist Party to keep its coalition alive. This situation increased the ire of
the extreme Right, who rallied around the slogan "Better Hitler than
Blum."[126] The sense of crisis was only furthered by the continued "invasion" of France by migrants from Central Europe. The royalist newspaper
Action Française echoed the opinion of much of the Right when it asked,
"How many of these allegedly persecuted individuals and refugees are in
reality spies working on behalf of Germany?"[127]

The intensification of conflict in Spain and the successes of Franco's
Nationalists on the frontier of France during the summer of 1937 made
matters no easier. Blum, to the consternation of the Communists and some
in his own cabinet, carefully steered clear of materially supporting Spain's
republicans. That did not stop Spanish republicans from flowing into
France with the victory of the Frente Popular's sister movement.[128] What
an inopportune moment for France to host the world's fair, which it had
been planning for years and which would attract tens of thousands of vis-
itors![129] In July, with the world's fair likely in mind, the director of the
Sûreté issued a confidential circular reminding prefects of the threat
posed by a "massive immigration" of "undesirables" who might try to
enter as tourists. Local authorities should thus "mercilessly *refouler* any
foreigner who tries to enter without a passport or other traveling papers."
Marx Dormoy, Salengro's replacement at the Interior Ministry, showed
how effective protectionist lobbying by merchants and artisans was when
he declared that these new arrivals were "in no way refugees, but individuals without work or resources," who would look for whatever work they
could find. The migrants "increasingly flood [*submerger*] our commercial
and artisanal professions, thus heavily burdening our general economy."
For this reason, Dormoy asked officials to increase their vigilance in controls at the border. Local authorities should *refouler* "all foreigners remaining illegally in France," although this did not apply, he hastened to
add, to "true political refugees," whose traditional right to asylum was
not in question.[130]

Within a couple of months, however, Dormoy's director of intelligence at the Sûreté, prompted by complaints from the Belgian government regarding the treatment of its nationals, called for a "most benevolent spirit" to be brought to bear on their cases. He also used the occasion to remind prefects of a more general policy whereby an order of *refoulement* could not rely merely on a foreigner's unemployed status or the rejection of his or her work contract. Reiterating portions of Charles Magny's April 1936 circular word for word, the director of intelligence insisted that immigrants with property or family in France should receive special treatment.[131] A week later, Camille Chautemps, who had taken over as premier in June, again differentiated such resident immigrants from "undesirables," and publicly warned foreigners to stay out of French domestic politics or suffer severe repression.[132] The Chautemps and Blum governments did make some effort to change policy, not just the tone for its implementation. A subsecretariat of state for immigration, under the leadership of Philippe Serre, was created in early 1938, and Serre's plans included, among other things, creating a *statut des immigrés*. But like many progressive projects, the Serre plan fell victim to the conflicting pressures faced by the Popular Front government and was never implemented.[133]

As so often had been the case, much came down to what local officials made of shifting government attitudes or how much attention they paid them. The fact that the Belgian government protested Dormoy's *refoulement* policy suggests that, at least in areas where Belgians made up a considerable share of the workforce, local authorities had taken seriously Dormoy's call for "merciless" rejections of residency authorizations, or perhaps had never abandoned an approach adopted under Flandin and Laval. Vicki Caron also argues that "police greeted Dormoy's crackdown with relief"; expulsions and *refoulements* reportedly rose.[134] Officials in Lyon and Marseille, meanwhile, seem to have settled into a pattern of taking family attachments and length of stay in the country into account before the Popular Front arrived in power, and there is no evidence that they diverged from this approach until after the Popular Front's collapse. For Marseille authorities, of course, there was nothing new about taking family considerations into account, though the scrutiny under which they fell after the October 1934 assassination had weakened their confidence in doing so. By contrast, while Lyon authorities had never ignored family, the formal attention they now paid to it represented a more dramatic shift in their outlook, from a guest-worker model of migration to a populationist one.

One sign of this was the prefecture's reconsideration of adjourned naturalizations. As Jean-Charles Bonnet has noted, naturalization rates did not change dramatically under the Popular Front.[135] Nonetheless, there is evidence that officials at the Justice Ministry made an effort to process languishing applications and to evaluate new ones more efficiently. Local authorities in Lyon received new inquiries from ministerial officials in 1936 and 1937 investigating applications that either had been officially postponed or had simply sat on the back burner, sometimes for years.[136] Just a few years earlier, Rhône department authorities had recommended rejecting the request of an Italian man married to a Frenchwoman because "after eight years of residency and five years of marriage to a French woman," he made the request "only out of fear that he will be laid off."[137] A new request was again postponed in August 1935 on the grounds that his only child was a girl and that his naturalization was therefore of no immediate interest.[138] It was only in 1937 that the prefect now recommended his naturalization wholeheartedly, noting that he was "head of a French family."[139] The keeper of the seals granted his naturalization in 1938. Naturalization files in Marseille, perhaps unsurprisingly, showed less of a shift in this regard, possibly because the new concerns with family resonated with attitudes that municipal officials had long espoused.

By the late 1930s, officials in both Lyon and Marseille were distinguishing between settled immigrants and migrants who were unsettling. To be sure, there was no precise definition of either, a fact that sometimes gave local authorities considerable influence in the power relations involved in negotiating rights. But as national authorities issued circular after circular curtailing the discretionary powers of local authorities, some immigrants drew strength from this changing relationship. They pointed to their employment and business interests in France, their property, their children enrolled in French schools or who would serve in French armed services, as well as other evidence of their "investment" in France, bargaining with state officials for recognition of the right to continue their participation in French society, where, they thought, they had earned a *droit de cité*. This new recognition emerged, paradoxically, from the efforts of central authorities to increase their control over the regulation of migrants.

Even as shifting power relations opened up new possibilities for some immigrants, it foreclosed possibilities for many migrants. The right to live in France became subordinated to a fairly narrow set of conditions that many migrants, especially the newly arrived or the single, could hardly hope to fill. To be sure, for many migrants, this was nothing new. Foreigners housed in Marseille's central districts, or who had no fixed residence at all, had long been excluded as unsettling, while their counterparts who owned property in the city's periphery and raised families there were seen as settled. Nothing since the Marseille assassination had changed this; if anything, the pattern became more pronounced. What was more, it was increasingly replicated the country over. Nationwide, officials saw their role as separating the "wheat from the chaff."[140] Rhetorically, the chaff were the "undesirable" or "criminal" elements in the foreign population; in practice, their crimes often amounted to little more than a lack of identity papers or an inability to prove a legal income.[141] Maurizio G., the Italian man who had evaded expulsion for seven years, would have been considered an "undesirable" migrant prior to earning his *sursis*. Afterward, he earned quasi-automatic *sursis* as a model immigrant with deep connections to France, a father of French children.[142] This development, like the bases of rights more generally, emerged as social, political, and diplomatic relations coalesced to transform a migration policy into an immigration regime.

French politics in the mid-1930s were extremely volatile. In the four years following the rightist riots of 6 February 1934, no fewer than 10 governments were formed, and these shifted from Right to Left to Center. Léon Blum formed the first government under Socialist Party leadership in French history in 1936. His experiment with governing was, by the measure of the times, relatively successful: Blum's first government was the longest since Raymond Poincaré had taken office for the fourth time in 1926.[143] But by the summer of 1937, unable to win the support of the conservative Senate, Blum turned the helm over to his electoral partners, the Radicals. By the time he resumed the role of premier for a month from March to April 1938, the coalition was not only attacked from the outside but also fracturing from within.

Such extreme political swings might have produced equally dramatic shifts in immigration policies had these depended on parliamentary debate. Instead, governments on both the Right and the Left studiously avoided bringing this issue forward for debate. To the extent that parliament discussed immigration, therefore, it was when they were supposed to be addressing other matters—such as the budget. Every effort was made by governments on both the Right and the Left to maintain tight control of migration within the ministries.

As they strove to maintain authority over migrant rights, central government policy makers discovered what local officials had long known—migrants were not chess pieces that could be manipulated at will. Yet central government officials were more intolerant of the idea that migration regulation could escape their control than they were committed to enforcing their original vision of migration restriction. Decreeing exceptions, in other words, was a way of maintaining authority. If France had become an immigrant nation, the central government wanted the criteria for inclusion in that nation to be its own, not the widely divergent and idiosyncratic choices of local officials. This is what led to circular reasoning, the practice of issuing circular after circular to fine-tune the boundaries of belonging in 1930s France.

Thanks to circular reasoning, authorities drew a new line between those admitted to work and those admitted to live. In practice, of course, the former had often become the latter. By setting new standards based on who had lived in the country five or 10 years, or who had established family connections there, policy makers designed a new immigration regime that favored groups that had been in France prior to the economic crisis and prior to Hitler's assumption of power in Germany. The Popular Front modified this, but it, too, established a threshold arrival date after which subsequent migrants, for all intents and purposes, could not become immigrants.

Meanwhile, officials all but ended the guest-worker migrant program by instructing prefectures to refrain from renewing residency papers for migrants in the country fewer than two years or, in the event that the migrant in question was indispensable for the economy, to limit his or her residency authorization to only a few months. Migrants therefore easily became illegal aliens, while immigrants—sometimes even those with illegal status, such as refractory expellees—found new legal grounds to be incorporated "automatically regardless of the labor market situation."[144]

The Flandin reforms and their progeny, then, turned France's migrant rights regime on its head. Where once all migrant rights had flowed from labor contracts, the right to residency now depended on residency, and the right to work depended on the right to reside in the country. In this upside-down guest-worker system, the possession of solely a labor contract was practically a ticket to *refoulement*.

Despite this inversion, the very claim immigrants could make to participate in the social contract had been facilitated by labor contracts. The groups that had benefited from labor treaties in the 1920s now figured among those able to claim a *droit de cité* in the mid-1930s. In both Lyon and Marseille, such treaties had, in the 1920s, allowed migrants to remain in the country despite opposition from organized labor. This had often come at a high price: In practice, migrants had a right to work as long as they did not protest their working conditions. In the early 1930s, moreover, migrants had invoked these treaties to a new purpose: in order to acquire social rights. This had been more successful in cities such as Lyon, which housed both advanced industries and advanced welfare programs. In this way, the very treaties that had been negotiated to ensure that migrants remained migrants helped some of them to become immigrants.

Those who remained without treaty protection, or who lived in cities where social rights were more difficult to acquire, faced greater vulnerability during the depression. If they succeeded in staying, they did so by shifting into new lines of economic activity, by relying on the support of extended family, or in some cases by hiding. But arrests, expulsions, and incarcerations of such individuals rose, and if they sought to normalize their status in the late 1930s, they often did so under the conditional regime of *sursis* to expulsion orders. Migrants who were not treaty-protected were not precluded from immigrant status, but they often faced greater obstacles to obtaining it, especially as policy treated nationality as a proxy for longevity in the country—as, for example, when Frossard instructed local authorities to give special treatment to Italians, Belgians, and the Swiss. Groups that had not benefited from treaties, such as Russians and Armenians, could claim immigrant status by virtue of their longevity in France—if they could prove it. Spanish nationals also fell into this group, despite the 1932 treaty between France and Spain.

What was peculiar about the development of this new immigration regime was that it did not call itself one. Rhetorically, immigrants remained the exception and migrants the rule. Even though "immigrant" status had obviously emerged from improvisation at the nexus between policy and practice, France's retention of a migration—rather than an immigration—policy cannot be regarded as purely accidental. Exceptionalism encouraged the notion that, to the extent that immigrants were accorded rights in the mid-1930s, these were really privileges. Like Old Regime privileges, they depended on the beneficence of the regime and, like them, they could be taken away.

To be sure, privileges often performed as rights, particularly once groups learned to invoke them. Still, these were different from rights that in the 1920s were based on principles of entitlement rather than recognition. The flip side of privilege was often arbitrary punishment. Recognition, or its removal, could mean the shift from one status to another within a matter of days. Since no one understood the fragility of such "privileges" better than refugees, it is to their story that we now turn.

Refuge or Refusal?

The Vicissitudes of Refugee Rights
between the Wars

Once they had left their homeland they remained homeless; once they had left their state they became stateless; once they had been deprived of their human rights they were rightless, the scum of the earth.[1]

More than many migrants, refugees understood the importance of official recognition, because it so frequently eluded them. The First World War and its resolution had triggered the twentieth century's first refugee crisis, but this hardly had led to consensus about what constituted refugee rights. Since 1951, international law has defined refugees as persons fleeing their country of citizenship due to a "well-founded fear" of persecution.[2] No such international norms existed in the period between the two world wars. Nationality had only recently become crucial to rights, making displacement from one's homeland newly problematic. What was more, national belonging hinged on international recognition. It was this that led Hannah Arendt to conclude that the plight of refugees was "not that they are not equal before the law but that no law exists for them."[3]

Arendt's reflections on the refugee condition between the wars are unmatched in their power, but they do not tell the full story. If statelessness marked refugees, this lack of legal recognition meant different things in different places and times. "Refuge" depended not only on one's legal status but also on whether or where one worked, the conditions in which one lived, the tenor of national or local politics, and the state of international affairs. As the relative weight of each of these factors shifted over time, so did the boundary line between refuge and refusal. While the refugee condition was unique in many ways, refugees' experiences also exemplified the degree to which rights in interwar France depended simultaneously on objective juridical criteria and on subjective factors that facilitated or blocked their implementation.

Migrant rights had diverged from their roots in postwar idealism as a guest-worker program was founded in the 1920s, and they shifted again in response to economic and political crises in the 1930s. This chapter traces those transformations from the perspective of refugees, whose arrival following the war challenged the guest-worker program from its inception, and whose continued influx in the 1930s tested practices aimed at discouraging the entry of new migrants.

In imagining migrants as temporary workers, French authorities had failed to anticipate the arrival and continued residency of individuals whose social profiles did not fit France's formulaic guest-worker program. Thus, while refugees did not come to France only to work, their ability to fit guest-worker expectations in the 1920s became crucial to their rights during this period. Russians, who were often young, unattached men, faced little opposition to their settlement in France prior to their conspicuous unemployment triggered by the onset of the depression. By contrast, Armenians, who frequently arrived burdened by minor, elderly, or infirm relatives, faced considerable hostility even during the expanding labor market of the 1920s. When the economic crisis changed their fortunes, Russians learned what Armenians already knew: Statelessness could become a liability. As the depression encouraged migrants to expand their claims from labor contracts to the social contract, Russians and Armenians alike increasingly found themselves excluded from both. This was the grim situation that prevailed when a new group of refugees—Jews from Germany—arrived during the depths of the depression.

Jews began to flee Germany fewer than six months after new legislation had been passed to limit French employers' reliance on foreign labor. Arriving in a political climate already prone to protectionism, they became easy targets of anti-Semitic propaganda that in turn encouraged the extension of protectionist measures from salaried labor to independent trades and professions. Jews' encounters with authorities in the 1930s thus accompanied and contributed to a major transformation in migrant rights. Whereas in the 1920s, refugees encountered difficulties if they were unable or unwilling to work, in the 1930s, the residency rights of new refugees were frequently predicated on their ability to prove that they did not need to work, would not compete with French businesses or professions, and would not become public charges.

As new bases for rights were invented in the mid-1930s, their impact on refugees was uneven. Refugees' lack of nation-state protection continued to severely limit their access to social rights and expose them to police repression. For some refugees, however, these risks now were mitigated partially by the families they had formed in France and the roots that they had set down. In the course of a decade and a half, what once was a liability for Armenians—large families and a relative lack of mobility—became an asset. During the same time, many Russians saw their fortunes reversed: While Boris M. seemed like the quintessential guest worker when he arrived in 1923, a decade later he was destitute. At the same time, as authorities increasingly discriminated between migrants and immigrants, new refugees found few bases for claiming rights as the latter, more privileged, group. Only the political will of the Popular Front coalition succeeded in breaking the vicious cycle of refugees' social and legal exclusion. Even then, its success in doing so was ephemeral.

THE IMPACT OF THE POSTWAR SETTLEMENT

The First World War had ushered in a new era of state involvement in labor recruitment and immigrant regulation in France. Already before the war was over, labor leaders planned for a postwar society where "workers of the world" would have the same rights, regardless of nationality. Organized labor's plans for internationalism based on universal rights gave way after the war to government-brokered bilateralism based on reciprocity. By definition, stateless and denationalized persons could not make claims on the French state on the basis of reciprocity. This was not the only manner in which their arrival perturbed the French guest-worker system. Refugees often possessed precisely the opposite qualities of what French policy makers were looking for in migrants. Authorities wanted single, mobile, young men who were eager to follow the labor market and who would subsequently return home. With refugees, they got families— or the remnants of them—who wished to rebuild their lives as much as they wanted to find work, and who, often much to their own regret, could not be sure that their relocation would be temporary.

The arrival of thousands of refugees in France also provided early evidence of the limits of the postwar settlement. In crafting postwar migration policy, French authorities drew on France's experience of recruiting workers for the war effort. Yet the war had displaced several million people for reasons having nothing to do with employment and left an unprecedented number of refugees in its wake. No one had planned for this.

Although the refugee problem initially was triggered by displacements occurring in the course of war, it was the international system emerging from the war's ashes that assured its place as an ongoing problem. The year 1922 proved to be a watershed. Bolshevik decrees stripped exiled Russians of their citizenship, and the Turks laid siege to Greek-occupied Smyrna, where many Armenians had taken refuge after the 1915 massacres. These events contributed to what Michael Miller aptly calls refugees' "post-war unsettlement."[4] Stripped of the protection of their home state, Russians would be able to return only in the event of a regime change, which many anticipated, in exile, for the remainder of their lives.[5] For Armenians, meanwhile, the Lausanne settlement, which ended the Greco-Turkish conflict, also foreclosed the possibility of an independent Armenia. In the face of this dizzying situation triggered by the war and exacerbated by the terms of the peace, France welcomed at least 135,000 Russian and Armenian refugees in the 1920s and early 1930s, more than any other Western European nation.[6] These influxes were only the beginning of an ongoing refugee crisis. Almost as soon as Hitler was named German chancellor in January 1933, the flow of refugees began again. In 1935, the results of the Saar plebiscite sent pro-French Saarlanders over the border. Refugee influxes from the German Reich peaked in 1938 after the Anschluss and Kristallnacht.

The refugee situation in France, as elsewhere, was complicated by the fact that the international system following the First World War differed greatly from the one that had preceded it. As empires dissolved into nation-states, and individuals whose nationalities "belonged" to new states were reshuffled, those whose nationalities were not politically recognized became either ethnic minorities or stateless. As the peace settlement gave formal recognition to the principle of national citizenship, passports emerged as necessary international travel documents, as well as a means by which to "verify" a person's national identity, now a matter of considerable importance. In a world where the new political logic obliged nation-states to defend the interests of their citizens living abroad but where the notion of political asylum was not yet entrenched, not belonging to a nation-state could be a considerable disadvantage.

Recognizing the importance that national protection had come to play in the postwar world, the League of Nations appointed Fridtjof Nansen High Commissioner on Behalf of the League in Connection with the Problem of Russian Refugees in Europe in 1921. In 1924, Nansen's purview was extended to Armenians, and in 1928 to "similars," meaning other Christian minorities of southern Kurdistan, who also had been displaced by the Turks.[7] The peculiar combination of post-Versailles international power politics and domestic political and economic concerns meant that France recognized only two other groups as legal refugees prior to the Second World War. Saarlanders who fled Germany after the plebiscite gained recognition as refugees in 1935, and immigrants fleeing Nazism could claim status as "refugees coming from Germany" from September 1936. This latter distinction came thanks only to the resolve of the Popular Front government and applied only to those who had immigrated between certain dates.[8] Italian antifascists never acquired the juridical status of refugee, and Spanish republicans did not until after the Second World War.

Not only was the recognition of refugee status highly politicized at the national and international levels, but it also frequently failed to confer rights on the local level. Nansen passports provided identity papers, but often little more. Although a 1928 League of Nations arrangement recommended relaxing expulsion orders against Nansen refugees in certain circumstances, records in Marseille and Lyon indicate that authorities readily expelled refugees and were quite willing to incarcerate refractory expellees, regardless of refugee status. Moreover, for most of the 1920s and 1930s, Nansen passports rarely entitled migrants to any social rights. Refugees did not belong to the class of most-favored foreigners whose access to work contracts, residency authorizations, and unemployment compensation—among other rights—was facilitated by bilateral agreement. When local budgets faced shortfalls, most-favored foreigners continued to enjoy welfare rights; refugees often did not. This, too, changed under the Popular Front, which softened its repression of illegal migrants and finally ratified the 1933 Geneva Convention, forbidding the *refoulement* of Nansen refugees and requiring that they be treated as most-favored foreigners.

THE FIRST REFUGEES, OR THE ECONOMICS
OF HOSPITALITY

During the years of economic expansion after the war, France welcomed refugees who were able to work, albeit with some reservations. A cynical observer might have noted that the French government provided asylum less in observance of French humanitarian traditions than in the hope that refugees might satisfy a more instrumental need for labor. A more charitable observer might have argued that the French labor shortage simply made it easier for the French to honor their traditions of hospitality. Either way, refugee rights often turned on employment.

Coming from the east, most of the early refugees, Armenians and Russians alike, disembarked in the same place: Marseille. From there, their paths diverged. Although both groups were housed in barracks loaned by the military—Armenians in "Camp Oddo" and Russians in "Camp Victor Hugo"—these "temporary" lodgings developed into distinct loci of

Armenian and Russian subculture. The similar housing agreements negotiated for each refugee group masked considerable differences between
them, distinctions that only the leveling power of the depression would
partially erase. Camp Oddo was placed under the direction of Tigran
Mirzayantz, a representative of the Armenian Republic at the Paris Peace
Conference. Mirzayantz was later replaced by Takvor Hatchikian, a naturalized French Armenian and former member of the French Foreign Legion who had been injured during the war. The administrative costs were
covered by the Armenian Aid Committee. Camp Victor Hugo was placed
under the direction of the Russian Serge de Becque, a former colonel
in Wrangel's "White" Army. It was administered under the auspices of
the Red Cross. An additional camp, "Mirabeau," which was comprised
mostly of tents, housed Armenians who supported themselves or received
allocations from the Union Arménienne.[9]

Intended as a temporary relocation center that would house refugees
until they found jobs in the interior of France, each camp soon took on its
own character. The Russian camp housed mostly soldiers and members of
the merchant marine, and it was run by a former colonel who had retained a military man's view of social order. Colonel de Becque was known
to run a tight operation in his camp. This had so impressed the special police commissioner Antoine Borelli that de Becque joined Borelli's personnel
when they boarded incoming ships, in order to screen Russians arriving in
the port city. As de Becque indicated which Russians he "recognize[d] as
suspicious," Borelli in turn refused entry to men so identified, especially if
they were "dangerous from the point of view of Bolshevik propaganda."
For Borelli, it was a way to supplement his personnel, "much reduced . . .
[and] preoccupied with controlling passports." For de Becque, it was a
way of screening who lived in his camp.[10]

Camp Victor Hugo itself was run by de Becque with similar circumspection. Divided into sectors, the camp was policed by a commander in
chief and three subcommanders who reported to de Becque.[11] Perhaps because of the extraordinary discipline subjected upon its inhabitants, the
camp largely met French expectations: Few of its residents, mostly young
men, stayed long; as soon as they found jobs, they left the camp, probably
with few regrets. Mostly born around the turn of the century, these men
were, according to Marina Gorboff, "ready to confront a new life [and]
accept all kinds of work" and became popular recruits for French industrialists who were "in search of an anticommunist and inexpensive" labor
pool.[12] Many were employed in the steel industry in northeastern France,
others in the automobile industry. The British refugee advocate Sir John
Hope Simpson reported that Russians comprised a third of the workforce
at Renault's Billancourt plant in 1930, an astonishing figure when one

considers that Russians made up no more than 2% of the foreign population and less than 1% of the total population in France.[13] Gorboff's assertion that certain shop floors of the Renault and Citroën auto plants were "sometimes entirely comprised of Russians" is probably an exaggeration, but it gives one an idea of the magnitude of their employment in this industry.[14] Others turned to service trades: As many as 8% of all Russian refugees were employed as taxi drivers or private chauffeurs, a profession that drew "soldiers, aristocrats and Cossacks."[15] Although the jobs that they accepted sometimes translated as a loss in status, Russian success in procuring employment, contracts, and identification cards was considerable. From the perspective of the French administration, they faded in with "other" European economic migrants.

From the outset, however, the situation faced by Armenian refugees was different. Unlike the mostly young male Russians, the Armenians included large numbers of women, elderly, invalids, and children, many of whom arrived on the verge of starvation.[16] Although many Armenians did move on to jobs in the interior, as their high concentration in metropolitan areas such as Lyon attests, they were often described as languid "orientals," ill suited for hard labor. In part, Armenians' reputations stemmed from the continual arrival of refugees, which gave the impression that the population was stagnating in the camps. As of December 1923, nearly six months after the Lausanne treaty and after many had already moved on to jobs elsewhere in France, Camp Oddo still exceeded its 2,000-person capacity, housing 857 men, 894 women, and 754 children under 15. The prefect, Louis Thibon, estimated that about 500 of the men were working and supporting families in Camp Oddo, while only seven or eight men from Camp Mirabeau went out each morning to look for work, usually on the docks.[17] Thibon never mentioned how many camp residents were able-bodied and in a position to look for work; regardless, he began to regard them as lazy, even fatalistic. Accusing them of "willingly accepting to live without worrying about the next day," he engaged in some fatalism of his own when he wrote that "nothing allows [me] to envision any end in sight if measures are not taken."[18]

Thibon had not always been so inhospitable. When the first refugees arrived after the siege of Smyrna, he seemed to take the complexity of the refugees' situation into account, writing that he had tried to find jobs "for those among them who want them and whose state of health allows." At the same time, he asked for additional funds to keep the project going. Thibon's wife, Marie-Andrée, even presided over a patronage committee established for assisting the Smyrna refugees originating from French-mandate Syria or Lebanon.[19] His patience, however, was apparently worn thin by the "continual arrival of these orientals." Between August and

December 1923, in his estimation, another 10,885 refugees had arrived.[20] The president of the Armenian Assistance Committee, Mirzayantz, claimed that many of these Armenians found willing employers but were then thwarted by an administration that refused to issue cards to them, effectively precluding them from accepting the jobs they had found. He also reported that those who had the means not to work were similarly refused identification cards and told that they must have labor contracts in order to receive cards.[21] Thibon, on the other hand, insisted not only that most of them did not seek work, but also that they were not sought after as employees.[22]

When more than 4,700 Armenian refugees arrived in the month of October 1923 alone, Thibon faced an increasingly urgent problem. Public opinion, too, began to turn against the refugees. Exemplifying this shift, the aid committee begun by Madame Thibon now called for authorities to "CONTROL THE ADMISSION of these refugees, SUPPORT THEIR PROVISIONAL NEEDS, and finally DISTRIBUTE THEM IN THE REGIONS WHERE THEY CAN BE USED."[23] Finding resources to provide for migrants who were too old, too young, or too invalid to work—a problem that in the 1930s would hit municipalities more generally—already preoccupied Bouches-du-Rhône authorities as early as 1923. In this experience could be glimpsed the seeds of later discussions about "dependent" immigrants.

Louis Thibon suggested on several occasions that the French authorities halt Armenian immigration to Marseille altogether. His superiors listened, having realized that Armenian migrants, contrary to authorities' initial assumptions, would stay permanently. After the Treaty of Lausanne foreclosed the prospect of an independent Armenia, repatriation no longer presented a viable possibility. Officials thus concluded that the only way to prevent unemployed and presumably idle Armenians from staying in France was to stop them from immigrating in the first place. Although the cities of Constantinople, Salonika, and Athens arguably faced an even greater refugee crisis than Marseille, Raymond Poincaré, the "*bloc national*" prime minister and minister of foreign affairs, ordered the French consulates in those cities to refuse all visas to Armenians.[24]

It is said that Poincaré "knew everything and understood nothing."[25] Certainly he had seriously underestimated the desperation and resolve of the Armenians. Not long after Poincaré's categorical denial of visas, Armenians found another way to enter the country. By procuring tickets to Spain and Italy on French vessels that docked in Marseille en route, they obtained French "transit" visas; instead of transiting, however, they stayed. Faced with the prefect's complaint of this "subterfuge," Poincaré telegraphed the consulates, instructing them to refuse transit visas to all Armenians whose final destination was Spain or Italy.[26] In the meantime, the prefect's cabinet director, on Thibon's behalf, ordered the special police commissioner, Borelli, to bar Armenians with transit visas from disembarking and instructed the head of the Foreigners' Service to "take the necessary measures so that they do not receive residency papers."[27]

Acknowledging the inefficacy of *refoulement,* "since the administration had no credits for evacuating [refugees] to the frontier or port of embarkation," the head of the Marseille Foreigners' Service instead advocated refusing identification papers, without which employers "cannot furnish work without exposing themselves to [legal] pursuits." Never mind that Marseille employers often flaunted these regulations. He still called for "exercising constant surveillance over this category of foreigners," who were, he claimed, "not at all without resources and who compete with our nationals in commerce and industry. Knowing they are being watched and followed," he continued, "it is not unlikely that they will decide to leave France."[28] This line of reasoning anticipated the protectionism experienced by many other migrants during the depression; it also treated Armenians as if they had come to France as voluntary economic migrants, and, as the historian Maud Mandel aptly points out, as if they had a national base to which they could return.[29]

From boom to bust, the economy served as the rationale for excluding Armenians. In 1925, the head of the Foreign Labor Service in Marseille, for example, presented Armenians living in Camp Oddo as deliberately inventing obstacles to accepting the work offered them; he therefore insisted that visas should require "refugees to accept work immediately upon their arrival in the territory."[30] There was such a thing as a non-worker identification card, but there was little room in the French bureaucratic imagination for a foreigner who was not also a manual worker. The very fact that Thibon's successor at the prefecture, Hilaire Delfini, referred to Armenians as having "come to the Bouches-du-Rhône in order to reinforce the labor [pool]," indicates that he saw little difference between refugees and other migrants.[31]

Perhaps, as Abdelmalek Sayad once suggested, an immigrant who did not work was a contradiction in terms.[32] In fact, however, refugees contributed to the French economy in many ways that were not officially sanctioned, a fact that displeased Delfini considerably. Having come "to reinforce the labor [pool]," he wrote, "[they] provide only relative satisfaction in this regard. Of a commercial spirit, [and] a tenacious and independent nature, these nationals quickly desert manual labor to compete with local commerce."[33] This was hardly surprising. Industrial factories had been uncommon in Armenia, whose population had engaged mostly in artisanal or agricultural occupations prior to arriving in France.[34] Many, perhaps most, Armenian refugees gave up these traditional occupations, at least initially. But their reputation as a social-climbing commercial class was nonetheless a tenacious one. As we shall see, similar objections were raised regarding the economic activity of Jewish refugees from Nazism some years later.

Ironically, after all the insistence on obliging Armenians to work, French consulates were stamping their visas in quite the opposite fashion only a few years later: "Authorized for entry into France under the condition of not accepting work."[35] Indeed, officials in the Ministry of Foreign Affairs specified in 1928 that "foreign workers can enter France to assume salaried employment only if they have a contract stamped by the Ministry of Labor or Agriculture. This regime applies to Russian and Armenian refugees as it does to other foreigners."[36] Where once officials wanted to force refugees to work, as early as 1928 they wanted to control immigration by limiting migrants' access to work permits.

In part this shift stemmed from some of the same concerns authorities had developed with regard to guest workers: keeping militancy to a minimum. Whereas the prefect reported in March 1925 that Armenians, for the most part, kept to themselves and did not engage in militant activity, two years later that was no longer true.[37] By March 1927, unemployment affected hundreds if not thousands of Armenians in Marseille and helped to politicize Armenian organizations.[38] Officials became concerned when the pro-communist HOK (Haistani Oknoutian Komité, or Armenian Aid Committee) held a meeting for unemployed Armenians at a movie theater in February 1927, at which they claimed attendance of 1,500.[39] At the meeting, which had been triggered by the nondistribution of 80,000 francs voted by the French government in 1924 in aid for Armenians, a "committee for aid to the unemployed" was established, and the organization of Armenian workers "on the basis of class concepts" was indicated as a goal.[40] Anticommunism was not the only factor motivating French officials' surveillance of this meeting; they were also concerned about avoiding clashes between pro- and anti-Soviet factions within the Armenian community. With funds from the CGTU, HOK competed with another association for the loyalties of unemployed Armenians in Marseille. The second group, led by Haik Serengulian, a baker and Unified Socialist Party (Second International) militant, had enrolled almost 600 members. Authorities' concerns were not entirely frivolous. A year earlier, clashes between Armenian nationalists and Soviet sympathizers in Lyon had resulted in an exchange of fire that had left one man dead.[41]

French reactions to HOK demonstrated the complexity of policing migrant politics. HOK was pro-Soviet, and, in line with Soviet nationalities policies of the 1920s, it favored repatriation to the Soviet Republic. French authorities would have liked to repatriate Armenians, but they hardly wished to do so in cooperation with a Soviet-sponsored organization. Accordingly, officials treated HOK much as they did the Communist Party and the CGTU—with hostility. While HOK lent ideological support to repatriation, and other organizations held out hope for eventual independence, French authorities slowly came to the conclusion that refugees probably "cannot be returned to their countries of origin."[42] This may explain why efforts turned toward discouraging immigration from Asia Minor.[43]

National labor director Charles Picquenard's move to limit new Armenian immigration was likely influenced not only by the growing reports of Armenian agitation but also by pressure from the League of Nations to recognize that "refugees cannot be repatriated to their countries of origin where the governments have declared them to have lost their rights of citizenship."[44] In November 1928 Picquenard reported that "the introduction of workers of Armenian, Lebanese, Chaldo-Assyrian, Syrian, Ottoman, Greek and Albanian nationality" was suspended because of various "drawbacks which their employment in France had created, particularly concerning their instability and the difficulties created for the eventual repatriation of undesirables." He went on to clarify that with respect to Greeks, the proscription aimed principally at "workers coming from Asia Minor" and had not been intended to apply to "European Greeks." Finally, he stipulated that, as of the date of his circular, Albanian recruitment could be resumed.[45] Armenians clearly were the principal targets of this policy. They were by far the largest group among the "nationalities" he mentioned, and of all of them, their repatriation posed the most difficulties. Moreover, Picquenard clearly lumped Armenians together with "Eastern" populations, while Albanians and "European" Greeks were perceived both as more desirable and as easier to repatriate, should the need eventually arise.

The phantasm of hordes of "Orientals" massed together in inadequate facilities turning communist no doubt also contributed to the move in 1925 to disband Camp Oddo, a year after the HOK was first established. Officials had known about overcrowding and poor housing conditions at the camp for some time; now the specter of a concentrated—and perhaps disenchanted—group of Armenians added to their worries. Worse, the inhabitants of Camp Oddo had split into rival religious factions, leading Assyro-Chaldeans to set up an independent, makeshift, and disease-ridden "Camp des Aygalades" on Oddo's edge. Thus, while fiscal concerns in 1922 had moved French officials to let both the Russian and Armenian camps be run independently, that parsimony had come with a price: Autonomous "republics" had emerged in the midst of Marseille. Meeting with Marseille officials to plan the evacuation of the camps, representatives from the Ministries of Labor, Foreign Affairs, and Interior agreed that Hatchikian had to be stripped of his "self-ordained" authority, and the camp had to be brought under state control.[46]

The sudden discovery of problems due to Camp Oddo's autonomy was not entirely genuine. Marseille and Bouches-du-Rhône authorities had been aware of the camp's organization for years. They knew that Hatchikian charged inhabitants only 50 centimes a day to cover expenses, and that he exempted large families, the invalid, and the unemployed from payment.[47] Similarly, they knew that the camp administration encouraged the maintenance of Armenian culture, since it supplemented the French instruction provided by one publicly funded French *institutrice* (at a time when children under 15 numbered a few hundred) with instruction provided by six Armenians who were paid out of the camp's operating budget.[48] It is hard to imagine, moreover, that they were unaware of the makeshift chapel in the camp, since they were known to ask the Armenian prelate Monsignor Mampre Clafayan to serve as an intermediary between the public administration and the Armenian population.[49]

Nor was the Armenian camp any more autonomous than the Russian one in this regard. Like the Armenians at Camp Oddo, the Russians in Camp Victor Hugo had established their own school and chapel, as well as a number of small businesses. In fact, once the initial wave of single men had left, the Russians had arguably gone farther than the Armenians in constructing an independent "village" in the middle of Marseille. The director succeeding Serge de Becque, his brother Vladimir, even had remodeled the French military barracks (using supplies from demolished barracks), then jacked up rent for families living there in order to cover his costs. Although the result was a better stock of housing than that provided by the "sordid" Oddo barracks, the original mission of the camp had been altered.[50] Vladimir de Becque had made it prohibitively expensive for indigent or transient persons to live in his camp; instead it became a privileged—and autonomous—"bourgeois" village complete with its own paid administration and police.[51]

In part because of the way in which Vladimir de Becque had changed the purpose of Camp Victor Hugo, it avoided some of the problems— such as overcrowding—that plagued Camp Oddo. Its inhabitants, however, were no more integrated into Marseille life than were the Oddo residents. Indeed, when the Camp Oddo commissioner Claude Montel wrote his report about the Russian camp, he recognized their "need" to remain unassimilated, for, by "living together, the refugees who in their country sometimes occupied a high social rank, can avoid to some degree the humiliating obligation of living in working-class neighborhoods, in contact with people from all nationalities, [who are] most often deprived of the most elementary education."[52] Montel's evaluation of immigrant groups in Marseille clearly collapsed the categories of class and nationality into one, as he contrasted Russians to the "working class."

If the popular journalist Ludovic Naudeau's view is any indication, Montel's class-infused vision of the differences between Armenians and Russians was far from unique. Comparing Armenians to Jews, Naudeau even invoked a supposedly Russian adage, claiming that the people of Marseille had begun to "wonder with concern how justified is the famous Muscovite saying according to which 'a Jew fools three Russians, while a Greek bamboozles three Jews, and an Armenian is more cunning than several Greeks.'" While he admired the preservation of Russian culture that he witnessed at Camp Victor Hugo, he disdained the "particularis[m]" of the "miserable" Armenians who "are obsessed with the idea of multiplying their kind" and who had transformed their barracks into a "veritable village of Asia Minor." Impressed by the children in Camp Victor Hugo, who "converse among themselves in Russian," he nonetheless accused the Armenians of "thwarting" French education laws by organizing private instruction in Armenian at Camp Oddo. Naudeau was also enchanted by the "*bakaleinaia lavka*" (grocery stand) and the "*traktir*" (tavern) he found in the more "lustrous" Camp Victor Hugo. Where the Armenians were perhaps "worthy of pity," he sympathized with the Russians, who, he wrote, had probably had servants back in Russia and had been accustomed to a refined life of frequenting salons with the "*tchinovniki.*"[53]

Perhaps because of conditions in Camp Oddo, Armenians' efforts to maintain community and to resist efforts to close the camp did not register as positively. In fact, however, many Armenians had been putting money aside regularly to buy land in the sparsely inhabited northern sectors of Marseille's fourteenth, fifteenth, and sixteenth arrondissements, where some had already begun to build small houses on the land they had purchased. Far from being the fatalists that Louis Thibon had once accused them of being, many Armenians had suffered the overcrowded conditions at Camp Oddo because they were planning for their future; living there had allowed them to save a little money and to build a new, more comfortable but still collective, life together in a new quarter of Marseille.[54]

Echoing the divisions local police regularly made between residents of the periphery and transients, Camp Commissioner Montel was willing to allow those who could prove they had purchased land to remain in the camp until they were able to move into their new homes; for the rest, he had little sympathy.[55] Faced with their refusal to move to other regions in France where work purportedly awaited them, Montel was exasperated by their "intransigent attitude," for which he blamed the lack of resolve shown by the French administration thus far. Since, he argued, the Oddo population was now convinced that the administration had no means to force their dispersal, it was crucial to prove them wrong. "The only sanction we have at our disposal in their case," Montel wrote, "is expulsion from the country. Two or three examples will be sufficient, on the condition that the measure is effective; it is indispensable that those affected are forced to leave France and that no deferments are granted."[56]

Effective expulsion of refugees from France was easier said than done, but that did not prevent local administrators from trying. While Poincaré's and Picquenard's policies to discourage Armenian emigration had been stimulated, at least in part, by their recognition that repatriation to the Soviet Union and Turkey would be nearly impossible, local officials in Marseille, as in other department seats, ignored the impracticality of expelling refugees and recommended their expulsion for myriad offenses, large and small. In this as in so many other affairs, city and prefectural officials used what powers they had to influence their superiors in the capital. Although the Bouches-du-Rhône prefect, as a border prefect, could have summarily expelled Armenians, he rarely chose to do so. Instead he referred Armenian expulsions to Paris, as if to call attention to the problems he felt Armenians perpetually posed his administration. Once an expulsion order was issued by the Ministry of the Interior, local police could and often did imprison anyone they discovered who had not complied.

Failure to obey expulsion orders was by no means limited to refugees, but they faced unique difficulties in complying. Because in the postwar world passports were a prerequisite for international travel, a foreigner living in France could not legally enter another country without a passport, and often a visa. But many refugees, precisely because they were refugees, did not have passports. Nansen passports only partially alleviated this problem. Available for Russians as early as 1922, the Nansen passport was not extended to Armenians until 1924, the year after the largest number of them had arrived in France. Obtaining a Nansen passport required being able to prove one's identity, something that was exceedingly difficult for people who had fled their homeland quickly.[57] In France, only one agency was officially allowed to certify Armenian identities, the Central Office of Armenian Refugees in Paris.[58] Moreover, although the distribution of Nansen passports was supposed to follow guidelines established by the League of Nations High Commission for Refugees, in effect each country issued the passports according to its own priorities. In the case of France, this meant that "Nansen passports are not issued to foreigners affected by an administrative measure," a euphemism for expulsion.[59] Even when issued, the Nansen passport served primarily to allow its bearer the right to reenter the country that had issued it. It did not guarantee access to jobs, social security, or the identification cards required of all foreigners living in France.

Refugees had few options when faced with expulsion orders. Those with passports could leave, provided that they could find a country that would assent to their immigration. The rest had to choose between entering another country illegally or remaining in France illegally. Decisions of this sort often led to other forms of illicit behavior, as refugees forged or bought fake identity papers, committed social crimes, or otherwise ran afoul of the law. Belnirari O.'s situation exemplified this dilemma. An Assyro-Chaldean refugee living with his elderly mother, widowed and terminally ill brother, and infant nephew in Camp Oddo, now under the control of the French administration, Belnirari allegedly resorted to dressing as a priest and soliciting alms in order to support his family. Arrested for his fraudulent behavior, he was expelled for possessing no valid identification papers. When officials notified Belnirari of the expulsion, he begged them to let him stay until his brother died so that he might take his nephew with him. Despite being warned that he would be arrested if he did not leave France immediately, Belnirari nevertheless remained in Marseille and worked as a stevedore while his brother's tuberculosis worsened. Although he was instructed to ask other countries for a passport since his native Turkey refused to issue one, this too proved impossible, given that the only identity papers in his possession were ones issued, according to his brother, by the "fake prince Cambar, . . . who was expelled from France for fraud and traffic in false passports and false certificates!"[60] As promised, he was arrested again, imprisoned this time for a month. The day after Belnirari's arrest pulled him off the docks and into prison, his brother, despite illness acknowledged as "critical" by local police, assessed the problem with considerable lucidity: "Finally, if ever the Authorities don't want to keep him in France, would someone at least issue him some sort of passport in order to go somewhere!"[61] Making "ordinary citizens who have the misfortune to be exiles into fugitives from justice,"[62] expulsions of refugees often ended tragically: "As I already said," one Armenian refugee told gendarmes visiting his residence outside Lyon in order to verify his departure, "I cannot leave French territory to go elsewhere. Sick and without money, and no longer having any country, I prefer to go to prison," which is where Ishag Y. died, three years later, at the age of 44.[63]

Cases like Belnirari O.'s were relatively isolated in the 1920s, but they became increasingly frequent as the economic situation pressured local officials to police not only the political but also the economic arena. In a complete turnaround from the assumptions that prevailed in the early

1920s, by the early 1930s officials presupposed that any Armenian who immigrated *would* work, and would therefore contribute to the clogging of an already saturated labor market. As we have seen, when Bedros T. requested to be able to bring his sister Takouhi to Lyon, the general secretary for police replied that his family did not have "the means to assure housing and a means of support for [Takouhi], *who will look for work.*"[64] Lyon officials routinely rejected requests like that made by Bedros, particularly when they were made for people still of working age. For the elderly, authorities finally recognized that they could not work, but this did not make them more inclined to approve their residency. Instead, officials reasoned that in the current economic climate there was no guarantee that their adult children would be able to sustain a job and remain able to support their kin. Avedis W., for example, a 29-year-old Armenian living in Lyon, asked local officials for permission to bring his parents, who were living at the Catholic Armenian Church in Aleppo (Syria), to join him. The chief of police in Lyon felt that his two-room apartment was large enough and the 3.3 francs an hour he earned at a synthetic fiber plant adequate for supporting his family. But the Rhône department general secretary for police concluded that "he does not appear to have the means to receive his parents."[65] In this way, the experience of Armenians living in Lyon paralleled that of many other foreign migrants, whose potential to become public charges caused new concern.

When permission was invariably denied "in view of the current economic situation," the family members very often entered France illicitly, as Avedis W.'s parents ultimately did.[66] If caught, they were generally asked to leave and then officially expelled if they did not obey. Once this happened, they joined Belnirari O. in having to make a decision about whether it was worth risking imprisonment in order to stay. Sometimes even those who had valid passports preferred remaining with family to a life of even more uncertainty elsewhere. With their homeland devastated, family became home:

My three sons and my married daughter have all been in Lyon for about 10 years [and] I have no one elsewhere, I am 66 years old. I came to France to join them to pass the last days of my life. You is not unaware of the life Armenians have had. Was enough to torture, massacre, burn by the Turkish barbarians. I endured all these events with my own eyes; I came to France to live in Peace but I don't know why I have suffered such consequences from the police [*agents de la sureté*], I have done no wrong to anybody I ask to live tranquil with my children.[67]

Pergrouhi L., unlike Ishag Y., was fortunate enough to persist until her expulsion order was repealed by the Popular Front interior minister on 31 December 1936.[68]

By the early 1930s, however, refugees from Armenia were far from alone in falling victim to what amounted to a criminalization of immigration. Russians, finding waged work easily, had earlier been spared the degree of insecurity that had initially plagued Armenians; now they suffered from this "success" since they were often among those laid off during the depression, particularly once the quota laws on foreign employment went into effect. Of the 47,721 Russians included on the 1931 French census, 3,143, or nearly 7%, of them were listed under the category "employees and workers without work." By 1936, the Russians included in this category had risen to 6,169, or almost 15% of the Russian population included in the census. Although Russians still only made up, according to the census, 6% of the foreigners without work, this represented three times their weight in the foreign population living in France.[69]

These figures probably understate the level of Russian unemployment, given that individuals—especially foreigners—are often reluctant to admit unemployment to census takers. In a study based on 34,174 unemployment compensation files from 1931, Russians represented 2% of the sample and nearly 14% of the foreigners included in it.[70] Because of their frequent ineligibility for unemployment assistance, real levels of Russian unemployment probably were considerably higher than available statistics suggest.[71] While the 1931 census indicates a total of only 392 Russian nationals in all of France who were without work in metallurgical and mechanical industries, the unemployment study—which covered only greater Paris, greater Lyon, and Mulhouse—cited 268 Russians in the same category that year.[72] Since the unemployment crisis worsened considerably for foreigners once the 1932 law placed quotas on their employment, it is reasonable to suppose that the worst period of unemployment for Russians came, as it did for other foreigners, after 1931. By that time, municipalities whose leaders sought ways to reduce welfare expenditures often eliminated foreigners without most-favored status. In this way, refugees suffered from what Michael Miller calls the "intrusiveness of international politics" during the interwar period.[73] No possibility existed for France to sign an agreement with Armenia, since there was no sovereign Armenian state. Similarly, even had the Bolsheviks not denationalized anti-Soviet refugees, a bilateral agreement with the Soviet Union to protect its nationals in France would have been implausible, since it was not in Soviet interests to encourage emigration to France, where opponents of Bolshevism were given safe harbor.

Russian unemployment, at an average of 257 days, also was longer than that of other foreign groups.[74] These were the unemployed who haunt Nina Berberova's fiction.[75] Suffering from extended unemployment and often with no family to turn to, Russians figured among the increased arrests for vagrancy during the depression years. As Armenians already had discovered in the 1920s, misdemeanors as minor as vagrancy could be used to justify expulsion orders, which in turn were impossible for denationalized persons to obey. This led to imprisonment, release, and the risk of repeated arrest and incarceration. Boris M. exemplified this problem: A single man with no fixed domicile, between 1932 and 1936 Boris was incarcerated as many as nine times for vagrancy and failing to honor his expulsion order. During the same time that Boris faced repeated incarcerations, Berj Y., an Armenian expelled for unemployment four days before Boris, was granted at least 17 *sursis*. Berj's ability to rely on the support of his sister and brother-in-law, who lived in Marseille, no doubt helps explain this discrepancy.[76] By contrast, one study estimated that fewer than a third of unemployed Russians had families to help support them. When families came to be privileged in the latter part of the 1930s, single Russian men despaired.

Although the expulsion archives that remain in Lyon and Marseille concern relatively few Russians, contemporary refugee advocates claimed that there were as many as 4,000 known expulsion orders pending throughout France for Russians as of September 1935.[77] Other contemporaries also suggested that life during the depression was difficult for many Russians living in these cities. In Marseille, for example, it was estimated that half the Russian refugees had been reduced to working as stevedores, placing them

amongst the dregs of the cosmopolitan population of Marseilles. These last have no identity cards. This is known to the police (with whom they are on good terms), who periodically make a raid and take a few off to jail where they serve a short term of imprisonment and then go back to work in the port.[78]

The fact that Russians suffered multiple arrests and incarcerations at the hands of Marseille police throws into question on just how good terms they really were with authorities.

As for Lyon, one refugee advocate, citing the Russian Emigré Committee as his source, argued that

not more than 1% of the refugees in Lyon are living what he [the committee representative] calls a normal life. Of the remainder, about 80% are just able to carry on, while the rest are living in great poverty, the lowest depths being reached by . . . the so-called "bridge dwellers," i.e. those who live under the bridges over the Rhone.[79]

This observation is consistent with the situation faced by at least two Russian migrants for whom we have verifiable information, Anatoly V. and Maxim Y., both of whom lived under a bridge on the banks of the Rhône. Four years after Anatoly V.'s first expulsion order had been issued, the Lyon police chief wrote that he still had not re-formed his ways:

He lives only by begging and he sleeps under the University Bridge; he is miserably dressed and it would be impossible for him to gather together the sum of five francs with which to purchase the sheet of taxed paper required to request a new residency authorization in France.[80]

Both refugees were arrested and imprisoned multiple times during the 1930s, and both were later sent to the concentration camp Vernet in 1940.[81]

The economy alone could not explain the distinction in Russian and Armenian experiences in the 1920s, but it took the depressed economy's effect on Russian employment and the conspicuous misery that resulted to revise received ideas of Russians. In contrast, Armenians had arrived in often obvious misery and were perceived either as lazy or as unwelcome social climbers. While the depression helped to shift the economics of hospitality with regard to Russians, it exacerbated the difficulties Armenians had faced since the early 1920s and, as we shall see, provided a particularly hostile context for the arrival of refugees from Nazism.

REFUGEES FROM NAZISM AND THE CLIMATE OF EXCLUSION IN DEPRESSION-ERA FRANCE

During the depression, refugee groups that had had very different experiences in the 1920s began to find themselves in similar circumstances. Even refugees who were able to find willing employers were often thwarted by the protectionist regulatory logic that was now in full swing in some parts of France. Refugee rights had always been connected to the economy in some ways. Like all other foreign nationals, refugees needed officially approved contracts in order to qualify for worker identification cards, and identification cards in order to work in all but the most temporary of jobs. But now the depression also created fear among merchants, artisans, and educated professionals. Foreigners became scapegoats, as protectionist policies were extended to new trades. Since refugees were often involved in commercial and artisanal trades, they became the privileged targets of this new animosity. If their identification papers were not in order, they became, like any other foreigner in a similar situation, illegal aliens. As such, they could be *refoulés* or expelled.

The coincidence of a new influx of refugees in 1933 and 1934 with the deepening of the French depression allowed xenophobia—and anti-Semitism in particular—to be cast in the "rational" language of economics, hardly the first time this had happened in France.[82] By the time that

Hitler ascended to power in January 1933, French unemployment was at a record high, with 316,300 persons receiving assistance.[83] Real unemployment was much higher; some estimated that there were as many as one million out-of-work individuals.[84] Although unemployment, no matter how it was calculated, hit a significantly lower percentage of the active population in France than it did in many other countries, French unemployment rates were nevertheless alarming in a country where there had been only 1,000 registered recipients of unemployment as recently as 1929.[85] Entrepreneurs suffered as well. Personal bankruptcy, as Eugen Weber puts it, "became a not overly significant commonplace of business life."[86] Moreover, the government's finances were in a shambles. By the end of January, the Treasury had exhausted almost all its available funds; by the third of February, the treasury deficit already had reached 350 million francs.[87] Financial crises had brought down two governments since mid-December. Hopes were pinned on Radical Party leader Édouard Daladier to save the day; he formed his new government the day after Hitler became German chancellor.

Daladier's job would have been difficult even without the emergence of a Nazi government next door. His ascent to prime minister had resulted from deadlock in the Radical Party, whose leadership had alternated between Daladier and Herriot since the formation of Herriot's ill-fated Cartel des Gauches government in 1924. Herriot had been discredited, as far as the left wing of the Radical Party was concerned, when he joined Poincaré's National Union government in 1927. More recently, as premier from June to December 1932, Herriot had pursued an intensely unpopular deflationary approach to the French economic and fiscal crisis. Daladier, who was among the deputies voting "no confidence" in Poincaré's government, earned a reputation as left-leaning by comparison to Herriot. Even so, uncertainty reigned about the sort of government Daladier would lead. On the day he formed his government, there were protests throughout France by civil servants concerned that the Daladier government would cut their salaries. Shopkeepers, small traders, and others who worried about a possible increase in taxes also took to the streets.[88] Both groups continued their protests periodically throughout the next few months. This provided the backdrop for the arrival of refugees from Germany, many of whom were engaged in similar professions.

Daladier's arrival in power at the same time as Hitler presented problems beyond those posed by balancing a budget and quelling internal opposition to new taxation and austerity measures. A decorated veteran of the First World War and two-time minister of war, Daladier was gravely concerned about the security threat posed by a new German leadership that actively advocated remilitarization.[89] Although later under Vichy he was placed on trial and imprisoned for "failing" to adequately prepare the country for war, in fact Daladier broke ranks early with the Radical Party's pacifism.[90] Upon learning in May 1933 that as many as 20,000 refugees had been admitted to France since Hitler's rise to power, Daladier expressed concern over the threat he felt they posed to national security. Admitting large numbers of refugees—and perhaps especially refugees from a vengeful Germany—was, he thought, tantamount to inviting "a Trojan Horse of spies and subversives."[91] Daladier also allegedly worried that a liberal refugee policy could stimulate xenophobic reactions among French workers and the unemployed.[92]

In spite of Daladier's concerns, however, France initially opened its doors more readily than any other Western nation to the refugees fleeing Germany. Following the purging of Jews from the German civil service and the first boycotts of German Jewish businesses in April 1933, Interior Minister Camille Chautemps and Foreign Minister Joseph Paul-Boncourt instructed the consular services in Germany to waive visa requirements for asylum seekers. Officials also instructed border police to allow free passage and told interior police to liberally grant residency permits and identification cards.[93] With the benefit of hindsight, the Daladier government's skeptical approach emerges as more liberal toward German refugees than that of any French government prior to the Popular Front.

By the time that Camille Chautemps became prime minister in November 1933, the tide had shifted and the standard visa regime had been reestablished. Moreover, an examination of how refugees were treated by local functionaries reveals that Daladier's vision of refugees as potentially undesirable was shared by many at various levels of the French administration, even before the conservative governments of Pierre-Étienne Flandin and Pierre Laval were formed. This lack of enthusiasm, to say the least, for refugees from Germany had considerable impact. Although an estimated 25,000 German refugees flocked to France in 1933, by 1935 only 10,000 remained.[94]

Confronting the human problem posed by refugees once they were in France was primarily a job for the Ministries of the Interior and Labor. Sympathy for refugees was often hard-won among the local representatives of these ministries, daunted by the seeming inundation of their towns. Local protectionist opposition to the refugees was so significant, in fact, that after 1 July 1933, movement out of the departments of the Alsace-Lorraine region was generally a prerequisite for residency approval. Exceptions were granted only after consultation with the local chambers of commerce and then only to those businesses that were regarded as noncompetitive.[95]

Almost certainly in response to the pressure local officials in the border departments placed on the upper echelons of the French administration, the labor minister François Albert issued a directive in which he expressed his suspicion that "certain foreigners [try] to pass as political refugees, with the objective of benefiting from a benevolent measure." As a result, Albert demanded that all applications for identification cards from supposed refugees, as well as all applications that included letters of support from a member of parliament or organizations such as the League of the Rights of Man, be submitted to him for final decisions; he further cautioned that the recommendations made by the regional labor offices had to be justified.[96]

In part these policies stemmed from the insistence of the protectionist lobby, whose center of gravity had shifted from the working class to the middle class, on the supposedly pernicious role that Jews allegedly played in French economic life. There was nothing new about portraying Jews as invidious or deceitful competitors. Such clichés had long circulated in France. The difference now was that these stereotypes were resurrected during a period of small-business failure, as Jewish businesses were under attack in Nazi Germany, and as thousands of new refugees arrived in France, hoping to reestablish themselves and their livelihoods. Often French business owners' fears were as much imaginary as real. But the fearful voices were heard in part because the middle classes, the core of the Radical Party's electorate, had political clout. The fact that the disaffected among them also risked being lured by the extremist politics of the rightist antiparliamentary leagues contributed to the receptiveness of mainstream politicians to their calls for protection. Aided by the revival of a virulently anti-Semitic press in the 1930s, their voices were heard loud and clear.

Between 1933 and mid-1936, local officials' conclusions to reject German refugee settlement rarely faced opposition from the Ministry of the Interior, which readily approved *refoulements* and expulsions. In Lyon, for example, of the 84 extant records of requests for residency from refugees, 70 persons (84%) claiming refugee status were *refoulés,* expelled, or both, many as early as 1933. Among the same files, only four applicants were clearly approved, one who was a traveling salesman of "pure German race," and three who unequivocally had "the means" to live in France without "displacing" French workers, including one who earned an extraordinary 5,000 francs a month as an engineer and who had been working in France since 1929![97] While there were undoubtedly more than 84 refugees from Germany who applied for residency in Lyon, the tenor displayed by Rhône officials in rationalizing the 70 rejections suggests a practice that was very likely much more widespread.[98]

Lyon mayor Herriot had, as a leader of the Radical Party, publicly denounced Nazism and the treatment of Jews in Germany.[99] But he had also encouraged a vigorously protectionist approach to immigration that rested uneasily with his more liberal proclamations. Even prior to the Jewish refugee crisis, he had concluded that immigration was "desirable for our countryside," but, "on the contrary, is filling our already overcrowded cities [with] undesirables."[100] This view, which probably motivated Herriot's later support for rigid quotas on foreign employment, became much more widespread in the 1930s. When later he headed Flandin's interministerial commission for the protection of national labor, Herriot proclaimed that legitimate refugees would have a right to reside in France but would not be allowed to work.

Lyon's police, as a *police d'état,* did not report to Herriot, but as a member of the national cabinet the mayor had a hand in developing the policies they were supposed to enforce, and the views of the Rhône department's leadership closely paralleled Herriot's protectionist outlook. Since the onset of the depression, the prefecture's reflex had been to deny immigrant claims on the grounds that they interfered with the national economy. Although some migrants earned subsequent reprieves, rejection was almost invariably the first course of action. This approach was firmly in place when Jewish refugees began to arrive. As authorities combined a predisposition to protectionism with stereotypes of Jewish economic competitiveness, legal Jewish settlement in Lyon was made exceptionally difficult.

Over and over again, Rhône officials wrote that new applicants for residency, almost all of whom were Jewish, were "not authentic refugees" but had left Germany "voluntarily" in order to look for work or establish a business in France. Although in the 1920s, authorities had often excluded refugees on the grounds that they were unable to work, now they excluded them because they did want to work or earn a living. In one case, for example, the Rhône prefect wrote that Herschel K., his wife, Freda, and their three children were "not refugees but undesirables in Germany because of their religion." He condemned their "attitude," which he said was "adopted by the majority of the so-called 'political refugees' who take advantage of the situation in Germany to come in search of a means of existence in our territory."[101] Similarly, the prefect argued that the members of another family "do not seem really to be refugees but to have taken advantage of the welcome given in France to Israelites coming from Germany in order to set up business in France."[102] Still another Jewish family had come to "exercise their profession more lucratively."[103]

Decisions such as these straddled a period when Rhône officials shifted from evaluating all migrants through a protectionist lens to bringing a more familialist approach to their considerations of some. Newly arrived Jewish refugees rarely could take advantage of policies that granted exceptions to those with French family connections, precisely because their arrival was so recent. Moreover, authorities still regarded Jews primarily in relation to the economy. The incessant media attention given to the alleged competition Jews posed to French artisans and businesses likely encouraged this. Authorities continued to focus on Jewish economic activity even as they began to evaluate other migrants on populationist grounds.

Was it this disjuncture that had led the one "pure race German" in the sample to earn residency, even though he declared his intention to become a traveling salesman, a profession that officials invariably deemed "encumbered by peddlers, draft dodgers and the unemployed" when evaluating requests from Jews?[104] Could this have been a fluke, perhaps the one traveling salesman who missed officials' attention? Or perhaps it provides corroborating evidence that anti-Semitic views of Jews as particularly invidious competitors had found new expression in the 1930s. Even consular officials who witnessed Jewish experiences in Germany evaluated their exile as primarily motivated by business interests:

A priori, his status as an Israelite is sufficient to classify him among those persons for whom the residency and professional or commercial activity in Germany is difficult. Nevertheless, one can place [Berthold I.] among those Israelites who, having nothing more to lose in Germany, rushed to leave the country counting on taking advantage of their status as more or less qualified political refugees in order to obtain our assistance. The information I was able to gather demonstrates that this foreigner . . . twice ceased business to the detriment of his creditors.[105]

In other words, the business practices of Jews were deemed inconsistent with purely political motivations for emigration. This perception of Jewish migrants was so pervasive that, as Vicki Caron shows, French Jews often opposed Jewish immigration, fearing that an influx of Jewish merchants or artisans would exacerbate domestic anti-Semitism, of which they might become the targets.[106]

Responding no doubt to pressure placed on them by French businessmen and artisans, Rhône officials deemed boycotts and raids of Jewish businesses in Germany as purely economic and therefore apolitical acts, and repeatedly concluded that the persons in question had been "neither threatened nor endangered by the Hitlerians."[107] In those cases where the refugees insisted that they had indeed been threatened, officials wrote instead that the so-called refugee had "no document to support his declarations."[108] Like earlier refugees who could not prove who they were or where they were born because of their refugee status, German Jewish refugees could not prove they had been threatened without a document from the Nazis stating as much.[109]

Considerations of family unity also entered into officials' evaluations of Jewish refugees. Refugees who still had family members in Germany were regarded as not having been genuinely endangered, for if they had been, surely the whole family would have emigrated. While threats to an individual certainly could be experienced as menacing to an entire family, police agents took it as a given that they ought to be, or used this notion as a convenient way to deny residency to new refugees. Assumptions about the national security threats posed by transnational families may also have entered into authorities' evaluations. In any case, the demands of local officials illustrated the often contradictory understandings of what a refugee was. On the one hand, authorities required documentation that a certain individual had been the victim of specific violence by "Hitlerians" or had been overtly and personally threatened by them. On the other hand, they reasoned that such threats ought to trigger the emigration of not just the person in question but his or her entire family, brothers and sisters living in other cities included. Yet, as Marion Kaplan shows, the prospect of emigrating from Nazi Germany often divided families. If Jews experienced what Kaplan calls "social death," women did so earlier or differently than did men, and children differently than their parents. Often only one or two family members felt the pressure to emigrate, and these were frequently the very young, who experienced discrimination on a daily and particularly brutal basis at school or university. In Lyon, most of the refugee files concerned individuals born between 1906 and 1916, evidence supporting Kaplan's claim that it was often young adults who had the courage and energy to leave and try to start a new life elsewhere.[110]

French officials' preoccupation with "proof" created other impediments to the acceptance of Jewish refugees in France. Many of the Jewish refugees had been born in territories that were now part of Poland, or in some cases the Soviet Union. They had lived in Germany for years, if not most of their lives, without gaining German citizenship. When faced with the pressures of Nazism, they did not flee to Poland, where, after 1934, "anti-Jewish voices received official sanction"; instead they fled to France and other Western countries.[111] But because French authorities were looking for ways to limit refugee settlement, they reasoned that Polish Jews could not be "German" refugees. Once again, therefore, the postwar logic of national citizenship prevailed.

The record in Marseille is more difficult to uncover, since expulsion files of foreigners initiated from 1933 through mid-1938 apparently have been lost. The only conclusive evidence regarding German refugees in Marseille dates from the Popular Front period, when refugees were invited to apply for—and almost always received—government-recognized refugee status. Some of the Marseille applications from this period have bits of information about the refugee experiences prior to June 1936, but it is difficult to draw any definitive conclusions as to whether the refugee experience in Marseille was qualitatively different from that in Lyon. Only 53 applications have been conserved in the archives. Of these, almost all of the refugees first arrived in France in 1933. The legality of these refugees' early status in France is unclear, however, in 38 of the files. Since 13 of the files specifically mention that the refugee had a legal identification card prior to the date that the Popular Front formed its first government, one might conclude that in the 38 files where this detail was not provided, the refugees had no valid identification cards. But to do so would mean drawing conclusions based on a lack of evidence. It is clear, however, that, compared to Lyon's files, a higher percentage of the Marseille files— 13 of 54, or 24%—show evidence of residency approval between 1933 and mid-1936. In only three cases is there clear evidence of *refoulement* or expulsion.[112]

Even so, the nature of the remarks made by local officials suggests that Marseille officials may have had similar reactions to German Jewish refugees as had been prevalent among Lyon officials. Even after the Popular Front recognized the special status of refugees coming from Germany, for example, Special Police Commissioner Sallet drew on popular stereotypes of Jewish commercial competitiveness as he argued that Koppel U. had been "in no way bothered" in Germany and that he came to France to study the possibility of establishing a dental prosthesis workshop. "It was only after this operation was completed in association with [Mr. X.]," Sallet continued, "and that the workshop was established, that he left Germany with his family, to come settle in our city." Because he deemed this behavior pernicious, Sallet recommended rejecting Koppel U.'s request to be recognized as a refugee.[113]

This outright rejection was, however, the exception that proved the new rules established by the Popular Front administration. After forming his coalition government in June 1936, Léon Blum, a Socialist and Jew, took a liberal stance on refugee policy and encouraged his administration to do the same. Among other things, he saw to it that the 1933 Geneva Convention, in which the expulsion of Nansen refugees was condemned, was finally ratified in France. In distinction to the position Herriot espoused as head of the interministerial commission for the protection of labor, Blum's labor minister, Jean-Baptiste Lebas, issued a statement that "the right of asylum" could not be separated from the "right to work."[114] More important, Blum's interior minister, Salengro, pushed for official recognition of a League of Nations agreement that proposed to give refugees from Germany a status akin to Nansen refugees. By decree dated 17 September

1936, France thus officially recognized the special status of "refugees coming from Germany." Even the nomenclature acknowledged the uniqueness of Jewish refugees' situation: Since the September 1935 Nuremberg laws, they were not "German refugees," but refugees from Germany. One wonders if even the liberal Popular Front would have been ready to acknowledge the special status of Jewish refugees had Jews not been completely stripped of their rights as German citizens. After all, the new policy explicitly excluded those who had lived in Germany but held citizenship in other countries.

In recognizing Jews from Germany as legitimate refugees, the Popular Front government tried to balance a humanitarian approach to refugees who had already arrived against a realpolitik stance regarding future refugees. To do so, the government limited the new status to refugees already in France. Those who had not succeeded in acquiring legal recognition of their residence would be permitted to "regularize" their status, provided they had arrived in the country before 5 August 1936. This date was later extended to 31 December and then to 31 January 1937. Significantly, however, Jewish refugees were never included in the special categories of foreigners who were granted residency rights "regardless of the labor market situation."[115]

The limits placed on applications for refugee status caused controversy then, and have stimulated scholarly debate since. With regard to the development of national policy, I have little to add to Caron's masterful study of the matter.[116] In terms of everyday local practices, the results are probably somewhat less linear. Rhône officials already had begun expelling Jewish refugees before hard-line policies under the Flandin and Laval governments were instituted.[117] Inversely, Marseille's special police commissioner still drew on received ideas about Jewish business culture after a special refugee status was created.

Still, the policy change did help to alter practices significantly. The prefect who had not recommended Gabriel C. on the grounds that he did not appear to be a "real refugee" in September 1933 was willing to authorize a repeal of his *refoulement* in November 1936. In response, the interior minister wrote that he "no longer opposed" authorizing Gabriel's residency based on the "new" information provided. In fact, no new information on Gabriel appeared in the file; the only thing that was new was the more indulgent spirit of local and national authorities. This, followed by a refugee certificate issued in 1937, bought Gabriel some time.[118] Herschel and Freda K., whom the Rhône prefect had accused in 1934 of "taking advantage" of the events in Germany in order to set up business in France, earned the prefect's recommendation in 1937.[119] Among the 43 of the 84 aforementioned refugees who had managed to remain in Lyon until the Popular Front's ascension to power, there were only two clear rejections of refugee status, whereas there were 25 approvals and five naturalizations.[120] The rejections were of a husband and wife on the grounds that their Polish citizenship made them ineligible for the new status.

The record in Marseille was similar. Of 54 files, only two (the husband and wife whose behavior was decried by Sallet) were rejected, while 51 were approved, and one had an unclear outcome.[121] The approvals included Jews as well as individuals who were not Jewish but who feared returning to Germany because of their (or a family member's) political opinions. Proof of a specific, individualized threat was no longer required. One Jewish man who had left Germany in 1930, "foreseeing the events," as well as for "commercial reasons," earned refugee status on the basis of having subsequently lost all his rights as a German.[122] Commercial interests also no longer categorically denied Jewish refugees a chance at legal residency. Even a Jewish man who entered France in 1933, then tried his luck in Italy, only to return to France in February 1935 having been "unable to establish his business in Italy," was approved for refugee status.[123] Nor was the fact that some family members remained in Germany any longer held against an applicant; migrants who admitted to wanting to summon their remaining family members were among those earning refugee status.[124] In addition to approving refugee status, the Interior Ministry under both Salengro and his successor, Dormoy, also repealed many of the expulsions that had been ordered against German refugees. This made it easier for refugees to find work or open businesses legally.

The Popular Front's recognition of League of Nations agreements not only helped Jews secure official recognition as refugees; it also finally removed the handicap that statelessness posed to the social and civil rights of Armenian and Russian refugees. The 1933 Geneva Convention exempted its beneficiaries (stateless Russians, Armenians, and "similars") from having to meet reciprocity requirements in order to benefit from social rights such as unemployment insurance.[125] In addition, at least in theory, it aimed to prevent the expulsions of stateless persons except in extraordinary circumstances. Still, local authorities were not eager to comply. When the government called for an end to exclusions of Nansen refugees from social rights, municipal officials balked.

In some French communities, the ratification of the Convention promised to make little impact. In Marseille, by contrast, conservative estimates placed Armenians at around 10% of the foreign population.[126] Moreover, by the time of ratification, Marseille was 233 million francs in debt. Some of the debt undoubtedly could be attributed to the bloating effect that patronage politics had on the city's payroll. Nonetheless, Marseille and neighboring La Ciotat protested, arguing that their budgets could not sustain the extra charges that providing unemployment relief to stateless persons would engender. Their complaints became the subject of discussion in interministerial committee deliberations early in 1937. There, Maurice Paz pointed out that a nationalized unemployment service would equalize the burden that social rights currently placed on municipalities. In the meantime, as the Interior Ministry's inspector general noted, the 1933 convention had a disproportionate impact on the Bouches-du-Rhône, "where its weight is felt all the more because [the convention] does not reflect public opinion." More than in any other department, Armenians were clustered there and, he continued,

constitute a sizable yet not very desirable element of its population. The municipalities in question find themselves imposed upon . . . in the middle of a crisis. . . . If the municipalities of Marseille and La Ciotat refuse to vote the necessary appropriations to pay for unemployment benefits to Armenians, the Interior Ministry will be obliged to impose these expenditures on them by fiat. Morally, can it do this?

The only reasonable solution, Paz retorted, was for the state to assume the costs of providing unemployment indemnities to stateless persons in Marseille. Unsurprisingly, the Finance Ministry's representative at the meeting opposed this proposal. The state already heavily subsidized unemployment assistance, he argued, and always had done so without regard to nationality. If it were to introduce an exception for Marseille and La Ciotat, other municipalities would demand the same.[127] Local exceptionalism was decreed over—at least in principle.

In practice, local divergences from national expectations probably continued, at least to some degree. Still, the change in tone under the Popular Front should not be discounted. Scholars have disagreed about the impact of Popular Front reforms on refugees. For Jean-Charles Bonnet, Blum's government was caught off guard by the strike movements and forced to make decisions hastily. Bonnet also underscores another effect of the mass mobilization; the masses, he claims, had other things on their minds than improving the rights of migrants. Rita Thalmann is less forgiving. Examining the efforts made by the government to create protections for refugees, she emphasizes the time limits they instituted, which, in essence, precluded any new refugees from settling legally in France. For Thalmann, this stemmed from a deliberate attempt to exclude new migrants and did not therefore constitute a departure from policies initiated under Flandin or Laval.[128]

Neither Bonnet nor Thalmann emphasizes the role that coalition politics may have played. The Radicals, even though undoubtedly diminished in power by the number of seats lost to the Communist Party in May 1936, were still crucial partners in the coalition. Many Radicals, as well as some Independent Socialists such as Frossard, had participated in the previous three governments; their leaders had been intimately involved in developing the hard-line immigration policy. A major reversal in policy might have alienated them, weakening the coalition. What was more, the citizens pushing for limits on refugees—the petty bourgeois and new middle classes—constituted the core of the Radical Party's electorate. The importance of coalition politics also suggests that it is misleading to treat Socialist Party ideals and Popular Front policies as one and the same. Marcel Livian's insider account from his days as general secretary of the Socialist Party's immigration commission therefore must be read skeptically. Livian insists that strict screenings of new refugees were performed mainly in order to keep out Nazis or fascists who might pose as refugees, and suggests that the stiffened punishments enacted with regard to refractory expellees were likewise aimed at penalizing Nazi and fascist infiltrators who tried to illegally remain in France.[129] Although espionage was a real problem, Livian might have considered what impact such policies had on those he regarded as "real" refugees. Overall Livian's tone is defensive and indignant that anyone would dare to question the Popular Front's record on immigration.

Despite Livian's defensiveness, his point regarding the relative gains under the Popular Front is valid. Even if it is true that the Popular Front placed limits on the degree to which it was willing to grant asylum to new refugees, this was a trade-off.[130] Popular Front policy makers secured a more liberal policy toward already present refugees in exchange for the promise to limit the arrival of new ones. As Vicki Caron points out, this was considerably different from the behavior pursued by Flandin and Laval, who "had been determined not only to close the borders to future newcomers, but to get rid of the vast majority of refugees already in France as well." Such changes, Caron adds, "cannot be dismissed as minor and superficial."[131] Refugee treatment was the one domain of migrant rights that changed considerably under the Popular Front. Even here, however, Popular Front leaders seemed to share a preoccupation of their predecessors: how to bring about change in immigration policy without exacerbating the conflicts it had already aroused.

As past chapters illustrate, the guest-worker system that French leaders crafted to manage migration in the wake of the First World War proved unworkable even on its own terms. Yet if guest-worker policies were impractical for many migrants from stable countries, they were extremely problematic—sometimes even catastrophic—for those who had no guarantee of returning home. It was one thing for labor migrants to defy French plans by working without contracts, moving before contracts expired, or shifting categories of work. It was yet another thing for authorities to cope with migrants for whom they had no plan, and who fell wholly outside the boundaries of existing migration law. This was the case of refugees, and with them, French administrators faced an entirely new problem.

The problem was in part due to the place refugees occupied in the postwar world, where citizenship in a nation mattered in new and profound ways. The guest-worker regime assumed a system of international relations where states would work together to solve an imbalance in the international economy. This assumption had effects far beyond the labor market. Because the guest-worker system was premised on maintaining relations with friendly states, France could hardly accord "refugee" status to the nationals of the same governments with which it had negotiated reciprocity treaties; doing so would have been tantamount to acknowledging the legitimacy of the migrants' dissatisfaction with their home regime. This is why Italians and Spaniards never earned official refugee recognition in interwar France. But it is also why Armenians did not gain Nansen status until after the Treaty of Lausanne foreclosed the possibility of an independent Armenia, and it is one reason that French authorities hesitated to recognize Jewish refugees from Nazism as legitimate refugees until 1936. If labor migrants drew their rights in part from international accords, refugees owed their predicament to international and internal discord. While the guest-worker system was predicated on the notion that states would protect the interests of their nationals living outside the home country's borders, refugees were those in whom no state took any interest. Their experience in interwar France proved how much that condition marked them, even after they had left their home countries.

At first, authorities confronted the refugee crisis by trying to force refugees to conform to policies invented for voluntary labor migrants. This determination to treat all migrants as temporary workers had an uneven impact on refugees because some fit the social profile of labor migrants more closely than others. By the late 1920s, however, policy makers at the national level had come to understand that many refugees were, if not exactly unwilling, often unable to return home to countries that either no longer existed or refused to recognize them as citizens. As this occurred, officials increasingly assumed that refugees, unlike guest workers, might never leave. They thus tried to find new ways to keep them from arriving in the first place. The Foreign Ministry used visas to control entries, and these visas often limited the bearers' right to work. Although

believing all refugees could or would work in the early 1920s had been un-
realistic, expecting them to be able to support themselves without working
in the 1930s presented sometimes equally vexing problems. Neither approach came to terms with the full complexity of the refugee predicament, and in both the 1920s and the 1930s, refugees unable to conform
to expectations found themselves on the wrong side of the law.

Refugees had always fallen outside the boundaries of French migration
policy, but in the 1930s, new visa regimes, employment quotas, as well as
novel forms of protectionism increased the prospect of contravening the
law just as a new wave of refugees arrived from Germany. As the economic crisis began to affect France's petty middle class, new forms of protectionism emerged. The impetus for protecting artisans, merchants, and
liberal professions stemmed in part from fears of downward mobility
harbored by the middle classes and in part from stereotypes that circulated about the latest refugees, who were predominantly Jewish. While
Jewish refugees presented many of the same problems as other refugees,
these were exacerbated by the resurrection of long-standing stereotypes
regarding Jews' economic activity; such clichés had considerable reso-
nance in a period of hardship in the commercial trades. Although ethnic
stereotypes had also contributed to perceptions of Russians and Armenians, public opinion had its clearest impact on public policy in the case of
Jews. Perhaps more than in the case of any other migrants, Jews' individual
rights were adjudicated by authorities who clearly had these stereotypes
in mind.

It took an extraordinary change in public policy, spearheaded by the
Popular Front, to turn these practices around. Even then, the new recognition of explicit refugee rights came at the price of limiting the definition
of who qualified. Nonetheless, refugee status alone did not necessarily
mean genuine refuge. As the comparison of Russians and Armenians
demonstrates, persons with the same status often had divergent experiences, and fortunes shifted over time as social and cultural expectations
changed. Moreover, classification as a "refugee" often worked against
migrants, since as *non*-nationals they could not invoke *inter*-national
treaties in their protection. If unemployed, they had to rely on one another unless they were fortunate enough to live in a municipality that included foreigners from nonreciprocity nations in its welfare programs,
something that fewer and fewer city governments were willing to do as
xenophobic pressure mounted from their French clients. As a result, statelessness often exacerbated precarious economic and social situations, increasing the likelihood that refugees would come into conflict with the
police. The Popular Front tried to address this, too, by exempting Nansen
refugees from most-favored foreigner requirements for social welfare.

Yet, perhaps anticipating the negative reactions it might cause both in France and in Germany, the government failed to implement plans to include "refugees from Germany" in the same social rights.[132]

Through stopgap measures instituted over the course of the 1920s and 1930s, a revolution in rights had occurred. Initially, refugee rights—beyond those conferred by Nansen passports, which proved to be limited in practice—were contingent upon the degree to which migrants fit the profile of the labor migrants, for whom migration policy had been designed. Increasingly, however, French authorities came to treat refugees as presenting unique problems by virtue of the fact that they were not free to leave. Refugees' right of non-*refoulement* would not be fully recognized internationally until after the Second World War, but its necessity was first demonstrated—primarily, albeit not exclusively, in France—by the crises caused by the First World War and the postwar "unsettlement." Even as refugees were finally recognized as needing unique protections, however, their presence in France remained profoundly unsettling in its own way. This was especially true of German refugees, not only because they were largely Jewish and France in the 1930s underwent an anti-Semitic revival, but also because they were from France's archrival, Germany. In this respect as in many others, Jewish refugees were about as far from the ideotypic guest worker as one could get.

Moreover, in part due to geopolitics, the first guest workers—those quintessentially temporary migrants—now could claim a more permanent stake in French society than could refugees. Circular reasoning led authorities to incrementally grant special privileges to some migrants, effectively recognizing them as immigrants. Many of the beneficiaries of circular reasoning in the 1930s were the same migrants who had enjoyed most-favored status in the 1920s.

What happened to refugees was rather different. While certain among them may have claimed privileged status by virtue of longevity in France or family ties, their special status as refugees did not, unlike membership in certain nation-states, confer any rights as permanent immigrants. In this, refugees had something in common, as the next chapter will show, with North Africans. However, North Africans' limited access to rights was produced not so much by a lack of legal protection as it was by a surfeit of legal impediments that their status as colonized persons placed upon them. They did not suffer from statelessness but rather from the interest that the French state had in maintaining hegemony over the territories from which they came. Like refugees, North Africans called attention to both the power and the limits of the nation-state system, but in a profoundly different way.

CHAPTER SIX

Subjects, Not Citizens

North African Migrants and the Paradoxes of Republican Imperialism

The colonized enjoys none of the attributes of citizenship.[1]

Unlike many refugees, North African workers in mainland France often epitomized the social profile of the migrant: young men detached from their families who retained ties in their home communities, to which they hoped to return. With few exceptions, however, the guest-worker policies designed for foreigners did not formally apply to them, for the majority of the North Africans who came to work in the metropole were French nationals. North Africans' experience as migrants, however, proved that their nationality was, as Patrick Weil has put it, "perverted, gutted" of the rights to which a French national ordinarily could lay claim.[2] Their experience in mainland France between the wars confirmed that they were still subjects of the empire, not citizens of an "imperial nation-state."[3] If the plight of refugees exemplified the important role that national belonging often played in shaping migrant rights in post-Versailles Europe, this chapter calls attention to the limits of formal membership in the nation. North Africans' civil and social rights were limited not because "no law exists for them," as Hannah Arendt wrote of refugees,[4] but rather precisely because of the legal and political ties that bound them, however unwillingly, to the French republic.

North Africans' civil liberties—to choose where they wished to live and to be able to freely circulate within metropolitan French territory or between the metropole and North Africa, for example—were fragile. The First World War had triggered unprecedented population flows from France's colonies to its battlegrounds and home-front industries. After the war, however, extraordinary measures were taken to curtail these flows. Many colonized subjects had hoped that their wartime sacrifices would lead to an extension of their rights, perhaps even to formal citizenship. However, during the course of several years following the war, the French government's attempt to defend the status quo in the empire led to novel forms of control in the metropole. Despite enduring legal distinctions in the nature of French imperial rule in Algeria, Morocco, and Tunisia, migrants from these three parts of the empire became collectively disadvantaged as *"indigènes nord-africains"*[5] in the 20 years following the war.

At the very moment that France was concluding treaties with European nations to facilitate the recruitment of their nationals as temporary workers, police were rounding up North Africans residing in mainland France in order to send them back home. In the early 1920s, these efforts were aided by arbitrary arrests and detentions of the kind that did not become systematic for European immigrants until the eve of the Second World War. Moreover, from about 1923, French authorities in metropole, protectorate, and colony alike worked together to raise obstacles to North African emigration, instituting what amounted to internal passports for Algerian French nationals.[6]

Like other migrants, North Africans faced the true test of their rights in the 1930s. Yet unlike many of their European counterparts, North Africans did not succeed in expanding the scope of their claims on the French state during the depression. To the contrary, while their unique relationship to the French state had already curtailed their civil rights, now it limited their social rights as well. Unlike earlier controls placed on their movement, however, there was little premeditation in the exclusion of North Africans from social welfare programs in the 1930s. As local governments looked for ways to reduce expenditures during the depression, North Africans, with little or no political clout, were simply the easiest beneficiaries to cut.

At the same time, French authorities recognized a political risk in leaving unemployed North Africans to their own devices, particularly as their rights became increasingly politicized in colony and metropole alike. North Africans received special, albeit not necessarily equal, treatment with respect to social rights. North African Indigenous Affairs Service (Services des Affaires Indigènes Nord-Africaines, SAINA) offices, established in Marseille, Lyon, and a few other large cities, served as intermediaries between North Africans and the public administration. Ironically, this attention meant denying colonial subjects the social and legal protections that were regularly accorded to metropolitan French citizens as well as many foreign nationals. Unlike similar services in Paris, which drew on subsidies

from colonial budgets and the Ministry of the Interior, and which under-
took major assistance projects including a state-of-the-art hospital, the
SAINA of Lyon and Marseille combined paternalism with penury. Social
assistance for North Africans in France's second and third cities thus differed not only in kind but also in substance. The failure of the SAINA to
adequately address the social dislocation of North African migrants led
authorities increasingly to resort to repatriation under the Popular Front.
This curtailment of North Africans' rights came as the government softened its approach to policing other migrants.

REESTABLISHING THE "STATUS-QUO ANTEBELLUM" AFTER THE GREAT WAR

In the wake of the war, the French Labor Ministry declared its preferences
for recruiting workers who would be needed to rebuild and sustain the
economy: Priority would go to "nationals from countries having fought
on our side or having demonstrated benevolent neutrality towards us."[7]
That meant recruiting Italian allies before neutral Spanish, and the Spanish before enemy Germans.[8] It did not mean appealing to the thousands
of colonial subjects who had fought in French regiments or worked in
French munitions plants.

During the war, French subjects had been called upon to make the ul-
timate sacrifice for the *patrie*: More than 26,000 Algerians gave their
lives or were missing in action, 72,000 were injured, and another
108,000 had served in the armed forces. All told, more than one-third of
Algerian males between the ages of 20 and 40 had served in the metropole in some capacity during the Great War.[9] The sacrifice reflected by
such statistics made a return to prewar inequalities unthinkable, or so
Muslim North Africans thought. In fact, however, postwar policies
quickly dashed hopes of equalizing the legal statuses of French nationals
on either side of the Mediterranean. Despite a 1914 law guaranteeing
free circulation between Algeria and mainland France, authorities set
about restricting Algerian residency in the metropole almost immediately
following the war.[10] Setting recruitment priorities for the workers who
would be needed to resurrect the French economy, officials called for "labor of European origin, in preference to colonial or exotic labor," which
was deemed "too ethnographically distinct from the rest of the population."[11] Intensified European recruitment and North African repatriation
were parallel activities.

Why send home willing workers only to recruit new ones? The prof-
fered explanation of avoiding "ethnographic" clashes in the metropole

was somewhat misleading; what really worried officials were ethnic relations in the colonies. As strike actions multiplied in Algeria after the war, colonists quickly blamed the exposure of "their" natives to radical elements of the metropolitan labor movement. Algerian nationalism, meanwhile, was growing, and with it, new polarizations within the colony.[12]

Settlers responded to mounting tensions with a politics of self-defense. This was only partially successful. Unable to entirely block political reforms that granted a limited local franchise to some Muslims,[13] they were more successful in their insistence that North Africans' exposure to the metropole was potentially dangerous to both the economic and political well-being of the colony. On the economic front, colonists worried that work in the metropole put upward pressure on wages and, worse, placed "*indigènes*" in a position to buy land from settlers, thus reversing the process of colonization.[14] At the same time that settlers feared displacement by enterprising North Africans, however, they also contended—and put pressure on the Indigenous Affairs Office at the Interior Ministry to argue on their behalf—that "*indigènes*" were neither mature nor independent enough to function outside the structured environment they claimed only settlers could provide. This paternalism probably said more about the threats settlers perceived to their own way of life than it did about the needs of Muslims. As much as anyone else, it was settlers who found the changes wrought by war destabilizing. And it was they, perhaps as much as the "*indigènes*," whom officials in Paris sought to placate.

Thus, Georges Clemenceau, the same premier who had advocated reforms in Algeria during the war, joined settlers in calling for a return to the *status quo antebellum* after it. In 1919, he instructed the commander of the Marseille colonial labor depot that from 15 May onward, "labor contract renewals for North Africans will no longer be accepted. The North African workers sent to the depot in Marseille will all be repatriated **without exception** and will not be authorized to renew their contracts."[15] In keeping with Clemenceau's autocratic style and the way in which North Africans initially had been recruited, the army was made responsible for ensuring that the repatriations occurred. Notwithstanding the 1914 law on free circulation, *indigènes* were not trusted to return on their own once their contracts expired. Instead, they were accompanied by gendarmes to the Marseille depot, from which they were escorted to ships crossing the Mediterranean. The same held true for Tunisians and Moroccans, whether on civil or military contracts.

Because of the "insufficiency of maritime transport," however, "the return of these 121,700 Indigènes *en bloc*" was impossible.[16] No doubt the delays were also due to concerns that too massive and rapid a return of potentially politicized subjects to the colonies threatened to exacerbate mounting tensions there. Either way, officials hoped for a "progressive disappearance via attrition," thanks to policies proscribing the renewal of labor contracts for North African workers.[17] Even with a policy of attrition, the Marseille colonial labor depot reportedly overflowed with the 7,000 North Africans it held awaiting repatriation at any one time, "in mud and disorder."[18] Despite massive repatriations following the armistice, the governor-general of Algeria complained a year later that a "relatively high figure" of 4,000 Algerian *indigènes* remained in the metropole.[19] This figure, probably inaccurate, actually represents a low percentage of the Algerians who had migrated to the metropole during the war. There were, however, new reasons that officials grew concerned about the presence of even a small group of North Africans in the metropole.

In 1920, government and industry collaborated to put down rail, mining, and general strikes. This crackdown seriously weakened the French labor movement, for the strikes were brutally repressed and the strikers replaced. Despite this, however, the "red threat" remained the rallying issue for police work throughout the 1920s. If this fact forced all migrants to carefully weigh their limited rights against the risks of exercising them, the government's fears about political subversion in the colonies often made the stakes of these calculations even higher in the case of North Africans. Although it is difficult to determine the degree of North African participation in the strikes,[20] the fact that the Ministry of the Interior relaunched its repatriation drive in their immediate aftermath suggests a concern either that North African militancy posed a threat to social peace in the metropole, or, in keeping with the earlier settler fears, that the continued exposure of North Africans to metropolitan working-class militancy was detrimental. Strikes began in February 1920 and continued on and off until May. Meanwhile, maritime transit requisitions for repatriates passing through the colonial labor depot in Marseille suggest that postwar repatriation efforts were launched in March and sustained through December 1920.[21]

A few of the repatriates had been convicted of crimes, but most appear to have been summarily arrested during raids on so-called Moorish cafes (*cafés maures*) and other locales they frequented, for "rupture of contract" or petty infractions of the penal code such as "vagrancy." As we have seen, vagrancy—a misdemeanor triggered by having no legitimate source of income and no proof of domicile—left a great deal of room for police interpretation. In one case, for example, gendarmes reported that they "questioned an individual of Algerian origin found wandering . . . in order to learn the motive of his travel and his means of existence." In another, they "saw an individual foreign to this area, who appeared to be a colonial worker" and arrested him.[22] Of course, as earlier chapters have demonstrated, North Africans were not the only ones arrested on charges of vagrancy. Due to postwar directives discontinuing their contracts, however, North Africans were more likely to find themselves without a legal source of income than were many Europeans. Moreover, unlike some European foreigners, North Africans were almost never acquitted of this charge. Expulsions sometimes ensued. Samples of expulsions from Marseille between 1919 and 1932 suggest that while total numbers of Moroccans and Tunisians expelled were very low, the likelihood that they would be expelled if they came into conflict with the law was high: Almost all (88%) of the Moroccans and Tunisians considered for expulsion in Marseille were expelled, and a considerable number of those expulsions (36%) were ordered summarily by the prefect without review by the Interior Ministry.[23] Algerians are not included in these figures since, as French nationals, they could not be subjected to formal expulsion procedures; nonetheless, arrest and incarceration were often used to encourage them to repatriate.

Patterns of detention also indicate that considerations of due process carried little weight. Although vagrancy was a misdemeanor for which offenders were routinely released on their own recognizance and asked to return to court on a given date, it was not unusual for North African "vagrants" to be detained prior to conviction, or even after a case had been thrown out by the *procureur*.[24] In those cases where due process initially was followed, there was no guarantee that it would continue. Saïd M., for example, served a court-issued sentence of one month for vagrancy. Instead of being released from prison after serving his sentence, however, he was turned over to gendarmes who escorted him directly from the St Paul Prison in Lyon to Marseille for repatriation.[25]

From Marseille, repatriation was not necessarily immediate, and in the meantime, North Africans were held alternatively at the colonial labor depot or in prisons. Though records are incomplete, it is clear that confinement in Marseille alone sometimes exceeded four weeks.[26] Larbi A., for example, served a four-month sentence in a Paris prison for engaging in a confidence game akin to three-card monte (*jeu de bonneteau*), while an order of immediate release was issued for his Algerian compatriot, Embareck M. After both were escorted from Paris to Marseille in March 1920, they jointly wrote to the governor-general of Algeria from Marseille's Eveché Prison, complaining that they and "a hundred [other] *Indigènes*" believed that, "as French citizens," they should have been released after serving their sentences. Instead they continued to be held pending repatriation. Three ships left weekly for Algiers, they wrote, and yet they had been detained for "29 days now [with] 600 grams of bread a day, only a board to sleep on, and no covers."[27]

The extended incarceration of North Africans awaiting repatriation also concerned the Marseille police, who complained:

The cost of nourishment, now reduced to the consumption of bread, falls under the police budget and the credit for it was only 4000 francs for 1920, [which] appears to already have been much exceeded.

I believe it is my duty to add that the health of these *indigènes* is generally poor and that their prolonged detention is becoming illegal.

Yesterday, I had to evacuate one to the hospital and today I will have to do so again for another.

Their embarkation is imperative therefore not only from an economic point of view but also from a legal one. . . . Moreover, they are becoming boisterous and threatening towards the guards.[28]

Whether or not it was an intended consequence of their detention, Algerians, Moroccans, and Tunisians alike pleaded for repatriation in personal correspondence intercepted by prison authorities. Although they all indicated that their detention was arbitrary and unjust, they also clearly preferred returning to North Africa to remaining in jail, where they were, in their own words, "starving to death [and] afraid that we too will become sick."[29] Only one wrote, in a letter apparently addressed to a close friend, that he would return to Algiers merely to legalize his papers, after which he planned to return to the metropole.[30] The fact that these letters remain in the Bouches-du-Rhône police files, of course, suggests that prison personnel never sent them to their intended recipients.

All over France, police targeted North African "enclaves" and raided their bars and cafés in an effort to gather as many North Africans as possible. These summary arrests, lengthy detentions, and repatriations of North Africans were simply the first instance in a series of events demonstrating that the formal "nationality" held by Algerians often came with fewer benefits than the foreign status of many Europeans. This discrepancy was not lost on North Africans themselves. Reacting to another repatriation drive in 1921, a petition from Algerians in Marseille complained that their compatriots were being "arbitrarily" and "summarily" forced to leave the city. The arrests, they claimed, occurred "at all hours in all locations." It was unacceptable that "simply because they are Arabs," these "citizens" who served their country during the war are forced to leave. "Nothing can allow them to be chased out against their will, like vulgar foreign trouble-makers against whom such summary procedures are not even employed."[31] The procedures were indeed extraordinary. As the prefect noted in a letter to the labor minister, he had ordered a search for "those Algerians without guaranteed work in order to return them to their country of origin" on the basis of an agreement he had made with the governor-general of Algeria.[32] Local unions also seized on this vulnerability. When the dockworkers reorganized in March 1922, their new contract aimed to ensure that "long-time dockers, even Italians, and veterans must benefit from priority hiring over the workers who have arrived on the docks since the war, almost all, by the way, foreigners or Arabs."[33] Italians were not foreigners to the dockers' union, but Algerian French nationals may as well have been.

Despite such exclusions, the central government's goal of repatriating all North Africans proved unobtainable. In response, settler lobbies—still concerned about the ramifications that migration would have once "*indigènes*" returned to the colonies—now sought to project their moral vision to the metropole. Philanthropic associations such as the Assistance Committee for Algerian Natives, which was presided over by the president of the Algiers Chamber of Commerce, lobbied the chamber of commerce in Marseille to open a "foyer" there, to provide "*indigènes*" with

material and moral assistance, spare them the temptations of the big city, and prevent their fraternization [*promiscuité*] with the "civilian" population [*population civile*], by concentrating them in a location where they would find the leisure activities they are used to.[34]

After establishing a "foyer" in Marseille, the Assistance Committee turned its attention to Lyon, where, they argued, a "sizable and permanent block" of North Africans remained, even after the "evacuation of last winter."[35]

From the early 1920s, then, organizations such as the Assistance Committee for Algerian Natives advocated the extension of foyers throughout the metropole. They argued that such foyers would allow Algerians, as "they leave the factory or workshop, [to] find shelter in an environment [*cadre*] that includes a few familiar objects recalling Algeria and its particular customs a little bit." These shelters would therefore prevent them from being "tempted to contract habits of intemperance and debauchery."[36] Although the settler lobbies behind such committees claimed to have North Africans' well-being foremost in mind, they were also aware of the political ramifications of such assistance. As the preamble to their 1920 bylaws noted,

the moral state of these *indigènes* has repercussions on that of the Algerian population, either by the influence exercised by soldiers and workers as they returned to their tribes, or by their correspondence, or by the rumors [*échos*] carried in the course of the constant back-and-forth of workers between France and the Colony. In this regard, the question is not only a simple one of assistance; it also touches the indigenous policies for which the Governor General of Algeria is responsible.[37]

Since repatriation could never keep up with emigration from North Africa, especially as famine spread across Algeria in 1920 and 1921, demands increasingly came from the colonies for both emigration control and moral assistance for *"indigènes"* in the metropole.[38]

A PASSPORT BY ANY OTHER NAME . . .

Just as settlers had first taken the initiative on "assistance" to *"indigènes"* in the metropole, so too settler interests left their mark on intensified regulation of emigration from Morocco, Tunisia, and Algeria. In the spring of 1922, scores of Moroccans arrived in Marseille each day without valid labor contracts. In response, authorities in France and the protectorate collaborated to toughen visa standards. As of that summer, Moroccans could embark for France only if they were able to produce "references issued exclusively by the controlling authorities in their place of origin or in the locality or city in which they have lived for the past six months."[39] These references, in turn, would not be issued unless the migrant in question produced a contract stamped by a representative of the French Ministry of Labor.[40] Tunisians faced similar restrictions. Invoking the foreign status of Moroccans and Tunisians, the French Ministries of Foreign Affairs and the Interior sought to limit their migration in much the same way that the premier, Raymond Poincaré, concurrently tried to limit Armenian emigration: by enacting tougher visa standards.[41] Moroccans and Tunisians represented the minority of native North Africans in the metropole, however, and by mid-1923 the French government, faced with widespread complaints from the settler lobby, sought to limit the departure of Algerian French nationals as well.[42] Looking for a reason to limit Algerians' emigration, the Directorate of Algerian Affairs in the Interior Ministry polled local authorities in July 1923 regarding the adaptation of North Africans to metropolitan life.

Prefects, overall, responded with cautious optimism, but the reports they attached to their letters revealed widely ranging views.[43] Not surprisingly, those holding negative opinions made more forceful arguments. A precinct commissioner in the Lyon suburb of St-Fons reported, for example, that North Africans were "unclean, sometimes even repugnantly so," and were also "liars, pilferers" who "conduct[ed] their quarrels in a brutal, even bloody, fashion, which seems natural to them."[44] This vision of them as both dirty and violent was common. They constituted, according to the police commissioner from the Part-Dieu precinct in Lyon, both a "foyer of uncleanliness" and a "danger for public security," since "cutlasses, daggers, [and] razors are the offensive arms normally used" by them, "even without any provocation." What was more, he added, they were "lazy, sluggardly to an extreme, [and] they prowl the streets, day and night, always looking for some foul play." Many of them, he concluded, "evade control. In sum, the Algerian population of Lyon, almost all of which arrived from Marseille, constitutes, for an urban center like ours, a public-health and social danger and a constant threat to public safety."[45] The more nuanced view—that North Africans looked "for employment in vain" and thus wound up "arrested for vagrancy, which gives them a very bad impression of the French administration," or even the positive spin that "they know how to make do with very little, which is one of the reasons that their work is appreciated"[46]—apparently held less sway, for by April 1924, the government established an interministerial commission in order to study the means by which the migration of North Africans, and especially Algerians, could be limited.

The commission, which was presided over by the Interior Ministry's director of Algerian Affairs, included officials from the Ministries of Labor, Agriculture, the Interior, and Foreign Affairs, as well as a number of "colonial experts." These included Lavenarde, the general secretary of the Franco-Muslim Committee of North Africa, the same group that had advocated opening what it called "protective" organizations for North Africans in 1923.[47] After deliberating over the legality of subjecting Algerians to identification controls, the commission established what were, in everything but name, passport requirements for Algerians. Meeting only twice before issuing recommendations, the commission agreed to limit Algerian migration to the metropole.[48] On 8 August 1924, the interior minister, following the recommendations of the commission, issued a policy directive to the governor-general in Algeria, who in turn issued a circular to Algerian prefects on 15 September outlining the new prerequisites for migration to the metropole. As a result, Algerian French nationals, like Tunisian and Moroccan foreigners, would now have to produce state-approved labor contracts, medical certificates, and photo-identification papers before being authorized to embark for mainland France.[49]

Muslim general councilors in the Department of Algiers, an elected group with little real power, claimed that this new regulation was "against the law,"[50] and "eight hundred Kabyle notables" protested the "measures [taken to] quell [the] exodus of indigenous workers."[51] These complaints had little impact. Despite second thoughts raised within the commission itself, the new director of Algerian Affairs at the Interior Ministry insisted that the instructions "do not restrict the right to free circulation in principle." Rather, he asserted, they were meant to "shelter [colonial subjects] from the cruel disappointment and life of deprivation that awaits those who come to France without sufficient resources or without having insured ahead of time that they had a well-paying job."[52] Only a Council of State decision in June 1926 forced the administration to abandon the circular, on the grounds that it was illegal for a circular to abrogate a law; even this did not prevent its revival, in modified form, only two months later.[53] The newly required transportation documents, an Algiers court ruled, were the "juridical equivalent" of passports.[54]

The impact of the 1924 circular on Algerian migration to the metropole was enormous. Whereas in September 1924, 7,640 Algerians were officially recorded as having entered the metropole, the following month this number declined to 331. In November, 384 made the trip; in December, 603. In 1925, 46,275 fewer entries were recorded than had been in 1924.[55] Although new European entries for 1925 (at 176,261) were also down, their decline of about 26% was considerably less dramatic than the 65% decline in legal Algerian arrivals that the Ministry of Labor recorded.[56] Clandestine emigration soon sent numbers rising again. However, the new formal prerequisites for migration meant that Algerians who thwarted the system became illegal residents—not to say "illegal aliens"—in the metropole. For those not dissuaded by the obstacles to "emigration," special state-subsidized services would take up the relay, providing social assistance that catered to them especially or, failing that, helped to repatriate them.

SEPARATE AND UNEQUAL WELFARE

Unique circumstances in the French capital had created a colonial "consensus," bridging differences between convinced imperialists and liberal republicans in order to forge support to open the inaugural SAINA office in 1925.[57] By contrast, efforts to establish SAINA branches in Lyon and Marseille were plagued by a lack of consensus. About the only thing local officials in these cities could agree upon was that unemployed North Africans and communist politics were a dangerous combination. As we shall see, both Marseille and Lyon established SAINA offices in the wake of political agitation. But disagreements abounded over the nature of political surveillance that SAINA would conduct, over who would be responsible for social services such as job placement and unemployment assistance, and, most especially, on whom the burden of fiscal responsibility for services to North Africans would fall.

Pleased with SAINA's results in the capital, Interior Ministry officials soon turned their attention to Lyon, Marseille, Bordeaux, Lille (Nord), and St-Étienne (Loire), all cities with considerable numbers of North Africans and in which unemployment was growing. Interior Minister Albert Sarraut insisted that public health and security, as well as the interests of the migrants, required that action be taken to prevent North Africans from being "left to themselves to fall into a state of destitution, engendering the most serious consequences."[58] One of the consequences he no doubt feared was that social strife would play into the hands of the nationalist party the North African Star (L'Étoile Nord-Africaine, ENA), established in Paris by Messali Hadj in 1926 with the express purpose of fighting for Algerian independence.

Although the Bouches-du-Rhône department formed a Marseille SAINA in 1928, for the next decade it suffered from underfunding and an unclear mandate. Meanwhile, in Lyon, fiscal disputes delayed the opening of a public SAINA until 1934. Fundamental disagreements remained, however, and they continued to color how the Lyon office functioned from then on—twice changing the nature of the services it provided and, ultimately, diluting their substance. In both Marseille and Lyon, political dissent among North Africans triggered the opening of the SAINA offices. In both cities, as well, North Africans' lack of political clout and local officials' lack of political accountability conspired to limit the social services available to these migrants from the French empire.

Those spearheading the SAINA initiative may have hoped that it could serve as a metropolitan "Arab Bureau." Arab bureaus were offices established by Maréchal Bugeaud as part of the pacification plans after the 1830 invasion of Algeria. Run by army officers, the bureaus were supposed to serve as intermediaries between the colonial military authority and the indigenous population. Their duties included providing colonial authorities information on the native Algerians' "state of mind" and resolving problems that the indigenous population might face. They served as interpreters, assisted with payment of taxes, ran public works projects, registered property, policed, settled disputes, rendered justice, and prepared for the intervention of troops.[59] Like Arab bureaus, the SAINA would act as a clearinghouse for all the administrative, legal, employment, medical, and assistance needs that North Africans might have. And, like the bureaus, they would be run by people "familiar" with indigenous life, usually former colonial administrators.

The trouble was that for all that settlers insisted that Algeria was part of France, the metropole was not Algeria. SAINA offices were not military establishments in colonial hinterlands serving as the sole source of colonial authority for miles around. Their budgets had to be voted by departmental councils and they competed for funds with other social services directly serving council constituents. Without the vote, North Africans were subjects, not citizens.

Recognizing the limits of local budgets, the Interior Ministry had suggested that new SAINA offices could—as in Paris—draw on money coming from the home "countries" of the "*indigènes*." In addition, they could attract contributions from surrounding departments and municipalities where concentrations of North Africans did not justify a separate office. Further subsidies would be provided by the Interior Ministry. To sweeten the deal, Sarraut virtually promised that "a noticeable decline in persons registered for unemployment assistance will, as in Paris, undoubtedly follow."[60] Local representatives in the Rhône remained unconvinced. In the fall of 1927, its departmental council rejected both a proposal to fund a local SAINA and the Loire prefect's request that the Rhône department subsidize the SAINA formed 60 kilometers away in St-Étienne.[61]

Rhône officials may have taken solace in the fact that, at least in Lyon, the CGTU reported having trouble organizing colonial workers.[62] The same could not be said of Marseille. In 1927, the Marseille branch of the Communist Party began demanding equal salaries, unemployment benefits, the right to organize, the eight-hour day, and freedom of circulation between colonies and metropole for North Africans.[63] The Communist Party's organizing efforts among migrants elicited concern from both the Interior Ministry and the Marseille special police; their worries were only augmented by the discovery that Arab nationalist newspapers, published in Paris, were distributed to Algeria via ships leaving Marseille.[64] Added to political concerns were a number of scandals surrounding North African migration to the port city. Since 1925, authorities had contended with labor contract counterfeiting rings, a fraudulent identification papers racket in which one of their own police commissioners was implicated, and the tragic deaths of five clandestine Moroccan migrants on one ship and 11 on another, as they stowed away in the coal bunkers, where temperatures reached as high as 70 degrees Centigrade (158 degrees Fahrenheit).[65]

Without such pressing concerns, Rhône officials continued to balk at the requests from the Interior Ministry and private associations to fund a local SAINA.[66] If anything, some of these appeals backfired. For instance, the pastor Émile Brès' energetic pleas on behalf of his Lyonnese Association for Aid to Immigrants and North African Workers, in which he alluded to the Paris SAINA's 4.1-million-franc budget and its plans to create a hospital costing 12 million francs, may have done more to frighten representatives from the Rhône than it did to convince them of the need to fund his cause.[67] At an April 1929 meeting, they voted to table the request, pending "a complete estimate" of the costs.[68]

Preferring not to take responsibility for special services to North Africans in Lyon, Rhône public officials let private organizations take the initiative instead. The idiosyncratic Julien Azario, a police clerk in Lyon's seventh arrondissement hall and a former colonial settler who was fluent in Arabic,[69] eagerly took the lead in transforming his Committee for the Protection of North African Workers into a "BUREAU Arabe Officiel."[70]

Operating this private organization out of a public building, Azario gave his activities the veneer of official approbation as he set about instituting "controls" of North African eating and drinking establishments, where, he suspected, nationalist and communist propaganda were circulated.[71] He also encouraged employers to dismiss people he viewed as troublemakers in the North African community, and apparently even had a hand in securing repatriations.[72] As a clerk in Lyon's seventh arrondissement, a district with a high concentration of North Africans, he had already begun providing his brand of special assistance some years before. The most spectacular of his endeavors occurred when, in 1926, more than 150 Algerians were transported from Lyon to jobs awaiting them, they thought, in Corsica. When their ship never stopped in Corsica and was instead diverted to Algeria, the Bône police commissioner noted that "the first impression given by these men at the moment of disembarkation was that they were extremely unhappy to find themselves back in Algeria (some very far from their homes), when they had left Lyon convinced that they were being taken to Corsica, where well-paying jobs awaited them."[73] Many of these men complained of their "expulsion," which they saw as especially unfair because "numerous 'foreigners' were allowed to remain" in France.[74]

Even before the Corsica incident, the Rhône prefect, Charles Vallette, was aware that Azario "had the reputation of liking commotion and of engaging in sometimes ill-thought-out maneuvers."[75] Yet it was not until 1934, when a scandal erupted in the wake of Azario's union-busting techniques, that a new prefect, Émile Bollaert, moved to take over the service.[76] The publicly funded SAINA that emerged nevertheless bore the imprint of this renegade clerk, and it never completely abandoned his repressive approach to managing the North African population of Lyon.

Azario had made political policing and the administration of social services part of the same process. An enemy of communism and syndicalism, he placed North Africans in jobs only after he had screened them for their political leanings; he also encouraged employers to fire migrants on his blacklist and to hire only those approved by him. In the summer of 1934, however, Azario's tactics proved better at creating friction than averting it. Conflict erupted when, in early August, Azario referred 19 Algerian workers to the Versillé construction company, which had the contract for channeling the city of Lyon's water supply. Work on the company's site had been disrupted since 24 July by the excavators' union, which insisted on a minimum wage of 6.75 francs per hour. When a new crew was hired at a lower wage, the union's action committee dispatched 30 members and successfully forced the work to stop.

Versillé, in search of workers who would accept wages below the union standard, turned to Azario, who readily obliged. At the end of the Algerians' first day on the site, they found union members waiting for them a short distance away. A fight broke out, and, according to Azario, the Algerians defended themselves with a revolver and knives. One union member was killed, and there was a critical injury on each side. The department's union conglomerate accused Versillé of having armed the North Africans, with Azario's complicity; the left-wing press, meanwhile, noted that at least part of the problem stemmed from a lack of rights among the North Africans, who should not have felt forced to work below the prevailing wage.[77] After the incident, Azario reported that other companies no longer accepted Algerians for fear of similar conflicts. This did not prevent him from referring Algerians to "Vesillet" [*sic*] again in October. In response, the excavators' union naturally mobilized to defend its wage; due to union pressure, the foreman dismissed the Algerians.[78]

Within days of the August 1934 incident, the Lyon branch of Messali Hadj's ENA drew record numbers to meetings held by its affiliate, the Association of Algerian Workers. Tracts circulated that accused Azario of exploiting the "destitution and deprivation of our compatriots" by enrolling them in jobs as strikebreakers. Reminding readers that it was Azario who "hired you to work in Corsica in 1926 . . . and who instead traitorously sent you to Algeria," the association went on to demand that Azario's office be closed, that Arabs be eligible for the public works projects instituted since the onset of the depression, that Algerian workers receive family allowances even if their families remained in the colony, and that they be guaranteed political and union rights, freedom of association and speech.[79]

The prefect satisfied one of these demands. He closed Azario's office. Citing the recent "excitability" (*effervescence*) of the some 10,000 North Africans in his department, Bollaert announced that he would assume responsibility for the SAINA "on a trial basis."[80] Operations moved out of the seventh arrondissement hall and into a building a few blocks away.[81] But, probably lacking other personnel fluent in Arabic, Bollaert proceeded to hire Azario as a SAINA clerk—ostensibly without decision-making powers, effectively as its director.[82] Azario's tactics, including his unpopular political policing, thus became state-sponsored practices once his private committee was folded into the SAINA.[83]

By taking this initiative, Bollaert fulfilled Herriot's wish that responsibility for special services to the North African population not fall to his municipality; some years earlier, Herriot had argued that it would be easier to "send home" the North Africans who were in need of aid.[84] Herriot's reluctance to shoulder any of the fiscal burdens for such an endeavor had been part of the reason that services remained private. But so too had the departmental council's insistence, as it rejected another request from the Interior Ministry to open a SAINA office in the Rhône, that responsibility for "assistance to North African *indigènes* lies with the state" and not local government.[85] Communication between the prefecture and the Interior Ministry suggests that Rhône officials maintained this outlook even after the SAINA opened.[86]

For a little more than two years, the Lyon SAINA secured jobs for North Africans with Lyon-area companies, albeit often below union rates.[87] In its first year of operation, the SAINA reported finding work for more than 2,000 North African residents of the Lyon area.[88] When out-of-work North Africans were eligible for unemployment compensation, SAINA officials worked with local municipalities to ensure that they received it. Since their migration was often seasonal, however, North Africans frequently had trouble meeting residency requirements for welfare. In such cases, SAINA initially helped get them indigent aid, usually food stamps.[89] During the same period, repatriations were de-emphasized.

As the depression continued to take its toll on public assistance budgets, however, these trends were reversed: Placements became almost nonexistent and repatriations skyrocketed. Aid to the unemployed was also significantly altered. Referrals for cash unemployment indemnities, even for those meeting residency requirements, became increasingly rare. Food stamps were discontinued and a special soup kitchen for the exclusive use of North Africans was opened instead. After a few months, even the new soup kitchen cut back on the number of meals it provided.

To be sure, Muslim French subjects were not the only ones to suffer from depression-era cutbacks in aid. Herriot had long sought ways to cut his city's welfare clients, alternately targeting foreigners from nonreciprocity states, the homeless, and single indigent men for reduced municipal aid or no aid altogether.[90] The depression also ultimately brought a number of Socialist municipalities that had abandoned eligibility requirements based on nationality to reinstitute restrictions on unemployment compensation and other forms of aid.[91]

Nonetheless, even without formal citizenship, many European foreigners were better represented politically than were North Africans. The

Ministry of Foreign Affairs' archives are filled with dispatches from countries such as Italy and Spain, where embassy officials reported with concern on the way that treatment of emigrants to France was covered in their respective presses.[92] While such reports did not guarantee good treatment of most-favored foreigners, at the very least they engendered immediate inquiries and resulted in prompt reports back to the embassies. North Africans did not earn the same consideration as Europeans in the metropole in part because it was the French government that claimed to represent their interests "abroad."

By contrast to complaints from Europeans, demands by the ENA's Committee for Unemployed Arabs to obtain full access to allocations, including payments for dependents living in North Africa, were dismissed as political extremism.[93] This was hardly to be unexpected. The French government had dissolved the ENA in 1929, following its attempt to incite revolt against colonial rule, only to witness it reconstitute itself in 1933. During the spring of 1935, French authorities watched with alarm as a resurgent ENA held 44 public meetings in Paris over the course of just four months.[94] Reactions to their mobilization in Lyon must be read against this backdrop.

Trying to undercut ENA politics, the Lyon SAINA did make an effort to improve job placements of North Africans. Placements remained steady through 1935 and 1936. But they could not keep pace with the depression. In March 1935, the SAINA succeeded in placing 201 North Africans in jobs but delivered a substantially higher 760 food stamps. In May, dispersals of food stamps reached a monthly total of about 2,400, whereas job placements were almost one-tenth this figure. By January 1936, placements had declined to 61, but food stamp allocations soared to 11,652. Although these numbers declined in the two subsequent months, they reached a new high of 15,304 in March 1936.[95] That, of course, did not mean some 15,000 claimants but rather the distribution of several hundred food stamps a day.

SAINA officials defended the expenditures, noting that food stamps were cheaper than unemployment indemnities.[96] Valued at 1.5 francs, the food stamps were a clear savings over the 8 francs per day granted to heads of household, the 4.5 francs granted to their unemployed spouses, and the 4 francs for each dependent under the age of 16 that were required by the unemployment regulations prevailing in Lyon.[97] Nevertheless, by June 1936, Herriot wanted to know how the city could be "relieved [*dégagée*] of its obligations with respect to Arabs."[98] Later that same year, he announced that he would cease authorizing food stamps for North Africans altogether.[99]

In response to this crisis, leadership of the SAINA—now renamed the North African Center (Centre Nord-Africain, CNA)—was assumed by the Departmental and Municipal Placement Office. With this reorganization, Julien Azario's methods were deemed "incompatible" with rational and disciplined administration, and he was dismissed.[100] Food stamps having been discontinued in Lyon, the CNA reopened with a soup kitchen that offered registered North Africans two meals a day. On opening day, 131 North Africans registered for services. By the end of January 1937, the service fed about 300 people twice a day. Yet financial problems were becoming, as before, an obstacle to the CNA's operation. In March, with 779 North Africans enrolled in the program, the second meal was discontinued "in order to prevent North Africans, well nourished at the noon meal, from bringing food back in the evening to distribute among their Comrades who, neither registered nor receiving assistance, can thereby prolong their stay in the Lyon area where nothing suggests that one will be able to employ them."[101] Thus the new CNA not only removed North Africans from the social services supplied to others, French and foreign; it also prevented them from making their own decisions regarding what to do with the food that they were provided. Responding to complaints that ensued from this decision, the CNA's administrators offered another reason: The evening meal was discontinued because "North Africans, for whom the typical meal is not as hearty and varied as that provided by the CNA, appeared to content themselves with this diet rather than return to their regions of origin."[102] Within six months of its reorganization, the CNA ceased providing any food at all, its funds depleted.[103] Requests for funds from the capital to keep the soup kitchen open were accommodated only after it closed.

The CNA proved more adept at repatriating North Africans than it had been in feeding them. Indeed, despite its initial pretensions as an assistance program, the CNA spent as much time repatriating North Africans as it did finding jobs for them or securing the unemployment compensation to which at least some of them were entitled. By the end of its first month of operation in its new facility, January 1937, the Lyon SAINA office had repatriated 55 people. On 17 March, center officials reported that "repatriation continues to be pushed," and indeed, some 133 had been repatriated, while 44 had been placed in agricultural jobs on the other side of France. Once meals were discontinued, repatriations accelerated. Between the end of July and the beginning of December 1937, 109 placements were recorded, while total repatriations reached 624. By 30 April of the following year— probably the halo effect of a February 1938 circular ordering local authorities to include North Africans in their social assistance programs—the CNA finally began placing a number of North Africans on unemployment compensation: a total of 32 since the office opened 16 months earlier. More tellingly, by the end of September 1938, they succeeded in repatriating 1,362, or about 34% of those registered, whereas they placed only 205, or

5%, on unemployment. From April to September 1938, the CNA made one job placement.[104]

By screening access to unemployment assistance, the CNA exacerbated North Africans' desperation, leading them to "volunteer" for repatriation. At the same time, local authorities authorized a considerable number of European foreigners to take vacations in their native countries and be assured legal reentry into France. Between 1 June 1937 and 1 March 1939, 2,163 such "recall letters" (*lettres de rappel*) were issued to European foreigners, of whom the majority were Italian. Meanwhile, between June 1937 and October 1938, Lyon authorities issued half-subsidized repatriation vouchers to a total of 27 Europeans.[105] By contrast, repatriations of North Africans had risen to 1,701 by March 1939.[106] This difference in treatment mirrored the concomitant shift in French migration policy more generally toward distinguishing between immigrants and migrants. Repatriation helped ensure that North Africans would remain migrants, while reentry authorizations helped Europeans increase their chances of becoming immigrants.

Unlike the SAINA office that opened in 1934, the reorganized CNA clearly focused more energy on repatriation than on social assistance. As if to confirm this, mutual aid societies such as the North African Muslim Workers' Aid Fund sprung up after the CNA discontinued its evening meal in March 1937.[107] At the same time, more European migrant groups gained a legal right to welfare provisions. Spaniards, who had complained of their exclusion from social assistance in the early 1930s, could no longer be refused after the December 1933 ratification of a reciprocity treaty between France and Spain. Similarly, in the fall of 1936, France finally ratified the 1933 Geneva Convention. This meant that, in principle, Russian and Armenian refugees, or any other refugees with Nansen passports, were included among the beneficiaries of local welfare programs.[108]

As other migrant groups were increasingly invited to take part in France's burgeoning social citizenship, North Africans were progressively excluded from it. In theory, Algerians, as French nationals, had a statutory right to assistance.[109] But when municipalities such as Lyon faced budget constraints, political expediency trumped nationality. The first evidence of this was the replacement of food stamps by the cheaper and easier-to-control soup kitchen in January 1937. A reduction from two meals to one per day quickly followed. This was a politics not of entitlement but of bare subsistence. Once meals were discontinued, it was not even that. The logic of this policy was reminiscent of the "less eligibility" principle behind English bans on outdoor relief in the nineteenth century—only here French authorities were not trying to encourage migration in search of work but rather repatriation to a land where jobs were also scarce.[110]

The Popular Front government did not directly order any of these repatriations, but its wavering on North African rights certainly did nothing to discourage them. North Africans initially welcomed the arrival of the Popular Front in power. In July 1936, shortly after taking office, the government issued a decree discontinuing restrictions from 1928 that required Algerian migrants to pay a repatriation deposit and clear other administrative hurdles prior to coming to the metropole. But North Africans quickly felt abandoned when the government yielded to settler pressure and reinstituted the identification card requirement in October. By December, it had restored the requirement of a repatriation deposit.[111]

With this signal coming from the capital, it is hardly surprising that Lyon's CNA began putting those repatriation deposits to use in January 1937, particularly as its requests for a larger assistance budget from the Interior Ministry generated no response until it was too late. Facing opposition to the use of local funds for North African assistance on the one hand, and inadequate subsidies from the central government on the other, officials in Lyon made decisions that effectively created a parallel and unequal system of welfare provision and job placement alongside that benefiting the metropolitan French and many European immigrants. There were occasional exceptions. The head of the Morocco office in the Lyon Chamber of Commerce somehow convinced the city of Décines to include Moroccans on its unemployment rolls.[112] Small towns such as St-Rambert-l'Ile-Barbe, in a semirural area just north of Lyon, seem to have been able to afford to treat all migrant residents as entitled to the same services.[113] And some Socialist and Communist municipalities probably, at times, made an effort to protect North Africans from abuse by the SAINA.[114] Even considering such exceptions, however, no other migrant group in the Rhône department suffered the same degree of systematic discrimination with regard to welfare rights as did North Africans. Nor was any other group repatriated at the same rate.

Whereas budget constraints led to a politics of retrenchment in Lyon, in Marseille they appear to have prevented the SAINA from taking much independent initiative at all. The original funds voted for the service by the Bouches-du-Rhône departmental council were allowed to lapse before the SAINA even opened. The lease on the housing facility for North Africans, which the SAINA assumed from the Assistance Committee for North African Natives, a settler association, was allowed to expire. The reassignment of ten officers from Marseille's *police d'état* to North African surveillance ushered in few practical changes to policing methods. And throughout its existence, Marseille's SAINA operated on a shoestring budget, never with more than three paid employees, in a small space that lacked heat and adequate office supplies.

The exact nature of early SAINA initiatives in Marseille is difficult to discern, given that virtually no records remain from the administration of its first director, Jean Zannetacci-Stephanopoli, a former administrator of a *commune mixte* in Algeria and director of the Marseille SAINA from 1928 until 1935.[115] From retrospective reports written after his departure, however, it is possible to reconstruct a reasonable picture of early Marseille SAINA operations. As with the first years of the public Lyon SAINA, the Marseille SAINA acted primarily as a liaison between North Africans and existing social services; it did not seek to serve as their substitute.

Unlike in Lyon, however, there is no indication that the Marseille SAINA developed the extensive preemployment political screening that first Azario and then the Lyon SAINA adopted. This may have been due to the nature of work in Marseille, where people often were hired for the half day, day, week, or month, usually without any contract. Comprehensive political screening hardly made much sense in a casual labor market. Nonetheless, in a city where the percentage of North Africans working as "indeterminate day laborers" had increased from 23% in 1911 to 36.2% in 1926, one of the hopes for the new SAINA office was that it might have better luck helping to refer North Africans to stable jobs. But the SAINA was faced with the fact that North African workers often had few skills, which made them especially susceptible to the rapid labor turnover that the Marseille economy favored. That the SAINA was unable to fight these obstacles is reflected in the high rate with which North Africans worked as "indeterminate day laborers" in 1931 and 1936: 64% and 60%, respectively.[116]

Even had the Marseille economy been structured differently, the resources placed at the SAINA's disposal limited the initiatives it could undertake. Its statutes provided for a small staff: one director, a clerk, a residence manager (discontinued with the expiration of the lease on the residence), a stenographer-typist, and a *"châouch."*[117] In fact, however, the Marseille office was always plagued by funding issues, and it never achieved even the modest staffing levels planned for it. When Jean Zannetacci-Stephanopoli ceased functioning as director in 1935, his assistant, a Monsieur Poussardin, became acting director. Serving as his own clerk, Poussardin never succeeded in filling his former position. For the next two years, Poussardin and Mohamed Ben Hadj, the *châouch indigène,* were SAINA's sole employees. This changed only when the position of typist, which had been discontinued in 1934, was reauthorized in 1938[118]—an improvement, to be sure, but the office still was housed in two small rooms with no waiting room and no heater. Filing cabinets were reportedly insufficient, and papers were piled on the floor.

Marseille's SAINA now had a typist, but its sole typewriter worked only intermittently.[119]

Judging from reports on its budget, the Marseille SAINA must never have undertaken surveillance and assistance programs on the level that its counterpart in Lyon had. As of 1938, the annual budget included 9,200 francs per year in rent, 29,736 in salaries, and 5,200 in office expenses, for a total of 44,136 francs per year.[120] Most notably, the budget lacked any mention of food stamps, soup kitchens, or other tangible forms of assistance. This contrasts to Lyon, where soup kitchen meals alone had cost the service almost 33,000 francs between early January and mid-March 1937.[121] Poussardin's reports on Marseille, rather, highlighted four categories of service provided: identification cards, complaints, repatriations, and miscellanea (*affaires diverses*).

With the exception of assuming responsibility for issuing identification cards to North Africans, the Marseille SAINA never tried to take on duties that could be performed by other branches of the local administration. And yet local administrations came to expect it to do just that. Its acting director complained bitterly about the trend to turn away North Africans, noting that it served the purposes of propagandists whose main line of argument was, "French subjects . . . you are treated as foreigners, although you went to war for France." Faced with what he characterized as the "extraordinary" ignorance of local administrations, Poussardin claimed that he frequently had to intervene in order to educate other branches of the French bureaucracy of their obligation to serve North Africans.[122] Yet, in the end, Poussardin's success in returning migrants to North Africa may have been a sign of what he could not accomplish in the metropole. When all else fails, as the Lyon SAINA also had come to conclude, repatriate. Repatriations from Marseille increased by more than 2600% between 1936 and 1937, the year they peaked.[123]

The higher rate of increase in repatriations from Marseille when compared to Lyon no doubt was due in part to the larger size of the North African population in the port city. But might it also have reflected that Marseille's SAINA was even less successful than Lyon's in garnering local and national support for assistance to North Africans? Certainly the two services had very different leadership. The SAINA directors in Lyon, especially but not exclusively Azario, welcomed—even sought—control over every aspect of North African affairs in that city. Signing his letters as the "chargé" of the North Africans, rather than as the director of the service designed to aid them, and frequently using the possessive adjective "our" in reference to the "natives" upon whom he was reporting, Azario clearly relished the sense of power the job accorded him. His hunger for power was not lost on the politicized elements in the North African population, whose tracts regularly derided Azario or his staff as a "Grrreat Qa'id," a "bandit," or "Hitler rivals [*émules*]."[124] Poussardin could not have been more different. Although he did not shy away from flaunting his "knowledge of Maghrebi Arabic, Egyptian, Syrian and Turkish, Berber and Arabo-berber dialects and expressions, of Persian even," which helped him to confront "all the questions that *indigènes* and Muslims might present,"[125] he actually begged, repeatedly, to share his responsibility with someone else. If anything, Poussardin's continuous appeals demonstrated the limits of his power; like those of the North Africans he sought to represent, his claims went unanswered. Azario, on the other hand—despite all his faults—had succeeded in defining the parameters of SAINA practices in Lyon for several years.[126]

Bollaert had dismissed Azario in May 1936 because he was too independent. But in assuming departmental responsibility for the SAINA without political support for doing so, Bollaert encountered other problems. Elected officials in the Lyon region had repeatedly expressed their conviction that responsibility for North Africans fell to central, not local, authorities. Skyrocketing expenditures for social services in the 1930s only reaffirmed their approach. When the budget of Lyon's CNA was nearly depleted in the spring of 1937, its director did not even bother to ask local authorities for help: Once the CNA agreed to substitute a soup kitchen for municipally administered food stamps, it became politically impossible to ask municipalities to resume the duty of providing social welfare benefits to North Africans. The director instead wrote, then cabled, the Interior Ministry that without immediate assistance the soup kitchen would have to close.[127] Assistance came, three months after meals had been discontinued.[128] The soup kitchen did not reopen.

Similarly, Poussardin's multiple pleas to increase funding for the Marseille SAINA went unanswered. Despite his requests to increase his staff and space, not to mention funds to institute some assistance with meals, the Bouches-du-Rhône departmental council voted SAINA only a single credit during Poussardin's tenure: 15,000 francs in 1939 to reorganize the service, with the caveat that the credit would be for one year only since "the operating expenses of this service should logically fall to Algeria's government general."[129] As we shall see in the following chapter, the timing of this credit probably had more to do with new expectations that SAINA offices serve as military screening centers than it did with Poussardin's own objectives. In both Lyon and Marseille, budget votes betrayed the priorities of local administrations: They showed whom officials regarded as constituents and clients, and whose aid they deemed politically dispensable.

On the surface, the repatriation drives of the late 1930s looked like a return to the practices of the immediate postwar period. But there was a crucial difference. This time, the repatriations were not ordered by any central state authority, nor did they fulfill any official policy. To the contrary, they resulted from decisions made by local authorities regarding the provision of social welfare within their jurisdictions. Significantly, officials in both Lyon and Marseille viewed North Africans as singularly different from other migrants. Despite free circulation laws, despite admonitions that Algerians were "French nationals," local authorities in France's second- and third-largest cities refused to regard North Africans as their responsibility. In essence, repatriations were an extreme form of disqualifying claimants from local welfare rolls.

REFORM AND REACTION

At the same time that many municipalities in the metropole refused to regard North Africans as their charges, mayors in Algeria mobilized to make clear whom they represented. At their December 1936 congress, the mayors of Algerian cities voted 300 to 2 to oppose electoral reforms proposed by Blum's Socialist minister of state, the former governor-general Maurice Viollette. The proposal, known as the Blum-Viollette plan, would have allowed an elite set of "evolved" (*évolués*) Muslim Algerians to exercise the full rights of French citizenship, including the right to elect deputies to the National Assembly, without having to renounce their Islamic personal status.

Compared to demands made earlier that year by the first Algerian Muslim Congress (Congrès Musulman Algérien, CMA), the Blum-Viollette project was a modest proposal. The project proposed to give the vote to at most 25,000 male Algerians who were cultured in French and often sympathetic to maintaining a French Algeria, at a time when Muslims accounted for 6.2 million of Algeria's population of 7.1 million. The demands of the CMA were more sweeping. It brought together delegates from Algerian political parties, the Federation of Muslim Elected Officials (Fédération des Élus Musulmans, FEM), and the Algerian 'Ulamâ (bodies of Muslim theologians) in an extraordinary set of meetings opening on 7 June 1936 in Algiers. Taking inspiration from the victory of the Popular Front coalition, the president of the FEM, Mohamed Bendjelloul, and the president of the Association of Algerian 'Ulamâ, 'Abd al-Hamid Ben Badis, saw an opportunity to bridge differences between heteroclite Algerian reform movements. The CMA issued a "Charter of Demands," which called for an end to the "exceptional regime" applying in Algeria

and demanded equal social, civil, and political rights. Its biggest demand
was for political citizenship: It called for an end to special electoral col-
leges, the institution of universal male suffrage with no obligation to renounce Islamic personal status, representation in parliament, and full integration of Algerian departments and communes into the French political
system. In addition, the CMA wished to abolish the office of the governor-
general, the exceptional status of "mixed communes," and the onerous tax
and financial codes that applied only to Algeria. Among the social rights
called for were equal salaries for equal work, equal access to free education, and an extension of French welfare entitlements to Algeria. As far as
civil rights were concerned, the CMA demanded the suppression of the
code de l'indigénat, amnesty for political prisoners, and respect of religious rights.

Like the Popular Front, the CMA initially spawned mass sympathy
demonstrations: Tens of thousands demonstrated in Algiers, Oran, Con-
stantine, and other Algerian cities.[130] Also like the Popular Front, however, the coalition of these groups was difficult to sustain. When Bendjelloul and Ben Badis returned from a meeting with Blum and Viollette, they
found Messali Hadj before a crowd at the Algiers football stadium attacking the CMA for supporting assimilation rather than independence.

By the end of 1936, it was becoming clear that the CMA and the Popular Front's ideas of reform had diverged. Governor-General Georges Le
Beau already had succumbed to settler pressure by not implementing a
July 1936 decree that promised to restore free circulation between the
colony and the metropole, and the Popular Front government responded
to this by issuing a new decree reinstating the restrictions it had lifted in
July. These concessions to settlers, however, did not stem the tide of their
opposition to Popular Front reforms. The following year, parliamentary
commissions holding meetings in Algeria on the Blum-Viollette project
had to be protected from violent settler mobs. When the project made it
out of committee, Algeria's mayors resigned en masse, returning to their
posts only when the reforms were tabled.

The combination of reduced social rights and increased repatriations
of North Africans from Lyon and Marseille in the months of vehement
settler opposition to the Blum-Viollette project probably stemmed neither from direct settler pressure nor from any overt policy issued in the
capital. But it did reflect the extent to which authorities at all levels of
administration had given up on trying to equalize rights, even in the most
limited way, between natives of the Maghreb and the metropolitan
French. While social citizenship, according to T. H. Marshall, helped to
breed a "new common experience" extending beyond the material benefits accorded by the state to affect the "qualitative aspects of social differentiation," decisions in Lyon and Marseille reinforced the notion that

North Africans were not party to the French social contract, even as increasing numbers of foreign Europeans were.[131]

Although official distinctions between French and foreign remained, many of these formal differences were erased in the social realm, as more and more European foreigners shared with the metropolitan French the experience of receiving unemployment insurance in the course of the 1920s and 1930s. Meanwhile, although many North Africans were French nationals, when local budgets were strained, they often were the first to be eliminated from social welfare programs. In some cases, local administrations even went so far as to establish entirely separate benefits for North Africans. By creating a parallel assistance system, one based on restrictions rather than civil liberties and on subsistence (or removal) rather than entitlement, authorities established something of an "exceptional regime" in the metropole.

As with many domains of migrant rights, this outcome had emerged from the confluence of multiple factors: budgetary constraints on the local level, international—and in this case, imperial—pressures on the administration, and the limits of parliamentary coalitions, among others. Even within Blum's own government, there was discord on the issue of Algerian rights. Although Viollette defended his proposals in January 1937 on the grounds that "Algeria will remain French only if France maintains the loyalty of its Muslim population," four months later, the secretary of state for the Direction of Algerian Affairs (DAA) in the Interior Ministry, the prominent Radical Raoul Aubaud, countered that "if we want to preserve our position, we must show our authority . . . we must show our fist."[132] Radical Party support for reform was, at best, lukewarm in the metropole. In Algeria, it was nonexistent. Radical senator Pierre Roux-Freissineng from Oran encapsulated the settlers' view when he declared the reforms unacceptable because "sooner or later," they would place Europeans "under native domination."[133] Might the Radical Party's and the DAA's ambivalence about reform in part explain why the Interior Ministry waited until Lyon's CNA closed its soup kitchen and accelerated repatriations before it allocated the credits requested by the CNA to keep the soup kitchen open? Could this also be why Poussardin's pleas for a larger staff and better infrastructure went largely unanswered?

Like the *statut des immigrés*, the Blum-Viollette bill could not overcome the divisions of the Popular Front coalition. Advocates for the reform were disappointed that Blum did not simply expand the Algerian electorate by decree, as some had tried to convince him to do. After all, Algeria's Jews had been naturalized collectively in 1870 by decree. Scholars generally have concluded that Blum was too much of a constitutionalist to ponder using a decree to enact this reform. Of his coalition partners, the Communists had pulled back from their earlier position supporting colonial liberation movements, and the Radicals never really had supported the project. This, on top of the settlers' violent reactions, led Blum to let the proposal die without ever coming to a vote on the floor of parliament. If the system of "circular reasoning" that developed in the second half of the 1930s had created a privileged class of foreigners, it also had exacerbated the exclusion of North Africans.

The social, civil, and political rights of North Africans in the metropole were profoundly intertwined. Denied the right to renew their labor contracts after the First World War, pressured to accept substandard wages, and discouraged (at best) from claiming unemployment compensation when jobs—even at low wages—became scarce during the depression, North Africans could hardly be said to enjoy anything resembling social citizenship. This was connected to North Africans' lack of civil rights as well, for it was their lack of success in exercising their right to free circulation—that is, their right to stay in mainland France—that made denying them social rights so easy. The threat of repatriation made it hard to turn down scandalously low wages, even when it meant employment as strikebreakers, and particularly when—with few exceptions—no social safety net was there to catch unemployed North Africans. And with no political accountability to North Africans, local authorities found excluding them from welfare rights the simplest and most politic way to balance their budgets.

Local officials often knew that their austerity measures were of questionable legality. Yet when it came to North Africans in the metropole, legal principles proved fungible, as Herriot, Azario, and the members of the Bouches-du-Rhône departmental council—among others—privileged expediency over legality when they made decisions regarding social welfare entitlement. Then again, they had not been discouraged from this view by the highest authorities in the government. After all, Interior Minister Albert Sarraut had suggested, in 1927, that one advantage of instituting SAINA offices was the reduction they would bring in the numbers of North Africans on local unemployment rolls. Even those who did not initially see "*indigènes*" as exempt from local responsibility came to regard the central state as primarily responsible—hence Poussardin's appeals to the director of Algerian Affairs rather than to the prefect.

Of course, in some ways this was nothing new. After all, metropolitan women were French nationals but enjoyed neither political citizenship nor, for that matter, the same civil rights as men.[134] But North African migrants were almost exclusively male, and for men, nationality and citizenship were supposed to be one and the same under the republic. Colonial law recognized a distinction between citizenship and nationality—in the colonies.[135] The experience of North Africans in Lyon and Marseille in the 1920s and 1930s proved that this distinction had significance in the metropole as well.

Unlike civil rights, which democracies do not ordinarily prevent non-nationals from exercising, social welfare systems are usually understood as restrictive. By definition they cannot include any and all, and, most often, nationality is used as the demarcation line of entitlement.[136] Yet the story told here suggests that, at least until France eliminated local welfare programs and established a nationwide welfare state after the Second World War, "nationality" did not confer the same social or civil rights to all able to claim that moniker.[137] Only mobilization for war brought national and local authorities to reconsider the exclusion of North Africans, potential soldiers, from social assistance in the metropole. Even then, as the next chapter illustrates, North Africans gained access to the rights of French citizens not so much because of the claims they could make on the French state but because France, unilaterally, made claims on them.

CHAPTER SEVEN

The Insecurity State

Migrant Rights and the Threat of War

Every day we search, we round up, we purge; our prisons can testify to this.[1]

During the nearly two years that the Popular Front had governed France, two imperatives had affected the government's approach to foreign policy. One was the objective of avoiding war at almost any cost; the other was the need to prepare for war in the event it broke out. Both had affected the coalition's alliances, its stance toward intervention in the Spanish Civil War, its openness toward refugees, and its reaction to settler opposition over proposed reforms in Algeria. It had been difficult for the Popular Front to balance these concerns against its domestic social agenda. The fact that the coalition partners were deeply divided on many of these issues had rendered governing especially difficult, as had the readiness of the opposition to exploit those divisions.

After the Popular Front collapsed in the spring of 1938, a new premier, Édouard Daladier, set the tone for the new government by declaring in his first speech to parliament that "all financial, economic, social and political problems are narrowly linked with the problem of our security."[2] Convinced of this, Daladier readily resorted to decree-laws. The Popular Front government had been reluctant to use decree-laws, and when it tried to resort to them, the result had been disastrous.[3] Migration clearly qualified as a social issue that Daladier linked to the country's security. In the same speech before parliament, he noted that France would "not permit foreign influences, unrest caused by undesirable foreigners, to interfere with the entire liberty of its decisions."[4] Within a month of assuming office, he issued two sweeping directives aimed at controlling immigration, the decrees of 2 and 14 May 1938.

Daladier's reliance on decrees has long been controversial. For some, he used them to save the republic. For others, he showed an authoritarian streak that presaged Vichy. Julian Jackson captures this ambiguity by using the term "authoritarian republic" to describe the Third Republic under Daladier.[5] It is of course impossible to know what might have transpired if Daladier had consulted parliament more readily. What seems clear, however, is that at least as far as immigration policy was concerned, the urgency with which it was addressed by Daladier and his cabinet generated new crises, which in turn required their own urgent solutions.

By attempting to codify the boundaries of rights through decrees, Daladier's government changed the relationship between migrants and the state, but not as originally anticipated. The decree-laws triggered highly visible attacks on migrants' civil liberties in both Lyon and Marseille, though officials in the latter, perhaps still avenging the reputation they had gained as a result of the 1934 assassination, sustained this zeal much longer. In both cities, repression flattened the distinctions among foreigners that had affected their rights over the previous few years. No foreigner, no matter how extensive his or her investment in France, was entirely safe from this new dragnet.

In many ways, the crackdown on migrants that began in mid-1938 typified what had emerged as France's approach to immigration policy: improvisation followed by fine-tuning after the fact. There was, after all, nothing new about a gap between policy development and implementation. Throughout the 1920s and 1930s, central state authorities had established policies, often without consulting parliament, and then relied on local authorities to execute them. When local practices diverged from the intentions of the central government, or when difficulties emerged with implementation, new policies were issued to modify the old. But the cycle through which equilibrium previously had been reached between policy and practice was now accelerated to such a degree that, for all intents and purposes, there was no equilibrium. This crisis mode of governing in many ways paralyzed the state.

In particular, new security pressures produced contradictory effects. Central state authorities endeavored not only to preserve peace but to prepare for war. Inasmuch as foreigners were perceived to pose a security risk as suspected spies, members of a fifth column, or deliberate warmongers, controlling the arrival of migrants or encouraging their removal aimed to keep the peace. Those preparing for war, on the other hand, did not entertain the question of migrants' threat to peace so much as their potential contribution to winning a war should one break out. War planners conscripted some of the same people whom the May decrees aimed to exclude. At the central government level, these two security imperatives emerged from different policy arenas. At the local level, however, they collided. No sooner had police officers rounded up foreigners in the wake of the May decrees than they faced recriminations from the capital that the repression had been too indiscriminate. Before expelling or incarcerating aliens, they now were ordered to take into consideration the military service that these foreigners might be able to provide. The same local authorities who issued expulsion orders also were called upon to rescind them in order that young men might be conscripted.

French obsessions with keeping the peace affected refugees the most. They were the principal targets of the 2 May decree, which had aimed to stem the arrival of new refugees and encourage the departure of those already there. The first migrants to be affected by the war-preparedness imperative, on the other hand, were North Africans. Ironically, after suffering a massive repatriation drive undertaken by local leaders during the Popular Front, North Africans now found that their strategic importance as soldiers gave them new rights in the metropole. In an effort to sustain North Africans in mainland France, local authorities finally began to include them in the social welfare programs from which colonial subjects often had been excluded earlier in the 1930s. When war was declared, North Africans were barred from leaving mainland France until their military status had been verified. While these reversals did not exactly amount to recognition of their civil liberties—instead of being pressured to leave they were now being forced to stay—it did protect them from the lengthy incarcerations to which many foreign migrants were now subjected.

North Africans were not the only migrants who "benefited" from the pressures that the war-preparedness imperative produced. Young, unmarried men, whose rights had proved particularly fragile during the depression, again became the privileged beneficiaries of certain types of rights. As potential soldiers, their expulsions were reversed and requests for naturalization were accelerated. Here, too, however, much depended on geopolitics and the judgment of local authorities. Although the war's outbreak did finally shift officials' focus from preserving the peace to mobilizing for war, the French entered the Second World War not certain, especially with regard to migrants, of who was on their side. The question of whether migrants posed a threat to national security or were vital to its protection remained unresolved when France fell to the Nazis in June 1940.

WAR OR PEACE

Daladier had formed his first government the day after Hitler came to power in 1933. This time, in April 1938, Daladier arrived on the scene after the Blum and Chautemps governments had failed, a month after Germany had annexed Austria, and in the wake of newly anti-Semitic legislation promulgated in Hungary, Poland, and Romania. The month he became premier, a new wave of boycotts against Jews began in Germany, and a Nazi decree required Jews to submit inventories of all property valued over 5,000 reichsmarks.[6] All these factors helped to set off a new wave of refugees and discouraged those refugees already in France from returning home. This would have been a delicate situation in any context, but at a time when French leaders were actively seeking a nonaggression agreement with Germany, the massive influx of refugees from German lands also interfered with France's security strategy.

Not only was France's role as protector of Nazism's enemies a potential stumbling block for negotiations with Hitler, but authorities also believed that refugees presented other security problems. There was always a vague fear that refugees might not have completely lost their loyalty to their home state or that, since so many of them traveled under false names or with forged identification cards, they might be spies. For all these reasons, Daladier wished to appear resolute. It was probably this desire that led him to make immigration regulation one of the chief areas he sought to reform through decree-laws. The 2 May 1938 decree authorized sweeping identification card checks, heightened surveillance of foreigners, stiffened punishments for illegal residence in the country, and instituted severe sentences for evading expulsion orders. This led to an unprecedented crackdown on migrants' civil liberties throughout France.

In the preamble to the 2 May decree, Sarraut, Daladier's interior minister, distinguished foreigners "whose conduct is irreproachable" and whose "attitude toward the republic and its institutions has been absolutely correct" from those "'clandestine' foreigners" or "irregular guests" who were "not worthy of our hospitality."[7] The decree required that foreigners carry identification at all times and specified that the following persons would be subject to punishment of one month to one year in prison and fined from 100 to 1,000 francs: foreigners who entered France illegally, those who failed to request an identification card, and any person who provided direct or indirect aid to someone entering or living illegally in France. It further specified that all persons lodging foreigners as employees, tenants, or even guests were required to declare this to the local police commissioner within 48 hours of their arrival or face fines. Foreigners also had to notify authorities if they changed addresses, even if they moved within the same city.[8] In an attempt to make expulsions more effective, the decree mandated a minimum sentence of six months to three years for any infraction of an expulsion order, and required that those arrested on this charge be escorted to the border after serving their sentence.

It gave foreigners in an "irregular situation" less than a month to apply for regularization; after 31 May they would be prosecuted if they fell into any of the above categories.

The newly strict stance on illegal aliens was backed up by changes in budget allocations. On the same day as the decree, Daladier declared in a report to the president that "not a day must be lost" in reorganizing the police to allow the 2 May decree to be implemented effectively. That report served as the introduction to another decree that allocated almost 15.3 million additional francs to the year's Sûreté budget, including 5 million francs for detention and repatriation, and another 3.25 million francs for the personnel of the Sûreté and the mobile police who would be needed in order to track down the foreigners.[9] In total, 16 million francs in credits were opened in mid-1938 for the Interior Ministry's newly decreed Service Central des Étrangers, and in 1939, 11 million francs were added.[10] Whereas the 1938 budget had accorded 900,000 francs for the Interior Ministry's section devoted to incarceration and repatriation of foreigners who had been expelled or *refoulés,* in 1939 this section reached 3.3 million francs.[11]

While the emergency budget reflected a desire to restrict migration, the May decrees were not entirely repressive. If the 2 May decree had instituted a newly intransigent approach to "undesirable" foreigners, the 14 May 1938 decree tried to define a "desirable" foreigner, introducing "a gradation of liberties" to be enjoyed by foreigners living in France.[12] First, the decree lengthened the validity of the "normal" identification card to three years, although worker identification cards would be limited to the dates of their labor contracts, and foreigners from certain countries would be limited to a two-year card.[13] Even more important, the decree allowed for differentiated rights to be granted to foreigners according to such factors as the amount of time they had spent in France or the family ties they had there. The most privileged of these foreigners would be issued "special worker" identification cards that authorized them to work in the profession of their choice throughout metropolitan France. The least advantaged would be limited to a specific profession in a certain department. In other words, different foreigners had different civil rights.

Interior Minister Sarraut took pains to remind prefects on 18 May that "it would be unthinkable, I emphasize, to proceed with massive expulsions or *refoulements* of every foreigner who appears in your offices or at police precincts in order to regularize his situation." Rather, the key was to discriminate:

to reject from the French collectivity those undesirable elements, condemned by common law, . . . agitators from all directions thus unworthy of our hospitality, and at the same time welcome with open arms those whose only fault was to have failed, by negligence or fear, to have fulfilled the administrative formalities required of them, or even those who, under the more summary regime practiced up to this point, have had the regularization of their status refused, without any solidly based motive.[14]

Although private administrative circulars throughout the second half of the 1930s had certainly hinted at this, the 14 May decree-law was the first public suggestion, with the force of law, that "discrimination" based on the social circumstances of particular foreigners was not only acceptable but expected. In a variation on the circulars issued under the Flandin and Laval regimes, "special worker" cards gave preference to foreigners who had lived in France for 15 uninterrupted years (precluding all but the earliest wave of refugees); those who had lived in France for five uninterrupted years, of which at least the last two had been spent married to a Frenchwoman; women of French origin who neglected to retain their French nationality when they married foreigners or who had married before this option became available; foreigners who had lived in France for five consecutive years and who were parents to French children, provided that all of their French-born children had been declared French nationals; foreigners who were volunteers in the French army; and foreigners who had served in the Foreign Legion, provided that they had received the recommendation of their *chef de corps*.[15] Privileged foreigners thus theoretically were able to "escape practically all restrictions on their activity and can freely exercise their profession of choice throughout the metropolitan territory."[16] Not only did they escape restrictions on their work; they also had earned an "incontestable right to the benevolence of the public powers" because they, "on their own and spontaneously, have demonstrated their attachment to the country from which they make a living."[17]

Sarraut distinguished the policies of the present regime from the "summary" judgments previously practiced. For the police charged with implementing the decrees, however, the line between dangerous foreign subversives and those with an "incontestable right" to remain in France was not so easy to draw. Sarraut's cautions notwithstanding, local authorities launched the largest crackdown on immigrants the republic had ever known. As they did so, jails filled up and correctional courts were overwhelmed with cases pertaining to identity card infractions, now handled to the detriment of other cases.[18]

Soon enough, the government realized there were problems with the 14 May decree as well. In an effort to ensure that migrant rights were based only on "real" family ties, a 12 November 1938 decree outlawed marriages between French citizens and foreigners who could not show that they had lived legally in France for at least a year. Sarraut also sent a chilling message in the November decree by envisaging the peacetime internment of foreigners "in the interest of order or public security." Finally, the 12 November decree activated a hitherto unused provision of the 1927 Nationality Code, allowing for naturalizations to be rescinded whenever a naturalized person proved "unworthy" of remaining French, because he or she either had engaged in activities injurious to national security or had naturalized under false pretenses. This measure was far less extreme than those being demanded by other politicians; Robert Schuman, later the architect of European integration, wanted to roll back all naturalizations that had occurred since 1919.[19] Instead, the Daladier administration was still trying to balance inclusion and exclusion, an approach Denis Peschanski has called "two-faced."[20] Within months of issuing the 14 May decree to grant special privileges to foreigners who had family connections to French citizens, the administration also cast doubt on those families and on French citizens themselves.

IMMIGRANTS INTO MIGRANTS

The May 1938 decrees launched an unprecedented crackdown on migrants' civil liberties throughout France. In both Lyon and Marseille, more attention was paid to the first decree and its repressive components than to the second and its call for inclusion. Given the urgency of the situation and the complexity of the 14 May decree, this was perhaps hardly surprising. Whereas the 2 May decree succinctly defined infractions and their punishments, the 14 May decree established intricate rules and exceptions to them.

Mounting numbers of correctional court hearings pertaining directly to laws on foreigners testified to the emphasis local authorities placed on repression. Cases pertaining to laws on foreigners (employment restrictions, identity card and residency rules, and enforcement of expulsions) grew in both absolute and relative terms. The likelihood that migrants would be imprisoned for infractions pertaining directly to their status as foreigners increased. While such cases constituted just under 4% of the Lyon court's docket in May 1938 before the decrees were implemented, by September 1938, almost 21% of the Lyon Correctional Court's cases concerned such infractions.[21] The transformation in Marseille was even more dramatic. As early as the second half of June 1938, the Marseille Correctional Court devoted more than 25% of its docket to cases pertaining to laws on foreigners; by August, the proportion had increased to almost 57%; in October, it was almost 62%. The rise in the relative importance of prosecuting laws on foreigners was also accompanied by an absolute increase in the number of cases heard in Marseille. Whereas July had been a more or less typical month, with 651 total hearings, in October the court heard 1,022 cases, of which some 633 pertained to the laws on foreigners. Although the Marseille court did not sustain this high level of hearings, cases pertaining to laws on foreigners continued to occupy the court heavily through the following year. Whereas Lyon cases dropped to 7% in November and just over 9% in December 1938, in Marseille, some 53% of the November cases and nearly 39% of the December cases still pertained to laws on foreigners.[22]

Not only did the courts try more cases pertaining to infractions of laws on foreigners, but also the punishments they meted out were more severe than previously had been the case. Sometimes, a disparity of a few days made all the difference. For instance, on Thursday, 19 May, the Lyon court sentenced Balthasar S., a Spanish national who had been arrested eight days earlier for failing to honor an expulsion order, to two months in prison, court fees, and enforced departure following his sentence.[23] The following Monday, 23 May, Lech T., a Polish man who had been arrested for the same infraction just a day after Balthasar had, was ordered to serve a six-month prison sentence, pay court fees, and be escorted to the border following his sentence. The difference? The 23 May case invoked the 2 May decrees, which increased the minimum sentence for violations of expulsion orders.[24] For a while, the court was inconsistent. No mention of the 2 May decree was made when a Swiss woman was tried on 30 May; she was sentenced to three months in prison. By the beginning of June, however, the Lyon court began applying the 2 May decree strictly, as almost all those found guilty of disobeying an expulsion order henceforth earned a minimum of six months imprisonment, longer in cases concerning recidivists. Around the same time, Lyon's main daily newspaper reported that the police were "purging" the city.[25]

Other shifts in prosecutorial practices also pointed to a change in priorities. In Lyon, foreigners were now vulnerable to state power in ways not witnessed since the crackdown of the early depression years. For example, more women faced prosecution. Belinda W., the Italian woman who was expelled following an expulsion order against her husband in 1934, on the grounds that she would be unable to support herself without him, was rediscovered only in November 1939, presumably because of the new measures.[26] Bettina M., who was expelled for allegedly working illegally in her aunt's bar in Lyon, was rediscovered in January 1940 when authorities informed her for the first time that she had been expelled since 1933.[27] This trend appears to have developed quite quickly after the institution of the 2 May decree: Between June and December 1938, about 30% of identity card infraction cases heard by the Lyon court concerned women, and of these, almost all pertained to women who had lived in

France for quite some time, either without a card or without having renewed an old card. The court sentenced to prison women ranging from
18 to 78 years old, making no differentiation among them. Only the case
against a woman of 88 was thrown out on account of her age and de-
mentia.[28] This intransigence was to be expected. Correctional courts, following strict procedure, could not "discriminate" based on social criteria;
they were merely to judge whether the law had or had not been broken.
As the police dragnet drew in a broader spectrum of the foreign population, a wider variety of immigrants were incarcerated. For Lyon mayor
Herriot, the solution to this problem was simple. France, he argued, had
three types of immigrants: "undesirables who must be expelled, those
whom it is necessary to keep provisionally and who have a residency permit, and those who have been in our country a long time who must be
naturalized."[29] What Herriot neglected to recognize was that these were
often one and the same. As more and more immigrants acquired police
records, more and more provisional and long-term residents became "undesirable."

The contribution that employers made to tipping this scale drew comparatively little interest from labor inspectors or the courts. Instead, both
cities demonstrated the degree to which the implementation of the laws
on foreigners targeted the migrants themselves, and not their employers.
While the Lyon court, perhaps in keeping with Lyon's tradition of more
rigorously enforcing labor laws pertaining to foreigners, brought more
employers to trial than did its Marseille counterpart, overall both the
numbers of cases and the punishments meted out demonstrated that it
was employees and not employers who were regarded as the perpetrators
of France's crisis.

Not only were punishments stiffer for foreign workers than they were
for those who illegally employed them, but also the former were more
likely to be caught and prosecuted. In both Lyon and Marseille in the wake
of the May decrees, police brigades had instructions to verify the identification papers of foreigners by stopping individuals on the street and by
inspecting short-term lodgings such as *garnis* and *meublés*. These methods allowed police to turn up foreigners who had lived illegally in France,
undetected, for years. Gawel S., a Polish man stopped in Villeurbanne on
16 July, had an identification card that had expired during the Flandin reviews, on 30 June 1935. He claimed to have been in France since 1926
and to have "completely forgotten" to renew his card. More likely, both
he and his employer, the Maison Favre, which had employed him since
September 1934, knew that a request for a valid identity card as a chemical worker in the summer of 1935 would have been turned down. For
this, Gawel was sentenced to a month in prison in October 1938. If his

employer was pursued as well, this has left no archival trace.[30] Another identity check in June 1938 turned up an Italian man with a card that had expired on 31 December 1935. Benito C. admitted that he had not renewed the identity card because he had no work certificate. He, too, spent a month in prison.[31]

In both Lyon and Marseille, police arrested, and then referred for prosecution, an increasingly broad spectrum of the foreign population, including individuals who had been resident in the country for some time. In both cities, judges increasingly relied on national policy prescriptions to guide their sentencing of foreigners. In Lyon and Marseille alike, long-term immigrants—especially those with families—felt renewed vulnerability, something they thought they had put behind them when authorities had distinguished them from migrants earlier in the 1930s.

It was in Marseille, however, that the shift appeared to be the most dramatic. Throughout the summer, labor conflicts had tried Daladier's patience with the port city. A two-month strike in the evenings and on weekends by dockworkers had greatly interfered with port traffic and had been settled only in September after Daladier's government placed Marseille's port under military control.[32] The dispute, along with Daladier's new insistence that the workweek be extended beyond 40 hours, prompted the remaining Popular Front sympathizers in Daladier's cabinet to resign. It was one of their successors, the new minister of public works Anatole de Monzie, who militarized the port. The following month, as the Radical Party held its congress in Marseille, what was already becoming evident was now recognized in principle: The Popular Front as such was no more. When the Radical Party condemned any future coalition with the Communists at the congress, Daladier abandoned what pretense remained of an antifascist coalition. Daladier's speech before the congress was scathing in its attack on the Communists, whom he accused of "sabotaging" the government's work and labeled as the agents of "foreign forces."[33]

Daladier also used his platform at the Radical Party congress to reiterate the security problems associated with immigration. If France were to continue to be a land of "refuge," he declared, it had a right to insist

upon respect for the fundamental law of hospitality, which is, not to intervene in the affairs of your host. Those who would not comply with this law would place themselves outside the bounds of French hospitality.[34]

With Daladier and the Radicals in town, local authorities redoubled their efforts to police the boundaries of that hospitality. However, other incidents occurring during the congress detracted attention from this zeal. A dramatic fire in the Nouvelles Galeries department store spread to the

Hôtel Noailles, where delegates to the Radical Party Congress were staying; the fire caused more than 70 deaths.[35] This seemed to confirm, four
years to the month after the murders of King Alexander and Louis Barthou, that Marseille still lacked an appropriate level of security and safety
services. Since Daladier had just finished reminding delegates at the Radical congress of Marseille's strategic importance, particularly regarding relations with the empire, the disorder of the city's administration was particularly worrisome.

Marseille and Bouches-du-Rhône authorities always had been defensive in their relations with the central government. In the context of imminent war, they became all the more so. No local official, least of all
in Marseille, wanted to be responsible for letting slip through his hands
another Vlado Cernozemski (aka Victor Georgiev), the assassin of King
Alexander and Louis Barthou in Marseille in 1934. With such incidents in
mind, local authorities increasingly adjudicated migrant rights with an
eye to what they understood to be their role in protecting the national interest. Only as local officials began worrying about this, rather than about
how immigrants fit into Marseille's social map, did they embark on an
all-out attack on Marseille's foreign population. Indeed, repression of foreigners reached its highest pre–World War II level in the month during
which national and local crises dovetailed: from the time of the Munich
crisis in September 1938 to the ineffectively managed fire in Marseille
during the Radical Party Congress the following month.

As if to avenge the lax reputation they had earned because of the 1934
assassination, the Marseille police used their newly buttressed powers
as a license to begin raids.[36] The first foreigners caught up in the dragnet
came from the social groups that had always proved most vulnerable to
police power: ragpickers, vagrants, sailors, traveling salesmen, and anyone without a stable residence or profession. But as the police cast their
nets more widely, they began to drag in those whose presence they had
long ignored: the residents of the periphery. A Spaniard who had lived in
Marseille's peripheral Les Caillols neighborhood for 24 years suddenly
found himself imprisoned for never having had a valid identification card.
Another who had lived in France since 1909 but who now had no verifiable address was imprisoned for failing to renew his card. Still another
who was born in France in 1918 was imprisoned for not having a card.[37]
Even an Italian man who had lived in the Montredon neighborhood for
53 years received a one-month prison sentence and a 100-franc fine.[38] Refractory expellees, some of whom claimed that they did not remember being expelled, turned up with expulsions dating back to the end of the
nineteenth century.[39] Perhaps it was not accidental that Hagop Z., the Armenian who had narrowly escaped being expelled in 1931, chose the fall
of 1938 to file for naturalization.[40]

As in Lyon, Marseille authorities not only prosecuted more foreigners as a result of the May decrees but also meted out stiffer punishments. Foreigners represented by an attorney seemed, until mid-June, to have a better chance at a shorter sentence. In early June, an Italian represented by an attorney received an eight-day sentence for violating an expulsion order; a Liberian with an attorney was sentenced to a month in prison, as was a Maltese. Meanwhile, those not represented by attorneys were sentenced a minimum of two months and as much as one year.[41] By mid-June, however, all refractory expellees found guilty by the Marseille Correctional Court received a minimum prison sentence of six months, whether or not they were represented by attorneys.[42]

Expellees were far from the only target of this new crackdown. Prosecutions for infractions of identity card regulations increased in frequency while the relative share of prosecutions for failing to honor an expulsion order declined. In August, identity card infractions constituted 41% of Marseille's Correctional Court docket (72% of the cases pertaining to laws on foreigners), while expulsion infractions represented approximately 15%. In October, identity card infractions had increased to 57% of the total docket (92% of cases pertaining to laws on foreigners), while expulsion cases had declined to 5%. Had refractory expellees gone into hiding? It is possible, although in absolute terms, the 5% was still higher than the 15% of two months' prior. What seems most likely is that, while police continued to arrest, as always, refractory expellees, they also redoubled their efforts with regard to other foreigners. Now their dragnet included persons who had never before been found to violate a law. The Marseille court no longer differentiated between migrants: All identity card infractions, whether they resulted from illegal entry or failure to renew a valid card, led to a month in prison and 100 francs in fines. These were the very people Sarraut thought deserved the benefit of the doubt as long as their identities could be verified and they had some way to earn their livelihoods. But accounting for such subtleties took time, and police, like Daladier himself, instead acted with urgency.

Marseille officials were not alone in emphasizing repression. Judging from ministerial reactions, this approach must have been widespread. Indeed, the director of the Sûreté admonished all prefects in September for recommending expulsions "based on poorly established facts or even on simple presumptions made from summary inquiries." The circular from the Sûreté director instructed them to, "from now on, . . . undertake detailed investigations, conducted with a concern for objectivity and precision," and reminded them to "gather information, as much on family attachments that the interested parties might have in French territory as well as on the length of their stay in France and, where applicable, the military service they might provide."[43] Clearly, neither the 14 May decree nor Sarraut's circular of 18 May had sunk in. As a result, the Sûreté now had to exercise damage control. In the context of increasingly polarized international politics, it was imperative, from the perspective of Interior Ministry officials, that expulsion be used to control people who were truly dangerous. But putting the lid back on Pandora's box was easier said than done; after this circular was distributed, repression of foreigners in Marseille intensified rather than decreased.

The threat of war and concerns over foreigners had only been heightened by events that had occurred since May. The concession at Munich of Czechoslovakia's Sudetenland to Germany in late September 1938 had stimulated another wave of refugees. Following Munich, the government's commitment to antifascism, the rallying cry of the Popular Front coalition in 1936, became rhetorical at best. In October, Sarraut again changed his tune, now ordering across-the-board expulsions of refugees who did not have visas or passports. Exactly one month later, and within days of Kristallnacht, Sarraut and Daladier went further by establishing a special border police and authorizing the creation of detention centers for dangerous foreigners who, although expelled, could not be forced to leave.[44]

Together, the increased arrests and stiffer sentences soon posed problems in prison space for the detainees. At the beginning of Marseille's crackdown on illegal aliens, all the accused were detained, usually three weeks to a month, pending their trial dates. By late July, however, the increasing numbers of "nondetained" on the court docket suggest that it had become impossible to continue the detention system. Because fewer were detained, more defaulted on their trials by failing to appear, which in turn increased their penalties if and when they were caught and referred for enforcement again. By November, this had posed such a problem that authorities opted for detention pending trial again. With the city's social boundaries less relevant in the context of impending war, legal standards also lost anchor. Instead of judging immigrants first and then incarcerating or expelling them, officials operated in reverse order. Marseille and Bouches-du-Rhône authorities had, even before the start of war, abandoned a central principle of the liberal republic. The following spring, the central government abandoned another republican principle: elected mayoral office. In the wake of the October 1938 blaze and the inquiry into it ordered by Daladier, an *administrateur extraordinaire* with the rank of prefect took over most of the duties that had previously fallen to Marseille's Socialist mayor, the son of Italian immigrants, Henri Tasso. The police came under the control of a new *directeur des services de police*, who reported to the new administrator; the latter reported not to the interior minister, as did most prefects, but to Daladier himself.[45]

If placing Marseille and its police under receivership initially added another confusing layer of hierarchy to Marseille's police structure, it did not prevent its later efficacy: After the outbreak of war in September 1939, Marseille police reportedly rounded up 13,000 "enemy aliens" by the first of October.[46]

With the outbreak of war, the port city attracted only more foreigners—especially refugees—who hoped to set sail from there and flee the continent altogether. Marseille's rooming houses and hotels grew crowded with migrants whose legal right to stay in the city became, incongruously enough, contingent upon their ability to prove to local authorities that they intended to leave.[47] Of course, the fact that many migrants were, after the war's outbreak, trying to leave rather than to stay says a great deal about how much the stakes had changed with the war.

SUBJECTS INTO SOLDIERS

The stakes had changed for the state as well, and this explains North Africans' reversals in fortune. As many European migrants were threatened with expulsion or internment, North Africans were called upon to aid the French war effort. Despite worrying throughout the 1920s and 1930s about colonial nationalism, military leaders never questioned whether North Africans should serve in the French army; it was understood that they would. As early as December 1937, authorities in the capital had begun to make plans to draw on the services of North Africans in the event of another war.[48] Opposition to the Blum-Viollette reforms had killed, for the time being, any possibility of offering suffrage in exchange for serving France. Instead, authorities seized on another of the Algerian Muslim Congress' agenda areas: social rights.[49]

Although North African associations in the metropole had long called for equalizing social rights, the idea that doing so was crucial to French interests appears to have been first articulated by the general secretary of the Nord department prefecture. Writing to mayors in his department in January 1938, he asked them to ensure that North Africans were not laid off by employers trying to meet the quota laws, for, as he put it:

We cannot allow North Africans to think that France is totally disinterested in their destiny. . . . If we are able to win their hearts with a benevolent policy by showing our interest in their destiny, we will have accomplished an important task, for which France will not tarry in reaping the benefits. Returning home, they will be our best collaborators. But if we do not fulfill our duty, there is every reason to believe that others will and will turn them against us through clever propaganda.[50]

The Nord department anticipated national policy: Fewer than three weeks later, an interministerial circular informed all unemployment offices that Algerians should be included in local assistance programs.[51]

It took longer, however, to convince local authorities that committing North Africans to a future war effort required reversing policies and practices that had actively discriminated against them. Excluding North Africans from social assistance had become a common means of budget management. In May 1938, for instance, the Bouches-du-Rhône departmental council proposed to "unclog" (*décongestionner*) its unemployment office by requiring North Africans to go through the SAINA office for their social assistance. Clearly, administrators in the Bouches-du-Rhône department did not share the solicitude of their colleague from the Nord department. The council dropped the proposal, but not because of any objection to its underlying principles.[52] It was not until war became imminent in the summer of 1939 that central authorities made a serious effort to break local habits and insist that the new policies be implemented. With the outbreak of war, officials went one step further; not only did they try to discourage repatriation of North Africans, but they also forbade it until migrants' status for requisition as workers or soldiers had been verified.

Like the Nord department official, the director of Marseille's SAINA raised concerns about the psychological impact that a lack of services for North Africans might have. Yet Poussardin's interventions seem to have had little impact. Instead, he derided clerks in the various municipal and departmental services, alleging that they were too ignorant to know the difference between a foreigner and a French subject. Turning sarcastic as he reported these details to the Interior Ministry, Poussardin mocked local administrations for telling North Africans "But no, you [*tu*] are foreign."[53] As a result, Poussardin was forced to, "little by little, substitute [him]self for all the [administrative] organisms that cause delays" in services to North Africans.[54] As his efforts to encourage solicitude for the "*indigènes*" within the local branches of state offices repeatedly failed, he tried, again in vain, to get a budget subsidy large enough to allow him to offer bread to the North Africans who visited his office after trying to tap every other resource.[55]

As North Africans increasingly turned to the SAINA office for their every need, complaints from neighborhood businesses grew regarding the "herds (there is no other word) of unfortunate" North Africans loitering outside the office.[56] Poussardin used such "perfectly justifiable" complaints as levers for launching complaints of his own: Insufficient resources in the face of high demand for SAINA services explained why migrants were forced to convene on the sidewalk as they waited to be served.[57] With each subsequent report on the state of the SAINA, Poussardin's language betrayed a growing impatience. In a May 1938 report to the Bouches-du-Rhône prefect, he accused the department of "never wanting to grant a subsidy" that would allow his service "to come to the aid of North Africans."[58] The fact that Poussardin's complaints peaked in the wake of the May decrees suggests that he was probably right; many probably did not know the difference between North Africans and foreigners, and the former probably were getting caught occasionally in the dragnet for the latter.

Certainly that difference had not raised many obstacles to repatriation—quite the contrary. Even as central state ministries had jointly admonished unemployment offices in February 1938 to cease refusing service to North Africans, the Interior Ministry still advocated repatriation as an alternative to social provision. In June, the ministry's director of Algerian affairs reminded the Bouches-du-Rhône prefect that, while it is "not legal to repatriate Algerian *indigènes* without their consent, you should . . . make an effort to persuade them . . . that it would be in their interest to return to the *douar* they came from rather than stay in FRANCE . . . where they risk being no longer able to obtain assistance from local sources because of a lack of sufficient resources."[59] With mixed messages like these, it is no wonder that repatriation continued while acquiring social assistance remained difficult. Lyon's Centre Nord Africain had registered only 246 North Africans for unemployment compensation during 1938, but its repatriations were 38% higher than in the previous year. Repatriations from Marseille had declined compared to their peak in 1937 but still numbered over 3,400 for the year.[60]

Mixed messages with respect to North Africans were of course nothing new. When parliament had debated establishing new limits on foreign employment in 1933, Henri Brière—a centrist republican deputy from Oran (Algeria)—had introduced an amendment: "Indigenous labor coming from the colonies, mandates, and protectorates shall not be considered foreign labor." The amendment was dropped when the government insisted that there was "no question"—natives could not be considered foreign.[61] But the establishment of visa requirements for North Africans and the creation of SAINA offices in a deliberate effort to decrease social welfare costs showed that at the highest levels of government administration, North Africans were indeed regarded as less than fully French.

Now, as France prepared for war, officials in Paris wished to cultivate the unique relationship of North Africans to France. A chain of reminders marked "very urgent" and "very important" sent in 1938 and 1939 admonished local administrations to treat North Africans as nationals. They reminded local officials that employers attempting to meet foreign labor thresholds must not do so by dismissing North Africans before Europeans. They insisted that Algerians receive all the same forms of social assistance given to the metropolitan French except for publicly funded allowances designed to encourage the national birthrate. They even eventually extended those same allowances to Algerians who had married French (read: metropolitan) women. Although initially this solicitousness extended mostly to Algerians, as war looked increasingly imminent in the summer of 1939, officials concluded that Moroccans and Tunisians—likely candidates for labor requisition—ought also to be treated as nationals with respect to unemployment insurance and other forms of assistance.[62] With these and similar directives, authorities in Paris attempted, for the first time since demobilization after the Great War, to facilitate North Africans' chances of staying in the metropole. Extending social citizenship to them was one way to do this, just as limiting it had been a way to encourage their repatriation.

The very fact that such reminders were necessary suggests the impact that a decade and a half of discrimination had had on the rights of North Africans. Far from establishing a clear-cut status for North Africans, the constant reminders begged a question: If their status as French subjects or protectees so clearly and automatically entitled them to social rights, why the need to reiterate this fact? The policy (re)affirmations were necessary because North Africans' relationship to the French state had not been sufficient to guarantee them rights with any regularity. North Africans had faced what were, for all intents and purposes, passport controls. Local officials, meanwhile, had regarded North Africans as the fiscal—and thus legal—responsibility of authorities in central state ministries or the colonies themselves.

With the war, things finally did turn around. Local authorities were called upon to conduct special censuses of the North Africans in anticipation of their contribution to the war effort. After war was declared, the Interior Ministry instructed local officials to cease repatriating North Africans and to deny travel authorizations until their eligibility for military service had been verified.[63] No doubt this explains why Poussardin's figures for "identifications and miscellanea" soared from 1,094 in 1938 to 11,929 in 1939, while repatriations secured by his office declined by more than 83% to 564. Records from the Rhône department suggest a similar shift in priorities. Of the more than 3,500 North Africans evaluated by the CNA as of 4 October 1939, almost 1,800 were deemed "available." Another 1,700 had been assigned military jobs, many at the arsenal.[64]

The onset of war unhinged an already flustered Poussardin. Informed that he could no longer repatriate Algerians who might be requisitioned for the war effort, he was left wondering what his service—which by that time did little besides repatriate—was supposed to do. He was still fighting his losing battle with public agencies in the Bouches-du-Rhône, complaining that North Africans "fan[ned] out to the other administrations, return[ed] to me, disperse[d] again only to return" because of the "incompetence" of the other administrations, which increasingly proved either "unable" to communicate with North Africans, or unwilling to assist those whom they argued were "foreigners."[65] Instructed to verify colonial subjects' military status, he became livid whenever a North African was subsequently arrested by Marseille police for lacking registration papers, apparently convinced that routine roundups of anyone appearing foreign were aimed directly at questioning the professionalism with which he had issued their papers.[66] By the late fall of 1939, Poussardin's reports showed a man at wit's end:

For the past hour, two assistants and I have been trying to fix the sole typewriter in the office, identified as unusable already three years ago, continually requiring expensive but ineffective repairs. And while this goes on, the guards chat with the crowd of claimants whom multiple administrations . . . discharge in my direction.

He continued, a bit further:

The effort I have put in, no matter how disinterested, the unrequited (or practically) self-sacrifice cannot, despite countless overtime hours put in, make up for the emptiness we confront.

"You are far away," he then told the director. "You no doubt think that this state of affairs, lamentable in peacetime, cannot last another hour in time of war. How can I get through to you?"[67]

Poussardin's struggle for recognition from Paris seems a fitting metaphor for the relationship of North Africans in the metropole to the central administration. While North Africa was vital to central state interests, individual colonial subjects were not. It was this that allowed them to be treated worse than most-favored foreigners for most of the 1920s and 1930s. Even the Popular Front had concluded that the interests of North Africa were better served by catering to the rights of colonial settlers rather than by extending those of colonized Muslims. By the fall of 1939, however, the issue had become not only saving French overseas possessions but France altogether. Some 157,000 North Africans were mobilized at the time of the fall of France; as many as 67,000 were captured by the Wehrmacht.[68] Of the tens of thousands requisitioned to work in war industries, 35,000 were sent home after the armistice.[69]

MIGRANTS IN WAR: ENEMIES OR ALLIES?

Perhaps surprisingly, given the paranoia about the security threat posed by foreigners, some 100,000 of them served either directly in the French army or in special foreign contingents.[70] More might have served, had it not been for fears regarding the incorporation of large percentages of foreigners, especially former Germans, into the foreign legion or other military contingents.[71] In fact, despite these remarkable numbers, French policy makers never completely overcame the tensions between seeing migrants as security risks and relying on them for support. As a result, mobilization for war led at once to the reinforcement of repressive measures toward migrants and to their reconsideration. Reinforcement came in the form of internment. Reconsideration came in the form of accelerating pending naturalizations and rescinding old expulsion orders to facilitate the military conscription of young foreign men. In part because the German attack did not come immediately, forcing France into several months of *drôle de guerre*, or phony war, authorities had time to second-guess themselves. By the time France fell in June 1940, however, they still had not completely resolved whether to regard foreigners as threatening or vital to the war effort.

The earliest internment camps had been established before the war to respond to an inundation of refugees from the Spanish Civil War after the final fall of Barcelona. In early 1939, more than 450,000 refugees had crossed into France from northern Spain. The first camp, Argelès, was little more than a beach surrounded by barbed wire with inadequate shelter and sanitary facilities. Like Marseille's camps Victor Hugo and Oddo in the 1920s, Argelès was intended to be transitional. Unlike Hugo and Oddo, which were run by the migrants themselves, Argelès and other camps like it were heavily guarded by the French military. Here the transition in mind was not settlement in France so much as return to Spain.[72] After France recognized Franco's government in February 1939, mainly in order to keep it neutral in the event of war, French leaders were hardly inclined to provide safe harbor to its opponents, particularly given growing antirefugee sentiment. Anticommunist politicians ranging from the Radical Party to the extreme Right pushed particularly hard for expulsion, and Sarraut, after insisting on distinguishing between "honorable" Spaniards and the "troubling or shady elements in the Spanish exodus, the criminals and outlaws, the derelicts who have lost all sense of morality and who will constitute a grave danger for us if kept in our territory," noted parenthetically that he did not know how "within such an inundation, one can differentiate between refuse and wrecks, but I won't dwell on this point."[73] French authorities drew a line in the sand, quite literally.

In doing so, they certainly gave new meaning to the Spanish republican slogan *"No pasarán."*[74] When war broke out months later, as many as 250,000 Spanish refugees were still living in the camps.

Spanish republicans were not the only ones considered for internment. Already in August 1938, authorities in the Ministry of the Interior had begun to grow concerned about the security problems posed by the mounting number of refugees being *assignés de résidence* as a result of the May decrees. Too lenient an approach to refugees might result, they worried, in a concentration of dangerous migrants in certain towns; a better solution might be detention centers, which some had advocated as an alternative to *assignation* as early as 1937.[75] The 12 November 1938 decree gave public voice to these plans, as it introduced the possibility of internment camps. Still, authorities hesitated. Almost as soon as they authorized sending refugees to "lodging centers," they reversed this decision and returned to using *assignation*.

With the war, this equivocation ceased, at least for a while. Sarraut, who had chastised local authorities in 1938 for not discriminating between good and bad foreigners, now argued before the Chamber of Deputies in December 1939 that selection was impossible. That is how, as the Hungarian-born writer Arthur Koestler vividly recounts his time in the Vernet concentration camp, "white" Russians came to be interned with "reds," while Italian communists and fascists shared barracks, as did German immigrants of opposing political stripes. Neutrals from countries such as Hungary, where Koestler was born, Czechs, Poles, Georgians, Spanish, and Senegalese, according to Koestler, all shared the experience of being interned despite the obvious differences among them.[76] In the Camp des Milles, "soldiers from the foreign legion who have their chest full of medals," Czechs, "who point out that they are French allies," Danzigers for whom the French had gone to war, and even an Alsatian were interned, according to the antifascist writer Alfred Kantorowicz.[77] In addition to Vernet and Milles, there were numerous other camps, each supposedly having a slightly different function but most in fact rather indiscriminately grouping so-called dangerous foreigners.[78]

Within weeks of beginning massive internments, central state authorities once again tried to discriminate between good and bad internees. "Sifting" (*criblage*) committees were formed to discern who really did pose a threat and who did not; on what criteria, it was hard to say. Thus, internment engendered a reconsideration process in some ways similar to that which followed the May decrees. In September 1938, the general director of the Sûreté Nationale had chastised local authorities for "the poorly established facts" and "simple presumptions made from summary inquiries" that informed the decisions they had made in the wake of the

May decrees.[79] A year later, officials faced a similar task but with even higher stakes. Authorities had, as with arrests in the wake of the May decrees, erred on the side of caution. According to Lion Feuchtwanger, the German writer who was interned at Les Milles, low-level officials "evidently had been instructed to lock up too many people rather than too few."[80] Prefectures apparently had come to rely so heavily on internment to rid themselves of troublesome foreigners that the Interior Ministry revoked the authority of prefects to intern, requiring that they clear such decisions with it first. Even then, the ministry still had to ask prefects to curtail their recommendations to intern, noting that excessive internments themselves posed a threat to public order.[81]

Rights had always been weighed against risks. Now, however, it was not only migrants who made this calculation but also the administration. The case of a Spanish man interned in Vernet exemplified this challenge. Julio Q. had never been officially expelled, though Lyon officials had long kept an eye on him as a labor militant with suspected communist leanings. Not taking any chances at the outbreak of war, the Rhône prefect had sent him to Vernet, the camp in the Ariège designated for those foreigners who posed the gravest threat to France.[82] Julio, meanwhile, allegedly had tried to volunteer for the French army. Lyon's chief of police recommended that he remain interned until a decision was made about his request to serve.[83]

The very fact that Julio's request to serve in the French army was taken at all seriously might call into question the appropriateness of interning him in Vernet. Clearly, Lyonnese police authorities were trying to play it safe. Even more remarkable, however, was a letter from the Rhône prefecture's general secretary to his counterpart in the Ariège department noting that Julio did indeed pose a "threat to public order" because, while he had never been a member of the Communist Party, he had been active in unions and was known as a communist "sympathizer." For all these reasons, he concluded that Julio should remain interned. This draft of the letter, however, was not sent. Instead, the recommendation of continued internment was crossed out and replaced with "Nonetheless, I am not opposed to his release, on the condition that he enlists in your department for the remainder of the war and is approved as able to serve."[84]

Identical facts had led the same office to come to two opposite conclusions. It is hard to know what precipitated the change in position over the course of four days. Had a lower-level bureaucrat drafted the letter, only to have the general secretary edit it at the last minute? Or had the general secretary himself changed his mind over the course of a few days? This seems likely, since the first draft was dated 19 April 1940 and that same day, Julio's wife, Nicole, a Frenchwoman, sent a letter to the prefecture.

In her letter, Nicole insisted that while Julio may have been a syndicalist, he was not a communist; as proof, she pointed out that he had not fought in the international brigades during the Spanish Civil War, which surely he would have done had he been a communist.[85] Nicole's letter does not seem to have changed the general secretary's mind with regard to Julio's political leanings. But perhaps it was enough that she was a Frenchwoman. Under political pressure, authorities at the national level had decreed that internees with French families were to be released.[86] Of course, having a French family in no way prevented an individual from potentially acting as a spy or subversive, but at a time when authorities hardly expected a lightning war, this concern had to be weighed against maintaining the morale of French citizens over the long term. Either way, the Rhône's general secretary took few risks. By writing a letter that spared few details about Julio's alleged political beliefs, he left ample room for Vernet authorities to make a decision either way.

In the end, Julio remained interned. But it could easily have gone the other way. Francesco M., a refractory expellee from Italy, very narrowly escaped being interned. When ordered to leave France in the fall of 1939, he asked to join the French army. Although the prefect had set his sights on interning Francesco in Vernet, an intervention from Senator Camille Rolland (Radical, Rhône), a member of the National Assembly's Army Commission, helped convince the Interior Ministry to give Francesco a *sursis* in May 1940 so that he might enlist instead.[87]

Bouches-du-Rhône officials faced similar quandaries. Orsino R. had left France in 1922 following the death of his brother, for which Orsino was convicted of involuntary manslaughter in 1923. After serving in the Italian military, he returned to France in 1928 and settled down with a Frenchwoman of Italian background. He was discovered in 1932, and authorities expelled him, then immediately tempered his expulsion with a *sursis*. Orsino requested a number of times to have the expulsion lifted, but it was not until 1939, when he volunteered for the French army, that local authorities were ready to oblige. The Interior Ministry, however, proposed another solution: Why not simply give him a 13-month *sursis* so that he could join the army?[88] The use of *sursis* in Francesco's and Orsino's cases was a remarkable development: It effectively said that the two Italian men still posed too much of a security threat for their expulsions to be rescinded but not so much of one that they could not enlist as soldiers in France's defense.

Although France's need for army recruits was a major factor in reversing and suspending expulsions, migrants found that not all pasts were so easily overcome. Whereas Orsino R. had been living under the regime of *sursis* since 1932, Ghazaros T., an Armenian, had been in and out of jail

during the same time. First expelled for vagrancy in 1931, and arrested as
a result of the May decrees, he was released from prison in January 1939
after serving an eight-month sentence. As he explained in a letter he sent
from the Armenian refugee office, he had been incarcerated 14 times for
vagrancy since coming to France. Instead of incorporating Ghazaros into
the French army (nearing 40 and allegedly "neurasthenic," he was not particularly fit for service), Bouches-du-Rhône authorities tried to force him
to emigrate, even going so far as to request visas on his behalf from Mex-
ico, Panama, and Venezuela. However, the same factors that classified
Ghazaros as an "undesirable" in France blocked his emigration to Latin
America. Confronting Ghazaros' lengthy police record, the Bouches-du-
Rhône prefect resorted to recommending his internment at Rieucros. Ultimately, Ghazaros was instead placed under house arrest in Arles, since
the relocation of "undesirable foreigners" to what the Interior Ministry's
seventh bureau chief, on 6 May 1939, euphemistically called "lodging
centers" had been "temporarily suspended."[89] By contrast, a fellow Armenian, the younger and fitter Berj Y. (b. 1912), whose police record was
clean, succeeded in having his expulsion repealed in August 1938 so that
he could enlist. Indeed, Marseille authorities began paperwork for his naturalization on 12 June 1940, two days before the Nazis entered Paris.[90] A
great deal turned on a migrant's police record, timing, and perhaps a little luck.

Similar motivations brought authorities to revisit pending or postponed
naturalization applications. Italians Roberto V. (b. 1918) and Marcello I.
(b. 1917) had both applied for naturalization in 1936; neither file was processed until the men volunteered for service.[91] Twenty-two-year-old
Luciano T. had likewise applied in 1936. Authorities had postponed his
case in 1938 because he was single, had been involved in a fraud case, and
had a "very bad reputation," all of which had nearly led to his expulsion.
After Luciano volunteered for the French army on 4 November 1939,
however, the director of the naturalization service finessed past accusations
of fraud against him, noting that he had "no known convictions against
him" and that he had good conduct and morality. Meanwhile, Nicolo R.
had been rejected as late as July 1939 on the grounds that he retained too
many family members in Italy. But when he volunteered for the French
army in the fall, his file was forwarded to Paris in December marked "Priority."[92] By mid-March 1940, Bouches-du-Rhône officials had created a
preprinted form: "[Name] registered for voluntary service on [date] for
the duration of the war and has been approved as apt for armed service."[93]
A rubber stamp was also newly minted for such men: "Priority—23 October 1939 circular," a reference to the policy memorandum that allowed
for accelerated naturalizations of enlistees.

Rhône officials pursued a similar course. As early as 1936, they had forwarded files to Paris for naturalization with the remark "Urgent—military service."[94] This imperative had brought them to violate some of their long-standing principles with respect to naturalization. Even their cardinal rule—to reject the naturalization of those who, although born in France and eligible to claim French nationality at adulthood, had instead repudiated it—now proved fungible. In December 1937, for instance, the Rhône's chief of police had opposed naturalizing the French-born Italian national Benigno F. because he had repudiated his French nationality and had served in the Italian army. But his superior crossed out this objection and replaced it with a favorable recommendation. In January 1938, Benigno's application was also forwarded with the statement "Urgent—military service," and he was naturalized in October of that year.[95] Similarly, Matteo I., 24 years old and a prime candidate for service, succeeded in having his expulsion repealed in order to naturalize.[96]

Indeed, even as politicians in some other parts of the country called for naturalizations to be rolled back, Lyon's municipal council adopted a resolution proposing to accelerate the process of granting naturalizations. Noting the "urgency with which an outcome should be reached on the requests from young men aged eighteen to thirty who wish to perform their military service under the French flag," it called for decentralizing the naturalization process and allowing for civil courts to decide them locally. The resolution passed, but not before the councillor Paul Charbin expressed reservations about overly hasty naturalizations: "The invasion of our territory by foreigners is utterly prejudicial to French interests."[97] A few minutes of municipal council debate in Lyon had summed up the crux of the tensions that foreigners posed in a period of national security crisis. Still, naturalizations jumped astronomically. In 1939, according to Patrick Weil, nearly 44,500 men and women were naturalized nationwide; more than 99,000 foreigners became French that year if children are included.[98] This represented an 89% increase over the previous year.[99] In the first half of 1940, more than 29,000 applicants were naturalized, or almost 56,000 when children are counted.[100]

Refugees in particular often hoped that volunteering for military service would bring them the benefits of naturalization. Indeed, from April 1939, such "volunteering" had become mandatory. Thenceforth, all holders of Nansen passports and all officially recognized refugees from Germany aged 20 to 48 had the same military obligations as native Frenchmen. This gave male refugees the responsibilities but not the rights of citizenship. Nonetheless, stateless persons continued to be considered special security threats, and this hampered their incorporation into the military.[101] In November 1939, the government extended its formal reservations to

Croatians and Slovenians, German exiles, Czechs, and even the Poles for whom they had gone to war.[102]

Although some stateless refugees did succeed in naturalizing in 1938 and 1939 on the basis of military service performed or promised, authorities appear to have been more concerned about granting naturalizations to persons who could be conscripted by other states. As stateless persons, refugees could not. From the onset of the war, authorities pushed the naturalization of young, able-bodied men who had lived in France at least five years, especially if they were Belgian, Swiss, Italian, or Spanish.[103] Accelerating Italian naturalizations accompanied the discontinuation of incorporating Italians into the French foreign legion, a practice that had angered Mussolini. Outwardly placating Mussolini, behind closed doors French authorities promoted the naturalizations of Italians; a secret circular issued by the Justice Ministry in 1939 urged local authorities to facilitate the naturalization of young Italians.[104] Of the more than 50,000 adult males naturalized in 1939 and 1940, about 57% of them were Italian, at a time when Italians represented 31% of the foreign population in France.[105] Russians and "Armenians and Turks" constituted fewer than 2% apiece of these naturalizations. And German and Austrian men constituted about 4% of adult males naturalized in 1939, but only one-fifth of 1% in 1940.[106]

As France mobilized for war, it became obvious how much had changed since demobilization after the First World War had brought labor leaders, employers, and state officials from France and emigrant nations to craft a migration policy that, they thought, would ensure the equitable treatment of French and foreign alike. In the wake of the Great War, a guest-worker regime had been established to favor short-term migration of workers. Although France had demographic problems that had been exacerbated by the war, migration was, at least initially, seen largely as a temporary palliative, not as a long-term solution to the country's anemic population growth. In 1918, rebuilding the country's army was just about the last thing anyone wanted to ponder. The Great War was supposed to have been *la dernière des dernières*, the war to end all wars. No one imagined that just over two decades later some of the same people who had been recruited to reconstruct France after the 1914–18 war would enlist to defend it in 1939–40.

No one imagined either the obstacles that would soon emerge to implementing postwar guest-worker policy as it had been designed. In the 1920s, the system was already challenged by regional differences in economy, social life, and public administration; the arrival of refugees whose chances of repatriation did not turn on the labor market so much as on politics at home; unpredictable regime changes in emigrant nations such as Italy, Germany, and Spain; and France's politics of maintaining its empire.

It was in the 1930s, however, that France's guest-worker system was truly put to the test. As authorities sought to enforce the provisions of migrants' temporary residency authorizations by enjoining the "guests" to go "home," migrants engaged in new strategies that demonstrated a longer-term investment in French society. Ironically, many migrants successfully used the very agreements on which their labor contracts had once been based to demand social rights once they were made redundant. Social expenditures skyrocketed.

New international crises also loomed—particularly in Germany, Central Europe, and Spain. The arrival of new refugees as the depression deepened led to renewed calls from central authorities to enforce labor regulations and protect French jobs. The very attempt to do this, however, created new obstacles to controlling migration effectively. As a result, state officials rationed their repressive resources, creating exceptions to guest-worker policy at precisely the time when pressure grew to enforce it. At the local level, officials had already learned to use repression selectively in their encounters with migrants. But while approaches to doing so had varied widely from prefecture to prefecture in the 1920s and early 1930s, a pattern developed by the mid-1930s whereby settled families with children earned privileges, while new migrants and the single faced increased prejudice. In the process, migrant rights, which had always been subject to great variation, became more stratified than ever. Authorities now called for local officials nationwide to distinguish between temporary migrants and permanent immigrants. A populationist immigration policy had developed. Workers of the world clearly no longer shared rights, if they ever had.

Only in the context of renewed international crisis did this new distinction lose its purchase. In anticipation of war, local authorities took little time to distinguish between a newly arrived migrant and a long-term immigrant. Intense repression equalized migrant rights—or the lack thereof. Immigrants who had developed profound connections to French society and institutions saw those links disintegrate as the polarized politics of the late 1930s increasingly demonized foreigners. Although national authorities were responsible for triggering the police crackdown on migrants in 1938 and 1939, they did not anticipate how their directives would be implemented. The ensuing frenzy often produced profound confusion both among migrants and among the petty bureaucrats and police charged with adjudicating their rights.

Although the declaration of war brought some clarity to the situation, particularly with respect to North Africans, who were readily incorporated into the army, it did not resolve the underlying ambiguity of migrants' status. Foreigners were interned, but they were also conscripted. Sometimes this was even true of the same individual. The decisions made in this regard were often quite arbitrary, but they also often bore witness to the ongoing effects of factors—international power politics, relationships between the local and national administration, family connections, and political proclivities, among others—that had influenced migrant rights for the past two decades. Ironically, while Italians earned most-favored foreigner status in 1919 because they had served as France's allies in the First World War, they earned privileged access to naturalization in 1939 precisely because this allowed France to deprive Italy of soldiers. Ironically, too, the most committed antifascists were also the ones French authorities deemed most dangerous, especially if they were communists, particularly following the Nazi-Soviet pact. As far as refugees were concerned, it is hard not to wonder, with Vicki Caron, whether the failure to overcome the fears about the risks refugees posed to French security may have constituted a "missed opportunity."[107]

Still, this chapter is not about the road not taken, but rather the one that was. In many ways, it was a well-worn path: National authorities issued policies, local authorities implemented them based on their own understandings of what was being asked of them, and new policies tried to correct for the errors of local implementation. What this meant for migrants was that their rights were enormously volatile during this time. Even more than labor contracts or welfare programs or family relations had been, national security was a moving target; to base migrant rights on it virtually invited arbitrary treatment. As a result, migrants and government officials entered the Second World War in a state of insecurity.

Republican France, One and Divisible?

After the Second World War, a provisional government led by General Charles de Gaulle set about reconstructing the republic and writing a new constitution. Because authoritarian government, and collaboration with Nazi Germany after the fall of France in June 1940, had discredited the Vichy government and divided the citizenry, reviving democracy and the promise of universal liberty and equality became vital to the task of postwar reconstruction. Migration policy, too, was overhauled. Or so it seems from a superficial glance: Regulations now explicitly aimed at encouraging permanent immigration, not just temporary migration, and a new National Immigration Office was founded to coordinate policy among ministries. As novel as these developments looked, however, France's postwar immigration regime built on practices that had emerged through the push and pull of interwar negotiations. Beneath the surface of the republican universalism reaffirmed after the war lies the history revealed in this book. The legacies of that history can be felt in the ongoing conflicts that trouble French society today.

The nature of these legacies has remained obscure for many reasons. The reinvention of the republic after the Nazi occupation masked the divisions of the late Third Republic. Since then, scholarship taking egalitarian rhetoric at face value has helped to perpetuate the republican myth. While all modern democratic republics claim liberty and equality before the law as core political principles, republican rhetoric in France implies that these are more perfectly realized there than elsewhere, for the republic recognizes no differences among its citizens. In short, France's republic is "one and indivisible" because all those things that breed division are deemed irrelevant to public life. This book, I hope, demystifies French exceptionalism by bringing to life the claims and confrontations that opened the republic's doors to some immigrants yet closed them to others.

MIGRANTS AND THE RESISTANCE MYTH

For more than a decade now, scholars have underscored the extent to which occupation-era France was a "murky moral universe," where the line between survival strategies and accommodation or even collaboration was often a fuzzy one.[1] In the immediate aftermath of the liberation, however, de Gaulle recast wartime choices as morally unambiguous: One had either aided the enemy or stayed true to the republic. Migrants' claims were evaluated through this Manichaean lens. Foreigners could reclaim a stake in postwar society if they became part of the resistance myth. This was hardly much comfort to the few surviving relatives of the 75,000 Jews, among them many foreigners, who had been deported by French authorities to Nazi camps. Their families could not be judged for their wartime choices, because they had been given no choice. But the imperative of reestablishing the republic produced a disregard for such categorical exclusions.[2]

Turning as it did on individual choices, the adjudication of residency rights after the liberation helped propagate the notion of a nation unified in its resistance to Nazism. Bertoldo S., who had been expelled in 1933 for antifascist activity, interned at Vernet, and turned over to Italian authorities for confinement on Ventolene Island, requested that his expulsion be repealed after the war on the grounds that he had participated in the Italian resistance after his imprisonment. French authorities complied in 1949.[3] Bedros B., an Armenian, referred to the "pillaging" of his home by German and French paramilitary forces in May of 1944 as evidence of his resistance when he applied for a "privileged resident" card after the war.[4] Antonio S. was reexpelled on the recommendation of Lyon police in 1946 because his return to Italy in 1940 was evaluated as proving his allegiance to an "enemy army." It was only after a known Lyon resistant vouched for him and said he had returned to France to participate in the resistance that his expulsion was repealed in 1947.[5]

While every resident of France who had lived through the war and occupation had to live with the moral burden of his or her wartime choices, migrants also had to live with the legal ramifications. Wartime survival strategies came back to haunt some migrants. Michele B.'s choice to work for the German forced-labor placement office in Marseille tracking down refractory "volunteers" in order to avoid his own requisition contributed to a postwar conviction for "violating the external security of the state."[6] Pietro E.'s infiltration of communist circles in Lyon in order to inform on them to the Italian consulate and the German occupation authorities, which had helped earn him *sursis* from Vichy authorities until he entered the Service du Travail Obligatoire in 1943, led to his reexpulsion from

France in 1946 as a collaborator.[7] Others tried to find ways to recast their pasts. Zita N. had left France for her native Italy the day after Germany invaded Poland, following an expulsion motivated in part by "injurious remarks" she had made toward France. After the liberation, when she tried to return to France, where three of her six children had been born, she claimed that she and her husband had left Italy in 1924 out of opposition to fascism. Finding that explanation unconvincing, since her husband had been a member of Lyon's Fascio between the wars, authorities repeatedly turned down her requests on the grounds of her alleged fascist sympathies.[8]

As the occupation episode was reinvented, so too was the republic. This helps to explain why the republic has become such a touchstone in contemporary France, particularly as politicians on the extreme Right have sought to downplay the ill effects of occupation and collaboration.[9] For mainstream politicians, Vichy provides a horrific example of what happens when republicanism is forsaken. From there, the view that republicanism abhors all forms of discrimination is not a difficult leap of logic.

For others, the origins of Vichy exclusion lie in the republic itself. This view has been most forcefully articulated by Gérard Noiriel, who argues that the republic forged the concept of a "national community" by giving a social content to French identity. But whereas under the republic this "community" had been an abstraction based on indirect relations—and especially rights—mediated by the state, the Vichy regime attempted to make that community "real," as if the nation were simply a "big family."[10] Through obsessive identification practices—residency cards and the like—the republic had created the means for realizing this discriminatory community, well before Marshal Philippe Pétain assumed full powers. Foreign identification cards prefigured the national identification card instituted in 1941; quotas placed on foreign workers easily led to outright bans on foreign and Jewish employment in the public sector. The *fichier* (central file) of foreigners in the 1920s proved to be the basis for the infamous *fichier juif*, which aided in deporting Jews from France. And the 1927 nationality code created the possibility of "denaturalization," put into practice under Vichy.

Neither the view that invents a republican tradition of egalitarianism nor the one that emphasizes the exclusionary aspects of republican nationalism, however, adequately captures the dynamics of France's encounter with immigrants in the 1920s and 1930s. As we have seen, migrant rights were highly contingent on variations in social, political, and administrative life. Even the most exclusionary decrees often engendered differences in implementation. Indeed, new opportunities for inclusion emerged from attempts made to exclude migrants. And, in the first months of the Second World War, some migrants were slated for both inclusion and exclusion. The republic, then, was not a monolith, nor should it be analyzed as such.

RESTORING THE REPUBLIC'S REAL STORY

As the First World War ended, there was great hope that international migration to France could be engineered to ensure that migrants and French nationals would share the same labor and social rights. After the First World War, however, bilateral treaties took the place of the imagined universal labor laws, and a guest-worker regime emerged that linked residency rights to labor contracts and privileged some nationalities over others in the acquisition of those contracts. Meanwhile, because the state retreated considerably from managing day-to-day industrial relations, the idea that worker identification cards could be used to "direct with surgical precision the flow of labor according to the needs of the national economy," as Noiriel puts it, proved largely illusory.[11] French economic planners confronted a national economy riddled with regional differences that made engineering population flows difficult, or perhaps impossible.

When migrants confronted activist state officials in Lyon who sought to enforce the guest-worker model by requiring them to leave as regional industries began reducing personnel in the 1930s, their responses—shifting from salaried work to independent contracting, moving to other departments, requesting naturalization, agreeing (at least officially) to live on partners' incomes, and invoking entitlement to the provisions of the welfare state—all demonstrated the limits of the guest-worker model of migration. The ability of foreigners to adopt these strategies hampered state attempts to exert constant control over them, forcing Lyon authorities to adapt their approach to regulating migrants.

Family ties also challenged the guest-worker program, as familial considerations started to penetrate relationships between migrants and officials in Lyon. Their meaning and importance, however, shifted over time. In the early 1930s, Lyon officials took family ties into account inasmuch as they regarded families as economic units that, they believed, should not be severed. If a male head of household were expelled, they reasoned, his wife and children should be as well. This same reasoning also led authorities to grant exceptions to the guest-worker policy by authorizing the residency of migrants—especially married women—who could, they believed, count on family support. Because this rationale was used to drive migrant women out of the labor market, it was not seen as inconsistent with protectionist objectives. Nor were residency authorizations granted to men who supported their families through business endeavors or independent contracting considered antiprotectionist, at least until pressure grew later in the 1930s to protect commerce and the professions, particularly from competition by Jews.

The notion of family that became central to rights negotiations later in the 1930s was different. By that time, at issue was not so much the family as an economic unit but rather the family as a demographic resource for the nation and its military. Now migrants claimed rights through their families, not just to support them. Because the family's role had shifted, how the family supported itself became less pertinent than how it was composed.

If this shift was less apparent in Marseille, it was probably because a rigid guest-worker model never had made much sense in the port city in the first place. Marseille authorities never warmed to regulating the economy as such; when they did, as when they tried to set limits on the numbers of foreigners allowed to play in a nightclub band, their efforts bordered on caricature. Rather, they were always more interested in policing public order. To this end, family had always been important, while the quintessential guest worker, a single unattached man with an intermittent income and precarious lodging, was more likely to be deemed a threat than a rights-bearing individual. Unlike their Lyon counterparts, Marseille officials cared less where a migrant was employed than whether he or she worked at all. Foreign transients in the city center of Marseille were targeted for repression by police, not because they had violated the terms of their labor contracts, though many undoubtedly had, but because they were regarded as social deviants.

What made a difference to Marseille's police in their negotiations with migrants was the appearance of stability in a city whose population was constantly in flux. Already in the 1920s, authorities evaluated residents of the city's outer districts as members of Marseille society, not just as workers in its economy. Of course, as migrants' coping mechanisms during the depression proved, the line separating the city's districts and populations was not clear. Many residents of the periphery had once lived in the central districts, and many returned to work on the city's docks when other sources of income dried up. Nonetheless, citywide crackdowns on migrants' civil liberties usually followed on the heels of political, not economic crises: the de Castelnau incident in 1925, the assassination in 1934, the placement of Marseille and the Bouches-du-Rhône administrations under receivership following the dock strike, and the October 1938 fire.

The line between temporary migrant workers and permanent immigrants had always been a fuzzy one. Nonetheless, differentiations between the two became, over time, an integral part of national policy. Increasing unemployment and political polarization helped, by the mid-1930s, to provoke a rationing of rights on a new basis. Migrants adjusted their strategies accordingly. Threatened with exclusion, they found that family and prolonged residence in France—rather than the more abstract labor contracts—became crucial criteria for claiming rights. Even militants who in the 1920s had rejected bourgeois family politics and nationalism found themselves party to both as they invoked their own family ties to protect their interests in France.

By the middle of the 1930s, the guest-worker model had been turned upside down. Instead of residency rights turning on labor contracts, the right to work increasingly depended on a prior residency authorization. In this way, a regime of exception, or privilege, developed under the surface of policy that remained outwardly committed to enforcing limits on all migrants. A new distinction emerged between those admitted solely to work and those admitted to live "regardless of the labor market situation." With guest-worker policies remaining on the books, the former could easily become illegal aliens if a contract were severed or an identity card rejected. This shift made pariahs of the single, mobile men whom France's migration policy had been designed to attract. So too it rendered new migrants, especially the increasing numbers of Jewish refugees. Meanwhile, those who had achieved precisely what French policy had aimed to avoid—long-term residency in France and lasting ties to the country—found new grounds for legal incorporation. Immigrants had arrived at this situation by following different paths, some more treacherous than others. The claims of some to participate in the social contract had been facilitated by labor contracts. For others, legal recognition came only after years of precariousness.

From the mid-1930s, the adjudication of migrant rights in Lyon and Marseille increasingly followed similar patterns, as officials in both cities distinguished between migrants and immigrants. Like the migrants themselves, authorities in each city arrived at this convergence after following different paths. Lyon adopted this bifurcated approach after a wholesale crackdown on foreign workers in the early depression years. Faced with the resistance of migrants, Rhône authorities began granting exceptions little by little. Marseille officials had always distinguished between the temporary migrants who dwelled in the central districts and the seemingly more rooted populations of the city's semirural periphery. When an enduring depression punctured by a stunning assassination in Marseille led the government to strive to eliminate the country's "superfluous" foreign laborers, national policy makers discovered what officials in both Lyon and Marseille already knew: Because an indiscriminate crackdown was impractical, they had to become discriminating. Marseille's idiosyncratic treatment of immigrants now became the rule.

With the crisis created by the collapse of the Popular Front and the escalation of international conflict, the state brought new resources and zeal to regulating migrants. Once again, however, policy prescriptions confronted unexpected developments in practice. As local authorities assumed new responsibility for adjudicating migrants' rights in the interest of protecting national security, they found it easier to err on the side of repression than to distinguish between undesirable and desirable foreigners, a distinction that constantly shifted anyway. As central administrators continually redefined the criteria for "desirable" foreigners, migrants found themselves more vulnerable to repression. At the same time that national security concerns produced new exclusions of migrants, however, they also led to new forms of inclusion, primarily as soldiers. The ambiguity that this "two-faced" rights regime engendered persisted until the fall of France.

LEGACIES AFTER THE LIBERATION

The changing fortunes of migrants who arrived in France between the world wars show that it is misleading to insist on the historical continuity of the unitary republic. As Miriam Feldblum has astutely noted, republicanism is a political ideology, not an analytical tool.[12] Uncovering the vicissitudes of migrant rights in interwar France restores complexity and historical contingency to the Third Republic's civic order. It also sheds light on how migrant rights have developed since the collapse of the Third Republic in 1940. The policies and practices that developed piecemeal over 20 years of trial and error—as unions and employers negotiated, migrants claimed rights, diplomats made deals, and officials fought bureaucratic battles—became principles in France following the liberation.

After the Second World War, France's new immigration regime made no pretense of workers of the world sharing rights. To be sure, the events of the war had helped render some of the explicitly racist views of some postwar policy makers politically unacceptable.[13] Still, postwar policy placed migrants into one of three categories. First, "temporary" migrants would be granted one-year residency contracts and would be forbidden to marry in France without authorization from the Ministries of Justice and Interior. Second, "ordinary" residents were authorized to enter for three years with the possibility of renewing their contracts. In both these cases, limits could be placed on the professions migrants were allowed to exercise and, resuscitating a restriction from the Flandin decrees, the department in which they could live. Third and finally, "privileged residents" would acquire residency permits lasting ten years with the possibility of renewal. This final category clearly was invented to redress a perceived demographic deficit rather than punctual economic needs, since it gave benefits to migrants of childbearing age and those with families. In particular, foreigners who had entered France before turning 35 could obtain privileged status after only three years. For those with children, the age threshold was raised by five years for each child.[14] What was more, foreigners married to French nationals or having French children were granted special privileges—they now could request the "privileged resident" card after only a year in France.[15] Changes in the nationality code reinforced the new migration policies. Five years' residence would now be required for naturalization instead of three, meaning that "temporary" and "ordinary" residents were by definition precluded from naturalizing unless their residency authorizations were renewed, or they met the criteria for exceptions. Exceptions once again followed a largely populationist logic: Foreigners married to Frenchwomen could naturalize after two years, and fathers of three legitimate minor children could apply for naturalization with no waiting period.[16]

The political scientist Vincent Viet has called the post–Second World War policies regarding family migration "very liberal" when compared to interwar legislation on foreigners. Without question, the new overtly populationist approach to migration exhibited more openness to permanent settlement than had the guest-worker policies of the 1920s. Nonetheless, the new laws clearly built on practices that emerged from negotiations between migrants and authorities and that shaped exceptions made to guest-worker policy in the mid-1930s. In fact, it was in part through the attempt to enforce guest-worker policy in a climate of growing xenophobia in the 1930s that authorities had begun to distinguish not only in practice but also in policy between temporary migrants and permanent immigrants. This development helped foster an ontological distinction between labor and settlement migration, one that, as Abdelmalek Sayad has suggested, is

no more than a disguised way of making, with a semblance of (ethical) neutrality and by using a supposedly objective vocabulary, a distinction between an "assimilable" immigration . . . which will be rapidly (and if need be, with our help) transformed into a "settler immigration," and an inassimilable immigration . . . that can only be and remain (and if need be, we will make sure that it is) a "labour immigration."[17]

After the Second World War, what had initially constituted exceptions to the rule gained the force of law. Indeed, more than at any time in the

1920s or 1930s, temporary labor migrants and permanent immigrants were distinguished by their formal rights. At the same time, distinctions between nationals and privileged residents diminished, as the latter were allowed free circulation and free choice of profession.

Suggestions from some members of the High Committee on Population that France institute national preferences never appeared in the final ordinances issued by the provisional government after the liberation. This confirms, for Patrick Weil, the "victory of republican values."[18] Nevertheless, what Weil calls the "action state" (*L'État acteur*) got around this "legal state" (*L'État de droit*) by installing special emigration offices in select countries, concluding labor agreements with European states, instituting new visa regimes, targeting some groups more than others for forced repatriation, and engaging in a number of other discriminatory practices.[19] Refugees and stateless persons no longer fell through the cracks in this system, since their *droit de cité* was recognized.[20] Refugees from the Spanish Civil War were retroactively subsumed into those protected by the 1933 Geneva Convention, despite protests from the Spanish government.[21] Meanwhile, North Africans increasingly challenged the underlying assumptions of France's migration policy.

With the liberation, General de Gaulle called upon the French to reconstruct not only national but also imperial unity. This required, he concluded, granting colonized peoples more of a stake in what was now called the "French Union." Although a distinction remained between France and its "associated" states, rights were expanded in what some would call a last-ditch effort at saving the empire. Ordinances issued after the war recognized French Muslims from Algeria (or FMAs, as they were now known) as "French citizens." Although these reforms still did not offer Muslims political rights identical to those enjoyed by the non-Muslim French, it did render Algerians free to come and go across the Mediterranean at will for the better part of two decades.

Precisely because of Algerians' facility in accessing mainland France, however, the French government shifted its policies to "encourage the spontaneous arrival of other nationalities by giving them the same rights as Algerians."[22] Although the Evian Accords ending the Algerian war (1954–62) reaffirmed the right to free circulation between what were now two independent nations, within a few years the French government concluded that this was against its interests, and new limits on Algerian migrants' movement to and residency in France were negotiated with Houari Boumediene's government.[23] This new restriction, of course, was profoundly different from the visa-type requirements imposed in the mid-1920s, because after 1962 Algerians really were foreigners, unless they had opted for French citizenship. After labor migration was officially halted in 1974 in response to rising unemployment, repatriation policies targeted Algerians. Exempted from repatriation were refugees (because they benefited from the non-*refoulement* clauses of international law), members of the European Community (long before the Schengen accords assured the free circulation of signatories' citizens), and Portuguese and Spanish nationals as "future Europeans."[24] In this way, as Vincent Viet has noted, "absolute" foreigners became, by virtue of bilateral treaties and European integration, "relative" foreigners, while those coming from France's former colonies shifted from being "relative" French citizens to "absolute" foreigners.[25]

As in the 1920s and 1930s, a thorough evaluation of migrant rights in France since 1945 would require an analysis of not only policy but also practice and lived experience. As the suburban riots of fall 2005 demonstrate, many of the same issues that affected the substance of citizenship between the wars continue to do so to this day: jobs, policing, family, housing, and welfare, not to mention the vicissitudes of international relations.[26] Discriminatory police practices and access to jobs affect citizenship on what Danièle Lochak and Aléxis Spire call an "infra-juridical" level.[27] So do housing conditions. The very lodging that was built to house temporary workers in the 1960s and 1970s has come to permanently mark France's built environment. In so doing, it has helped turn social stratification into spatial segregation so manifest that in 2003 the French minister for urban policy characterized the most notorious housing projects as existing "on the margins of national territory."[28] In the aftermath of an earlier wave of suburban violence outside Lyon, children of immigrants set off in 1983 from housing projects in Vénissieux on a march "for equality and against racism" that traversed France and grew to be 100,000 strong.[29] Politics in these "hot zones" or "difficult neighborhoods"—as the French press often refers to the suburbs of Lyon, the *cités* of northern Marseille, and other suburban housing compounds populated predominantly by immigrants and their descendants—has changed significantly in the more than 20 years since the march, but feelings of disenfranchisement among their residents remain acute. Meanwhile, deteriorating suburban housing conditions and radicalized—especially Islamist—politics have contributed to some radical measures on the government's own part: Low-income housing towers are being imploded at the planned rate of 40,000 units per year, in the hope that by removing the physical barriers of exclusion, civil society can be revitalized. One is reminded of the smaller-scale evacuation of Marseille's Camp Oddo beginning in 1926 when, after years of neglect, authorities suddenly realized that it had become its own "autonomous republic."

The fact that downtrodden housing projects within France are perceived as existing outside the country's national boundaries, or that scholars of immigration invent terms such as "relative" and "absolute" nationality, and distinguish between the "legal state" and the "action state," or between juridical rights and "infra-juridical" ones, suggests how limited the unitary republican model is for understanding the distribution of rights in France since the advent of mass immigration. Scholarship on the diversity of French regional cultures has proved that France is a pluralistic country, despite the legacies of Jacobinism.[30] However, this appreciation has yet to penetrate reasoning about France as an immigrant nation. Indeed, one scholar has argued that France is a "country" but not a "nation" of immigrants, despite the fact that almost a quarter of French citizens have at least one foreign-born grandparent.[31]

The tendency to write diversity and difference out of what is meant by the "nation" in France is exacerbated by a French political culture that, in the past two decades, has insisted that the republican model "only recognizes nationality" and not social, religious, or cultural distinctions.[32] Within this framework of understanding, differences are treated as aberrations of French norms rather than as complex products of French and transnational societal relationships. Relying on this particular vision of republicanism's capacity to shape French social life presents a number of drawbacks. Because this line of analysis assumes that legal principles structure society virtually autonomously, it also assumes that all nationals have access to the same substance of citizenship—and that all foreigners do not. I have demonstrated that this was not true in interwar France and have suggested that it remains false today.

Scholarship that sees citizenship as an "instrument of social closure," where nationality is depicted as an "internally inclusive" and "externally exclusive" "membership system," has inadvertently perpetuated the French republican myth.[33] In practice, the adjudication of legal rights in France, as we have seen, has been neither entirely exclusionary nor entirely inclusive. Legal norms did provide an instrument of social closure in interwar France, but they proved more powerful in some circumstances than in others. Legal closure was easier to enforce against those who were already socially vulnerable, as residents of Marseille's central districts and women in depression-era Lyon both learned. At the same time, the relationship between legal and social norms was not unidirectional but dialectical. At the very moment when French lawmakers in the 1930s demanded a wider application of exclusionary policy, some migrants successfully drew on family life and long-term residency to modify the legal limits of inclusion. The "citizenship of aliens" emerged from intersecting legal, political, social, cultural, diplomatic, and imperial relationships that allowed some migrants to enjoy "thick" citizenship, whereby they enjoyed a substantial set of enforceable rights, while the citizenship of others was comparatively "thin."[34]

The boundaries of citizenship depended not only on how officials viewed migrants but also on how migrants related to authorities and what resources they brought to bear on those relationships. Some migrants were able to exploit divisions within French bureaucracy with regard to their residency rights, thereby proving that citizenship depended not only on their own relationships with government authorities but also on relationships between various ministries responsible for migration. The experience of citizenship also depended on the degree of resolve, force, coercion, or manipulation authorities were willing to use in their interactions with migrants. That is why North Africans often ended up with thin social welfare rights even though their legal relationships to the French state were thick.

The argument that states are membership systems also attributes more coherence to the state than it ever had. Despite the intense administrative centralization for which modern France has long been known, the state did not function as a unitary entity pursuing a single clear objective. Nor is the story of rights within a democratic nation-state ever wholly about the internal politics or culture of that state alone, for while international relations in theory concern affairs between states, they also affect intrastate relations in profound ways, as we have seen.[35] If this was already true in interwar Europe, it has never been truer than in today's expanding European Union.

And yet while we should not overestimate the state's capacity to pursue coherent policies regarding inclusion and exclusion, neither is it accurate to characterize migrant rights as emanating from some open-ended civil society that knows no national boundaries. According to this view, an expansion of rights among immigrants signifies a weakening of the nation-state vis-à-vis global forces such as human rights norms.[36] To the extent that universal ideals exist, however, they are always put into practice within nations, regions, cities, or even neighborhoods. Moreover, while scholars positing the expansion of migrant rights in conjunction with the development of international law see this development as linear and progressive, this book demonstrates that rights do not just expand; they also contract. They become thicker and thinner, not only over time, but across space and among people.

In interwar France, universal ideals were modified by migrants' interactions with coworkers, employers, neighbors, consulates, union and political leaders, local bureaucrats, and the police, as well as by the vicissitudes of international and imperial affairs. In Europe's new millennium, such contingent relationships will continue to shape the contours of rights. In addition, migrant rights now depend on novel and equally complex relationships established through constitutional and jurisdictional battles, growing judicial activism in the domain of rights, increasing labor mobility, intensifying religious conflict, mounting social welfare crises, and transnational political and cultural organizing within civil society. Will France face these new challenges with a "self-deluding, rearguard, nationalist *repli sur soi-même*," insisting on the "peculiarities" of its republican political culture, as Adrian Favell suggests?[37] Will it "re-ethnicize" citizenship, as Christian Joppke has put it, while most of northwest Europe moves in the opposite direction?[38] The social history of migrant rights at an earlier historical watershed moment—the end of the First World War—suggests that the answer will not depend solely on decisions made in parliament or in government commissions. Access to rights will likely remain, as has been the case historically, contested territory. To be sure, battles over rights will be waged in parliament, the United Nations, and European institutions. But they will also be fought in precinct houses and courts, schools and hospitals, the workplace and the street. The results may be unpredictable, uneven, or even ephemeral. They may also change the boundaries of belonging in France and Europe. Surely they already have.

Abbreviations Used in the Notes

ADBR	Archives Départementales des Bouches-du-Rhône
ADC	Archives Départementales du Cher
ADR	Archives Départementales du Rhône
AMAE	Archives du Ministère des Affaires Étrangères
AML	Archives Municipales de Lyon
AMV	Archives Municipales de Villeurbanne
AMVx	Archives Municipales de Vénissieux
AN	Archives Nationales
BMT	*Bulletin du ministère du travail*
Bur.	Bureau
CAOM	Centre des Archives de la France d'Outre-Mer
CC	Commissaire Chef
CCP	Chef du Cabinet du Préfet
CGT	Conféderation Générale du Travail
CGTU	Conféderation Générale du Travail Unitaire
Circ.	Circulaire
CPS	Commissaire de Police Spéciale
CS	Chef de la Sûreté
DAA	Direction des Affaires Algériennes
DGSN	Direction Générale de la Sûreté Nationale
Dir. T.	Direction du Travail
DSG	Direction de la Sûreté Générale
Exp.	Expulsion
IS	*L'information sociale*
JODCD	*Journal officiel, débats parlementaires, Chambre des Députés*

JODP	*Journal officiel, documents parlementaires*
JOLD	*Journal officiel, lois et décrets*
MAS-CRDM	Ministère des Affaires Sociales, du Travail et de la Solidarité: Centre des Ressources Documentaires Multimédia
Min. AE	Ministère des Affaires Étrangères
Min. HAP	Ministre de l'Hygiène, de l'Assistance et de la Prévoyance Sociales
Min. I.	Ministère de l'Intérieur
Min. J.	Ministère de la Justice
Min. T.	Ministère du Travail
MOE	Main-d'Oeuvre Étrangère
ODMPST	Office Départemental et Municipal de Placement et de la Statistique du Travail
ODP	Office Départemental de Placement
Prés. Cons.	Président du Conseil (prime minister)
SCMO	Service Central de la Main-d'Oeuvre
SGP	Secrétaire Général pour la Police
SMOE	Service de la Main-d'Oeuvre Étrangère

Notes

PREFACE

1. Lewis, *America, Nation or Confusion*. Inscribed copy in the private collection of Griff Lewis.
2. On this point, see Hollifield, *Immigrants, Markets and States*.

SOURCES AND ACKNOWLEDGMENTS

1. For the text of the Geneva Convention on the Status of Refugees of 1951, see United Nations Office of the High Commissioner for Human Rights, "Convention Relating to the Status of Refugees," http://www.unhchr.ch/html/menu3/b/0_c_ref.htm (accessed December 14, 2004).

INTRODUCTION

1. Statistics from *BMT* 1–3 (January–March 1924): 93. Information on Boris and Bruno is from their expulsion files, respectively found in Archives Départementales des Bouches-du-Rhône (hereinafter ADBR) 4 M 1959 and Archives Départementales du Rhône expulsion files silo 1, travée 154 et suivantes (hereinafter ADR Exp.), box 2. Throughout this book, names of individuals have been changed.
2. Noiriel, *Creuset*, 21, 253; Schor, *Histoire de l'immigration en France*, 125; Guichard and Noiriel, *Construction*, 287.
3. Statistics from Cross, *Immigrant Workers*, 181.
4. Tilly, "Citizenship," 8.
5. Hollifield, *Immigrants, Markets and States*, 3; see also Polanyi, *The Great Transformation*.
6. Weber, *Economy and Society*, esp. 43–46; on social closure in relation to immigration, see Brubaker, *Citizenship and Nationhood*, 23.
7. Rosenberg, *Policing Paris*.
8. The United States and Argentina, prime destinations for European labor migrants until the war, instituted legal limits that severely curtailed immigration thereafter; the United Kingdom also raised barriers to immigration from the turn of the century forward.

9. On liberalism's dim prospects, see Mazower, *Dark Continent*.

10. The average cabinet's life span ranged from four to eight months between 1914 and 1940.

11. Soviet decrees in 1922 stripped exiled Russians of their nationality.

12. ADBR 14 M 23_21: Circ. Min. T. (Dir. T., 1st bur.) to prefects, 2 December 1926. Scholars have since shown that the French were more mobile than was once thought. See esp. Chatelain, *Les migrants temporaires*; Lequin, *Les ouvriers de la région lyonnaise*; Moch, *Paths to the City*; Rosental, *Les sentiers invisibles*.

13. Ibid.

14. Attributed to Max Frisch. See Philip L. Martin, "Germany: Reluctant Land of Immigration," in Cornelius, Martin, and Hollifield, Eds., *Controlling Immigration*, 192.

15. Rosenberg, *Policing Paris*, xiv. His chap. 3 explores the limits on this seemingly total control.

16. Rosenberg asserts that Paris had some 12,000 police in the 1920s and some 20,000 by 1939. *Policing Paris*, 9. The door-to-door verifications of immigrant status he describes and the Paris police force's ability to routinely check businesses for illegal employment of foreigners simply had no parallel in any part of France outside the capital.

17. ADR Exp., box 2: Prefect to Min. I., 25 April 1934; reply, 4 May 1934.

18. Kreher's name appears in other files I have examined concerning other foreigners.

19. Such trends in scholarship are too vast to enumerate; for an excellent overview, see Green, *Repenser les migrations*. For the culture clash argument, see esp. Huntington, *Who Are We?* Huntington makes a similar argument about immigration to France in his *Clash of Civilizations*, 67–68.

20. See esp. Noiriel, *Les origines républicaines*. For a more extreme version, see Deschodt and Huguenin, *La république xénophobe*. For subtler reflections on continuities with Vichy, see Paxton, "Gérard Noiriel's Third Republic"; Marrus and Paxton, *Vichy France and the Jews*, chap. 2; Peschanski, *La France des camps*, chap. 1; Caron, *Uneasy Asylum*, chaps. 9–11; Rosenberg, *Policing Paris*, 199–212.

21. See esp. Weil, *La France et ses étrangers*; idem, *Qu'est-ce qu'un Français?*; Cross, *Immigrant Workers*; Noiriel, *Creuset*; idem, *La tyrannie du national*; Bonnet, *Les pouvoirs publics français*; Viet, *La France immigrée*. For an approach that looks at enforcement, albeit only with respect to Paris, see Spire, *Étrangers à la carte*.

22. These studies on specific regions and/or national or ethnic groups are nonetheless indispensable in their detail. A partial list follows: Noiriel, *Longwy*; Ponty, *Polonais méconnus*; Milza, *Voyage en Ritalie*; Rygiel, *Destins immigrés*; Blanc-Chaléard, *Les Italiens dans l'est parisien*; Massard-Guilbaud, *Des Algériens à Lyon*; Temime et al., *Migrance*. See also Caron, *Uneasy Asylum*, a rare example of a work that examines both the specific experience of an ethnic group and the changing nature of national policy. Only one major work has been comparative: Green, *Ready-to-Wear*.

23. Noiriel, *Les ouvriers,* 141.

24. In contrast to the North and Northeast, which attracted larger concentrations of Poles and Belgians.

25. For a theoretical discussion of such narrative "fictions," see Davis, *Fiction in the Archives*; and Sahlins, *Unnaturally French,* esp. chap. 3, "The Use and Abuse of Naturalization." See also Fassin, "La supplique."

26. See, e.g., Todd, *Le destin des immigrés*; Brubaker, *Citizenship and Nationhood*; Schnapper, *La France de l'intégration.* Other scholars, meanwhile, invoke France's "republican" model but make no explicit comparison to other countries. See Hollifield, "Immigration and Republicanism"; for critiques, see, in the same volume, Feldblum, "Reconsidering the 'Republican' Model"; Weil, "From Hidden Consensus to Hidden Divergence"; and Tapinos, "Questioning the Hidden Consensus," 177–88.

27. Schain, "Minorities and Immigrant Incorporation in France"; and Fassin, "Good to Think"; Favell, *Philosophies.* Fassin's article has an excellent summary of the development of French thinking on this matter. See also Lebovics, *Bringing the Empire Back Home,* 115–42.

28. Favell, *Philosophies,* 44.

29. Comte Stanislas-Marie-Adélaide de Clermont-Tonnere, cited in Hyman, *The Jews of Modern France,* 27. Citizenship was granted to Jews on 27 September 1791.

30. Tribalat was widely condemned for proposing a census category of "Français de souche" (French of French "stock"). On the issues involved, see esp. Blum, "Comment décrire les immigrés"; Calvès, " 'Il n'y a pas de race ici.' "

31. This was widely reported on in the French and international news media, for which the references are too numerous to cite. For a comprehensive and critical overview, see Tévanian, *Le voile médiatique.* Parliamentary debates were held in the chamber on 3–5 February 2004 and in the Senate on 2–3 March 2004. For the law, no. 2004-228 of 15 March 2004, see *JOLD,* 17 March 2004, 5190.

32. Debré cited in Philippe Ridet, "Le camp chiraquien a réservé un accueil glacial aux propositions de Nicolas Sarkozy," *Le monde,* 13 January 2005. Sarkozy presented his objectives in a "Voeux de la presse" on 13 January 2005. See also "M. Villepin répond à M. Sarkozy sur les quotas d'immigration," *Le monde,* 14 January 2005; Philippe Ridet and Jean-Louis Saux, "Dominique de Villepin se rapproche de l'idée des quotas," *Le monde,* 19 January 2005; Christophe Jakubysyn, "Présentation du projet de loi sur 'l'immigration choisie," *Le monde,* 30 March 2006, 15. Labor migration as such has been barred with very few exceptions since 1974, leaving "family reunification" and asylum applications as the main legal means for entering the country permanently. Clandestine labor migration has soared.

33. Tocqueville, *Democracy in America,* 98. Tocqueville saw in Jacobinism an extension of tendencies that had begun under absolutism.

34. Crozier, *La société bloquée.* Before Crozier, Stanley Hoffmann had made a similar argument about the "stalemate society." See Hoffmann, "Paradoxes of the French Political Community." For an updated version, see idem, *Decline or Renewal?* For an alternative analysis, see Suleiman, *Private Power.*

35. Sahlins, *Boundaries*; Ford, *Creating the Nation*; Woloch, *The New Regime*; Nord, *The Republican Moment*. Both Sahlins and Ford can be read as critiques of Weber, *Peasants into Frenchmen*.

36. See esp. Cooper, *Decolonization and African Society*; Conklin, *A Mission to Civilize*; Emmanuelle Saada, "La 'question des métis'"; idem, "Citoyens et sujets"; Blévis, "La citoyenneté Française"; idem, "Les avatars"; Shepard, *The Invention of Decolonization*.

37. This argument has been made most forcefully by Brubaker, *Citizenship and Nationhood*. While scholars disagree about the specifics of Brubaker's analysis with respect to France and Germany, the underlying premise of the book—that the state is not just a territorial organization but a membership system—has been widely accepted.

38. Brubaker, "Membership without Citizenship"; Hammar, *Democracy and the Nation State*; and idem, "State, Nation, and Dual Citizenship," in Brubaker, *Immigration and the Politics of Citizenship*, 81–95; Soysal, *Limits of Citizenship*; for a similar, albeit less sanguine, argument about the internationalization of rights regimes, see Jacobson, *Rights across Borders*. For a critical perspective on this argument, see Joppke, *Immigration and the Nation-State*; idem, "Immigration Challenges the Nation State," 5–46, and Virginie Giraudon, "Citizenship Rights for Non-Citizens: France, Germany and the Netherlands," 272–318, both in Joppke, *Challenge to the Nation-State*; and Morris, *Managing Migration*.

CHAPTER 1

1. Castles, "The Guest-Worker in Western Europe," 762.

2. Zola, *Germinal*.

3. Perrot, "Les rapports des ouvriers français et des ouvriers étrangers," 4–9; Dornel, *La France hostile*, 33–37.

4. The most comprehensive history of modern French nationality law is Weil, *Qu'est-ce qu'un Français?* See also Brubaker, *Citizenship*; and Noiriel, *Creuset*. For the codes themselves, see Ministère de la Justice, *La nationalité française*.

5. Noiriel, *Creuset*, 76–95; Dornel, *La France hostile*, esp. 95–132.

6. The workers the government recruited included 186,000 Spanish and Portuguese, 7,500 Italians, 25,000 Greeks, 78,500 Algerians, 18,000 Tunisians, 35,500 Moroccans, 4,500 Malgaches, 49,000 Indochinese, and 36,000 Chinese. Viet, *La France immigrée*, 36n3. Viet's calculations, drawn from Direction de la Population et des Migrations archives, closely match the estimations of colonial recruits found in Nogaro and Weil, *La main-d'oeuvre étrangère et coloniale*, 25. His statistics for European recruits, however, far surpass the 81,000 estimated by Cross, *Immigrant Workers*, 33. European and "colonial" immigrants were administered separately during the war. The former fell under the authority of the Ministry of Armaments and subsequently the Ministry of Labor. The latter— including the Chinese, although China had no colonial relationship to France— fell under the authority of the Ministry of War. See also Stovall, "The Color Line behind the Lines," 741–42, 737–69. Numbers of colonial migrants are also con-

firmed in AMAE K—Afrique, 1918–40—Questions Générales, vol. 30, folio 106: "Au sujet d'économies réalisables sur la main-d'oeuvre coloniale."

7. Horne, *Labour at War,* 303.

8. Ibid., 333.

9. On the plans for postwar recruitment, see esp. Ibid., chaps. 3, 4, and 8.

10. On the growth of the CGT, see Kriegel, *La croissance de la C.G.T.*

11. AN F[14] 11337: Circ., Min. Public Works, Central Service of Military and Commercial Exploitation in the Maritime Ports, 20 December 1918. See also Lewis, "Une théorie raciale des valeurs?" 223–40.

12. There is no extant record of polls to other public authorities besides the ports. For the port authority responses, see note 11. For Algerian repatriations, see Chapter 6.

13. The term is borrowed from Manela, "Wilsonian Moment."

14. Comité Confédéral National, "Programme minimum de la C.G.T.," 170.

15. Bilateral migration and/or labor and assistance treaties or conventions were initially concluded with Poland (3 September 1919); Italy (30 November 1919; ratified 10 January 1921); and Czechoslovakia (20 March 1920). Bilateral treaties also were concluded with Luxembourg (4 January 1923) and Belgium (24 December 1924). Belgium also had an early treaty regarding miners from 14 February 1921. The 1924 Belgian treaty remained unratified for more than three years; the Luxembourgian treaty was ratified after a year and a half but then rarely invoked in policy memoranda mentioning the treaties. A treaty with Spain was signed in 1932 but not ratified until December 1933.

16. The Italian treaty spelled these out most explicitly; many of the other treaties had more blanket provisions. No treaty, including the Italian one, regulated the minutiae of labor relations to the extent implied by Catherine Collomp, "Immigrants, Labor Markets, and the State."

17. Cross, "The Structure of Labor Immigration," 87.

18. Director of Spanish Emigration (1928), cited in Denéchère, *La politique espagnole,* 107–8.

19. Marshall, "Citizenship and Social Class," 72.

20. See esp. Esping-Andersen, *The Three Worlds of Welfare Capitalism,* 55ff.

21. AMAE K—Afrique, 1918–40—Questions Générales, vol. 31: P. Hémery, avocat, à M. le Maréchal Lyautey, Commissaire Résident Général à Rabat, 7 December 1922.

22. ADBR 4 M 948: Port-de-Bouc mayor to Bouches-du-Rhône prefect, 30 January 1923, and handwritten comments in margin; prefect to Port-de-Bouc mayor, 5 February 1923.

23. AML 0747 WP 162_3: Note relative au voeu proposé par M. l'Adjoint Leghouy au sujet des taxes sur les étrangers, n.d. [1924].

24. AML 0747 WP 162_3: Fonds Municipal du Chômage, Règlement Adopté par le Conseil Municipal, 27 December 1926.

25. AN F 1a 4524: Inspection Générale des Services Administratifs.

26. AML 0747 WP 145_1: City of Marseille, assistance office. Deputy mayor of Marseille to mayor of Lyon, 26 April 1928; emphasis in original. The advantages and disadvantages of special "Nansen" refugee passports are discussed in Chapter 5.

27. ADBR 1 M 1782: Prefect to Min. HAP (Cabinet du Directeur), 12 December 1923.

28. ADBR 1 M 1775: Multiple exchanges and, esp., Le Représentant de la République Arménienne à Marseille au Préfet (Bouches-du-Rhône), 18 January 1923.

29. ADBR 1 M 1775: CS to prefect, 22 June 1924; CCP to CPS 28 June 1924; CCP à Castres, 28 June 1924; Chef du Service des Étrangers, Note au Sujet des Orientaux Entrés Clandestinement en France, 28 June 1924.

30. *L'information ouvrière et sociale* 99, 24 April 1924, 4.

31. *L'information ouvrière et sociale* 86, 24 January 1924, 5. All foreign workers and their employers had to pay into the pension plans. Only those foreigners from treaty nations, however, were guaranteed to receive pensions. This provision was in place to prevent employers from privileging the employment of foreign over French workers to cut their payroll taxes.

32. Comité National de la CGTU, 19–20 September 1924, "Main d'oeuvre étrangère," reprinted in *IS* 122, 23 October 1924, 6.

33. Ibid. *Bicot* is a derogatory term, usually used with reference to Arabs. Here the CGTU representative, Monsieur Rousseaux, seems to be using the epithet more generally.

34. ADR 4 M 415: Commissaire de Police à St-Fons, 26 May 1925.

35. ADR 4 M 415: Eysseric [*sic*; Eysséris], Secrétaire des Syndicats des Maçons et Aides de Lyon et sa Banlieue à M. le Préfet du Rhône, 3 June 1925. Pencil underlining. Gustave Eysséris was known to be hostile to the communist influence on the masons union. See Maitron, *Dictionnaire biographique*.

36. On the Société Générale de l'Immigration, see esp. Cross, *Immigrant Workers,* 58ff.

37. For example, of the several hundred reports filed by labor inspectors for the Marseille jurisdiction in 1928, only 20 regard infractions of employment laws pertaining to foreigners. None of these, however, pertains to salaries. See ADBR 14 M 22_56. National files on labor inspection showed a similar lack of focus on foreign employment prior to 1933. See AN F^{22} 301, 551, 556, 562, 576, 577, 579, and 580. Beginning in 1933, labor inspection files contained copies of the new regulations implementing the thresholds on foreign employment in certain industries required by the 10 August 1932 law, but they still showed little evidence of actual inspection. See AN F^{22} 580. A review of the labor inspection bureau's bulletin during the period also suggests little concern with immigrant labor prior to the 1932 law. See *Bulletin de l'inspection du travail et de l'hygiène industrielle,* années 27–40 (1919–32). Files on labor inspection for the Lyon jurisdiction have not been archived.

38. ADBR 14 M 23_4: Dir. ODP to Dir. Agence Blanc, 7 April 1926.

39. As Marcel Roncayolo argues, industries so reliant upon the vicissitudes of worldwide supply, demand, and pricing had little incentive for investment in modernizing techniques. Roncayolo, *Les grammaires,* 168–69.

40. ADR 4 M 418; ADBR 4 M 946.

41. Échinard and Temime, *Migrance,* vol. 1, *La préhistoire de la migration*; Lopez and Temime, *Migrance,* vol. 2, *L'expansion Marseillaise.*

42. This section draws significantly from material appearing in Lewis, "The Strangeness of Foreigners," 75–107.

43. On this point see esp. Roncayolo, *Les grammaires*; and Lambert, *Marseille*. As Lambert astutely points out, when the rare industry did modernize, it tended to employ fewer foreigners. The reluctance to innovate is not exclusive to port economies; see, for example, Green, *Ready-to-Wear*.

44. Temime and Attard-Maraninchi, *Migrance*, vol. 3, *Le cosmopolitisme*, 7. See also Fletcher, "City, Nation and Empire," introduction.

45. Loew, *Les dockers de Marseille*, 6–7. Based on observations made in the 1930s.

46. Londres, *Marseille*, 54.

47. Claverie, "Les dockers à Marseille," passim.

48. Loew, *Les dockers de Marseille*, 1.

49. Londres, *Marseille*, 55.

50. Loew, *Les dockers de Marseille*, 20.

51. Lambert, *Marseille*, 114.

52. The weight of development on Marseille's periphery can be seen in the percentage increases in population there between 1926 and 1931. While the population of the Marseille periphery as a whole increased by 78% during these five years, the population of the northeastern "suburbs" increased by 109%. In some districts, increases were over 200%. See Lambert, *Marseille*, 118.

53. Called *meublés* or *garnis* in France and comparable to what are known in the United States as SROs. Migrants in particular often shared these tiny spaces, which sometimes lodged several persons in a room intended for one or two.

54. In the 1931 census, for example, foreigners comprised 26.8% of the inhabitants of the fourth canton of Marseille, where population density was figured at 28.5 persons per building. Bontoux, *Le problème du logement*, 147. In that same canton, the native French constituted the majority of unskilled workers and the unemployed. See Jankowski, *Communism and Collaboration*, Appendix 1, 153–59.

55. See Camiscioli, "Intermarriage"; Childers, *Fathers*; Roberts, *Civilization without Sexes*, esp. chap. 4; Schneider, *Quality and Quantity*. The literature on France's declining population and associated social pathologies is too vast to cite in its entirety here. For a general introduction, see Dupaquier, *Histoire de la population française*; Ogden and Huss, "Demography and Pronatalism"; Offen, "Depopulation."

56. For population statistics, see Jankowski, *Communism and Collaboration*, 5.

57. In Marseille and in other *police d'état* cities, the central state set the police budget but expected the municipality to cover 50% of the operating costs. By contrast, in Paris, the city's police set its own police budget and then was reimbursed 50% by the central state. Paris' budget autonomy allowed its active police personnel to nearly double from 1914 to 1939, reaching as many as 20,000. This facilitated the capital police's tracking of migrants. Berlière, *Le monde des polices*, 112. See also Rosenberg, *Policing Paris*.

58. Bergès, *Le syndicalisme policier*; Kitson, "The Marseille Police." For detail on the structure of the Marseille police, see Lewis, "The Company of Strangers," 91–98.

59. Lipsky, *Street-Level Bureaucracy*. A similar point is made by Bruschi and Bruschi, "Le pouvoir des guichets."

60. Kitson, "The Marseille Police," 16.

61. On the association of Marseille's central districts with both transience and crime, see Temime, *Marseille transit*; and Fletcher, "City, Nation and Empire."

62. On the connections between the legal and social vulnerability of migrants, see esp. Calavita, *Immigrants at the Margins*.

63. Merriman, *The Margins of City Life,* passim. Today, a considerably different social geography prevails in Marseille, as many of the peripheral districts are no longer associated with small houses but more spectacularly with huge housing projects and apartment complexes, home mostly to immigrants and their children.

64. On the relationship between "rootedness" and national identity as well as the dangers posed to the latter by "rootlessness," see Stoler, "Sexual Affronts"; on contemporary associations between rootedness and national identity, see Taguieff, "The Doctrine of the National Front."

65. Robert Ripa, interview by Maurice Lemoine, "Le petit peuple de Don Roberto," in Baillon, "Marseille," 66, 64–71.

66. See Bourdieu, "The Forms of Capital."

67. For court proceedings, see ADBR 403 U 838: Jugements Correctionnels. Weapons possession was one of the most common offenses adjudicated by the Correctional Court during this period. It was considered a minor offense, punishable by a few days in prison (often even a suspended sentence) or a fine. While the fine in this case was not insignificant—it was probably about what Larbi could have earned in a couple of days—it remains the case that this was a misdemeanor that was not deemed to require punishment by incarceration.

68. ADBR 4 M 1389: Prefect to Min. I., 16 September 1919.

69. Years later, some 80 clandestine Arab immigrants all claimed to be living at 7, rue des Chapeliers, and the restaurant at this address became implicated in a false identification card ring. ADBR 4 M 950.

70. Jankowski, *Communism and Collaboration,* 5.

71. Londres, *Marseille,* 23. North African immigrants in France during the interwar period were almost exclusively male. The 1931 census, for example, shows that women made up only 3.71% of the North African residents of the Bouches-du-Rhône department, as compared to 47.51% of the Italian population, 44.49% of the Spanish population, 43.58% of the Armenian population, and 33.27% of the Russian population. For statistics, see "Atlas de l'immigration en France entre les deux guerres," *Actes de l'histoire de l'immigration,* http://barthes.ens.fr/atlasclio (accessed 14 December 2004).

72. Naudeau, "Enquête sur la population," quote on 181. This article was one in a series on the population in various French departments. Also reprinted in Naudeau, *La France se regarde,* 147.

73. Montand, Hamon, and Rotman, *You See.*

74. ADBR 4 M 1389.

75. ADBR 4 M 1929: Chef's report, 27 August 1931. File solicited for naturalization on 15 September 1938.

76. ADBR 4 M 1389: Letter from P.M., 29 May 1919, with blue grease pencil emphasis, referencing an Italian migrant who, it was also noted, was "the father of 3 children who have been declared French."

77. See, for example, ADBR 4 M 1497.

78. Naudeau, *La France se regarde,* 147.

79. Data compiled from sampling of over 1,300 files in ADBR 4 M 1389 through 4 M 1981. For discussion of the sampling and the distinction between periphery and center, see Lewis, "The Strangeness of Foreigners," note 61.

80. Naturalizations, granted, in ADBR 6 M 746 through 6 M 1283; naturalizations, adjourned, in ADBR 6 M 1306 through 6 M 1355. Many cases were rejected for naturalization in Marseille because the applicant was "single" or because the applicant had a "household without children." It was not uncommon for naturalization cases to be adjourned "until foundation of a French family."

81. Here I am informed by Stoler's discussion of elastic conceptions of race in "Sexual Affronts," 521.

82. For elaboration on this point, see Lewis, "The Company of Strangers," 81–82.

83. Perret, "Dans la banlieue."

84. Ibid. On the effect of the eight-hour day and the war on the labor needs of these industries, see A. Chatelain, "Les étrangers dans l'agglomération lyonnaise" (draft of thesis, L'Université de Lyon, Institut des Études Rhodaniennes, 1940), 18 (AML 1120 WP 001_2, Cabinet du Maire).

85. Perret, "Dans la banlieue," 32.

86. A. Chatelain, "Les étrangers," 53.

87. Videlier, "Banlieue sud," 140.

88. Bonneville, *Naissance,* 66.

89. Perret, "Dans la banlieue," 32; Chatelain, "Les étrangers," 69.

90. Estimates range from 40.75% to 43.4%. Meniri, "Les immigrés dans la commune," 3; Videlier, "Banlieue sud," 216. Videlier modified this figure ever so slightly, to 43.9%, in his "Les Italiens de la région lyonnaise," 671.

91. Videlier, "Les Italiens," 671.

92. For the figures, see Chatelain, "Les étrangers," 19.

93. Foreigners comprised an estimated 40% of construction workers in the Lyon area by 1929. Chatelain, "Les étrangers," 61.

94. Lewis, "The Company of Strangers," 96–98.

95. Legrand, *Le logement populaire,* 105. The reference in this quotation is to the "Cité de la Soie" in Décines.

96. Legrand, *Le logement populaire,* 101. The reference here is to Gillet's "cité des textiles artificiels du sud-est."

97. Contrast to the situation in the steelworks of the Lorraine as described by Noiriel, *Longwy,* passim.

98. ADR 4 M 459: Dénombrement des maisons garnies ou hôtels meublés (by street address for 1924).

99. Navel, *Travaux,* 36–39. Thanks to Laura Downs for alerting me to Navel's writings on Lyon.

100. AML 0349 WP 5: Mayor to prefect, 30 November 1925; director of public health office to mayor, 30 June 1923. See also ADR 5 M 16 and 5 M 17 for similar reports on overcrowding.

101. AML 0349 WP 5: Director of public health office to mayor, 30 June 1923.

102. AML 0349 WP 5: Translations provided in 1924.

103. AML 0349 WP 5: Constructions en bois pour habitations. Rapport du chef du 7e bur., 25 July 1929.

104. ADR 5 M 16: Président de la Cooperative des "Jardins et Foyers," letter to Madame [illegible], 19 September 1923.

105. ADR 5 M 16: Multiple complaints dated 1923–29. For similar reports on neighboring Décines, see Videlier, *Décines,* 110–17.

106. "Le Recensement à Lyon," *Le guignol,* 10 April 1926. This slang is full of deliberate errors in the original French, including accent marks going the wrong way. The following is the best possible translation of the meaning, but it cannot convey the color: "When one thinks of all the Spaniards who set down roots among us, who find the means to rent large barracks and then to pile in their compatriots, piling them on top of one another like sardines in a can . . . and if Public Health existed as one claims it does at City Hall, one had better well rid us of these poisons. . . . Mister Edward [addressing Lyon's mayor, Édouard Herriot], I don't give a damn about being the second city of France, but I would prefer to see you work for all my fellow citizens than to see grow all the time this shambles of foreigners who will finish by swallowing us one day if we don't watch out." Gnafron was mistaken. Lyon briefly earned the status of France's second city due to what were probably deliberately inflated census statistics. See Bienfait, "La population de Lyon."

107. For evidence of immigrant businesses in these neighborhoods, see police reports in naturalization, expulsion, and identification card files.

108. ADR Exp., box 23.

109. ADR Exp., box 15.

110. ADR Exp., box 3.

111. ADR Exp., box 1: Prefect to Min. I. (DSG, 2nd bur.), 21 September 1926.

112. ADR Exp., box 3: SGP report, 19 October 1927.

113. Léon Jouhaux, cited in "Le problème de l'émigration Italienne: Le nouveau traité entre la France et l'Italie," *L'information ouvrière et sociale* 92, 26 January 1919, 3.

114. *L'humanité,* 30 January 1921.

115. Loi relative à la création des syndicats professionnels, 21 mars 1884, Article 4. *JOLD,* 22 March 1884, 1577.

116. "Le gouvernement de la police," *L'humanité,* 10 November 1920; emphasis in original.

117. AN F^7 14654: États signalétiques des étrangers expulsés de France. On the dismissals: ADBR 14 M 23–21: Rapport du chef de brigade de 3e classe BEYET sur la fermeture éventuelle d'une usine à Gardanne; report no. 15, 25 February 1921. On the expulsions of strike militants: ADBR 4 M 1517.

118. ADBR 1 M 1830: CPS, report no. 5055, 12 October 1922.

119. AMAE Z—Europe 1918–40—Italie, vol. 382: "Note au sujet des réfugiés politiques," 17 November 1924; emphasis in original; Camille Chautemps, Min. I.

to Prés. Cons., Min. AE, reporting on the 23 November 1924 meeting of their two departments, 27 December 1924.

120. For accounts of the incident see ADBR 1 M 1800: CPS, report no. 1795, 29 May 1926; *JODCD*, 2e séance du 11 Février 1925, 756–66; "Les incidents à Marseille," *Le temps*, 13 February 1925, 1; "À Marseille, les bandes fascistes provoquent une bataille de rue," *L'humanité*, 11 February 1926, 1; "Les incidents de Marseille. De Castelnau fait couler le sang," *L'humanité*, 12 February 1926, 1.

121. Rousso, *The Vichy Syndrome*, 4–8.

122. Alsace-Lorraine continues to fall under a different regime with respect to France's secular laws.

123. On the Taittinger-Castelnau connection, see Soucy, "Centrist Fascism."

124. *JODCD*, 2e séance du 11 Février 1925, 756–66.

125. Ibid.

126. AN F[7] 12976: Bouches-du-Rhône prefect to Min. I., 17 March 1925. See also, in the same file: Min. I. to Bouches-du-Rhône prefect, 9 March 1925, marked "Confidential and Urgent"; CPS, report no. 753, 6 March 1925; M. le Procureur Général de la Cour d'Appel (Aix-en-Provence) à M. le Garde des Sceaux, 27 February 1925; CPS, report no. 629, 25 February 1925.

127. AN F[7] 12976: Reports from 22 and 23 February indicated that during the two previous nights, some 7,551 interrogations took place, nearly half of which concerned foreigners. Regarding the first of the two sweeps, *L'humanité* reported numbers identical to those of the police report (5,236 interrogations, of which 2,330 concerned foreigners). "Rafles monstres à Marseille," *L'humanité*, 23 February 1925, 2.

128. AN F[7] 12976: CPS, report no. 753, 6 March 1925. *L'humanité* claimed that there was indeed a counterdemonstration at the Millerand event of about 5,000 to 6,000 persons, but it gave no indication of whether foreigners participated. "La journée fasciste de Marseille," *L'humanité*, 2 March 1925, 1.

129. Milza, *Voyage*, 233.

130. AN F[7] 12976: Congrès de la CGTU, 17e région, reported in CPS, report no. 114, 13 January 1925.

131. "Emigration temporaire ou permanente?" *La vie syndicale* 17 (March–May 1925), 422–23.

132. ADR 4 M 260: CPS report, 3 March 1925, on the subject of the Réunion du Comité Général Élargi de l'Union des Syndicats Unitaires, 1 March 1925.

133. Martin A. Schain, "Immigration and Trade Unions in France," 101. See also Leah A. Haus, *Unions, Immigration, and Internationalization*.

134. Ponty, *Polonais méconnus*, 205.

135. On unionization, see esp. Noiriel, *Longwy*, 233–35; Milza, *Voyage*, 352. On antifascist militancy, see Milza, *Voyage*, 223.

136. Characterization of foreign workers by Marius C., cited in Auzias, *Mémoires libertaires*, 133.

137. ADR Exp., box 2: CS, 14 April 1925, responding to inquiry from Ligue Internationale des Droits de l'Homme.

138. ADR Exp., box 2: Prefect to Min. I., 22 April 1925.

139. Auzias, *Mémoires libertaires,* 183–84.

140. "Les expulsions des travailleurs étrangers," *Secours Rouge, Bulletin du Comité Exécutif de Secours Rouge International* (February 1925), 2; CGTU militant cited in Noiriel, *Longwy,* 244.

141. The list in the text gives just a sampling; emphasis in original. ADR Exp., boxes 2, 5, 6, 7, 10, 13, 15, 17, 18, 29; Expulsion files, ADBR 4 M 1389–1981.

142. Auzias, *Mémoires libertaires,* 73.

143. For naturalizations in the Rhône, see ADR Naturalization files, 1927–38. For the Bouches-du-Rhône, see ADBR 6 M 746–1355.

144. Mauco, *Les étrangers en France,* 132n. While Mauco relegates this remark to a footnote, it has been cited repeatedly as one of his central insights. The book, a published version of Mauco's geography thesis, has often been used as an authoritative source on interwar immigration. However, Mauco's own thesis adviser Albert Demangeon criticized the thesis for "sentimental exaggeration in an analysis that ought to rely on precise description" (*Annales de géographie,* 15 May 1932, 409). The problems of interpretation in Mauco's work are discussed in Mary Lewis, "Drawing Distinctions: Georges Mauco, Immigrants, and the Social Ascension of Both, 1926–1942" (unpublished manuscript, 1996). Karen Adler's discussion is also very illuminating. Adler, *Jews and Gender.*

145. Indeed, Mauco decries this lack of control elsewhere in the thesis.

146. Noiriel, *Longwy,* 274.

147. Letter from an Armenian who began working at the Société Lyonnaise de Soie Artificielle in Décines in 1927, cited in Videlier, *Décines,* 151.

148. See Chapter 5 and Mandel, *In the Aftermath,* 100–102.

149. Information on Armenian and Italian in latter's expulsion file contained in ADR Exp., box 4: CC report, 8 October 1928; prefect (SGP) to Min. I., 23 October 1928; CC reports, 2 September 1940 and 21 September 1940. Reports on strike and union victory in ADR 10 MpC 75.

150. Depiction of the Spanish immigrant Jaume P. in Auzias, *Mémoires libertaires,* 131.

151. ADBR 4 M 1827: Letter from employer, Huilerie Léonce VIAL, on taxed paper dated 5 March 1930; CPS Dhubert, report, 5 April 1930.

152. ADBR 4 M 1827: Evidence of *sursis* in multiple reports. Expulsion repealed 5 April 1938.

153. ADR Exp., box 3: CPS to prefect (Secrétaire Général), 13 June 1928.

154. ADR Exp., box 3: Expulsion, 9 July 1928, with note from the director of the Sûreté.

155. ADBR 4 M 1890: Matteo's jobs prior to his arrest were long-term by Marseille standards. He worked the Compagnie de petroles from 1922 to 1925 and at the Raffinerie de sucre de St Louis from 1925 to October 1927, according to one account, and to March 1928 according to another. In 1931, he found work again in a refinery, this time at the Huilerie Rocca-Tassy. Matteo always maintained that he had stumbled upon the anarchist demonstration "by accident." Even the CPS questioned how dangerous he was, noting that he had been allowed to emigrate by fascist authorities. (See ADBR 4 M 1890: Reports, 4 April 1928 and 13 April 1928; expulsion order, 23 April 1928; letter from wife, 8 May 1928; CPS

report, 26 May 1928; letter from [Matteo], 18 June 1928; CPS report, 4 July 1928.)

156. ADBR 4 M 1890.

157. ADBR 4 M 1867: Letter to Deputy Henri Tasso, 6 December 1932. Tasso did, however, follow up on her inquiry since she also claimed that police were harassing her and threatening her with expulsion as well. On the circumstances motivating the original expulsion: CS report, 26 June 1928. On the painting incident: *Procès-verbal,* 8 January 1932; CPS report, 30 March 1932; expulsion reactivated per Sûreté order, 15 April 1932.

158. Guillen, "L'antifascisme," 215. See also Sugier, "Les mines du Gard"; Milza, *Voyage,* 347–48.

159. Milza, *Voyage,* 351. Milza asserts that the "golden legend" of Italian integration is of recent vintage, only "perhaps twenty years old" at the time he was writing; the myth is circulated in part for polemical purposes, as a countermodel to Maghrebin immigration. See Pierre Milza, "L'immigration italienne en France d'une guerre à l'autre," in Milza, *Les Italiens en France,* 4.

160. Noiriel, *Longwy,* 227–48.

161. Ibid., 237, 248–63.

162. Sirot, "Les conditions de travail," 85. We return to this issue in Chapter 6.

163. Becker and Berstein, *Histoire de l'anti-communisme,* vol. 1, *1917–1940.* As they point out, new jurisprudence from this period likened communism to anarchism in terms of the threat it posed to the nation.

164. Baker, "The Surveillance of Subversion," 496, 486–516.

165. See ADR Exp., multiple files.

166. Mandel, *In the Aftermath,* passim.

167. In European Union parlance, a "third-country national" is a person living in the European Union who does not originate from one of the member states. These migrants often cannot make the same claims on labor, social, or even civil rights as their counterparts who benefit from belonging to the European Union, a fact that underscores the degree to which EU rights, like the rights of guest workers in post–World War I France, are the product of negotiations between nations.

CHAPTER 2

1. Sayad, "Qu'est-ce qu'un immigré?" 7.

2. Herriot, "Lettre-préface," 5.

3. Chamber debates, cited in *IS* 444, 14 April 1932, 8.

4. Adolphe Landry addressing the Chamber of Deputies in its 15 December 1931 session. Reprinted as "Travaux préparatoires de la loi du 10 août 1932," *Bulletin de l'inspection du travail et de l'hygiène industrielle,* année 40 (1932), 315; Édouard Herriot in "Travaux préparatoires," 315.

5. Cross, *Immigrant Workers,* 194.

6. The automobile industry was one of the first to show the effects of the crises, its production peaking in 1929. Automobile production fell another 29% between May 1929 and September 1931. By that time, textile production was also 35% below its prewar level. Sauvy, *Histoire économique,* vol. 1, 264.

7. ADR 10 Mp D5: CPS Brun to prefect, marked "Confidential," 13 February 1931.

8. ADR 10 Mp D5: CPS to prefect, 31 December 1931 and 30 January 1932.

9. ADR 10 Mp D5: CPS to prefect, 25 September 1934, 24 October 1934, and 26 November 1934.

10. Laferrère, *Lyon*, 217.

11. Henri Baroin, *La main-d'oeuvre étrangère*, 145. Statistics appear to be from the first part of 1935. Given that some foreigners had no legal claim to unemployment insurance and others may have been unaware of their rights, actual unemployment compensation may well have been even more heavily foreign than the figures suggest. As we shall see, these statistics may also reflect differences in immigrants' access to compensation by municipality.

12. Percentages derived from figures given by Baroin, *La main-d'oeuvre étrangère*, 55. Even so, the decline of the foreign population in Villeurbanne and Villefranche was still a significant 19.5%.

13. ADR Exp., box 8. First appearing in 1931, this form left blanks for name, nationality, address, and number of days in which named individual had to leave. It was sent to the police commissioner of the neighborhood in which the foreigner reportedly lived.

14. Orwell, *The Road to Wigan Pier*.

15. Jahoda, Lazarsfeld, and Zeisel, *Marienthal*, 22.

16. Humphries, *Hooligans or Rebels?* 172. For influential analyses of "social crime," see esp. Hobsbawm, *Primitive Rebels*; idem, *Bandits*; idem, "Social Criminality," 5–6; Thompson, *Whigs and Hunters*; Hay, Thompson, and Linebaugh, *Albion's Fatal Tree*; Linebaugh, *The London Hanged*.

17. Michelle Perrot, cited in Wright, *Between the Guillotine and Liberty*, 153. Original in Perrot, "Délinquance et système pénitentiaire en France au XIXe siècle" (1975) in idem, *Les ombres de l'histoire*, 169–70.

18. Perrot, *Les ombres de l'histoire*, esp. the articles "Du vagabond au prolétaire" (1972), 305–15; "La fin des vagabonds" (1978), 317–36; "Délinquance et système pénitentiaire en France au XIXe siècle" (1975), 163–91; Wright, *Between the Guillotine and Liberty*; Wagniart, *Le vagabond*.

19. Hugo, *Les misérables*.

20. Based on samplings from August and September in consecutive years throughout the 1930s. See ADR Jugements Correctionnels.

21. ADR Jugements Correctionnels, August–September 1931 and 1932.

22. On this shift, see Mary D. Lewis, "Les pratiques d'expulsion dans le Rhône durant la crise," in Rygiel, ed., *Le bon grain*, 245–262.

23. ADR Exp., box 21: CS report, 12 January 1933; prefect to Min. I., 20 January 1933.

24. Despite the fact that nationwide, they were employed largely in agriculture, which survived the throes of the depression better than industry did, Spanish were repatriated in disproportionate numbers. Entries of Spanish agricultural workers in 1931 outnumbered entries of Spanish industrial workers by 29 to 1; yet in that same year, 18,924 Spanish were repatriated, a figure equivalent to 94%

of the Spanish agricultural entries. As a comparison, in the same year, only 13,046 Italians were repatriated, although Italians made up a much larger percentage of the total population in France. *BMT*, année 39, nos. 1–3 (Jan–Mar 1932): 128.

25. A Spanish man enjoined to fence in his pigeons declared he would do so only once French nationals were also required to enclose theirs. See ADR Exp., box 15: CPS de Lyon to prefect (SGP), 25 June 1932.

26. ADR Exp., box 15: Teyssier report, 23 August 1932.

27. Marie-Claude Blanc-Chaléard points out that it was only as the old encampments were finally destroyed in the 1950s and public housing provided for their occupants that the new term "*bidonville*" came into circulation to refer to new encampments, housing North Africans almost exclusively. The use of different terms for makeshift housing serves, according to Blanc-Chaléard, to downplay the "family resemblance" between *baraques* and *bidonvilles*. Blanc-Chaléard, "Des baraques aux bidonvilles," in Lemire and Samson, *Baraques*, 89–92.

28. See ADR Exp., boxes 15–46.

29. ADR Exp., box 29: Letter, 6 January 1934.

30. This is made especially clear when compared to the clemency shown a male migrant who was guilty of the same infraction but had other sources of income. ADR Exp., box 12: Warning of 27 July 1932.

31. ADR Exp., box 37: Letter from Jacques Locquin, 19 June 1934. Handwritten comment on attached note: "She wants to stay—What decision to give?" followed by a reply: "Unfavorable."

32. ADR Exp., box 37: Prefect to Min. I., 5 July 1934.

33. ADR Exp., box 4. In all likelihood, this order also extended to her children. Under the French civil code, women were obligated to live wherever their husbands chose. In this case, the husband did not choose but was forced to leave France; it was thus assumed that his wife would follow. On this point, see Camiscioli, "Intermarriage."

34. ADR Exp., box 31: SGP to Min. I., 16 July 1931.

35. Multiple reports in ADR Exp., box 31.

36. ADR Exp., box 20: SGP to Min. I., 18 October 1932.

37. ADR Exp., box 34: Prefect to Procureur, 3 August 1933. Expulsion, 30 October 1933.

38. ADR Exp., box 37: Mayor of Montmorot (Jura) to Mayor of Lyon, 30 August 1934.

39. ADR Exp., box 37. The Rhône prefect's response to the inquiry from the Jura was negative; 18 September 1934. The Interior Ministry authorized her *sursis* in Jura on 7 June 1935. By 1936, Roberta had returned to the Lyon area. Her expulsion was repealed in 1944, and there is evidence that she still lived in the Rhône in 1956.

40. ADR Exp., box 11: Représentant en France de l'Office International NANSEN pour les Réfugiés to SGP, 13 February 1932.

41. ADR Exp., box 11: Prefect to Min. I., 3 March 1932.

42. ADR Exp., box 11. This was discovered after the fact. Finally leaving Lyon in 1935, he returned again in 1937 and ultimately succeeded in having his expulsion repealed after the war. The particular situation of Armenians is examined in depth in Chapter 5.

43. ADR Exp., box 11. Although expulsion files often include information on the spouse's profession, there is no indication in this file that his wife, a 17-year-old, worked.

44. ADR Exp., box 11: Min. I. to prefect, 31 March 1932, and trace of penciled reaction in margin.

45. Archives Départementales du Cher (ADC) M 7167: Min. I., DSG, Service Central des Cartes d'Identité des Étrangers, Circ. no. 202 (2 June 1932). My thanks to Philippe Rygiel for this and subsequent sources from the ADC.

46. Doumer was assassinated on 6 May 1932.

47. ADC M 7167: Rapport au Président de la République Française, 21 May 1932. Décret modifiant l'article 3 du décret du 10 juillet 1929 concernant le régime des cartes d'identité d'étrangers (21 May 1932).

48. ADR Exp., box 19: Prefect to Min. I., 28 February 1933.

49. ADR Exp., box 19: 24 March 1933.

50. Olivier Brillaut, "L'expulsion des étrangers en France" (PhD thesis, Université de Nice, 1982), 171, cited in Gordon, "The Back Door," 203.

51. For elaboration of this point, see Lewis, "Les pratiques."

52. Chautemps, Laval, Sarraut, and Dormoy all served in more than one cabinet.

53. ADR Exp., box 11; ADR Exp., box 19.

54. ADR Exp., box 20: Prefect to Min. I., 8 November 1932; ADR Exp., box 4: Sursis périodiques granted November 1939; ADR Exp., box 34: CS, 22 January 1940.

55. Industrialist (1872) cited in Lequin, *Les ouvriers,* vol. 1: *La formation de la classe ouvrière régionale,* 136.

56. Lyon's diverse economy and the flexibility of work trajectories within it are underscored by Lequin, *Les ouvriers.*

57. ADR 10 Mp D5: CPS to prefect, 30 March 1931.

58. ADR Exp., box 13.

59. Although no specific offenses were ever required for expulsion recommendations, it was not until May 1932, in the wake of the assassination of President Doumer, that national policy officially mentioned identification card inadequacies as a rationale for expulsion orders.

60. Bonnet, "Étude des petits commerçants," 5, 18.

61. ADR Exp., box 7.

62. According to French census figures, there were 390,095 fewer foreign "workers" in 1936 than there had been in 1931, while there were 23,770 more foreign "chefs d'établissements." The strategic nature of such a move is corroborated by an opposite trend among naturalized citizens. Among foreigners who became naturalized French nationals, there was an *increase* of 31,036 in the number of workers, while "chefs d'établissements" increased by only 9,112 among naturalized citizens. Figures reprinted in Guichard and Noiriel, "Annexes," in *Construction,* 278–368 passim.

63. Bonnet, "Étude des petits commerçants," 1–40.

64. ADR Exp., box 11: Reports, 24 February 1932 and 7 April 1932. Employment certificates from 1936 and 1937.

65. John Maynard Keynes developed his analysis of aggregate demand in the *General Theory of Employment, Interest and Money*. This characterization as "Keynesian" is mine; I am not suggesting that Rhône authorities would have been familiar with macroeconomic theory.

66. ADR Exp., box 13: Report, 5 January 1933.

67. ADR Exp., box 25: Official warning issued 14 December 1934; prefect to Min. I., 6 December 1935; reports on size of personnel and additional labor-code infractions dated 1936 and 1937.

68. See esp. Patricia Russell Evans, "Likely to Become a Public Charge."

69. See Chapter 6.

70. This clause was present in Article 4 of the treaty with Italy (30 November 1919), Article 10 of the treaty with Poland (3 September 1919), Article 9 of the treaty with Czechoslovakia (20 March 1920), and Article 4 of the treaty with Belgium (24 December 1924). The Luxembourgian and Spanish treaties, which pertained exclusively to assistance, did not have a similar clause, though they did address repatriation of long-term assistees.

71. On this, see esp. Ponty, *Polonais méconnus;* Yves Frey, "Le basin potassique de Haute-Alsace, laboratoire des rapatriements massifs de Polonais" in Rygiel, ed., *Le bon grain,* 157–90; Slaby, "Industry, the State," esp. 293–301.

72. Municipalities accepting the state's conditions for aid were accorded a 33% subsidy, as long as they did not exceed certain ceilings. See Daniel and Tuchszirer, *L'état face aux chômeurs,* 107–10. Departments also often subsidized local unemployment bureaus, but this aid was more variable.

73. Work on this aspect of French social welfare has flourished in the past 15 years. See esp. Pedersen, *Family, Dependence, and the Origins of the Welfare State,* and Dutton, *Origins of the French Welfare State.* For the shift from private charity to public assistance, see Smith, *Creating the Welfare State in France.*

74. AMV Chômage 1927–37: "Conséquences du Chômage sur la Situation Financière de la Commune de Villeurbanne," 22 February 1932.

75. Lyon spent some 114 million francs on unemployment assistance and public works relief between 1930 and 1934. The state and the department kicked in an additional 50 million francs during that time. Smith, *Creating the Welfare State in France,* 175.

76. AMV Chômage 1927–37: Circular from Mayor Goujon to local employers, 10 September 1931.

77. AMV Chômage 1927–37: Residency requirements were raised from three to six months as of 23 September 1932. Foreigners from nontreaty states were excluded as of 18 May 1934. This was reversed the following year (19 May 1935) when the three-month residency requirement was reinstated and the restrictions on foreigners removed.

78. AML 0747 WP 162_3, Ville de Lyon: Fonds Municipal de Chômage. Règlement Adopté par le Conseil Municipal, 27 December 1926; AML 0005 WP 058: Règlement, n.d. [early 1931]. AML 0981 WP 398: ODMPST Service Chômage,

"Instructions au Service du Fonds de Chômage," 22 July 1931. See also Héreil, *Le chômage en France,* 160. Héreil astutely notes that the Lyon municipality drew a "rigorous distinction" between different types of foreigners, but he erroneously attributes the two-thirds policy to the 27 December 1926 rules. The 1926 rules gave no indemnity rights to nonreciprocity foreigners. The policy adding this provision appears to date from early in 1931, but it was quickly amended by a circular dated 22 July 1931.

79. AML 0981 WP 398: ODMPST Service: Chômage, "Instructions au Service du Fonds de Chômage," 22 July 1931.

80. A year after Lyon had adopted its policy to exclude nonreciprocity foreigners from unemployment benefits, the minister of labor issued a circular informing local authorities throughout France that they had "every right to admit or exclude foreigners" from the benefits of unemployment insurance as long as they included foreigners from reciprocity nations "under the same conditions as the French." The appearance of the circular suggests that procedures had varied among localities and that some had sought policy guidance. See AMV Chômage 1927–37: "Situation des étrangers en France en ce qui concerne les secours de chômage. Instructions générales," Circ., Min. T., 20 June 1932.

81. "Les Étrangers en France: Faut-il renvoyer la main-d'oeuvre étrangère?" *IS* 554, 20 December 1934, 11.

82. AML 0981 WP 398: ODMPST Service Chômage, "Instructions au Service du Fonds de Chômage," 22 July 1931. No time limit was placed on French beneficiaries, while time limits were placed on both treaty beneficiaries and refugees. Foreign beneficiaries also were accorded different rights based on whether they were single or married; this distinction was not made for French nationals.

83. AML 0981 WP 398: Le Maire de Lyon à MM. les Adjoints Délégués aux Mairies d'Arrondissements LYON, 28 November 1931.

84. AML 0981 WP 398: Maire de Lyon. Office Municipal du Travail. Adjoint Délégué pour le Maire de Lyon, à MM. les Adjoints Délégués aux Mairies d'Arrondissement LYON, 29 December 1931.

85. Ibid. For the 1928 appeal, see AML 0747 WP 145_1: Le Maire de Lyon à Monsieur le Maire de Marseille, 17 March 1928.

86. AML 0981 WP 398: Office Départemental et Municipal de Placement Gratuit. Service: Chômage, "Note de Service," 27 May 1932.

87. AML 0981 WP 398: Le Maire de Lyon à M. l'Adjoint Huguenin et à MM. les Adjoints Délégués des Mairies d'Arrondissements, [illegible day] November 1932.

88. Smith, *Creating the Welfare State in France,* 174–75; 104.

89. AML 0981 WP 398: Office Municipal du Travail, 7 August 1933.

90. AML 0981 WP 398: Le Maire de Lyon à MM. les Adjoints Délégués des Mairies d'Arrondissement, 24 March 1934. See also Huguenin pour le Maire, à MM. les Adjoints Délégués aux Mairies d'Arrondissements LYON, 23 November 1933; and responses of district offices, 30 November 1933 and 28 March 1934.

91. Smith, *Creating the Welfare State in France,* 48.

92. Berthet, *Contribution,* notes that immigrants rarely benefited from the new housing construction. My guide from the Musée Urbain, Tony Garnier, who

toured me around the complex in June 2003, confirmed that foreign migrants were unlikely to have qualified for the apartments.

93. On Villeurbanne's urban projects, see esp. Bonneville, *Naissance.*

94. On the preference in Vénissieux for privately endowed housing projects over municipally funded ones, see Corbel, *Vénissieux la rebelle,* 138. For evidence of immigrants' access to assistance in the municipality, see AMVx 7 F 55, 7 F 56, and 5 Q 253. Corbel notes that Vénissieux even resorted to borrowing money to pay for unemployment assistance, "until the prefect forbade the use [of loans]." Corbel, *Vénissieux la rebelle,* 151.

95. ADR 3494 W 117: [Leandro N.] to prefect, 15 May 1936. Underlining in red pen.

96. ADR 3494 W 117: Swiss consul to prefect, 22 May 1936. The Popular Front took office in June 1936, and there is no trace of this particular kind of summons continuing past the fall of that year.

97. ADR Exp., box 7: [Savio] to prefect, 11 February 1931. Emphasis mine.

98. ADR Exp., box 7: CS reports, 14 June 1935, 23 September 1935, and 27 April 1936. In the April 1936 report, the CS expressed his opinion to the SGP that "this foreigner, being a public charge for our country, and having shown no proof of francophile sentiment, I am of the opinion that the expulsion order against him should be reactivated." Since the scribbled notes at the bottom of the page contradicted this position, we must assume that the penciled remarks originated in the office of the SGP, to whom the CS's reports were sent when completed.

99. ADR Exp., box 7: Commissaire de Police à Villeurbanne to SGP, 4 June 1936.

100. ADR Exp., box 7: CS to SGP, with penciled recommendation, 16 March 1937.

101. ADR Exp., box 7: CS to SGP, penciled recommendation, 22 September 1937; CS to SGP, 17 November 1937. ADR, Exp. box 16: Penciled note on CS report, 14 December 1939.

102. Figures reprinted in Guichard and Noiriel, "Annexes," in *Construction,* 278–368.

103. These edits included indicating that the applicant still socialized primarily with foreigners (in cases where the initial report had indicated that they interacted primarily with French nationals); that their spoken or written French was not as good as originally thought; that the applicant's political attitude is "correct" (where the initial report had indicated that the applicant was uninvolved in politics); that it is "unknown" whether the applicant still hopes to return to his or her native country; and so forth. See ADR Naturalization files, 1927–38.

104. In many other parts of France, the first level of review was conducted by municipal employees.

105. The 1927 law came only a year after labor regulations pertaining to immigrants were tightened, and it exhibited the ambivalence of French legislators toward immigrants. While the law loosened some restrictions on naturalization, it also introduced the possibility of revocation and barred newly naturalized citizens from holding electoral office for 10 years.

106. Lambert, *La France*, 78. This book was published after the law was passed but contained Lambert's principal arguments in its favor. See also his arguments before parliament in *Annales de l'Assemblée Nationale, débats de la chambre*, esp. 31 March 1927.

107. Lambert, *La France*, 75.

108. Ibid.

109. For an overview of these policies, see Ngai, *Impossible Subjects*, chap. 1.

110. Law of 10 August 1927, reprinted in Ministère de la Justice, *La nationalité française*, 88–92.

111. On the concept of legal fiction, see esp. Sahlins, *Unnaturally French*; also Sayad, "Naturels et naturalisés."

112. ADR Naturalization files, 1927–38, E: Secrétaire Général, 11 April 1932.

113. ADR Naturalization files, 1927–38, FERR-GAS: Prefect, responding to inquiry from Garde des Sceaux regarding an unemployed man who had applied for naturalization, 29 June 1933.

114. ADR Naturalization files, 1927–38, FERR-GAS: Secrétaire General, 20 December 1932.

115. ADR Naturalization files, 1927–38, IA-KAL: Prefect, 23 May 1934.

116. This analysis is consistent with Jean-Charles Bonnet's finding that 66% of the "unfavorable" recommendations issued by the general secretary for police between 1927 and 1938 came during the years 1931–33. Bonnet, "Naturalisations," 59.

117. ADR Naturalization files, 1927–38, W-Z: Secrétaire Général, 1 March 1932.

118. ADR Naturalization files, 1927–38, CAB-CHA: Prefect's opinion, 12 June 1932.

119. ADR Naturalization files, 1927–38, CAB-CHA: Préfet au Garde des Sceaux, 29 August 1933. In fact, his wife was no longer French, as she had become a Spanish national by marrying him and had not requested reintegration (allowed by the 1927 Nationality Code) into her French nationality until now.

120. ADR Naturalization files, 1927–38, CAB-CHA: Naturalization, 26 November 1933.

121. This was true even though justice ministers changed even more frequently than interior ministers—there were 16 justice ministers between 1930 and 1938, as opposed to 13 interior ministers.

122. ADR Naturalization files, 1927–38, D.

123. By virtue of the August 1927 Nationality Law, French women who married foreigners no longer automatically lost their French nationality. Instead, they were asked to declare at the time of marriage which nationality they intended to take. The law also provided that women who married foreigners prior to 1927 could ask to be "reintegrated" into their birthright French nationality. The intention of this clause in the law was to increase the number of children who would automatically become French, without the right to repudiate, because born to a French parent. (Children born in France to foreigners became French at their majority but had the right to repudiate their French nationality in preference of their parents' nationality.) The intentions behind the 1927 law did not prevent the

Lyon authorities from treating French-born women as foreigners. In one case, for example, the CS argued against reintegrating a woman into her birthright nationality because "the petitioner only seeks to reclaim her French nationality at the moment of the economic crisis in order to find work." See ADR, Naturalization files, 1927–38, IA-KAL: CS, 5 October 1932.

124. Algerian Jews, like his wife, were collectively granted full rights of citizenship by the Cremieux Decree of 1870.

125. ADR Exp., box 15: Dictated letters, 17 March and 18 August 1932.

126. ADR Naturalization files, 1927–38, E: Prefect to Min. J., 14 November 1933. Three of his brothers had requested naturalization in 1927 and had received favorable recommendations at the time from local officials.

127. Frequent refrain found in ADR, Naturalization files, 1927–38. See also Bonnet, "Naturalisations," 43–75.

128. ADR Naturalization files, 1927–38, FERR-GAS.

129. ADR Naturalization files, 1927–38. We should also not discount the fact that the prerequisite for naturalization was reduced, by virtue of the 1927 Nationality Law, from ten to three years.

130. ADR Naturalization files, 1927–38, SCHM-TAU: Wife of applicant to prefect, 2 September 1933.

131. Depoid, *Les naturalisations en France,* 75.

132. There are countless examples from the 1910s and 1920s of policy makers comparing migratory flows to laws of physics. In 1926, for instance, International Labor Office director (and former French Armaments minister) Albert Thomas argued that migration occurred as if "by force of natural law, so often compared to the law of communicating vessels." Thomas, "Preface," in Paon, *L'immigration en France,* 9.

133. Repatriation figures calculated from tables in *BMT,* année 39, nos. 1–3 (January–March 1932): 128; *BMT,* année 40, nos. 10–12 (October–December 1933): 486; *BMT,* année 42, nos. 10–12 (October–December 1935): 521. Official departures calculated from *BMT,* année 43, nos. 7–9 (June–September 1936): 290–91. It should be noted that during the same time, 423,639 labor migrants also legally entered France (a majority authorized for agricultural work), while an unknown number did so illegally.

134. In *BMT,* année 43, nos. 7–9 (June–September 1936): 294–95, it is claimed that the official departure figures represent probably around one-third of the real departures. The author makes no such caveat about official entries, although it seems plausible that real entries also far exceeded official numbers.

CHAPTER 3

1. Londres, *Marseille, porte du sud,* 21.

2. Chambre de Commerce de Marseille, *Correspondance et documents* (Marseille: Société Anonyme du Sémaphore de Marseille, 1931), 1118.

3. Ibid., 1123.

4. Sauvy, *Histoire économique,* vol. 2, 64.

5. ADBR 14 M 22_23: Société du Gaz et de l'Électricité de Marseille, Note annexe à la lettre 8.638/D, 8 December 1932.

6. ADBR 14 M 22_22: Multiple reports.

7. "Face aux défis de la rénovation (1914–1945)," in Daumalin, Girard, and Raveaux, *Du savon à la puce,* 219–55.

8. Lambert, *Marseille,* 486.

9. Commercial trade with Syria, a French mandate, for instance, rose from nearly 29,000 tons in 1930 to just over 50,000 tons in 1933. But then between 1933 and 1934, Marseille's exports to the Levant dropped by 18,000 tons; between 1934 and 1935, they dropped by another 14,000 tons. Courdurie and Miege, *Marseille colonial,* 122, 159.

10. The term in French was "En panne." Lambert, *Marseille,* 485–86.

11. In 1962, the active population employed in major Marseille industries was 114,438. It was 132,443 in 1931 and 125,317 in 1936. See Lambert, *Marseille,* 306.

12. ADBR 4 M 1928: CS au CC, 6 October 1931; ADBR 4 M 1959: CS au CC, 1 June 1932.

13. ADBR 4 M 1942: CS au CC, 5 February 1932.

14. ADBR 4 M 1942: CS au CC, 5 February 1932.

15. ADBR 4 M 1959: CS, recommendation of warning, 21 June 1932.

16. Londres, *Marseille, porte du sud,* 54.

17. Reassignments in Toul, even more so than initial placements, were kept to a bare minimum: 15 in 1930, 13 in 1931, 2 in 1932. In Lyon, too, they dropped some 93% between 1931 and 1932. All statistics from *BMT*; annual data for previous year in January–March edition.

18. ADBR 14 M 22_22: Chambre Syndicale des Margariniers et Fondeurs Margariniers à Monsieur le Préfet des Bouches-du-Rhône, 1ère Division, 3e Bur., 29 January 1935.

19. ADBR 14 M 22_22: Responses to questionnaire issued by Société pour la Défense du Commerce et de l'Industrie de Marseille (January 1935).

20. ADBR 14 M 22_22: S. Petit le Roy, manager of the Compagnie de Traitements Chimiques et Industriels, to Monsieur Abeille, Président du Syndicat des Produits Chimiques, 19 February 1934.

21. Ibid.

22. See Chapter 4.

23. AN F[7] 13533.

24. This is consistent with national trends; see statistics in Chapter 2.

25. Ville de Marseille, *L'œuvre municipale,* 377.

26. Guerry, "Le genre de la naturalisation," 6.

27. AN F[7] 13533.

28. Alain Hayot, "Populations et territoires," in Pinol, *Atlas historique,* 194.

29. Levy, "The Marseilles Working-Class Movement," 46. I am grateful to David Levy for sending me his thesis.

30. In choosing the term "populationism," I share Karen Adler's definition. Adler, *Jews and Gender,* 72.

31. See Alliance articles and tracts such as: "Immigration et naturalisation" (September 1923); "Interventions" (December 1923); Haury, "Natalité, mortal-

ité, immigration: Le doctrine de l'Alliance Nationale" (January 1925); "Interventions" (January 1925); and "Suppression des droits de naturalisation" (February 1925), all in *Revue de l'Alliance Nationale pour l'Accroissement de la Population Française*; and Haury, *La vie ou la mort*.

32. On Marseille's clientelist politics, see esp. Jankowski, *Communism and Collaboration*, passim.

33. Ibid., 14.

34. Ibid., 12.

35. The business cards of all these gentlemen are contained in some files, often with recommendations penned on the back, or letters attached recommending the candidate. Both Tasso and Vidal had also served as deputy mayor in their careers.

36. In the 1920s, Italians were also overrepresented. According to statistics culled by the inspector general's office, Italians represented more than 78% of the successful naturalizations in Marseille between 1922 and 1928. In real terms, their representation may have been even higher, since members of the same family naturalized at the same time as the head of household were counted as one naturalization. AN F^{1a} 4524.

37. ADBR 6 M 746 through 6 M 1283: Naturalizations, granted. Success rates from naturalization files compared to ADBR 4 M 941, 4 M 942, 4 M 944, 4 M 945, 4 M 946, and 4 M 947 (tableaux statistiques des étrangers en résidence dans la commune de Marseille).

38. ADBR 6 M 746 through 6 M 1283: Naturalizations, granted.

39. ADBR 6 M 1296: Adjoint, avis favorable, 11 February 1936; 3e division, avis favorable, n.d.; Certificat d'indigence, 10 January 1936.

40. ADBR 6 M 1196: Adjoint, avis favorable, 9 July 1936.

41. ADBR 6 M 1306: Adjoint, avis défavorable, 14 June 1934.

42. ADBR 6 M 1316: Adjoint, avis défavorable, n.d. [1935].

43. ADBR 6 M 1243: Application filed in 1935; adjoint, avis favorable, 14 September 1936.

44. ADBR 6 M 946: Adjoint, avis favorable, n.d.

45. ADBR 6 M 946: Min. J., Conseiller d'État, Directeur des Affaires Civiles et du Sceau, le Sous-Directeur, to prefect, 3 October 1929.

46. ADBR 6 M 946: Adjoint Délégué (pour le Maire) au Préfet, 14 November 1929; naturalization issued 1 July 1930 by Justice Ministry.

47. ADBR 6 M 1046: Adjoint, avis favorable, 24 March 1931; 3e division, avis favorable, 18 September 1931.

48. ADBR 6 M 1046: Min. J. (Affaires Civiles et Sceau), 1 April 1932; adjoint au préfet, 9 May 1932; naturalization granted 4 September 1932.

49. ADBR 6 M 1146: Adjoint, avis favorable, 14 November 1933; Min. J. to prefect, 8 September 1934; 5 November 1934.

50. ADBR 6 M 1306: 3e division, avis favorable, 7 November 1933; Min. J. decision, 5 December 1933.

51. ADBR 6 M 1306: Adjoint, avis, 12 April 1934 and 30 June 1936. 3e division, recommendations, 17 May 1934 and 22 February 1937; Min. J. postpones "until foundation of a hearth" on 10 July 1934 and then definitively rejects the application on 17 June 1938.

52. ADBR 6 M 1296: Letter to prefect, 23 December 1937. Blue grease pencil underlining.

53. ADBR 6 M 1296: Adjoint, avis défavorable, 4 January 1935; 3e division, avis défavorable, 3 February 1935.

54. ADBR 6 M 1336: Adjoint, avis défavorable, 13 December 1932.

55. See, e.g., ADBR 6 M 1355: Adjoint, avis défavorable, n.d. (application first filed in 1935); 6 M 1326: Adjoint, avis défavorable, 24 May 1937; 6 M 1336: Adjoint, avis défavorable, n.d. [appears to be 1935]; 6 M 1355: 3e division, avis défavorable, 25 January 1938.

56. ADBR 6 M 1336: Adjoint, avis favorable, 26 July 1929; 3e division, avis favorable, 1930.

57. ADBR 6 M 1336: Adjoint, avis favorable, 14 December 1935.

58. ADBR 6 M 1336: 3e division, avis défavorable, 17 April 1936.

59. ADBR 6 M 1346: Adjoint, avis favorable, 22 June 1931; 3e division, avis favorable, 3 October 1931; interventions of Vidal and Tasso, 3 September 1931 and 11 August 1931, respectively; adjoint, avis défavorable, 9 March 1937; 3e division, avis favorable, 21 March 1937; rejet du ministère, 24 October 1938.

60. ADBR 6 M 1346: Adjoint, avis favorable, 9 September 1936. Communications regarding Ira's case also include applications filed in 1932, 1934, and 1936. Joseph Vidal recommendation, 20 February 1932; adjoint, avis favorable, 29 June 1932; adjoint, avis défavorable, 13 March 1934; 3e division, avis défavorable, 13 March 1933 and 8 June 1937. Official postponement issued 25 July 1939. I am well aware of the trap of assuming confessional affiliation by name and am discomfited by the extent to which this suggestion puts me in a position similar to that of the decision makers in these cases. However, given that the persons in question here are Turkish nationals with first and last names of either Hebrew or Sephardic origins, the inquiry seems a fair one.

61. ADBR 14 M 22_24: Reference to this vote in Souc to Min. T., 25 January 1936.

62. ADBR 14 M 22_24: Souc to Min. T., 25 January 1936.

63. ADBR 4 M 946, Tableau statistique des étrangers en résidence dans la commune de Marseille, December 1932.

64. Conseil Municipal de Lyon, *Procès verbaux des séances*, 25 January 1932, 29 February 1932, 11 April 1932, 23 May 1932, 4 July 1932.

65. ADBR 14 M 23_21: Rapport du préfet, "Lutte contre une crise éventuelle de chômage," December 1926.

66. AMAE Z—Europe 1918–40—Italie, vol. 17: Prés. Cons. Min. AE to René Besnard, French ambassador in Rome, regarding nomination of vice-consuls in the South of France. Confidential minute, no. 109, 4 February 1926, stamped 6 February 1926; French embassy in Italy, direction of political and commercial affairs, Europe. Minute no. 35 to Aristide Briand, 20 January 1927.

67. The shift of unemployment services for foreigners from the regular unemployment office to the Dépot des Travailleurs Étrangers is dated to "the beginning of the crisis" without further specificity. At the latest, this system was in place by early 1933. ADBR 14 M 23_6: Report, 9 January 1933.

68. Décret du 28 Décembre 1926, cited in Héreil, *Le chômage en France,* 93.

69. On protests, see Ville de Marseille, *L'œuvre municipale,* 279–82. On food aid, see idem, *Budget primitif,* 1934 (with retrospective accounting to 1932).

70. Règlement de la Commission Paritaire en faveur des dockers, cited in Claverie, "Les dockers," 317.

71. Décret du 28 Décembre 1926, Bouches-du-Rhône, cited in Héreil, *Le chômage en France,* 163.

72. This crackdown is discussed in Chapter 4.

73. ADBR 4 M 1964: CS au Commissaire Central, 30 July 1932.

74. ADBR 4 M 1929: CS au Commissaire Central, 22 August 1931.

75. ADBR 4 M 1909: CS, 10 July 1931.

76. ADBR 4 M 1919: CS au Commissaire Central, 8 July 1931.

77. ADBR 4 M 1949: CS au Commissaire Central, 15 March 1932. On "gleaning" as a common practice among workers, see esp. Linebaugh, *The London Hanged.*

78. ADBR 4 M 1964: CS, 10 June 1932, reporting on theft of 16 March; ADBR 4 M 1964: CS, 27 July 1932.

79. See esp. ADBR 4 M 1887, 4 M 1899, 4 M 1928, 4 M 1943, and 4 M 1959. Dairy farmers all lived in Marseille's peripheral districts such as St Julien, Merlan, Caillols, St Louis, Montredon, La Pomme, St André, St Antoine, and La Valentine. Some also lived in nearby towns, such as Aix-en-Provence, Granettes, St Cannat, or St Martin de Crau. See also Lewis, "The Company of Strangers," 148–50.

80. See, e.g., ADBR 4 M 1964: Letter, 9 January 1933. Bouches-du-Rhône authorities were not alone in threatening delinquent taxpayers with expulsion, but they did so more frequently than their counterparts in the Rhône.

81. ADBR 4 M 1959: Letter addressed to prefect, 9 May 1932. Underlining is in blue grease pencil; exclamation points and "Ah non!" in pencil with illegible initials next to them.

82. Ibid. Underlining in pencil.

83. ADBR 4 M 1959: Letter addressed to Interior Ministry, 15 June 1932.

84. ADBR 4 M 1942: Trésorier payeur général withdraws recommendation for expulsion from 17 February 1932 when he receives payment on 1 March 1932.

85. ADBR 4 M 1943: Payment of 200 francs received 26 February 1932; warning issued 26 February 1932; full payment received 9 March 1932.

86. ADBR 4 M 1959: Préfet (Chef de Division) au Min. I, 16 June 1932; Min. I. (DSG) au Préfet, 4 juillet 1932 (blue grease pencil underlining).

87. ADBR 4 M 1959: Min. I. (DSG) au Préfet, 4 July 1932 (underlining in original type); sentence also highlighted in margin; reply, 11 July 1932.

88. On the *statut des immigrés,* see esp. Harouni, "Le débat." See also Livian, *Le parti socialiste.* The *statut* is discussed more fully in Chapter 4.

89. One observer, Rebecca West, was so concerned that she launched an investigation into the Balkan conflicts. See West, *Black Lamb, Grey Falcon,* prologue. See also Brown, "The King Is Dead."

90. Seton-Watson, "King Alexander's Assassination"; Brown, "The King Is Dead"; Broche, *Assassinat de Alexandre Ier.*

91. Left- and right-wing sympathizers quickly labeled the crime alternately as a "fascist" or "communist" plot. See the review of press contained in *IS* 545, 11

October 1934, 3; 546, 18 October 1934, 6; and 547, 25 October 1934, 3. For discussion of de Castelnau, see Chapter 1.

92. Philippe Henriot, *France d'abord*, 15 October 1934, cited in Temime and Attard-Maraninchi, *Migrance*, 71. For other examples of the scapegoating of immigrants following the assassination, see Schor, *L'opinion française*, esp. 636; André-Jean Tudesq, "La presse et la mort de Louis Barthou," in Papy, *Barthou*, 249–54.

93. *L'Action Française*, 13 October 1934, cited in *IS* 547, 25 October 1934, 3.

94. *Jeunesses Patriotes'* poster, cited in *IS* 545, 11 October 1934, 3, emphasis in original.

95. Léon Blum in *Le populaire*, 10 October 1934, cited in *IS* 545, 11 October 1934, 3.

96. *L'ami du people*, 10 October 1934, cited in *IS* 545, 11 October 1934, 3.

97. *Le matin*, 10 October 1934, cited in *IS* 545, 11 October 1934, 3.

98. De la Rocque in *Le jour*, 11 October 1934, cited in *IS* 547, 25 October 1934, 3.

99. Cited in *IS* 545, 11 October 1934, 3.

100. Seton-Watson, "King Alexander's Assassination," 28. See also the *New York Times* report from 12 October 1934, featuring the following headline and subheadlines: "Inadequate Guard for King Stirs New Crisis in France; Yugoslavs Attack Italians—Police Sparse in Marseilles, Film Shows; Shots and Crowd's Cries Ring in Newsreel." See Brown, "The King Is Dead," for a link to the newsreel.

101. Seton-Watson, "King Alexander's Assassination," 28.

102. Cited in André Ulmann's press review entitled "L'attentat de Marseille: Après ses compromissions c'est la désorganisation de la police qui apparaît," *IS* 546, 18 October 1934, 6. For similar accusations, see Adamic, "Who Killed the King?"

103. *Je suis partout*, 13 October 1934, cited in *IS* 546, 18 October 1934, 6.

104. *La république*, cited in *IS* 546, 18 October 1934, 6.

105. The first interior minister to replace Sarraut, Paul Marchandeau, indicated by circular dated 17 October 1934 that all Spanish refugees should be required to live north of the Loire River, so as to avoid "incidents" on the Franco-Spanish border. In particular, Spanish refugees were to be excluded categorically from Marseille. The principles behind this directive were reiterated in another circular signed by Marchandeau from the Direction Générale de la Sûreté Nationale to Prefects, 31 October 1934 (ADBR 4 M 959). See also Temime and Attard-Maraninchi, *Migrance*, esp. 74–78. The day before the assassination in Marseille, the Spanish army had landed in the Asturian port cities of Avilés and Gijón and had begun to put down the local resistance they met. See Jackson, *The Spanish Republic*, 157–59; Radcliff, *From Mobilization to Civil War*, esp. chap. 10.

106. The other one had been the ruling in the summer of 1933 to limit the settlement of German Jewish refugees in the departments of the Alsace-Lorraine region, although there this had primarily been in response to pressure from small businesses, which regarded the refugees as unfair competitors. See Caron, "The Antisemitic Revival," 38; idem, *Uneasy Asylum*, esp. chap. 2.

107. Cited in Adamic, "Who Killed the King?" 417–18.

108. "L'attentat de Marseille: Après ses compromissions c'est la désorganisation de la police qui apparaît," *IS* 546, 18 October 1934, 6.

109. ADBR 4 M 11: Prefect to DSG, 17 February 1934.

110. ADBR 4 M 14.

111. See Chapter 7.

CHAPTER 4

1. Saint-Exupéry, *The Little Prince,* 32.

2. The definitive work on the Stavisky scandal is Jankowski, *Stavisky.*

3. The term "guerre franco-française" is used by Henry Rousso, *The Vichy Syndrome,* 6; Robert Paxton also refers to "long-festering French internal conflicts" in Paxton, *Vichy France,* 5.

4. On the interdiction of public demonstrations, see Tartakowsky, "Stratégies de la rue," 45n53.

5. Eden, *Facing the Dictators,* 119.

6. Herriot devotes a chapter of his memoirs to the circumstances that led to his decision to resign from the Doumergue cabinet. Herriot, *Jadis,* vol. 2, 455–80.

7. See Chapter 2.

8. *JODCD,* séance du 13 Novembre 1934, 2291.

9. *JODCD,* séance du 13 Novembre 1934, 2292.

10. *JODCD,* 1ere seance du 15 Novembre 1934, 2335.

11. *JODCD,* 2e seance du 16 Novembre 1934, 2399–2400.

12. *JODCD,* 1ere séance du 20 Novembre 1934, 2457; 2464–63.

13. *JODCD,* 1ere séance du 22 Novembre 1934, 2508.

14. *JODCD,* 2e séance du 23 Novembre 1934, 2590–2604 and esp. 2593.

15. *JODCD,* 2e séance du 27 Novembre 1934, 2721.

16. *JODCD,* 3e séance du 27 Novembre 1934, 2728.

17. *JODCD,* 3e séance du 27 Novembre 1934, 2726.

18. *JODCD,* 3e séance du 27 Novembre 1934, 2731.

19. *JODCD,* 3e séance du 27 Novembre 1934, 2731.

20. *JODCD,* 3e séance du 27 Novembre 1934, 2735.

21. "Paris Police Seize Hundreds in Cafe Raids in Drive to Rid City of Undesirable Aliens," *New York Times,* 26 November 1934, 6; "Paris Raids Continue. Drive to 'Purify' City Is Being Made by the Police," *New York Times,* 27 November 1934, 10.

22. "La protection de la main-d'œuvre française: Les décisions gouvernementales," *Le temps,* 21 November 1934, 8.

23. Ibid.

24. Ibid.

25. Coutel, Speech to the Chamber of Deputies, 15 December 1931, in "Travaux préparatoires de la loi du 10 août 1932," *Bulletin de l'inspection du travail et de l'hygiène industrielle,* année 40 (1932): 344.

26. See Fette, "Xenophobia"; Caron, *Uneasy Asylum,* esp. chap. 2; Ralph Schor, *L'opinion Française,* 600ff.

27. "Proposition de loi tendant à protéger la main-d'œuvre artisanale nationale," *JODP*, annexe no. 4148, session extraordinaire—1ere séance du 22 Novembre 1934, 131.

28. Ibid.

29. ADR 4 M 448: Circ. no. 238, Min. I. (DGSN, Sous-Direction de la Police des Étrangers, Courses et Jeux, 8e Bur.—Cartes d'Identité), signed Marcel Régnier, 18 December 1934.

30. See esp. Chapter 2.

31. ADR 4 M 448: Dutrion speaking at International Conference of Traveling Salesmen held in Villefranche-sur-Saône (Rhône), 11 July 1933. Comments contained in Special Police Commissioner's Report.

32. ADR Exp., box 40: Prefect to Min. I., 9 August 1933. A protracted battle over this family's fate ensued. The family sought assistance from the League of the Rights of Man and various refugee associations and remained in the country, despite the Interior Ministry's repeated refusal to grant their appeals. Ultimately, their expulsion was ordered in March 1934, but they refused to leave. Their expulsion was repealed by the Socialist interior minister under the Popular Front, Marx Dormoy, in 1937.

33. Cross, *Immigrant Workers,* 70.

34. See Articles V, VI, and VII of 6 February 1935 decree. Provisions were also made for full-time students and the severely ill (both of whom had to provide proof of this status and both of whose cards would be valid only as long as this status prevailed). *JOLD*, 8 February 1935, 1673.

35. Ibid., Article II.

36. ADBR 14 M 22_24: Min. T., Dir. T., SCMO, no. 34. Min. T. to prefects (ODP), 25 January 1935.

37. By June, 19,000 of 49,000 had been completed. See ADBR 14 M 22_24: Prefect to Min. T. (Dir. T., SCMO), 13 September 1935. The labor minister acknowledged this snowball effect, while still chastising the local administration for its slow progress. Despite this admonition, the Labor Ministry had taken almost two months to reply to the prefect's report, suggesting that it, too, was swamped. ADBR 14 M 22_24: Min. T. (Dir. T., SCMO) to Bouches-du-Rhône prefect, 3 December 1935.

38. Berlière, "La professionalisation de la police"; idem, *Le monde des polices en France*; Kitson, "The Marseille Police"; Vogel, "Politiques policières." See also Jankowski, *Communism and Collaboration,* 11.

39. MAS-CRDM: Min. T., Dir. T., SCMO, Circ. no. 39, *CONFIDENTIEL,* Min. T. to prefects (ODP) and regional labor office directors, 12 February 1935.

40. This last innovation may have resulted from a suggestion by Aléxis Léger, the general secretary of the Foreign Affairs Ministry. Léger proposed to modify the application of the new policy that "departmental placement offices will immediately reject requests for renewal concerning professions that are experiencing unemployment," by adding the qualification "except if the person concerned has lived in France for at least ten years" (Aléxis Léger, lettre du ministère des affaires étrangères C/259, cited in Deschodt and Huguenin, *La république xénophobe,* 117).

41. Circ. no. 39, 12 February 1935; see note 39.

42. ADC M 7168: Min. T., Dir. T., SCMO, no. 49, Min. T. Paul Jacquier to prefects (ODP) and Messieurs les Chefs de Offices Régionaux de la Main-d'Œuvre, 3 April 1935.

43. Ibid.

44. MAS-CRDM: Min. T. Dir. T., SCMO Circ. no. 56, Min. T. to prefects (ODP) and regional labor office directors, *CONFIDENTIEL,* 11 May 1935.

45. Ibid.

46. Shorrock, "The Tunisian Question."

47. Circ. no. 39, 12 February 1935, see note 39.

48. MAS-CRDM: Min. T., Dir. T., SCMO, no. 76, Min. T. L.-O. Frossard to prefects (ODP) and regional labor office directors, *CONFIDENTIEL,* 9 September 1935.

49. Ibid.

50. See, e.g., AMAE Z—Europe 1918–40—Italie, vol. 398: Note "demandes de naturalisation de sujets italiens," 15 May 1934.

51. Circ. no. 76, 9 September 1935, see note 48. Underlining in original.

52. MAS-CRDM: Min. T., Dir. T., SCMO, no. 80, Min. T. to prefects (ODP), 12 September 1935.

53. Rapport au Président de la République Française, 30 October 1935, *JOLD,* 31 October 1935, 11489–90.

54. Décret du 30 Octobre 1935, *JOLD,* 31 October 1935, 11490–91.

55. ADC M 7168: Min. I., DGSN, Dir. de la Police du Territoire et des Étrangers, 6e bur., cartes d'identité, no. D-15, Circ. no. 303. Prés. Cons., Min. I. (Pour le Président, le Directeur de la Sûreté Nationale, Ch. Magny), to prefects, 28 April 1936.

56. MAS-CRDM: Min. T., Dir. T., SCMO, *Renouvellement des cartes d'identité des travailleurs étrangers,* no. 108. Min. T. to prefects (ODPs), 8 May 1936.

57. Ibid.

58. MAS-CRDM: Min. T., Dir. T., 3e Bur., no. 146, Min. T. (for the minister and, by authorization, the general director of labor Marcel Bernard) to labor inspection directors (copy to prefects), 18 February 1937.

59. These policies had hardly been applied since being decreed in August 1935. MAS-CRDM: Min. T., Dir. T., 3e Bur., MOE, no. 128, Min. T. (Minister of State, interim labor minister Paul Faure) to prefects and labor inspection directors, 3 October 1936; Min. T., Dir. T., 3e Bur., MOE no. 134, Min. T. (for the minister and, by authorization, labor director Ch. Picquenard) to prefects and labor inspection directors, 27 November 1936.

60. Conseil Municipal de Lyon, *Procès verbaux des séances,* 19 Novembre 1934, 200.

61. These included the following: hotels, textiles (silk and synthetic), metals, clothing, rubber, dairy, fabric printing, ceramics, gem polishing, carbonated beverages, chemicals, paper and cardboard, biscuits and pastries, and metals (revised). See *BMT, actes officiels* (1935): 185*; 215*–220*; 312*.

62. ADR 3494 W 97: Letter on taxed paper, 29 October 1935.

63. ADR 3494 W 97: Avis favorable du Directeur de l'ODP, Perret, 18 December 1935; avis favorable stamp from SGP, 17 January 1936.

64. ADR Exp., box 37: She was first granted a sursis in the Jura on 7 June 1935; this was extended to the Rhône department on "16 January 1935" [*sic*; it must be 1936 since the *sursis* had to be granted first before it could be extended; this is probably the not uncommon error of incorrectly dating documents at the beginning of a new year]. For Roberta's story, see Chapter 2.

65. ADR 3494 W 107: Ain prefect (Secrétaire Général Délégué) to Rhône prefect, 29 February 1936; CS to SGP (Rhône), 12 March 1936, with penciled question and response at top.

66. These protocols are cited in Circ. no. 56, 11 May 1935. See note 44.

67. ADR 3494 W 97: ODP, 6 January 1936.

68. ADR 3494 W 97: Letter on taxed paper requesting move to Rhône due to high cost of transit, 4 November 1935; Rhodiaceta work certificate, 15 October 1935, indicating work since 19 January 1934; avis favorable, Commissaire de Police de Décines, 14 December 1935; ODP decision, 6 January 1936. For another similar case, see ADR 3494 W 97: Letter on taxed paper, 23 September 1935; Préfet (SGP) du Rhône au Préfet de l'Isère, n.d., with handwritten note on bottom indicating that it was forwarded to office for approval 19 October 1935; Ville de Décines-Charpieu (Isère), Commissariat de Police au Préfet de l'Isère no. 1269, 8 October 1935.

69. ADR Exp., box 13. This is discovered when the Isère prefect, noting that Guillermo is the father of seven children (six born in France) and that he cannot return to his country in civil war, requests the Rhône prefect's agreement that he be authorized to stay in France. St Priest is now in the Rhône department.

70. ADR Exp., box 28. Diego lived "*maritalement*" with their mother. The Rhône prefect approved his move back on 10 September 1936.

71. On the register, tone, content, and effectiveness of individual petitions to state officials, see Fassin, "La supplique."

72. ADR Exp., box 40: "*Sursis non-renouvelable,*" 10 November 1934; declaration of children's nationality 29 February 1936; report, sous-chef de la sûreté, 27 August 1936. The final decision was made after the election of the Popular Front, but the process began beforehand. Expulsion repealed 1943.

73. For the cases of Savio and Gaetano, see Chapter 2.

74. ADR Exp., box 39: Letter, 17 September 1936; note, Conseiller de préfecture délégué, 13 October 1936; Min. I. (Direction de la police du territoire et des étrangers, chef du 6e bur.) to prefect, transmitting request, 31 October 1936; prefect to Min. I., 14 December 1936. *Sursis* granted 18 December 1936.

75. ADR Exp., box 38: Recommendation of expulsion, 2 August 1934; St-Fons mayor to prefect, n.d.; response, 11 January 1935; St-Fons police commissioner to SGP, 13 September 1935; prefect to Min. I., 5 October 1935, my emphasis.

76. ADR Exp., box 38: Letter to prefect, 8 January 1935; letter to Herriot, 5 January 1935 (this interpretation of her letter is supported by the fact that other documents in the file corroborate her pregnancy); forwarding of letter to prefect, 10 January 1935.

77. ADR Exp., box 38: Min. I., 6 December [1935]. Her first letter to the Interior minister had led to his "not favorable" response, 6 December 1934.

78. On the concept of the transnational family and its effect on migrant rights, albeit in a different context, see Ngai, *Impossible Subjects,* 87.

79. Nonetheless, Luis remained in France until at least 1942, much of the time illegally. ADR 3494 W 97: Verrerie de Vénissieux, work certificate, 15 November 1935, noting employment since 24 August 1935 as mechanic earning 28 francs/day; St-Fons police commissioner to SGP, no. 414, 20 November 1935, noting his residency history; Jean Perret (ODP), avis défavorable, 3 December 1935; note de Préfecture (4e division, 3e bur.), SGP (J.-F. Bussière) to St-Fons police commissioner, 4 January 1936; report, 23 February 1942.

80. The term is from Caron, *Uneasy Asylum,* 45.

81. Herriot had called for a lowering of all industries whose foreign-worker thresholds were above 10%; in Marseille, this meant a review of all industries.

82. On maintaining the status quo, see ADBR 14 M 22_22: Bouches-du-Rhône prefect to Min. T., 4 February 1935; on modifications voted, see Dir. ODP au Préfet, 14 January 1935. For additional decrees modifying quotas, see *BMT, actes officiels* (1935): 200*, 203*–04*; 211*–12*; 265*–66*; 298*.

83. ADBR 14 M 22_23: Prefect, "Suite à ma note marginale," 5 August 1936.

84. ADBR 14 M 22_23: Handwritten notes in response to dir. ODP to prefect (1ère division, 3e bur.), 11 February 1937. For elaboration on this story, see Lewis, "The Company of Strangers," 60–64.

85. ADBR 6 M 1146: 3e division, avis favorable, 12 February 1935; naturalization, 24 May 1935.

86. ADBR 6 M 1146: 3e division, avis, 17 April 1935. Min. J. approved their naturalization on 18 June 1935. On the parity commission, see ADBR 14 M 22_22: Dir. ODP to prefect, 14 January 1935.

87. ADBR 6 M 1216: Adjoint, avis favorable, 1 February 1935; 3e division, avis favorable, 12 March 1935.

88. ADBR 4 M and 6 W. I arrived at this figure from the numbers assigned to expulsion files for the period leading up to 1933 and then beginning again in 1938. These numbers are sequential, and there is a gap of 9,801 numbers in the middle. No explanation is available for the archival lacunae.

89. Beginning with files starting in 1919, I have calculated an average of 1,481 expulsion inquiries initiated by the Bouches-du-Rhône prefecture per year. Not all inquiries led to expulsion, and some represented follow-up on older expulsions initiated outside the Bouches-du-Rhône. Meanwhile, the missing files represent an average of 1,960 expulsion files initiated per year.

90. ADBR 4 M 1941: CS to Commissaire Central, 11 December 1934.

91. ADBR 4 M 1941: Min. I. (DGSN), 18 January 1935.

92. ADBR 4 M 959: DGSN to prefects, 31 October 1934.

93. ADBR 1 M 1737: Subprefect to prefect, 5 November 1934.

94. Prost, "Les manifestations."

95. ADBR 1 M 1737: CPS (Dhubert) to Bouches-du-Rhône prefect, report no. 3985, 15 December 1934.

96. ADBR 4 M 1968: Fernand Maille to Jacquemart, 29 May 1935; reply from SGP, 4 June 1935.

97. ADBR 4 M 1968: New request filed 15 June 1935; response, 5 July 1935.

98. ADBR 4 M 1968: Summons, 10 September 1935. In fact, he had probably just received word of the policy that day. Frossard's confidential circular was dated 9 September 1935.

99. ADBR 4 M 1968: SGP to Min. I., 16 September 1935.

100. The expulsion, dated April 1927, had resulted from a failure to honor a *refoulement*. Maurizio had been granted *sursis* for two years following the expulsion order, until he was accused of knowingly harboring stolen goods in 1929, at which time the expulsion was finally enforced.

101. ADBR 4 M 1659: The prefect's recommendation and the Interior minister's decisions had crossed in the mail. On 3 August 1927, the prefect recommended lifting the *refoulement* order (he noted that debts relating to a minor infraction had been paid); the following day, evidently before receiving the prefect's opinion, the Interior Ministry issued a formal expulsion order. For protracted negotiations between the wife and authorities, see her letters dated 12 November 1929; 25 August 1930; 19 November 1930 (date of receipt); 10 January 1931 (date of receipt); 19 October 1931; 30 September 1932; 19 January 1933 (date of receipt); 25 August 1933; 13 December 1935; and 19 March 1936. CS reports, 22 August 1930; 25 September 1930; 27 November 1930; 30 October 1931; 20 September 1933; 5 October 1934; and 20 September 1935. Prefect to Min. I. (DSG, 2e bur.), 12 September 1930; Min. I. (2e bur.) to prefect, 22 December 1930.

102. ADBR 4 M 1659: CS to Commissaire Central, 20 September 1935, reporting the wife's admission.

103. ADBR 4 M 1659: CS, n.d., reporting the 5 December 1935 arrest.

104. ADBR 4 M 1659: Min. I., 6th bur. chief (direction de la police du territoire et des étrangers) to prefect, 29 May 1936.

105. ADBR 4 M 1659: He earned *sursis* of six months each until 23 June 1938, when his *sursis* were extended to one year. In June of 1940, he signed a declaration of loyalty to France. His expulsion was repealed on 20 July 1943 (signed by René Bousquet). As of 2 June 1956 he was an electrician for the same company that hired him after his residency was approved in 1936. For T. H. Marshall reference, see Marshall, "Citizenship and Social Class," 72.

106. ADBR 14 M 22_24: Syndicat Général des Ports et Docks de la Ville de Marseille's complaint paraphrased in Min. T., Dir. T., Charles Picquenard, dépêche no. 5624 to prefect, 28 March 1936.

107. The Popular Front coalition was comprised of the Socialists, the Communists, dissident members of the neo-Socialists, and, crucially, the Radicals, those swing centrists who had also participated in the "truce" governments that leaned more to the right.

108. Prost, "Les grèves."

109. The standard work on this subject is Jackson, *The Popular Front in France.* A contrarian interpretation can be found in Rossiter, "Popular Front Economic Policy," which suggests that employer interests shaped the initial negotiations at Matignon more than has been previously acknowledged.

110. Nora, *Les lieux de mémoire.*

111. Bonnet, *Les pouvoirs publics français,* 315.

112. Harouni, "Le débat."

113. *JODP*, annexe no. 937, session ordinaire—2e séance du 31 Juillet 1936, 1581–83.

114. Ibid., 1581.

115. Ibid., 1581–83.

116. For details, see Chapter 2, note 70.

117. Harouni, "Le débat," 67.

118. *JODP*, no. 1288, 2e séance extraordinaire—séance du 12 Novembre 1936, 481.

119. Léon Blum cited in Rossiter, "Popular Front Economic Policy," 663 (my translation).

120. This is as true today as it ever was, but as Christian Joppke and Elia Marzal show, courts now increasingly intervene to protect immigrant rights, even (or especially) in a climate where the masses "are generally opposed, if not hostile to immigration." See their "Courts," 823.

121. Rapport au Président de la République Française, 14 October 1936, *JOLD*, 24 October 1936, 11107.

122. Article 2—Décret du 14 Octobre 1936, *JOLD*, 24 October 1936, 11107. This new article modified Article 13 of the 6 February 1935 decree. Marcel Livian calls Barbara Vormeier "mistaken" for claiming that the Popular Front continued this policy, saying that the 14 October 1936 decree modified the requirement. It did, but not in the way Livian implies. See Livian, *Le parti socialiste*, 78–79.

123. ADC M 7168: Min. I., DGSN, Direction de la Police du Territoire et des Étrangers, 6e bur., cartes d'identité, no. C-3-3-/F, Circ. no. 315, Min. I. (for the Min. I., the DGSN) to prefects, 22 October 1936.

124. *JODCD*, 1 October 1936, 2898; also cited in Livian, *Le parti socialiste*, 116.

125. On remilitarization of the Rhineland and German foreign policy from 1936 to 1937, see Craig, *Germany*, 688–96.

126. On the use of this and similar slogans, see Jackson, *The Popular Front in France*, 250–51; also Caron, *Uneasy Asylum*, 269–70.

127. "France, terre d'asile," *Action Française*, 25 August 1936, cited in Caron, *Uneasy Asylum*, 271.

128. Between July 1936 and December 1938, anywhere from 200,000 to 340,000 Spanish refugees crossed the French border. See Stein, *Beyond Death and Exile*, 6.

129. The 1937 World Exposition in Paris opened in May.

130. ADC M 7168: Min. I., DGSN, 6e bur., Service de la Carte d'Identité et des Passeports, no. B-56/9, Circ. no. 338. Min. I. Marx Dormoy to prefects, 9 July 1937, stamped "CONFIDENTIEL."

131. ADC M 7168: Min. I., DGSN, 6e bur., Service de la Carte d'Identité et des Passeports, no. B-8-5, Circ. no. 341. Min. I. (for the Min. I., for the DGSN, the director of intelligence Chevreux) to prefect, 8 September 1937. For the previous circular, see note 55.

132. On this point see Caron, *Uneasy Asylum*, 162.

133. On the Serre plan, see esp. Weil, *La France et ses étrangers*, 35–37; idem, "Racisme"; Racine, "Une expérience à reprendre"; Caron, *Uneasy Asylum*, chap. 7.

134. Caron, *Uneasy Asylum*, 164.

135. Bonnet, *Les pouvoirs publics français*, 327. Bonnet notes, for example, that there were 16,525 naturalization decrees issued in 1937, a mere 125 more than had been issued in 1935.

136. An application waiting since November 1934 was approved in July 1938; one first filed in 1933 and approved locally in October 1935 was approved in November 1937; an application approved by the CS in 1933 and by the prefect in 1935 was approved in November 1936; and so forth. ADR Naturalization files, 1927–38.

137. ADR Naturalization files, 1927–38, FER: Secrétaire Général, 3 December 1932.

138. ADR Naturalization files, 1927–38, FER: Prefect, recommendation of postponement, 9 August 1935. The CS in Lyon had been favorable, 28 January 1935.

139. ADR Naturalization files, 1927–38, FER: Prefect, 12 November 1937.

140. For multiple examples of this distinction, see Rygiel, ed., *Le bon grain*, passim.

141. Henri Baroin's study of foreigners in the Rhône department demonstrated that, when infractions for misdemeanors relating directly to one's foreign status were removed from consideration, foreigners' rate of trial before the Correctional Tribunal was comparable to that of French nationals. Baroin, *La main-d'oeuvre étrangère*, 162–64. For a longer discussion of Baroin's findings, see Lewis, "The Company of Strangers," 188–89.

142. Even Vichy authorities apparently thought so, repealing his expulsion in the summer of 1943. ADBR 4 M 1659: Order to repeal expulsion dated 20 July 1943 and signed Bousquet. The expulsion was repealed even though he had been arrested in 1942 for trafficking of ration cards. Of course, this no doubt also had to do with the careful approach Vichy authorities took with respect to Italy, which was occupying a portion of southeastern France.

143. Poincaré's fourth stint as premier lasted from July 1928 to November 1928. He then formed a new government in November, which lasted until July 1929.

144. Circ. no. 39, 12 February 1935 (see note 39); Circ. no. 108, 8 May 1936 (see note 56).

CHAPTER 5

1. Arendt, *The Origins of Totalitarianism*, 267.

2. Geneva Convention, 28 July 1951, Chapter I, Article I, Paragraph A, Section 2.

3. Arendt, *The Origins of Totalitarianism*, 277.

4. Miller, *Shanghai on the Metro*, 143.

5. Ibid., 130.

6. This represents a conservative estimate. Skran, *Refugees in Inter-war Europe,* 37 and 36n18. See also discussion of figures in Lewis, "The Company of Strangers," 221n10.

7. For the history of the High Commission and the refugee situation during and after the war, see esp. Skran, *Refugees in Inter-war Europe;* Marrus, *The Unwanted;* Noiriel, *La tyrannie;* and Marrus and Bramwell, *Refugees in the Age of Total War.*

8. Russians received international "refugee" passports, known as "Nansen passports," by virtue of the arrangement of 5 July 1922; Armenians were granted access to these passports by the arrangement of 31 May 1924; Assyrians, Assyro-Chaldeans, Turkish, and "assimilated" refugees, by the arrangement of 30 June 1928; and Saar refugees, by the arrangement of 24 May 1935. The decree of 17 September 1936 implemented the July 1936 international arrangement for refugees coming from Germany.

9. See reports in ADBR 1 M 1782.

10. ADBR 1 M 1780: CPS, report nos. 3564 and 3565, 29 September 1923.

11. ADBR 1 M 1782.

12. Gorboff, *La Russie fantôme,* 44.

13. Simpson, *The Refugee Problem,* 309.

14. Gorboff, *La Russie fantôme,* 44. Georges Mauco wrote that in 1930, 1,000 of the 7,550 immigrants working for an unnamed auto plant were Russian. Mauco, *Les étrangers en France,* 572. Olivier Le Guillou, meanwhile, offers no precise calculation, though he does argue that Simpson's figures are exaggerated. Although he acknowledges that "several thousand" Russians worked at the Renault plant in Boulogne-Billancourt between the wars, he says that there was also fairly frequent turnover of workers in this industry. Le Guillou, "L'émigration russe en France," 230–31.

15. Gorboff, *La Russie fantôme,* 33, 44–45.

16. Women, especially the many widows, were perceived as more likely to become a "charge" than were men. See ADBR 1 M 1776: Directeur de l'Hôtel du Levant au Président de la Société Protectrice de l'Enfance de Marseille, 17 January 1923; ADBR 1 M 1775: Minute, prefect to Min. HAP, 19 January 1923.

17. ADBR 1 M 1782: Prefect to Min. HAP (Assistance et Hygiène Publiques, Cabinet du Directeur), 12 December 1923.

18. Ibid. A portion of the Smyrna refugees included persons whose Lebanese or Syrian origins offered them French protected status.

19. ADBR 1 M 1782: Prefect to Min. I., 3 October 1922.

20. ADBR 1 M 1775: Minute, Prefect to Min. HAP, 19 January 1923; ADBR 1 M 1782: Prefect to Min. HAP (Assistance et Hygiène Publiques, Cabinet du Directeur), 21 December 1923.

21. ADBR 1 M 1775: Le Représentant de la République Arménienne à Marseille au Préfet, 18 January 1923.

22. ADBR 1 M 1775: Minute, Prefect to Min. HAP, 19 January 1923; ADBR 1 M 1782: Prefect to Min. HAP, Cabinet du Directeur, Secours aux Arméniens Réfugiés en France, 22 December 1923.

23. ADBR 1 M 1782: Office Central de Charité et de Bienfaisance, extrait du procès-verbal de la séance du 30 Octobre 1923, concernant le VOEU emis par la réunion au sujet des 'réfugiés.' Capitals in original.

24. ADBR 1 M 1782: Prefect to Min. HAP, Cabinet du Directeur, Secours aux Arméniens Réfugiés en France, 22 December 1923, where he refers to a telegram from Poincaré to consuls. For size of refugee populations in Greek cities, see Marrus, *The Unwanted*, 103.

25. Popular jibe cited in Paxton, *Europe in the Twentieth Century*, 194.

26. ADBR 1 M 1775: Prefect to Min. AE, Pres. Cons. (direction des affaires administratives et techniques, sous-direction des affaires administratives et des Unions Internationales), 7 June 1924; reply, 17 June 1924.

27. ADBR 1 M 1775: For quote: Chef du Cabinet (pour le préfet), note de service pour M. Castre, 28 June 1924. For instructions to Borelli, Chef du Cabinet (pour le préfet), note de service pour M. Borelli, 28 juin 1924. Borelli's report to prefect, precipitating these responses, 22 June 1924.

28. ADBR 1 M 1775: Chef du Service des Étrangers, Note au Sujet des Orientaux Entrés Clandestinement en France, 28 June 1924.

29. Mandel, *Aftermath*, 33.

30. ADBR 4 M 957: Min. T. (Chef de la MOE à Marseille) to Min. I. (DSG), 4 July 1925.

31. ADBR 4 M 951: Prefect to Min. I. (DSG, Contrôle Général des Services de Police Administrative), 19 March 1925 (response to latter's questionnaire to prefects, 26 February 1925).

32. Sayad, "Qu'est-ce-qu'un immigré?," 7.

33. ADBR 4 M 951: Prefect to Min. I. (DSG, Contrôle Général des Services de Police Administrative), 19 March 1925 (response to latter's questionnaire to prefects, 26 February 1925). Note that he refers to them erroneously as "nationals."

34. Mandel, *In the Aftermath*, 88.

35. See, e.g., files contained in ADR Exp., boxes 1–46.

36. AMAE SDN, vol. 1799: Min. AE, reply, n.d., to questionnaire, 31 January 1928, from High Commissioner for Refugees Fridtjof Nansen.

37. ADBR 4 M 951: Prefect to Min. I., 19 March 1925, see note 31.

38. The unemployment rate is difficult to determine since these figures usually come from statistics regarding those receiving benefits, and Armenians were eligible for benefits. Some groups estimated it at 2,000 in March; *L'humanité* estimated it at 1,000. *L'humanité*, 25 March 1927.

39. HOK was also known as HOG, the Haistani Oknoutian Gomidé.

40. ADBR 1 M 1820: Commissaire Central to prefect, 1 February 1927. See also AN F[7] 13524: "Le H.O.K. et les sans-travail à Marseille," note, 3 March 1927; Borelli's report, 21 March 1927. For Picquenard on Armenians, see MAS-CRDM: Circ. no. 7827, Min. T. (Dir. T., SMOE), Dir. T. (Charles Picquenard) [for the minister and by authorization] to directors of regional labor offices, 8 April 1929.

41. AN F[7] 13436: CPS (Lyon) to SGP (Rhône), 3 May 1926.

42. AN F[7] 13522: Note on "Rapatriement des chômeurs étrangers," n.d. (addendum to "Note du ministère du travail sur les étrangers et les secours de chômage," 17 January 1927).

43. MAS-CRDM: Circ. no. 7827, 8 April 1929, see note 40.

44. AMAE SDN, vol. 1799: Comité des Experts Juristes Russes et Arméniens, memorandum presented to the Conférence Intergouvernementale pour le Statut Juridique des Réfugiés, held 28–30 June 1928. As a result of the meeting, the commission recommended a resolution encouraging member countries to refrain from expelling Russian and Armenian refugees who did not have authorization to enter another country. NYU League of Nations Collection: Procès-verbaux des séances. LSC 15/1928. XIII Refugiés. The arrangement of 30 June 1928 recommended the relaxation of expulsion orders against Nansen refugees in certain circumstances. Simpson, *Refugees, Preliminary Report,* 106.

45. MAS-CRDM: Circ. no. 7827, Min. T., 8 April 1929. See note 40.

46. ADBR 4 M 957: Report to Min. I., filed by the Inspecteur Général Adjoint des Services Administratifs, Gravereaux, 10 March 1926, in which Gravereaux writes, "The present system cannot be maintained, and it is necessary to remove from the current 'director' of the camp, M. TAKOOR-HATCHIKIAN [*sic*], his self-appointed authority and powers." Gravereaux also indicated that it was extremely urgent to "eliminate the second so-called dissident 'Camp des Aygalades,' which borders a putrid stream carrying excremental material and which risks becoming an epidemic hotbed." Procès-Verbal de la Commission pour la liquidation, 23 February 1926.

47. ADBR 1 M 1782: Prefect to Min. HAP (Cabinet du Directeur, Secours aux Armeniens Refugiés en France), 22 December 1923. Interestingly, the low "rent" charged by Hatchikian has not always been remembered this way by Armenians who lived there. In one oral history, a man who immigrated as a child with his family and lived in Oddo for a couple of months remembered his family feeling extorted by rents paid to the French government. There is no evidence that this occurred, yet it is interesting that this man associated *feeling* exploited by the French government with the time he spent living in Oddo. "Récit de vie" of Haroutioun Kieusseian, in Hovanessian, *Le lien communautaire,* esp. 111, "on nous faisait payer une somme dérisoire parce que c'était le gouvernement" (We had to pay an exorbitant amount because it was the government).

48. ADBR 4 M 957: Réfugiés Arméniens, report to prefect, 28 May 1926.

49. See, e.g., ADBR 1 M 1820: CPS report no. 4118, 31 December 1925.

50. It was the Communist Party organ *L'humanité* that used the term "sordid" to describe the Oddo barracks. "Mornes aspects de Marseille éclatante," *L'humanité,* 25 March 1927. Kieusseian also recalled overcrowding, beds made from planks, and blankets hung as walls between families. Hovanessian, *Le lien communautaire,* 111.

51. ADBR 1 M 1782: Commissaire Special chargé du Camp Oddo, à Monsieur le Prefet des Bouches-du-Rhône, Enquête sur le Camp Russe, dénommé Camp Victor Hugo, 21 August 1927. According to this report, the residents remaining in Camp Victor Hugo belonged "in majority to the bourgeois classes . . . especially former officers, magistrates, engineers, liberal professions, etc." De Becque reportedly paid himself 850 francs per month for his role as director. His "commandant" was paid 500 francs per month, the secretary 400, the "mail orderly" 100. Three subcommandants were paid commissions for securing monthly rent from the in-

habitants, a job they performed in addition to their regular work. Camp employees did not have to pay rent. Although this report on Camp Victor Hugo makes no explicit comparison to Camp Oddo, the tone of the special commissioner's discussion is more positive than it is in his reports on Oddo. After briefly acknowledging that de Becque's move to charge rent caused considerable dissension within the community, he concluded that "the energy deployed by the director succeeded in the end to impose order and calm the effervescence, but it was necessary after these incidents to proceed with the eviction of the agitating parties." The lodgings, he wrote, "are decorated with considerable taste and are kept very clean."

52. Ibid.

53. Ludovic Naudeau, "Enquête sur la population de la France: Bouches-du-Rhône," *Illustration* Vol. 174, No. 4512, 24 August 1929, 181. This article was one in a series on the population in various French departments, and continues in *Illustration* Vol. 174, No. 4513, 31 August 1929, 198–201. Naudeau's use of Russian words is indicative of his different approach to the Russian population, with whom he clearly sympathized. Although he provided rough translations of *bakaleinaia lavka* and *traktir,* he left *tchinovniki* (dignitary, Russian official under the tsarist regime) untranslated, as if transparent in meaning.

54. See ADBR 4 M 957: Commissaire Spécial chargé du Camp Oddo, à M. le Préfet (Bouches-du-Rhône), 14 June 1926, for Montel's description of their real estate plans in his report. Armenians were known to have done this in the other parts of France they settled in as well. See Hovanessian, *Le lien communautaire.*

55. ADBR 4 M 957. Oddo residents immediately presented him with around 150 certificates attesting to their ownership of property or homes.

56. ADBR 4 M 957: Commissaire Spécial chargé du Camp Oddo, à M. le Préfet (Bouches-du-Rhône), 14 June 1926.

57. This may explain the low numbers of applications for Nansen papers. In the years 1926–46, fewer than 100 persons on average applied each year for Nansen passports. Mandel, *In the Aftermath,* 224n44.

58. "The Central Office for Armenian Refugees, whose central office is located at 7, rue Copernic in Paris 16e is the only organization officially authorized" to issue birth, death, or marriage certificates (état civil) to Armenian refugees in all of France. ADBR 1 J 479. This did not prevent other agencies from trying. For instance, the special commissioner in Lyon noted the importance birth and marriage certificates had in the Armenian community. It was enough to create a scission in the Regional (Armenian) Administrative Council over its leadership, since the leadership was believed to have the authority to issue birth and marriage certificates, certificates whose validity, the commissioner noted, "was questionable and for which members of the Administrative Council receive honoraria, as much for personal profit as for that of the association." AN F[7] 13436: CPS (Lyon) to prefect SGP, 10 November 1928.

59. AN F[7] 14759 (dossiers excerpted under derogation): Min. I. to Bouches-du-Rhône prefect, n.d. [1932 or 1933]. Dossier: Correspondance départ, émanée de la police judiciaire et relative à des étrangers expulsés, extradés, assignés à résidence, etc. et à des Français interdits de sejour.

60. ADBR 4 M 1692: Letter to prefect, 31 July 1926.

61. Ibid. See also the exchanges between the special Oddo commissioner Montel, the prefect, and the Ministry of the Interior contained in the same file. At one point (18 October 1926), Montel recommended letting Belnirari O. stay until he could place his nephew with Public Assistance, a suggestion that indicates the level of bureaucratic investment that went into enforcing an expulsion, regardless of the desirability of its side effects. No doubt Marseille officials under other circumstances would have wanted to avoid placing foreign children in publicly funded orphanages. From Montel's perspective, however, his job was to carry out the expulsion; once the child was placed in the public welfare system, the case would fall under someone else's jurisdiction.

62. League of Nations Union, "Refugees and the League," 32.

63. ADR Exp., box 18: *Procès-verbal,* gendarmes (Rhône), 2 October 1933. Ishag died in prison on 7 July 1936, after several prison sentences. Prior to a workplace accident, Ishag had worked at the Berliet auto plant. In all likelihood, as a stateless person, he had received no accident compensation.

64. ADR Exp., box 31: SGP to Min. I., 16 July 1931, my emphasis. For more detail, see Chapter 2.

65. ADR Exp., box 5: SGP report, 19 February 1929.

66. "In view of the current economic situation" was a common refrain in expulsion recommendations in the Rhône department beginning around 1931.

67. ADR Exp., box 7: Letter to prefect, n.d. [approx. January 1931], in broken French. Emphasis in original.

68. ADR Exp., box 7.

69. Figures gleaned from "Annexe" in Guichard and Noiriel, *Construction,* 278–368.

70. Letellier, Perret, Zuber, and Dauphin-Meunier, *Enquête sur le chômage.*

71. John Hope Simpson notes, for example, that the Russian population in Billancourt (site of the Renault factory) declined considerably in the late 1930s, in part due to deaths, in part because Billancourt did not offer any unemployment relief. "This means that the unemployed have, when possible, moved to some other commune where the dole is given (e.g. Paris—15th arrondissement)." Simpson, *The Refugee Problem,* 309. Moving did not always resolve the problem, however, since most municipalities required six months' residency for unemployment eligibility.

72. Letellier, Perret, Zuber, and Dauphin-Meunier, *Enquête sur le chômage,* 25, 337; also "Annexe," in Guichard and Noiriel, *Construction,* 329. One of the authors of the *Enquête* was the director of the Lyon Public Placement Office during the interwar period, Jean Perret.

73. Miller, *Shanghai on the Metro,* 80.

74. Letellier, Perret, Zuber, and Dauphin-Meunier, *Enquête sur le chômage,* 50, 265. Italians had the shortest period of unemployment at 213 days; this was followed by Poles, at 247 days, and Spanish, at 250 days.

75. See esp. Berberova, *Billancourt Tales,* and idem, *The Tattered Cloak and Other Stories.*

76. See the Introduction for Boris' story. For Berj, see ADBR 4 M 1968: Berj received his first three-month *sursis* in October 1932, his first six-month *sursis* in April 1935, and his first yearlong *sursis* in early May 1936.

77. League of Nations Union, "Refugees and the League," 33. This document also estimated, without attributing the source, that in the last two years (1933–35), the French had spent about 12 million francs to keep refugees in prison.

78. Simpson, *Refugee Problem,* 307.

79. Ibid., 306.

80. ADR Exp., box 32: CS Marcel Foex to prefect, 13 September 1937.

81. ADR Exp., boxes 32 and 11.

82. On earlier incidents, see Nord, *Paris Shopkeepers,* 372–92; and Green, *The Pletzl of Paris,* 42–67.

83. Sauvy, *Histoire économique,* vol. 3, 305. More were "without work" on the census: 452,000 in 1931; 864,000 in 1936. See Salais, Baverez, and Reynaud, *L'invention du chômage,* 77.

84. Jackson, *The Politics of Depression,* 88; Maga, "Closing the Door," 428. Source of Jackson's and Maga's calculations not attributed.

85. Jackson, *The Politics of Depression,* 30. The low 1929 figure was due partially to the fact that assistance was locally administered and not nationally mandated. Few municipalities or departments had *"fonds de chômage"* prior to the 1930s. On the depression in general in France, see, in addition to Jackson, Kemp, *The French Economy*; Sauvy, *Histoire économique,* vol. 3.

86. Weber, *The Hollow Years,* 35.

87. Jackson, *The Politics of Depression,* 66.

88. Ibid.

89. Indeed, when he became *président du conseil* on 31 January 1933, Daladier took the war portfolio rather than the foreign affairs portfolio, the standard choice of most premiers.

90. This represented a shift from his earlier pacifist stance (Daladier had opposed the occupation of the Ruhr by French troops in 1923). For his rearmament efforts, see Chapman, *State Capitalism*; also Hoffmann, Foreword to Daladier, *Prison Journal.*

91. Daladier, cited in Maga, "Closing the Door," 429.

92. Maga, "Closing the Door," 428.

93. Caron, *Uneasy Asylum,* 17.

94. Simpson, *Refugee Problem,* Appendix 6, Tables 65 and 66.

95. Caron, *Uneasy Asylum,* 28.

96. MAS-CRDM: Min. T., Dir. T. SCMO Circ. no. 1383, Min. T. to directors of regional labor offices, copy to directors of immigration and foreign labor control offices, 3 August 1933.

97. Three cases pertaining to Jewish applicants and one to a "pure German," in ADR, Foreigner files, silo 5, travée 85. In addition, for six of the 84 cases, the legality of their status in the country was unclear prior to the arrival of the Popular Front in power. Another two, who immigrated prior to 1933 but who claimed refugee status on the basis of being unable to return, were instructed to leave. Four immigrants who arrived from Germany after 1933, but whose reason for emigrating was not indicated in their files, met the same fate.

98. Only 84 cases are available in the archives. As of 28 December 1933, there

were a total of 300 German men, women, and children of whatever religion officially living legally in Lyon. This is undoubtedly an undercount, since it reflects only those Germans who successfully acquired identification cards. By December 1934, the official number of Germans had risen to 350. ADR 4 M 418 and 419.

99. See Caron, *Uneasy Asylum*, 402n35, for text of the Radical Party resolution.

100. Herriot, "Lettre-préface," 5.

101. ADR Foreigner files, silo 5, travée 85: Prefect to Min. I., recommending expulsion, 23 July 1934.

102. ADR Exp., box 42: Prefect to Min. I., 15 November 1933; expulsion ordered 30 April 1934.

103. ADR Exp., box 40: Prefect to Min. I., 9 August 1933; expulsion ordered 29 March 1934.

104. ADR Foreigner files, silo 5, travée 85: Min. I. to prefect, 28 May 1935. Quote regarding the case of Teman and Eliana H. For other examples, see ADR Exp., boxes 43, 44, and 46. For the "pure race German" traveling salesman, see ADR Foreigner files, silo 5, travée 85.

105. ADR Exp., box 45: Consul in Baden, Guerrin, to Rhône prefect, 16 March 1934.

106. Caron, *Uneasy Asylum*, 94–116; see also Schor, *L'opinion Française*, 193–96.

107. ADR Exp., box 41: CS, 12 December 1933. The CS also wrote that his claim of being threatened because he was Jewish "appears unbelievable since his brothers and sisters are still in Germany."

108. See ADR Exp., boxes 41 and 42, as well as ADR, Foreigner files, silo 5, travée 85.

109. For a more general discussion of this problem, see Noiriel, *La tyrannie*.

110. Kaplan, *Between Dignity and Despair*. Kaplan draws on Orlando Patterson's concept of "social death" (p. 5n2).

111. Marrus, *Unwanted*, 143. Marrus notes that the international community concerned with refugees was particularly worried about the possibility of a large Jewish emigration, not only from Germany, but also from Poland, in the 1930s as conditions for Jews worsened in both places. He notes that after Josef Pilsudski's death in 1935, Polish leadership "drifted to the right, and anti-Jewish voices received official sanction. From 1935 to 1939, a kind of 'war against the Jews' existed in Poland, involving economic boycotts, the segregation of Jewish university students, and exclusion of Jews from certain professions. Pogroms flickered across Poland in 1935 and 1936, recalling the anti-Jewish riots of the tsarist era. Although officially opposed to anti-Jewish violence, the Polish government became increasingly committed to the idea of removing large numbers of Jews from the country" (p. 143).

112. This does not preclude the possibility that some of the 38 "unclear" cases were expelled.

113. ADBR 4 M 948: Sallet to Min. I., 18 March 1937.

114. Cited in Simpson, *Refugee Problem*, 275.

115. For this policy, see Chapter 4.

116. Caron, *Uneasy Asylum,* passim.

117. See, e.g., notes 102 and 103, above. Caron dates the first expulsion of refugees without papers to January 1934; however, local-level recommendations to expel Jews, beginning almost immediately upon their arrival in 1933, predated the central government's shift toward advocating them. Caron does note that *refoulement* began in the summer of 1933. Caron, *Uneasy Asylum,* 34–42, 106.

118. ADR Foreigner files, silo 5, travée 85: Prefect, 20 September 1933; *refoulement,* 15 February 1934; prefect, 23 November 1936; Min. I. response, 12 December 1936; application for refugee certificate fowarded by prefect on 7 January 1937 and approved by Min. I. on 4 August 1937. This refugee was interned in 1943 or 1944, then deported to Auschwitz. Affidavit in this regard granted to nephew, 14 February 1951.

119. ADR Foreigner files, silo 5, travée 85: Prefect to Min. I., recommending expulsion, 23 July 1934; prefect to Min. I., recommending residency approval, 6 January 1937.

120. Eleven refugees (of whom seven were from the same nuclear family) had unclear outcomes, although the family of seven clearly found a way to stay in the area, because they were, tragically, deported from it during the war. It is not clear whether they and the persons concerned in the four other ambiguous cases applied for the special refugee status. See ADR Foreigner files, and ADR Exp., boxes 40–46). Officials had lost track of many of the other 84 original applicants; some appear to have returned to Germany, others to have emigrated to Holland, South America, or Palestine. Still others may have moved to other parts of France.

121. ADBR 4 M 948.

122. ADBR 4 M 948: CPS to Commissaire Central, 15 January 1937. Approved 15 November 1937.

123. With some delay, however. ADR 4 M 948: File forwarded to Min. I. 4 February 1937; ministerial authorization, 15 March 1938.

124. See multiple cases in ADBR 4 M 948.

125. Refugees from Nazism were not included in this category.

126. Ten percent represents the approximate figure for those identified in censuses and surveys as "Armenian." But Armenians were often identified as "Turkish" or, if they spent time in the Levant after the massacre and before migration to France, as "Lebanese" or "Syrian."

127. AMAE C, vol. 271: Procès-verbal de la réunion interministerielle, 20 April 1937.

128. Thalmann, "Jewish Women"; idem, "L'immigration Allemande"; idem, "L'émigration Allemande."

129. Livian, *Le parti socialiste,* passim and esp. 97 and 109. For an interesting critique of Livian, see Gordon, "The Back Door," 220; 201–32.

130. Caron, *Uneasy Asylum,* 119. Caron also has a more detailed discussion of the Bonnet, Thalmann, Livian debate.

131. Caron, *Uneasy Asylum,* 119.

132. On the Popular Front's plan to include refugees from Germany in social rights, see Caron, *Uneasy Asylum,* 138–39.

CHAPTER 6

1. Memmi, *The Colonizer*, 96.
2. Weil, *Qu'est-ce qu'un Français?* 225. Weil borrows the concept of a perverted (*dénaturée*) nationality from Boushaba, *Être Algérien*.
3. The term is from Wilder, *The French Imperial Nation-State*.
4. Arendt, *The Origins of Totalitarianism*, 277.
5. "North African natives." In the chapter that follows, I endeavor to use the terms that historical actors themselves employed. Both settlers and indigenous Algerians referred to themselves as "Algerian." To avoid confusion, I refer to the European population of the colonies as settlers (*colons*). Meanwhile, readers should understand "North African" as Muslim North African. In the rare cases where I refer to Jewish North Africans, I specify this. The term "*indigène*" is pejorative and was used almost exclusively by the metropolitan French and the administration. Thus, when it appears in the chapter, I use it to convey their outlook. I use geographic terms when such specificity is important. Occasionally, I employ the term "subject," also in common usage at the time.
6. These did not apply to Jewish natives of Algeria, who were collectively naturalized by the Crémieux Decree of 1870. Jews from Morocco and Tunisia would be, strictly speaking, like Muslims, considered foreigners. Although the Lyon suburb of St-Fons did have a few Moroccan Jewish families, most North Africans in the metropole were Muslim.
7. "Main-d'oeuvre étrangère," *BMT* 1–2 (January–February 1920): 20–21.
8. Ibid.
9. Including industrial workers. For figures, see Ruedy, *Modern Algeria*, 111.
10. The 15 July 1914 law removed restrictions on Algerian travel.
11. *JODP*, Chambre, session extraordinaire 1920, annexe no. 1540, séance du 25 Septembre 1920, 688; see also "Main-d'oeuvre étrangère," *BMT* 1–2 (January–February 1920): 20–21.
12. Meynier, *L'Algérie révélée*, part 5, chap. 4.
13. The so-called Jonnart Law. See Ageron, *Les Algériens Musulmans*, 1190–227; and Ruedy, *Modern Algeria*, 100–113.
14. See Ageron, *Les Algériens Musulmans*, 1167–73, and MacMaster, *Colonial Migrants and Racism*, 143; 134–52. Both Ageron and MacMaster point out that Muslim "buyback" of land was in fact very limited and had a disproportionate impact on settlers' anxiety levels.
15. Clemenceau, cited in Massard-Guilbaud, *Des Algériens à Lyon*, 50. Massard-Guilbaud does not indicate whether the emphasis is hers or Clemenceau's. The directive from Clemenceau stipulated that renewals would be allowed only for existing regiments, not for new positions, and that even these would be extended for only six months. Clemenceau wanted all repatriations to take place by the end of 1919.
16. AMAE K—Afrique 1918–40—Questions Générales, vol. 30: Note "au sujet d'économies réalisables sur la main-d'oeuvre coloniale," n.d. [Spring 1919].
17. Ibid.
18. Viala and Panza, "L'immigration Nord-Africaine," 78.

19. Governor-general of Algeria, cited in Massard-Guilbaud, *Des Algériens à Lyon,* 51.

20. In her authoritative work on the strikes, Annie Kriegel mentions that foreign and colonial workers were employed by the railroads during the war and that after the war, the Belgian rail workers returned to Belgium. She does not, however, indicate whether or to what degree colonial migrants participated in the strikes. Kriegel, *La grève des cheminots,* esp. 25.

21. ADBR 4 M 2214: "État des indésirables Nord-Africains et autres à rapatrier" ("Register of undesirable North Africans and others to be repatriated"). Statistics gleaned from this document indicate 15 transit requisitions for repatriation in March, 16 in April, 65 in May, 66 in June, 98 in July, 69 in August, 3 in September, 9 in October, 19 in November, and 4 in December, for a total of 364 in 1920. This record is not exhaustive, but it provides a glimpse into the overall patterns of North African repatriation during 1920.

22. ADBR 4 M 2214: *Procès-verbal,* Joigny (Yonne), 8 October 1920; *procès-verbal,* brigade de Lezoux, arrondissement de Thiers (Puy-de-Dome), 29 August 1920.

23. Files sampled from ADBR 4 M 1389 through 4 M 1981. Only 7% were warned, and 5% had inconclusive outcomes. The vast majority of the North Africans considered for expulsion were deemed to have "no fixed domicile" by local authorities.

24. ADBR 4 M 2214: This was the case in at least 39 of the 364 cases cited in note 21. Of the 39, there were 28 orders of "immediate release," 4 orders of "non-lieu," 4 orders of "main-levée," and 3 cases that "were not pursued by the *parquet.*" A *procureur* is similar to a district attorney.

25. ADBR 4 M 2214: *Procès-verbal,* gendarmerie de Lyon-Suchet, 24 November 1920. The gendarmes had been informed of his imminent release by the overseer at the St Paul Prison.

26. ADBR 4 M 2214. It has not been possible to determine the length of detentions prior to arriving in Marseille in most cases.

27. ADBR 4 M 2214: Letter addressed to Gouverneur Général de l'Algérie, 7 April 1920.

28. ADBR 4 M 2214: Commissaire Central, Mathieu, report to prefect, 6 April 1920; underlining in original.

29. ADBR 4 M 2214: Letter from two detainees addressed to prefect, 1 April 1920.

30. ADBR 4 M 2214: Unsigned letter "to my dear friend," 20 April 1920.

31. Letter to Bouches-du-Rhône prefect, Marseille, 20 January 1921, with 21 signatures. Stamped as received 22 January 1921; underlining in original. Reproduced in Viala and Panza, "L'immigration Nord-Africaine," annexe. This document may be what the prefect refers to when he writes the Interior minister on 23 January 1921 that "I must inform you that I have received a protest letter, on this issue, from Arab subjects who are originally from Algeria and are living in Marseille." ADBR 14 M 23–21.

32. ADBR 14 M 23_21: Prefect to Min. T. (Dir. T., 1er bur.), 8 January 1921.

An almost identical remark appears in the prefect's report to the Interior Ministry: Prefect to Min. I. (Cabinet), 23 January 1921.

33. ADBR 1 M 1830: CPS Borelli, report no. 835, 4 March 1922. As remains the case today, the term "Arab" was frequently used to refer to all Muslim Algerians, though many were in fact Berbers.

34. Algiers chamber of commerce president to Marseille chamber of commerce president, 17 July 1919, stamped as received 21 July 1919. Document reproduced in Viala and Panza, "L'immigration Nord-Africaine," annexes. "*Civile*" as used here appears to have several meanings: used this way "*civile*" usually refers to "civilian," as in nonmilitary. But it could also suggest the "city's population," since in the colonies, most "*indigènes*" lived outside of the city, or only in certain sections of it. Finally, one cannot help but wonder whether a third meaning of "civil" might have been intended here, one suggesting "civilized." Regardless, the fears expressed here suggest that the so-called civilizing mission required, from the *colons*' point of view, controlling access to metropolitan "civilization." Note also that "promiscuity" in French connotes interaction but not necessarily sexual impropriety.

35. ADR 4 M 598: Assistance Committee for Algerian Natives to Rhône prefect, 30 November 1921. In response, the prefect replied, on 27 December 1921, that after consulting Mayor Herriot, he had come to the conclusion that the numbers of North Africans had diminished so much since 1919 that it was currently not worth pursuing the construction of a foyer.

36. ADR 4 M 598: *Statuts du "Comité d'Assistance aux Indigènes Algériens," sous le haut patronage de Monsieur le Gouverneur Général de l'Algérie* (Algiers: Ancienne Maison Baside-Jourdan, Jules Carbonel, Imprimeur, 1920).

37. Ibid.

38. For example, AMAE K—Afrique 1918–40—Questions Générales, vol. 31. In 1923, the Comité d'Action Franco-Musulman de l'Afrique du Nord advocated opening what it called "protective" organizations for "*indigènes*" in Paris, Marseille, and the Nord department. Comité d'Action Franco-Musulman de l'Afrique du Nord à Monsieur le Président du Conseil, Ministre des Affaires Étrangères, 15 November 1923, transmitting letter sent to Interior Ministry regarding developing protective agencies.

39. AMAE K—Afrique 1918–40—Questions Générales vol. 31: Resident General of Morocco, note au sujet de la main-d'oeuvre indigène, 25 July 1922.

40. AMAE K—Afrique 1918–40—Questions Générales, vol. 31: Min. T., Dir. T., Service de l'Inspection et du Contrôle de la Main-d'Oeuvre Étrangère au Ministre des Affaires Étrangères, 8 September 1922.

41. On Armenians, see Chapter 5.

42. On the pressure exerted by settlers' groups: CAOM, 9 H 113, *Rapport sur l'émigration des indigènes,* n.d. [1924]; complaints received since October 1923 from multiple municipal councils in Algeria and groups such as the Confédération des Agriculteurs du Département d'Alger, the Chambre Consultative d'Agriculture. See also "L'exode des travailleurs algériens vers la métropole," *Bulletin du Comité de l'Afrique Française—Renseignements coloniaux et documents* (February

1925): 95, for a typical municipal council resolution from 1923, which took several paragraphs to emphasize the benefits to the metropole of greater emigration control, only adding at the end what was perhaps the bottom line: "reserving at the same time for Algerian agriculture, whose production is so necessary for the nourishment of the Metropole, a labor force [that is], certainly, mediocre but nevertheless usable in Algeria, only in Algeria." See also Stora, *Ils venaient d'Algérie*, 16–17.

43. See ADR 4 M 415 and CAOM, 9 H 112, for reports responding to the Interior Ministry inquiry of July 1923.

44. ADR 4 M 415: Commissaire de Police de St-Fons à M. le Préfet du Rhône, 8 August 1923.

45. ADR 4 M 415: Commissaire de Police de Lyon-Part-Dieu à M. le Préfet du Rhône, 9 August 1923.

46. ADR 4 M 415: Commissaire de Police du Quartier St-Louis à M. le Préfet du Rhône, 28 July 1923; Commissaire de Police, Quartier de la Bourse, à M. le Préfet du Rhône, n.d. [Summer 1923].

47. The other members were Gérard, the director of the Algerian governor-general's Paris office; Colonel Chardenet, a former chief of military personnel and indigenous services for the Algerian governor-general; Geoffroy de Saint Hilaire, the director of the Tunisian government office in Paris; Hardeman, the head of the foreigner identification card service in the Interior Ministry; Marius Moutet, a Socialist deputy to the National Assembly; de Beaumarchais, the director of the Africa section of the Foreign Affairs Ministry; Lebelle, the head of the Service de la Main-d'Oeuvre in the Labor Ministry; Marcel Paon, the head of the Service de la Main-d'Oeuvre Agricole; Faivre, a health official; Pierre Godin, a municipal councilor in Paris; and Christian Cherils, an "homme de lettres." For additional information on the commission, see Rosenberg, *Policing Paris*, 143–45.

48. AMAE K—Afrique 1918–40—Questions Générales, vol. 31: *Procès-verbal*, Réunion de la Commission Interministérielle de la Main-d'Oeuvre Nord-Africaine, 26 June 1924. There remained some quibbling about how to enforce the newly proposed provisions; for example, would police have to check people in all classes of service on the ships that shuttled between Algeria and mainland France? But the main principles of establishing prerequisites for emigration were conceded by all at this point.

49. The Rif rebellion in Morocco prompted additional visa prerequisites, followed by a complete ban on French work visas for Moroccans as of 6 October 1925. On new prerequisites for Moroccans, see AMAE K—Afrique 1918–40—Questions Générales, vol. 31: Résidence Générale de la République Française au Maroc. Secrétariat Général du Protectorat. Circ. no.15, Objet: Règlementation de la sortie de la main-d'oeuvre marocaine, 7 March 1925; CAOM, 9 H 113: Min. T. to Prés. Cons., Min. AE, 2 April 1925, no. 7205. On discontinuation of visas, see also Viala and Panza, "L'immigration Nord-Africaine," 47.

50. AMAE K—Afrique 1918–40—Questions Générales, vol. 31: Resolution of Conseillers Généraux au Titre Musulman du Département d'Alger, in *Procès-verbal, Réunion de la Commission Interministérielle*, 28 October 1924. The Jonnart reform of 1919 had expanded the Muslim franchise in Algeria to allow a

greater number of Muslims to elect municipal and departmental councilors. Unlike the European franchise, the Muslim franchise concerned only local elections and was filtered by an electoral college. Muslim representation on local councils was limited to one-third for the municipal councils and one-fourth for the departmental councils.

51. AMAE K—Afrique 1918–40—Questions Générales, vol. 31: Telegram, 8 November 1924. See also other complaints reproduced in "L'exode des travailleurs algériens vers la métropole," *Bulletin du Comité de l'Afrique Française—Renseignements coloniaux et documents* (February 1925): 96.

52. AMAE K—Afrique 1918–40—Questions Générales, vol. 31: On second thoughts, see *Procès verbal,* Réunion de la Commission Interministérielle de la Main-d'Oeuvre Nord-Africaine, 28 October 1924. On director's response: Min. I. (DAA) to Min. AE, 27 November 1924.

53. CAOM 9 H 113: Council of State decision no. 86601, 18 June 1926, ruling that a circular could not abrogate a law. After this decision, the Interior Ministry merely replaced the circular with a policy that was equally if not more restrictive. It removed the contract stipulation and replaced it with a minimum amount of money, so that the *"indigène"* could support himself while looking for work (4 August 1926 decree). The August 1926 decree was then updated in April 1928, when Algerian emigration was subject to the following prerequisites: (1) an identification card with a photograph; (2) a copy of the *indigène*'s conviction record; (3) a medical certificate; (4) a receipt for 125 francs as a deposit for eventual repatriation; (5) a ticket for the passage to the metropole with proof of payment; (6) at least 150 francs in cash to live on while looking for a job. This brought the total outlay—*not* including transportation or other costs (photographers, for example, were few and far between and very expensive in Algeria)—to 275 francs, an amount equal to at least two weeks' wages in the metropole and four to five times that in Algeria. See also Massard-Guilbaud, *Des Algériens à Lyon,* 101–5.

54. Arrêt du 27 juillet 1927, Cour d'Alger. In Collot, *Les institutions de l'Algérie,* 303.

55. A total of 24,753 Algerian entries were recorded for 1925, down from 71,028 in the previous year. *BMT* 4–6 (April–June 1926): 248. See also Neil MacMaster, *Colonial Migrants and Racism,* 147; Talha, *Le salariat immigré,* 81; and ADBR 4 M 950 for reports on *"refoulements"* of *"indigènes"* not meeting the new requirements.

56. *BMT* 1–3 (January–March 1926): 126 and *BMT* 1–3 (January–March 1925): 119.

57. Rosenberg, "The Colonial Politics of Healthcare Provision."

58. ADR 10 M 222: Min. I. to prefect, 11 August 1927. Similar appeals were made to other prefects.

59. On the history and structure of the *bureaux arabes,* see Julien, *Histoire de l'Algérie contemporaine,* 330–41. See also Ruedy, *Modern Algeria,* 72–73.

60. ADR 10 M 222: Min. I. to Rhône prefect, 11 August 1927.

61. ADR 10 M 222: Minute (Rhône prefect to Loire prefect), 30 November 1927.

62. ADR 4 M 261: Maurin, "Rapport sur la Main-d'Oeuvre Coloniale," 6e Union Régionale des Syndicats Unitaires (Lyon), Congrès Régional, 12–13 November 1927.

63. See ADBR 1 M 1801: CPS, report no. 100, 12 January 1927, on meeting of the Communist Party's Colonial Commission in Marseille in January 1927, during which they called for equal unemployment and family allocation rights for colonial workers, end to the *"indigénat,"* free circulation between Algeria and the metropole, a ban on repatriation, and a ban on eviction of the unemployed. They also indicated that the party would begin increased mobilization in Marseille to this end. See also "Les revendications votées par la Conférence des Ouvriers Nord-Africains," *Al-Raïat-al-hamra: Organe du Parti Communiste* (Section Française de L'Internationale Communiste), no. 8 (April 1927).

64. On the organization of North Africans: ADBR 1 M 1800 and 1 M 1801; AN F^7 13523. Officials were also concerned about communist agitation in Marseille among other migrants. See AN F^7 12736; F^7 12976; F^7 13436; CAOM 3 SLOTFOM-2. On newspaper circulation: ADBR 1 M 1800.

65. See ADBR 4 M 950 for multiple reports on the labor contract counterfeit cases and the identification card racket. See ADBR 1 M 1781, CPS reports, 9 April 1926, 10 April 1926, and 29 April 1926 on the deaths of Moroccan stowaways. The first of the stowaway affairs had prompted the suicide of the quartermaster, Guidicelli, who had apparently accepted money for allowing the illegal passengers to hide. See also *Le petit marseillais,* 29 April 1926; and *(Les) étrangers à Marseille,* 172–73.

66. ADR 4 M 222: Min. I. (Conseiller d'Etat, Secrétaire Général, Direction du Contrôle de la Comptabilité et des Affaires Algériennes) to prefect, 15 April 1929.

67. ADR 4 M 222: Letters to prefect, 24 January 1929 and 18 April 1929. The Paris hospital ended up costing closer to 25 million francs.

68. ADR 4 M 222: Conseil Général du Rhône, Première session ordinaire de 1929. Extrait du procès-verbal de la séance, 25 April 1929.

69. In a report to the Interior Ministry, Charles Vallette indicates Azario's birthplace as Soukahras, Tunisia. AN F^7 13521: Préfet (Rhône) au Min. I., 30 November 1926. Vallette no doubt meant Souk Ahras, Algeria, near the Tunisian border.

70. ADR 10 M 222: Retrospective characterization of Azario's organization as a "bureau arabe" in Directeur des Offices départemental et municipal de placement gratuit de la main-d'oeuvre et de la statistique du travail, "Notes sur le Centre de Lyon d'Accueil, d'Immatriculation, d'Aide et Protection, de Placement et de Rapatriement des Nord-Africains," 4 December 1937, 1. For a detailed account of Azario's committee, see Massard-Guilbaud, *Des Algériens à Lyon.*

71. ADR 10 M 226: Les Commerçants Arabes Cafetiers, Restaurateurs de Lyon et Banlieue, petition to prefect, 31 March 1934. See also ADR 10 M, Affaires Algériennes.

72. According to Geneviève Massard-Guilbaud, Azario secured nine convoys of repatriates during a less-than-two-month period (2 December 1926 to 20 January 1927). Massard-Guilbaud, *Des Algériens à Lyon,* 354.

73. CAOM 9 H 113: Commissaire Central, Ville de Bône, à M. le S/Préfet de Bône, 14 December 1926. Although the report does not mention Azario specifically,

later references to this incident implicate Azario as the mastermind behind the diversion to Algeria.

74. Ibid.

75. AN F[7] 13521: Rhône prefect to Min. I., 30 November 1926.

76. Bollaert had become prefect in Feburary 1934.

77. ADR 10 Mp C80: Union Départementale des Syndicats Ouvriers du Rhône au Préfet du Rhône, 7 August 1934; *L'humanité*, 7 August 1934. See also the prefect's letter to Min. I., 7 August 1934; the CPS reports, 7 and 10 August 1934; letter from Versillé Frères to SGP, 28 September 1934; and the *procureur*'s report to the prefect on the legal pursuits emerging from the incident, 5 November 1934. For other evidence of using North Africans to settle labor disputes, see ADR 10 M, Affaires Algériennes: Commissaire Divisionnaire au SGP, 5 and 10 April 1935.

78. ADR 10 Mp C80: Azario to SGP, 10 October 1934. Complaints about other firms refusing to hire North Africans in same letter. See also SGP to director of regional and departmental placement office, 17 October 1934, as well as the reply from Jean Perret, 22 October 1934.

79. ADR 10 M, Affaires Algériennes: Tract issued by Association des Travailleurs Algériens, transmitted from CS to SGP, 14 August 1934. For discussion of rising attendance at ENA and ATA meetings, see also ADR 4 M 235.

80. ADR 10 M 222: Préfet (Rhône) au Min. I. (1: Cabinet du Ministre; 2: Direction du Controle de la Comptabilite et des Affaires Algériennes), 24 September 1934.

81. Lyon papers announced the opening of the SAINA office in early November. *Le progrès de Lyon*, 3 November 1934; *Le salut public*, 3 November 1934; *Le nouvelliste*, 5 November 1934.

82. ADR 10 M 222: SGP à M. le Commissaire Divisionnaire de Police Spéciale à Lyon, 18 December 1934.

83. See ADR 10 M 222 for complaints from "victims" (workers and café owners) of Azario's political screenings in 1935.

84. ADR 10 M 222: Le Maire de Lyon au Préfet, [?] July 1931. See also prefect's transmission to Interior Ministry of Herriot's letter, 18 July 1931; Le Maire de Lyon à M. Peillod, adjoint délégué du 7e arrondissement de Lyon, 31 July 1930; ADR 10 M, Affaires Algériennes: Le Maire de Lyon à Monsieur le Ministre de l'Intérieur, Président du Conseil, 30 July 1930, signed by Herriot himself.

85. ADR 10 M 222: *Procès-verbal*, Conseil Général du Rhône, 9 May 1931 session, Augros, rapporteur.

86. ADR 10 M 222: Prefect to Min. I. (Direction du Contrôle, de la Comptabilité et des Affaires Algériennes, 4e bur.), 30 October 1934; SGP to Min. I. (Direction du Contrôle, de la Comptabilité et des Affaires Algériennes), 16 February 1935; Min. I. (Directeur Adjoint Chargé des Affaires Algériennes) to prefect, 8 March 1935; Prefect to Min. I. (Direction du Contrôle, de la Comptabilité et des Affaires Algériennes, 4e bur.), 21 March 1935; Min. I. (Directeur Adjoint Chargé des Affaires Algériennes) to prefect, 10 April 1935.

87. Evidence of below-standard wages can be found in ADR 10 M, Affaires Algériennes, Commissaire Divisionnaire au Secrétaire Général pour la Police, 5 and 10 April 1935.

88. ADR 10 M 222: Préfet (Rhône) à M. le Maire de Lyon, 17 juillet 1936.

89. Often North Africans' ineligibility stemmed not from a failure to meet length-of-residency requirements but rather from an inability to prove eligibility, such as through showing receipts for rent. This, in turn, was due to the precarious conditions in which they lived as well as their frequent changes in lodging.

90. AML 0981 WP 398. Of course, North Africans often fell into many of these categories.

91. AMV Chômage: Règlements 1932–34. The Villeurbanne Municipal Council later reversed this decision.

92. See, e.g., AMAE Z—Europe 1918–40—Espagne, Vol. 267: Jean Herbette, ambassadeur de la République Française en Espagne, à Pierre Laval, Min. AE, Report no. 42, regarding "doléances concernant le traitement des travailleurs espagnols en France," 27 March 1935. Similar reports, 2 and 18 February 1935, 25 March 1935. Also reply, Min. AE à Herbette, no. 1028, 3 July 1935.

93. ADR 10 M, Affaires Algériennes: "Aux Chômeurs et à Tous les Musulmans Nord-Africains de Lyon et de la Région," November 1935.

94. Stora, "Avant la deuxième génération."

95. ADR 10 M 224: Statistical reports, 5 April 1935; 2 May 1935; 9 May 1935; 1 June 1935; 1 July 1935; 18 July 1935; 1 October 1935; 4 November 1935; 1 December 1935; 2 February 1936; 2 March 1936; 3 April 1936; 2 July 1936; and 1 August 1936.

96. ADR 10 M 224: Report, 25 December 1935. The report noted that "Arabs" had a legal right to unemployment compensation but that many did not receive it because they had trouble producing proof of residency (due to their precarious living conditions). Given their statutory right to unemployment assistance, aid via food stamps represented considerable savings to municipalities.

97. For the cost of the food stamps, see ADR 10 M 224: Prefect to mayor of Lyon, 17 July 1936. For the cash indemnity rates, see AML 0747 WP 162–63: Commission Administrative de l'ODMPST, Séance du 20 Janvier 1937. Annexe 15—Barèmes appliqués par les fonds de chômage en activité pour l'attribution de secours (1936).

98. ADR 10 M 224: Lyon mayor to prefect, 21 June 1936. In the letter, Herriot makes reference to an earlier complaint lodged by him on the same subject dated 5 November 1935.

99. ADR 10 M 224: Lyon mayor to prefect, 28 December 1936; ADR 10 M 225: Prefect to Prés. Cons. (Secrétariat Général), au sujet du Haut Comité Méditerranéen et de l'Afrique du Nord, 4 February 1937.

100. ADR 10 M 224: Thibaud à Monsieur le Chef du Bureau, Service des Bons de Soupes, et des Nord-Africains, "Rapport sur les services des Nord-Africains," 2 May 1936.

101. ADR 10 M, Affaires Algériennes: "Rapport sur la situation et le fonctionnement" [du SAINA], 13 March 1937.

102. ADR 10 M 222: ODP, 22 March 1937, response to inquiry from SGP, 19 March 1937, enclosing complaint dated 18 March 1937. The response also indicated that the meal offered at the center included soup made from fresh vegetables

and the meat for the evening meal; a piece of meat; a plate of legumes, grains, or pasta; and 200 grams of bread.

103. ADR 10 Mp D43: Procès-Verbal, Deuxième Session Annuelle de la Commission Administrative Commune à l' ODMPST, 2 July 1937. Meals ceased in June.

104. ADR 10 Mp D59 and ADR 10 M 224: Daily and weekly service reports.

105. ADR 10 Mp D44: Commission Administrative de l'Office Départemental et Municipal de Placement. Ordre des Travaux. 1ère session annuelle 1938, figures for period between 1 June 1937 and 15 May 1938; ADR 10 Mp D47: Commission Administrative Commune à l' ODMPST. Ordre des Travaux. 2e session annuelle de 1938, figures for period between 16 May and 15 October 1938. ADR 10 Mp D44: Commission Administrative de l'Office Départemental et Municipal de Placement. Ordre des Travaux. 1ère session annuelle 1938.

106. ADR 10 Mp D45: ODP. Ordre des Travaux, 1939.

107. ADR 4 M 415: Report no. 6144, transmis par l'Inspecteur Lapierre au Procureur, 23 April 1937; Président de la Caisse de Secours, Behloul Mohamed, au Procureur, 13 March 1937. Attendance at the remaining meal also declined propitiously after March. ADR 10 M, Affaires Algériennes.

108. See Chapters 4 and 5.

109. ADR 10 M 224: A Lyon official even acknowledged this in a report: "According to a strict construction of the law, Arabs have a right to unemployment in Lyon." Report, December 1935.

110. On England's poor laws, see esp. Englander, *Poverty and Poor Law Reform,* and Lees, *The Solidarities of Strangers.*

111. CAOM 9 H 113: A decree dated 17 July 1936 discontinued the 14 April 1928 restrictions. The Popular Front's commitment to free circulation was short-lived. An October 1936 decree reinstituted an identification card and a 9 December 1936 decree required *"indigènes"* to pay a 125-franc repatriation deposit.

112. "Placement et aide aux travailleurs marocains en France," *Compte rendu des travaux de la Chambre de Commerce de Lyon,* année 1934, 108. At the time, the Lyon suburb of Décines was in the Isère department, not the Rhône.

113. AML 0005 WP 214-2.

114. AMVx 7 F 56-1. Judging from the nature of the back-and-forth correspondence between the Vénissieux municipality and the CNA, it seems that the latter was not pleased with efforts made by the former to give Algerians unemployment compensation. It is possible that, when the CNA summoned Vénissien Algerians, a municipal administrator in Vénissieux may have alerted the Algerians to the potential for repatriation that this entailed. In any case, the CNA reported back to Vénissieux complaining that the men never appeared. The Vénissieux municipality was alternately Socialist and Communist during the interwar period.

115. In one reference, he is called Zannetacci-Stephanopol, but Zannetacci-Stephanopoli is more frequently used.

116. Viala and Panza, "L'immigration Nord-Africaine," 121–22.

117. *"Châouch"* is a term used for a sergeant in the Turkish army; in this context, it means a guard. For guidelines to the administrative organization of the Marseille SAINA, see decree dated 27 October 1928, in *JOLD,* 30 October 1928,

11551; and Arrêtés, 3 November 1928, in *JOLD*, 8 November 1928, 11846. See also Ray, *Les Marocains en France*, 341.

118. AN F¹ᵃ 4526: Note de M. l'Inspecteur Général CAPART concernant le fonctionnement du service des affaires indigènes nord-africaines de Marseille, à Marseille, May 1942.

119. On the conditions of the SAINA office and the number of people it served, see ADBR—SAINA, Poussardin to Prefect, 16 May 1938; Reports written by Poussardin, 13 October 1939 and 2 November 1939; also prefect's notes on confidential letter from Ministry of the Interior, DAA, 1 June 1938; Préfet des Bouches-du-Rhône au Min. I (DAA, 4e bur.), 21 June 1938.

120. ADBR SAINA: Rapport sur le service des affaires indigènes nord-africaines de Marseille, 17 June 1938.

121. ADR 10 M, Affaires Algériennes: Rapport sur la situation et le fonctionnement au 13 March 1937.

122. ADBR SAINA: Rapport sur le service des affaires indigènes nord-africaines de Marseille, 17 June 1938. See also the Interior and Labor ministries' recognition of this problem, in their joint circular, "Le Président du Conseil, le Ministre de l'Intérieur délégué pour la coordination et le contrôle des Administrations de l'Afrique du Nord, le Ministre du Travail, le Ministre de la Santé Publique à Messieurs les Préfets de la Métropole (en communication à Monsieur Gouverneur Général de l'Algérie), reprinted in the *Recueil des Actes Administratifs de la Préfecture des Bouches-du-Rhône* no. 3, 41 (March 1938): 112.

123. ADBR SAINA: Chef du SAINA au Directeur des Affaires Indigènes, 2 November 1939, and AN F¹ᵃ 4526: Note de M. l'Inspecteur Général CAPART concernant le fonctionnement du service des affaires indigènes nord-africaines de Marseille, May 1942. Poussardin's presentation of these statistics was misleading. He gave the impression, even to the Vichy inspector who admitted being unable to verify Poussardin's figures, of "a noticeable and continuous increase in the number of cases handled since 1935." In fact, however, Poussardin had compounded the figures, so that that numbers for 1939 included those from 1938; those from 1938 included those from 1937; and so on. This appears to be a deliberate attempt to illustrate how overworked he was. The figure 2600% is based on the calculations I have done to deconstruct Poussardin's compound figures.

124. *El Ouma* (June–July 1934), 4; ADR 10 M, Affaires Algériennes, multiple tracts.

125. ADBR SAINA: SAINA director to prefect, 7 October 1939, marked "Personal and confidential."

126. And in fact, with the war, Azario was named "Secrétaire de police, chargé sous les ordres directs de M. le Secrétaire Général pour la Police et M. le Secrétaire Général pour l'administration, du contrôle, de la surveillance et de l'administration des Nord Africains (Algériens, Tunisiens, Marocains) de l'agglomération Lyonnaise et du département du Rhône." ADR 10 M 222.

127. ADR 10 M 223: Directeur des Offices de Placement, 25 May 1937; Prefect to Min. I. (Affaires Algériennes), 19 May 1937; Prefect to Min. I. (Affaires Algériennes), 31 May 1937, marked "very urgent"; telegram, 12 June 1937.

128. ADR 10 M 223: Credit of 20,000 francs authorized 20 August 1937.

129. ADBR SAINA: Henri Tasso, rapporteur, characterizing the opinion arrived at by the departmental commission considering the subsidy. "Affaires Indigènes Nord-Africaines, Rapport au Conseil Général," Extrait des Procès-Verbaux des deliberations, 2e session ordinaire de 1939, Séance, 9 Novembre 1939.

130. Aoumeur, "Les fédérations socialistes Algériennes," 6; El-Mechat, "Le gouvernement du Front Populaire," 86.

131. Marshall, "Citizenship and Social Class," 33.

132. Viollette, interview in *Le populaire,* 7 January 1937, cited in Aoumeur, "Les fédérations socialistes Algériennes," 10. Aubaud in *Le temps,* 10 April 1937, cited in Cohen, "The Colonial Policy," 383. On Viollette, see also Nouschi, "La politique coloniale."

133. Roux-Freissineng, Speech before the Senate on 29 January 1937, cited in Cohen, "The Colonial Policy," 381.

134. On women's citizenship, see Fraisse, *Reason's Muse*; Smith, *Feminism and the Third Republic*; Scott, *Only Paradoxes to Offer*; idem, *Parité!*

135. The best work on this subject is Saada, "La 'question des métis'"; and idem, "The Empire of Law." See also Blévis, "Les avatars."

136. In postslavery democracies, civil rights and nationality are decoupled. In practice, of course, foreigners often feel more vulnerable to civil rights' infringements—witness the targeting of immigrants as terrorists since 11 September 2001 in the United States. By contrast, social rights are often linked to nationality, both practically and theoretically. On the boundaries of social entitlement programs, see esp. Freeman, "Migration and the Political Economy"; Noiriel, *Creuset,* esp. 110–16; and idem, *La tyrannie,* esp. 90–95.

137. And, perhaps, not even then. See Lyons, "Invisible immigrants"; Math, "Les allocations familiales." See also Cole, "Discipline and Punish or Preserve and Protect?"

CHAPTER 7

1. Albert Sarraut, *JODCD,* 2e séance, 14 March 1939, 958.

2. Daladier, Speech before parliament, 13 April 1938. Reprinted in Daladier, *In Defense of France,* 41–42.

3. Blum's first government failed when he resigned as premier after a foiled attempt to assume decree powers on financial matters; he took the Senate's opposition as a vote of no confidence, although some of his supporters believed that he need not have resigned.

4. Daladier, Speech before parliament, 13 April 1938, in Daladier, *In Defense of France,* 43.

5. Jackson, *France,* 102.

6. Decree Regarding the Reporting of Jewish Property, 26 April 1938, referred to in Craig, *Germany,* 635.

7. "Rapport au président de la République Française," 2 May 1938, *JOLD,* 3 May 1938, 4967.

8. Provided that the city's population was over 10,000. ADBR 4 M 953: Décret-loi du 2 Mai 1938.

9. "Décret relatif aux modalités d'application des mesures prises en ce qui concerne la police des étrangers," 2 May 1938, *JOLD,* 17 May 1938, 5530–31.

10. Decree establishing the Service Central des Étrangers, 13 August 1938. Statistics on credits from Bonnet, *Les pouvoirs publics français,* 252.

11. Bonnet, *Les pouvoirs publics français,* 253.

12. Interpretation of 14 May decree in ADBR 14 M 22_24: Circ. no. 194, Min. T., Direction Générale du Travail et de la Main-d'Oeuvre, to prefects, labor inspectors, et al., 4 June 1938.

13. Foreign nationals who were required to obtain visas for entry into France were not eligible for three-year cards. ADC M 7169: Décret du 14 mai 1938 sur les conditions de séjour en France. Article 2, paragraph 2, discussed in *Actes de la préfecture,* no. special, June 1938, 7–8.

14. ADC M 7169: Min. I. (Cabinet du Ministre) à Messieurs les Préfets, Signed Sarraut, 18 May 1938.

15. Décret-loi du 14 Mai 1938. *JOLD,* 15 May 1938, 5492ff.

16. Min. T. Circ. no. 194, 4 June 1938. See note 12.

17. Ibid.

18. See, e.g., ADBR 403 U 1288–1312; ADR Jugements Correctionnels.

19. Caron, *Uneasy Asylum,* 237.

20. Peschanski, *La France des camps,* 29.

21. ADR Jugements Correctionnels. On the trends, see also "Une rafle d'épuration à la Guillotière," "L'Épuration," "L'épuration de Lyon," and "Une vaste opération de police au 'village nègre,'" all in *Le progrès de Lyon,* 26 July 1938, 4; 13 August 1938, 4; 31 October 1938, 4; 18 December 1938, 3.

22. ADBR 403 U 1288–1312; ADR Jugements Correctionnels. In making these calculations, I have not included rehearings of defaulted trials; instead, I counted all rehearings on defaulted trials in the "other" category, though some of these undoubtedly would have included cases involving the May decrees and infractions of expulsion orders.

23. This and similar cases suggested that Laval's 30 October 1935 decree, making six months a minimum sentence for this infraction, had not been applied systematically.

24. ADR Jugements Correctionnels, May 1938.

25. ADR Jugements Correctionnels, May–June 1938. "La Sûreté épure la ville," *Le progrès de Lyon,* 5 June 1938, 4.

26. ADR Exp., box 4. See Chapter 2 for Belinda's original expulsion.

27. ADR Exp., box 34. See Chapter 2 for Bettina's original expulsion.

28. On appeal, a few other elderly women subsequently benefited from a "grâce."

29. Conseil Municipal de Lyon, *Procès verbaux du séances,* 28 November 1938, 154.

30. ADR U cor 999: Procès-Verbal, 10e brigade de police mobile (Lyon). Bergeret Auguste, inspecteur, no. 4784 A. 363, 16 July 1938. Tried and sentenced on 11 October 1938.

31. ADR U cor 1000: Procès-Verbal, Gendarmerie Nationale no. 290, 26 June 1938. Sentenced 25 October 1938; arrested 1 January 1939 to serve his sentence.

32. "Réquisition du port de Marseille—Les dockers ayant refusé les nouvelles propositions," and "La réquisition du port de Marseille et en quoi elle consiste," both in *Le petit marseillais,* 7 September 1938, 1, and 8 September 1938, 3. See also Colton, *Compulsory Labor Arbitration,* 126.

33. Before the Radical congress in Marseille, 27 October 1938. Reprinted in Daladier, *In Defense of France,* 112, 122. On the Radicals' anticommunism, see Larmour, *The French Radical Party.*

34. Speech, 27 October 1938, in Daladier, *In Defense of France,* 123.

35. *Le petit marseillais,* 28 October 1938.

36. ADBR 4 M 953: Circ., prefect to mayors, 24 May 1938, authorizing "surprise police operations" to round up foreigners.

37. ADBR 403 U 1288: Jugements Correctionnels, audiences des 22, 24, et 27 juin 1938. All foreigners age 15 and over were required to have identification cards. This foreigner was just 20. In a year, he would be French if he did not decline his right to French nationality. He was nevertheless imprisoned for infraction of the 2 May decree.

38. ADBR 403 U 1290: Jugements Correctionnels, audience du 26 Juillet 1938.

39. One case dated to 1893; see ADBR 403 U 1312: Jugements Correctionnels, 23 August 1939. The case in question concerned a Spanish man expelled on 25 March 1893, first notified on 4 April 1895, and found to be in infraction of the expulsion only on 24 March 1939. As a result, he was sentenced to six months in prison. For similar cases, see multiple entries in ADBR 403 U 1287–1312, Jugements Correctionnels.

40. See discussion of Hagop's case in Chapter 1. On the climate as he requested naturalization, see "L'application du décret-loi sur les étrangers," "Lutte contre la pègre—Les mesures d'épuration se poursuivent," "L'épuration de Marseille se poursuit," all in *Le petit marseillais,* 18 September 1938, 3; 12 October 1938, 3; 13 October 1938, 3. The more moderate *Petit provençal* had almost no coverage of the crackdown, other than the occasional "notice" (*avis*) to foreigners regarding the new requirements.

41. ADBR 403 U 1287.

42. ADBR 403 U 1288.

43. ADC M 7169: Min. I., DGSN, Direction de la Police du Territoire et des Étrangers, Sous-Direction des Étrangers, Circ. no. 125, à Messieurs les Préfets, le Préfet de Police et le Gouverneur Général d'Algérie, 5 September 1938.

44. "Décret relatif à l'organisation des brigades de gendarmerie-frontière," 12 November 1938, *JOLD,* 13 November 1938, 12920; "Décret relative à la police des étrangers," 12 November 1938, *JOLD,* 13 November 1938, 12920–23. The November 1938 decrees also barred foreigners from getting married in France if they had not been living there legally for at least a year. This was a way of trying to prevent "unsettling" foreigners from falling under the arbitrary qualifications of "settled" foreigners dictated by the 14 May 1938 decree, which included marriage to a Frenchwoman.

45. Decrees placing Marseille under receivership in *JOLD,* 21 March 1939, 3671, and 20 April 1939, 5030. See also Kitson, "The Marseille Police," 42.

46. Sûreté report of 1 October 1939, referenced in Ryan, *The Holocaust,* 82, 236n6. On confusion caused by changes to police structure, see Kitson, "The Marseille Police," 42–44.

47. For a superb exposé of this absurdity, see the novel by Anna Seghers, *Transit* (1940), trans. Jeanne Stern (Paris: Éditions Alinéa, 1986). On the impact of new refugee influxes on Marseille's resources, see Ryan, *The Holocaust,* esp. chap. 1.

48. For example, the minister of colonies had plans to send sub-Saharan Africans to North Africa and North Africans to the metropole in the event of war. AMAE K, Questions Générales, vol. 36–37: Ministre des Colonies au Ministre du Travail, Sous-Comité de la Main-d'Oeuvre Coloniale, 21 December 1937, marked "Secret."

49. For the Congress platform, see Chapter 6.

50. MAS-CRDM: Nord Department Prefecture, Cabinet of the Secretary-General. Circular to mayors, 25 January 1938.

51. AML 0005 WP 060: Interministerial Circular of 15 February 1938, cited in Dir. ODMPST to mayors, marked "*VERY URGENT,*" 30 June 1939.

52. ADBR 14 M 2964: Conseil Général des Bouches-du-Rhône, Séance, 12 May 1938; Directeur de l'ODP à M. le Préfet, 27 August 1938.

53. Note the use of the condescending *tu* as opposed to the formal *vous.* ADBR SAINA: *Rapport sur le service des affaires indigènes nord-africaines de Marseille,* 17 June 1938.

54. Ibid.

55. ADBR SAINA: *Rapport sur le service des affaires indigènes nord-africaines de Marseille,* 17 June 1938; SAINA director to prefect (5e division), 16 May 1938.

56. See, for example, ADBR SAINA for complaint from Mr. Auguste Bassi, who owned the café next door. Bassi to prefect, 5 May 1938. Neil MacMaster notes that the mere sight of Algerians hanging out was enough to provoke vehement "not in my backyard" sentiments. MacMaster, *Colonial Migrants and Racism,* 130–31.

57. ADBR SAINA: SAINA director to prefect (5e division), 16 May 1938.

58. Ibid.

59. ADBR 14 M 2964: Min. I. (Directeur du Contrôle de la Comptabilité et des Affaires Algériennes) to prefect, 20 June 1938.

60. For Lyon, see ADR 10 Mp D59: Office Départemental et Municipal de Placement. Service Nord-Africains, monthly statistics; for Marseille, see AN F¹ᵃ 4526: État Français, Min. I., Inspection Générale des Services Administratifs, Vichy, 20 May 1942. Note pour M. le Conseiller d'État Secrétaire Général pour l'Administration (Sous-Direction des Affaires Algériennes). Includes retrospective statistics. On interpreting these statistics, see Chapter 6, note 123.

61. *JODCD,* 10 December 1933 session, 11 December 1933, 4600–4601.

62. MAS-CRDM: Min. T. (Paul Ramadier), Circ. no. 206 to prefects, ODP, copy to labor inspectors, 20 August 1938; AML 0005 WP 060: Interministerial Circulars of 15 February 1938 and 19 June 1939, cited in Dir. ODMPST to mayors,

marked "*VERY URGENT,*" 30 June 1939; ADR 10 Mp D45: Min. T. Circ. to prefects, 7 August 1939, cited in Dir. ODMPST to mayors, 19 August 1939. Previous communications had stated that Moroccans and Tunisians were to be excluded. See AML 0005 WP 060: Dir. ODMPST to mayors, marked "*VERY IMPORTANT,*" 12 July 1939.

63. ADBR SAINA: Min. I. (Affaires Algériennes, 4e bur.) to prefects, 23 October 1939.

64. ADR 10 Mp D 59: Office Départemental et Municipal de Placement. Service Nord-Africains. Monthly statistics.

65. ADBR SAINA: SAINA director to prefect, marked "Personal and confidential," 7 October 1939.

66. See, in particular, the following exchange in ADBR SAINA: SAINA to prefect, 12 December 1939; Commissaire de Police S/Chef de la Sûreté to CS, 16 December 1939; CS to Commissaire Central, 17 December 1939.

67. ADBR SAINA: SAINA director to Min. I. (affaires indigènes), 2 November 1939.

68. Rivet, *Le Maghreb,* 351.

69. Viet, *La France immigrée,* 63

70. Weil, *La France et ses étrangers,* 40.

71. Incorporation of German refugees into the foreign legion was suspended in May 1940 for this reason. See Crémieux-Brilhac, *Les Français de l'an 40,* vol. 1, *La guerre oui ou non?* 490–91.

72. According to John Hope Simpson, Spanish refugees peaked in early 1939 at 453,000, of whom approximately 350,000 remained in France as of June 1939. Simpson, *Refugees: A Review,* 49. Gabriel Jackson estimated their numbers at half a million. Jackson, *The Spanish Republic.* Efforts to return refugees began almost immediately.

73. Sarraut in chamber debates, *JODCD,* 2e séance, 14 March 1939, 958. Those pushing for intransigence toward the refugees included, on the extreme Right, Philippe Henriot, Xavier Vallat, and Jean Ybarnégaray. Among the Radicals were J. Montigny and Marcel Régnier, the former interior minister under Flandin.

74. *No pasarán* means "they will not pass," where "they" refers to the "moors brought by Franco." From the republican song of the same name. For lyrics, see "The Music of the Spanish Civil War" at http://lacucaracha.info/scw/music/index .htm (accessed December 2, 2004).

75. See, for example, the proposal for establishing concentration camps. AMAE C—Europe Administrative 1908–40, vol. 271: Procès-Verbal de la Réunion Interministérielle, 20 April 1937.

76. Koestler, *Scum of the Earth,* esp. chap. 2, "Purgatory."

77. Alfred Kantorowicz, cited in Vormeier, "La situation des réfugiés," 191. See also Feuchtwanger, *The Devil in France.* Men age 17 to 50 from the Reich (including Austria), regardless of their refugee status, were instructed to report immediately to internment camps under the authority of a decree issued 5 September 1939. On 14 September, this requirement was extended to men age 50 to 65. On 17 September, a circular extended the possibility of internment to

all "suspicious, dangerous, or undesirable foreigners and *apatrides*" who posed a threat to war mobilization. Circ. Min. I., 17 September 1939, reproduced in Vormeier, "La situation des réfugiés," 204–7.

78. Until, of course, concentration camps were established specifically for Jews and served as stations on the way to German camps.

79. ADC M 7169: Circ. no. 125, Min. I, DGSN (Direction de la Police du Territoire et des Étrangers, Sous-Direction des Étrangers) to prefects, prefect of police, and governor-general of Algeria, 5 September 1938, signed Berthoin.

80. Feuchtwanger, *The Devil in France,* 41.

81. Badia, ed., *Les barbelés de l'exil,* 296, 310.

82. ADR Exp., box 5: Internment order, 25 October 1939.

83. ADR Exp., box 5: CS au Secrétaire Général, 6 January 1940.

84. ADR Exp., box 5: Rhône prefect (general secretary) to Ariège prefect, 19 April 1940. Retyped with changes, 23 April 1940.

85. ADR Exp., box 5: Letter to prefect, 19 April 1940.

86. In practice, many were not.

87. ADR Exp., box 44: Expulsion, 11 October 1934; Min. I. DGSN, 3 August 1939 order to send him to Gurs if he refuses to leave territory; intervention of Rolland, 11 May 1940. *Sursis,* May 1940. Senator Rolland was also one of the 80 members of parliament who voted against granting full powers to Pétain on 10 July 1940.

88. ADBR 4 M 1964: Expulsion, 27 August 1932; letter requesting repeal of expulsion to work in other departments, 11 May 1936; response of CS, 29 May 1936; recommendation from prefect to repeal expulsion in order to serve, 4 October 1939; reply of Min. I. with 13-month *sursis,* 11 November 1939.

89. ADBR 4 M 1692: Prefect to Min. I., 7e bur., reporting on lack of success with Latin American visas and recommending internment at Rieucros in the Lozère, 7 April 1939; Min. I. (chef du 7e bur.) to prefect, 6 May 1939, instructing him to pursue assignation instead; assignation in the Arles vicinity, barring Arles itself, ordered 13 July 1939.

90. ADBR 4 M 1968: CS report, 2 May 1938; Min. I. to prefect, transmitting request from expellee, 17 May 1938; prefect's recommendation, 19 May 1938, and confirmation of same, 27 May 1938; expulsion repealed 12 August 1938; naturalization inquiry instigated 12 June 1940. Berj had been expelled in 1932 as a result of unemployment.

91. ADBR 6 M 1283: S/prefect's comments, 28 June 1938; naturalization, 11 March 1940; and 6 M 1243: file opened 20 May 1936; avis favorable, adjoint, 9 June 1938; naturalization, 13 May 1939.

92. ADBR 6 M 1346: Adjoint, 2 September 1937; chef de service, avis favorable, 15 December 1939. Adjoint, avis défavorable on grounds of family in Italy, 6 May 1938; 3e division, avis d'ajournement, 17 January 1939; enlists for army, 15 November 1939; administrateur par interim, chef de service, avis favorable, 22 December 1939. This is stamped "Priorité circulaire du 23 Octobre 1939."

93. ADBR 6 M 1283.

94. See multiple files in ADR Naturalization files, 1927–38.

95. ADR Naturalization files, 1927–38, GED.

96. ADR Exp., box 17: 2 January 1940, prefect recommends repeal of expulsion in order to naturalize. Expulsion repealed.

97. Conseil Municipal de Lyon, *Procès verbaux du séances,* 6 February 1939, 35–36. Charbin, who later served as supply minister under Philippe Pétain's fifth government, was put on trial for collaboration after the war. "Six Vichy Ministers Go on Trial Today before Reorganized French High Court," *New York Times,* 11 March 1946, 9.

98. Weil, *Qu'est-ce qu'un Français?* 92.

99. Caron, *Uneasy Asylum,* 256.

100. Weil, *Qu'est-ce qu'un Français?* 92.

101. Circ. no. 162, Min. I. to prefects, 11 November 1938, cited in Kitson, "The Marseille Police," 48.

102. Contrôleur Général des Services de la Surveillance du Territoire to Commissaires de la Surveillance du Territoire, circ. nos. S/358 dated 26 August 1939 (regarding Croatians and Slovenians); S/359 dated 3 September 1939, N-C/C374 dated 3 November 1939, and S/412 dated 3 January 1940 (regarding Germans and Germans "of Israelite origin"); N-E/C374 dated 3 November 1939 (regarding Czechs); S/387 and S/396 dated 15 November and 4 December 1939 (regarding Poles). All cited in Kitson, "The Marseille Police," 48.

103. Weil, *Qu'est-ce qu'un Français?* 92; Crémieux-Brilhac, *Les Français de l'an 40,* 489.

104. Weil, *Qu'est-ce qu'un Français?* 92. Weil indicates that a reference to the secret circular became shorthand on applications. He identifies the date of this circular as 13 April 1939, but I believe he must mean the 23 October 1939 circular, which I saw used in this way. This is corroborated by Weil's footnote 57, p. 298, where he suggests that the circular responded to complaints that Mussolini had registered over the summer of 1939. Thus, the circular must postdate these complaints. Crémieux-Brillhac also identifies a decree of 22 October 1939, on which this circular must be based. See *Les Français de l'an 40,* 489. The date mentioned by Weil, 13 April 1939, is significant because it was on this date that a decree was issued requiring stateless foreigners to serve in the army to the same extent as Frenchmen. The same decree permitted nonstateless foreigners to contract a special engagement (such as with the foreign legion). It was not until October 1939 that nonstateless foreigners were required to volunteer.

105. Naturalization figures calculated from statistics in Depoid, *Les naturalisations en France,* 52.

106. Ibid.

107. Vicki Caron entitles a chapter devoted to equivocation about mobilizing refugees "The Missed Opportunity." See Caron, *Uneasy Asylum,* 240–67.

CONCLUSION

1. Gildea, *Marianne in Chains,* 16; Burrin, *France à l'heure allemande*; Veillon, *Vivre et survivre en France.*

2. A similar point is made by Mandel, *In the Aftermath,* chap. 2, where she discusses the problems of Jewish property restitution after the war.

3. ADR Exp., box 18: Original expulsion, 12 January 1933; testimony, 22 November 1948; repeal of expulsion, 1949.

4. ADR Exp., box 42: Inspecteur MOLTER au Chef du Service Départemental des Renseignements Généraux, 26 July 1944; undated application for "privileged resident" card, claiming to have been "pillaged by the Germans in May 1946 [*sic*; 1944] during a raid at my home to arrest me for resistance activity"; naturalization, 24 September 1948.

5. ADR Exp., box 25: Proposition de remise en vigueur de l'expulsion, Conseiller de préfecture du Rhône VEYRET, 8 March 1946; expulsion, 23 April 1946; Min. I. DGSN, Service des Renseignements Généraux du Rhône, 9 December 1946; expulsion repealed 9 May 1947.

6. ADBR 4 M 1954: Commissaire de Police Chef de la 4e Section to Commissaire Principal Chef du Service Départemental des Renseignements Généraux, 20 May 1952.

7. ADR Exp., box 11: Original expulsion from 1932 for family abandonment; *sursis*, 1939–43; Service du Travail Obligatoire, 18 October 1943 to 28 May 1945; testimony of ex-wife, 1946; prefect to Min. I., request to reactivate expulsion order and reply, 1946; L'Officier de Police André Giraud à M. le Commissaire Principal Chef de la Sûreté Urbaine de Lyon, reports, 25 October 1954 and 3 June 1955.

8. ADR Exp., box 32: Prefect to Min. I. (DGSN, 6e Bur. expulsion), 12 May 1939; note du Sous-Chef de la Sûreté, 11 August 1939; expulsion, 21 August 1939; border-crossing police report (Modane), 14 September 1939; Service des Renseignements Généraux à Lyon, 22 December 1947.

9. Timed to coincide with the 60-year commemoration of the liberation of Nazi camps in January 2005, National Front Party president Jean-Marie Le Pen made headlines when he remarked in a magazine interview that "in France at least, the German occupation was not particularly inhumane, even if there were a few hitches, inevitable in a country of 550,000 square kilometers." Le Pen cited in Christiane Chombeau, "Pour M. Le Pen, 'l'occupation allemande n'a pas été particulièrement inhumaine,'" *Le monde,* 13 January 2005. Calls immediately came to prosecute Le Pen under antinegationism legislation. In response to the ensuing furor, Bruno Gollnisch (deputy-general of the National Front) defended Le Pen by noting that Auschwitz "was also the responsibility of the Soviet Union." Gollnisch cited in "Gollnisch: 'Auschwitz était aussi de la responsabilité de l'URSS,'" *Le monde,* 31 January 2005.

10. Noiriel, *Les origines républicaines,* 98. Deschodt and Huguenin, *La république xénophobe,* make a similar argument, but, unlike Noiriel, they often take historical evidence out of context to make their case. These arguments differ considerably from that advanced in 1981 by Michael Marrus and Robert Paxton (*Vichy France and the Jews*), which also saw some continuities between the Third Republic and Vichy. Marrus and Paxton emphasize the changing nature of anti-Semitism and xenophobia, showing how conflict escalated in the late 1930s, whereas Noiriel locates the problem in the "republican compromise" of the late nineteenth century and then traces its development through the 1930s. See also Paxton, "Gérard Noiriel's Third Republic."

11. Noiriel, *Les origines républicaines,* 194.

12. Feldblum, "Reconsidering the 'Republican' Model," 177–79. See also Feldblum, *Reconstructing Citizenship.*

13. See Patrick Weil's account of how George Mauco's and Albert Sauvy's suggestions for postwar policy were tempered by other members of the Haut Comité de la Population. Weil, *La France et ses étrangers,* 59.

14. Thus, a foreigner entering France would have access to privileged status within three years at age 40 if he or she had one child, 45 if two, 50 if three, and so on. See Adler, *Jews and Gender,* 98. See also Viet, *La France immigrée,* 142.

15. Ibid.

16. Weil, *Qu'est-ce qu'un Français?* 152. Exceptions were also made for foreigners holding certain advanced diplomas and having fought in the French or Allied armies.

17. Sayad, "An Exemplary Immigration," in idem, *The Suffering of the Immigrant,* 71.

18. Weil, *La France et ses étrangers,* 59.

19. Ibid., 62. See also idem, *Qu'est-ce qu'un Français?* 166.

20. Weil, *La France et ses étrangers,* 54. Of course, major disputes continue about what constitutes a refugee under international law, but unlike in the interwar period, "asylum" is recognized as a legitimate claim on residency.

21. Viet, *La France immigrée,* 267.

22. Weil, *La France et ses étrangers,* 65.

23. Ibid., 65–67.

24. Ibid., 111. Viet, *La France immigrée,* 387. The Schengen accords of 1990 crowned a long process of removing barriers to the free movement of European Union citizens, a right recognized in principle under Article 48 of the Treaty of Rome but limited in practice.

25. Viet, *La France immigrée,* 293.

26. The press coverage of the fall 2005 riots is too vast to list here. For an excellent reflection on the unrest, see Paul Silverstein and Chantal Tetreault, "Urban Violence in France," *Middle East Report Online* (November 2005), http://www.merip.org/mero/interventions/silverstein_tetreault_interv.htm (accessed 21 November 2005).

27. Lochak, *Étrangers, de quel droit?* 214; Spire, *Étrangers à la carte,* 13.

28. Jean-Louis Borloo cited in Bertrand Bissuel, "Le gouvernement prévoit la démolition de 40000 logements par an," *Le monde,* 19 June 2003.

29. Mustapha Kessous, "La longue dérive de Vénissieux," *Le monde,* 14 January 2005.

30. For work on French pluralism, see esp. Ford, *Creating the Nation;* Peer, *France on Display;* Rogers, *Shaping Modern Times;* Sahlins, *Boundaries.* These books all respond in some way to Eugen Weber's now classic *Peasants into Frenchmen,* which posited that as France modernized and as the French state encroached into wider and wider spheres of French life, people lost their regional identities and became "Frenchmen."

31. Hollifield, "Immigration and Republicanism," 144. Hollifield argues that the difference between a "nation" and a "country" of immigrants is crucial. Here

he draws heavily from the analyses of Gérard Noiriel in arguing that immigration in France is not part of what de Tocqueville would have called a "founding myth," making France unlike the United States, Canada, and Australia, where immigration coincided with nation building. See Noiriel, "Immigration."

32. Hervé Le Bras, cited in Gauthier, "La guerre des démographes." This remark was made with reference to the prospect of recording ethnicity in the French census.

33. These terms all emerge from Brubaker, *Citizenship*.

34. The term "citizenship of aliens" is from Bosniak, "The Citizenship of Aliens"; for "thick" and "thin" citizenship, see Tilly, "Citizenship," 8.

35. For a vivid example of how international relations have affected domestic citizenship rights, see Dudziak, *Cold War Civil Rights*.

36. See esp. Soysal, *Limits of Citizenship*; Hammar, *Democracy and the Nation State*; Jacobson, *Rights across Borders*. See also Castles and Davidson, *Citizenship and Migration*.

37. Favell, *Philosophies*, 240–41.

38. Joppke, "Citizenship between De- and Re-ethnicization." By citizenship Joppke means membership rather than the wider constellation of rights to which I refer; the overall trend he observes is nonetheless germane here.

Bibliography

ARCHIVAL SERIES

Archives de la Chambre de Commerce (Marseille)

Correspondance et Documents

Archives de la Chambre de Commerce et de l'Industrie (Lyon)

Letters Collection
Procès-Verbaux des Séances 1919–39

Archives Départementales des Bouches-du-Rhône (Marseille) (ADBR)

1 J	Prélature des Arméniens à Marseille (Box 479)
1 M	Cabinet du Préfet
2 M	Administration
4 M	Police
6 M	Naturalizations
14 M	Travail
3 N	Budget
6 W	Expulsions (Post-1940 Deposit)
403 U	Jugements Correctionnels
1 Y	Camps de Concentration

Uninventoried "Événements Politiques Étrangers Afrique du Nord 1927–39" (SAINA)

Archives Départmentales du Cher (Bourges) (ADC)

M   Police (courtesy of Philippe Rygiel)

Archives Départementales du Rhône (Lyon) (ADR)

2 M	Administration
4 M	Police
5 M	Hygiène
10 M	Travail
3494 W	Dossiers d'étrangers
U cor 939	Dossiers d'instruction, tribunal correctionnel

Jugements Correctionnels
Uninventoried Expulsion Files Silo 1, travée 154 et suivantes, boxes 1–46
Uninventoried Foreigner Files Silo 5, travée 85, loose files and unlabeled boxes
Uninventoried Naturalization Files Silo 2, travée 285, 1927–38, 16 boxes

Archives du Ministère des Affaires Étrangères (Paris, Quai d'Orsay) (AMAE)

C—Europe Administrative 1908–40
K—Afrique 1918–40
    Questions Générales
M—Maroc
Z—Europe 1918–40
    Italie
    Espagne
Correspondance Politique et Commerciale
Direction des Affaires Commerciales, Europe 1919–44
Sociéte des Nations (1917–40)

Archives Municipales de Lyon (AML)

0005 WP—Fonds Municipal de Chômage
0349 WP—Hygiène; Baraques en Bois
0747 WP—Office Municipal du Travail, Fonctionnement
0981 WP—Bureau de Bienfaisance; Aides aux Chômeurs, 1931–42
1120 WP—Cabinet du Maire

Archives Municipales de Marseille

1 D   Déliberations du Conseil Municipal
5 D   Correspondance du Maire au Préfet

Archives Municipales de Vénissieux (AMVx)

7 F 55, 7 F 56, and 5 Q 253

Archives Municipales de Villeurbanne (AMV)

Chômage 1927–37

Archives Nationales (Paris) (AN)

BB   Ministère de la Justice
F^{1a} Inspection Générale des Services Administratifs
F^7 Ministère de l'Intérieur
F^{10} Ministère de l'Agriculture
F^{12} Ministère du Commerce et de l'Industrie
F^{14} Ministère des Travaux Publics
F^{22} Ministère du Travail

Centre des Archives de la France d'Outre-Mer (Aix-en-Provence) (CAOM)

9 H (Gouverneur Général de l'Algérie)
SLOTFOM (Service de Liaison entre les Originaires des Territoires d'Outre-Mer)

Ministère des Affaires Sociales, du Travail et de la Solidarité: Centre des Ressources. Documentaires Multimédia, uninventoried circular collection (MAS-CRDM)
New York University, Bobst Library
League of Nations Collection

NEWSPAPERS, PERIODICALS, AND PUBLISHED
GOVERNMENT DOCUMENTS

Al-Raïat-Al-Hamra: Organe du parti communiste (SFIC)
Annales de l'Assemblée Nationale, débats de la chambre
Annales de l'Assemblée Nationale, débats du sénat
Budget primitif (Marseille)
Bulletin de l'inspection du travail et de l'hygiène industrielle
Bulletin du Comité de l'Afrique Française—Renseignements coloniaux et documents
Bulletin du Ministère du Travail (1918–40) *(BMT)*
Chambre de Commerce de Lyon, *Comptes rendus des travaux*, 1919–39
Chambre de Commerce de Marseille, *Correspondance et documents*, 1931-38 (Marseille: Société Anonyme du Sémaphore de Marseille).
Conseil Municipal de Lyon, *Procès verbaux des séances*
El Ouma
(Les) études Rhodaniennes
(Le) guignol (ADR Pér. 415)
L'humanité
Illustration
L'information ouvrière et sociale (becomes *L'information sociale* in 1921) (1918–1935) *(IS)*
Journal officiel de la République Française
  Débats parlementaires, Chambre des Députés (*JODCD)*
  Documents parlementaires (*JODP)*
  Lois et décrets (*JOLD)*

Marseille, revue municipale (post–World War II)
Le matin
Le monde (post–World War II)
New York Times
Le nouvel observateur (post–World War II)
L'oeuvre
Le petit marseillais
Le petit provençal
Le peuple
Le progrès de Lyon
Revue de l'Alliance Nationale pour l'Accroissement de la Population Française
Rouge-midi
Le temps

La vie syndicale, Bulletin officiel de la Confédération générale du travail unitaire.
La voix du peuple (Lyon)

CONTEMPORARY PUBLISHED MATERIAL

Adamic, Louis. "Who Killed the King?" *The Nation,* 10 October 1936, 417–18.

Baroin, Henri. "La main-d'oeuvre étrangère dans la région lyonnaise." Thèse de droit. Université de Lyon. Lyon: Bosc Frères, M. et L. Riou, 1935.

Barthélemy, Xavier. "Des infractions aux arrêtés d'expulsion et d'interdiction de séjour." Thèse de droit. Paris: Éditions Domat-Montchrestien, 1936.

Bontoux, Henri (adjoint au maire). *Le problème du logement à Marseille. Résumé des travaux de la Commission Municipale de l'Habitation.* Marseille: Imprimérie Municipale, 1932.

Chambre de Commerce de Marseille. *Marseille, le port—la ville—la région. Répertoire memento de chiffres et de faits.* Preface by Hubert Giraud. Marseille: Imprimérie du "Sémaphore" Barlatier, 1922.

Le Comité Confédéral National. "Programme minimum de la C.G.T." (15 Décembre 1918). In *La Confédération Générale du Travail et le mouvement syndical.* Paris: Fédération Syndicale Internationale, 1925.

(La) Confédération générale du travail et le mouvement syndical. Paris: Fédération Syndicale Internationale, 1925.

Daladier, Édouard. *In Defense of France.* New York: Doubleday, Doran, 1939.

Depoid, Pierre. *Les naturalisations en France (1870–1940).* État Français, Ministère des Finances, Service National des Statistiques, Direction de la Statistique Générale, Études Démographiques. No. 3. Paris: Imprimérie Nationale, 1942.

Feuchtwanger, Lion. *The Devil in France: My Encounter with Him in the Summer of 1940.* Translated by Elisabeth Abbott. New York: Viking Press, 1941.

Girault, Arthur. *Principes de colonisation et de législation coloniale.* Vol. 4, *L'Afrique du Nord I. Algérie.* 1926. Paris: Recueil Sirey, 1933.

Gomar, Norbert. *L'émigration algérienne en France.* Paris: Les Presses Modernes, 1931.

Haury, Paul. *La vie ou la mort de la France.* Paris: L'Alliance Nationale pour l'Accroissement de la Population Française, 1923.

Héreil, Georges. "Le chômage en France: Étude de législation sociale." Thèse pour le doctorat, Université de Paris, Faculté de Droit. Paris: Librairie de Recueil Sirey, 1932.

Herriot, Édouard. "Lettre-préface." In *La France et les étrangers (dépopulation—immigration—naturalisation),* by Charles Lambert. Paris: Librairie Delagrave, 1928.

Jahoda, Marie, Paul Lazarsfeld, and Hans Zeisel. *Marienthal: The Sociography of an Unemployed Community.* 1933. Translated by the authors with John Reignall and Thomas Elsaaesser. Chicago: Aldine-Atherton, 1971.

Jouhaux, Léon. "Appel à l'action méthodique." 1915. Reprinted in Confédération générale du travail, *XIXe Congrès National Corporatif.* 1918. Paris: Paris: Imprimérie nouvelle, 1919.

———. *La C.G.T., ce qu'elle est, ce qu'elle veut.* 25th ed. Paris: Gallimard, 1937.

Koestler, Arthur. *Scum of the Earth.* 1941. London: Eland, 1991.

Lambert, Charles. *La France et les étrangers (dépopulation—immigration—naturalisation).* Preface by Édouard Herriot. Paris: Librairie Delagrave, 1928.

Larnaude, Marcel. "L'émigration temporaire des indigènes algériens dans la Métropole." *Revue de géographie marocaine* 8, 7 (1928): 45–51.

League of Nations Union. "Refugees and the League." Publication no. 389 (September 1935).

Letellier, Gabrielle, Jean Perret, H. E. Zuber, and A. Dauphin-Meunier. *Enquête sur le chômage.* Vol. 1, *Le chômage en France de 1930 à 1936.* Preface by Charles Rist. Paris: Librairie de Recueil Sirey, 1938.

Lévy, Bernard. "Les arrêtés d'expulsion." Thèse pour le doctorat d'état (science juridique), Université de Strasbourg. Clermont-Ferrand: Imprimérie Mont-Louis, 1941.

Lewis, Edward Rieman. *America, Nation or Confusion. A Study of Our Immigration Problems.* New York: Harper and Brothers, 1928.

Loew, M.-R. *Les dockers de Marseille: Analyse type d'un complèxe.* 2nd ed. L'Arbresle, Rhône, France: Économie et Humanisme, 1945.

Londres, Albert. *Marseille, porte du sud.* 1927. Paris: Le Serpent à Plumes Éditions, 1994.

Marcel-Rémond, G. *L'immigration italienne dans le sud-ouest de la France.* Paris: Dalloz, 1928.

Marseille, City of. *L'œuvre municipale (1929–1935).* Marseille: Imprimerie municipale, 1935.

Masson, Paul. *Marseille pendant la guerre.* Publications de la Dotation Carnegie pour la Paix Internationale. Paris and New Haven: Les Presses Universitaires de France and Yale University Press, 1926.

Mauco, Georges. *Les étrangers en France: Leur rôle dans l'activité économique.* Paris: Colin, 1932.

Naudeau, Ludovic. "Enquête sur la population de la France: Bouches-du-Rhône." *Illustration* 174, 4512 (24 August 1929).

———. *La France se regarde: Le problème de la natalité.* Paris: Hachette, 1931.

Nogaro, Bertrand, and Lucien Weil. *La main-d'oeuvre étrangère et coloniale pendant la guerre.* Publications de la Dotation Carnegie pour la Paix Internationale. Paris and New Haven: Les Presses Universitaires de France and Yale University Press, 1926.

Orwell, George. *The Road to Wigan Pier.* 1937. London: Folio Society, 1998.

Oualid, William. "L'immigration algérienne en France." *Documents du travail* (October 1927): 10–16.

———. *L'immigration ouvrière en France.* Les Cahiers du Redressement Français 23. Paris: Éditions de la S.A.P.E., 1927.

Paon, Marcel. *L'immigration en France.* Preface by Albert Thomas. Paris: Payot, 1926.

Pasquet, Louis. *Immigration et main-d'oeuvre étrangère en France.* Paris: Éditions Rieder, 1927.

Perret, J. "Dans la banlieue industrielle de Lyon: Vaulx-en-Velin." *Les études Rhodaniennes* (1937): 23–33.

"Programme de la Charte Internationale du Travail." Adoptée à la Conférence Syndicale Internationale à Berne, 5–9 February 1919. Reprinted in Confédération Générale du Travail, *XXe Congrès National Corporatif.* 1919. Villenueve-Saint-Georges, France: Imprimérie L'Union Typographique, 1919.

Racine, P. "Une expérience à reprendre: Le sous-secrétariat d'état a l'immigration, et les projets de Philippe Serre." *Esprit* 82 (July 1939): 609–19.

Ray, Joanny. *Les Marocains en France.* Collection des Centres d'Études Juridiques, Vol. 17. Paris: Librairie du Recueil Sirey, 1938.

Seghers, Anna. *Transit.* 1940. Translated by Jeanne Stern. Paris: Éditions Alinéa, 1986.

Seton-Watson, R. W. "King Alexander's Assassination: Its Background and Effects." *International Affairs* 14, 1 (January–February 1935): 24–47.

Simpson, John Hope. *Refugees, Preliminary Report of a Survey.* New York: Oxford University Press, 1938.

———. *The Refugee Problem: Report of a Survey.* New York: Oxford University Press, 1939.

———. *Refugees: A Review of the Situation since September 1938.* New York: Oxford University Press, 1939.

Thomas, Albert. Preface to *L'immigration en France,* by Marcel Paon. Paris: Payot, 1926.

Ulmann, André. *Le quatrième pouvoir. Police.* Paris: Éditions Montaigne, 1935.

Ville de Marseille. *L'œuvre municipale (1929–1935).* Marseille: Imprimerie Municipale, 1935.

West, Rebecca. *Black Lamb, Grey Falcon: A Journey through Yugoslavia.* New York: Viking, 1941.

Wlocevski, Stéphane. "Y a-t-il trop de travailleurs étrangers en France?" *Revue d'économie politique* 49e année, 2 (March–April 1935): 324–59.

SECONDARY MATERIALS

Adler, Karen. *Jews and Gender in Liberation France.* Cambridge: Cambridge University Press, 2003.

Ageron, Charles-Robert. *Les Algériens musulmans et la France (1871–1919).* Paris: Presses Universitaires de France, 1968.

Alexander, Martin S., and Helen Graham, eds. *The French and Spanish Popular Fronts: Comparative Perspectives.* Cambridge and New York: Cambridge University Press, 1989.

Aoumeur, Mouloud. "Les fédérations socialistes algériennes et la question nationale au moment du Front Populaire." *Maghreb Review* 23, 1–4 (1998): 2–23.

Arendt, Hannah. *The Origins of Totalitarianism.* 1950. Rev. ed. San Diego, New York, and London: Harcourt Brace, 1979.

"Atlas de l'immigration en France entre les deux guerres." Actes de l'Histoire de l'Immigration. http://barthes.ens.fr/atlasclio.

Attard-Maraninchi, Marie-Françoise. "Prostitution et quartier réservé à Marseille au début du XXe siècle." In *Marseillaises: Les femmes et la ville,* edited by Yvonne Knibiehler, Catherine Marand-Fouquet, Régine Goutalier, and Éliane Richard. Paris: Côté-Femmes, 1993.

Attard-Maraninchi, Marie-Françoise, and Émile Temime. *Migrance: Histoire des Migrations à Marseille.* Vol. 3, *Le cosmopolitisme de l'entre-deux-guerres (1919–1945).* Aix-en-Provence, France: Édisud, 1990.

Auzias, Claire. *Mémoires libertaires: Lyon 1919–1939.* Collection: "Chemins de la Mémoire," edited by Alain Forest. Paris: L'Harmattan, 1993.

Azéma, Jean-Pierre. *From Munich to the Liberation.* Translated by Janet Lloyd. The Cambridge History of Modern France. Cambridge and Paris: Cambridge University Press and Éditions de la Maison des Sciences de l'Homme, 1984.

Badia, Gilbert, ed. *Les barbelés de l'exil: Études sur l'émigration allemande et autrichienne (1938–1940).* Grenoble: Presses Universitaires de Grenoble, 1979.

———. *Les bannis de Hitler: Accueil et luttes des exilés allemands en France (1933–1939).* Paris: Études et Documentation Internationales, Presses Universitaires de Vincennes, 1984.

Badie, Bertrand, and Pierre Birnbaum. *The Sociology of the State.* 1979. Translated by Arthur Goldhammer. Chicago: University of Chicago Press, 1983.

Baillon, Jean-Claude, ed. "Marseille: Histoires de famille." Special issue. *Autrement* hors série, no. 36 (February 1989).

Baker, Donald. "The Surveillance of Subversion in Interwar France: The Carnet B in the Seine, 1922–1940." *French Historical Studies* 10 (1978): 486–516.

Balibar, Étienne. " 'Rights of Man' and 'Rights of the Citizen.' The Modern Dialectic of Equality and Freedom." In *Masses, Classes, Ideas: Studies on Politics and Philosophy Before and After Marx,* by Étienne Balibar. Translated by James Swenson. New York and London: Routledge, 1994.

Bardakdjian, Geneviève. "La communauté arménienne de Décines (1925–1971)." *Bulletin du Centre d'Histoire Économique et Sociale de la Région Lyonnaise* (1972): 55–65.

Barou, Jacques. "Genèse et évolution d'un village urbain. Un groupe d'émigrés algériens dans un ensemble d'îlots du XVIe arrondissement de Marseille." *Ethnologie Française* 16, 1 (1986): 59–76.

Becker, Jean-Jacques. *Le Carnet B.* Paris: Klincksieck, 1973.

Becker, Jean-Jacques, and Serge Berstein. *Histoire de l'anti-communisme.* Vol. 1, *1917–1940.* Paris: O. Orban, 1987.

Begag, Azouz. *Place du Pont ou la médina de Lyon.* Collection Français d'Ailleurs, Peuple d'Ici. Paris: Éditions Autrement, 1997.

Berberova, Nina. *Billancourt Tales.* Translated by Marian Schwartz. New York: New Directions, 2001.

———. *The Tattered Cloak and Other Stories.* Translated by Marian Schwartz. New York: New Directions, 2001.

Bergès, Michel. *Le syndicalisme policier en France (1990–1940).* Paris: L'Harmattan, 1995.

Berlière, Jean-Marc. "La professionnalisation de la police en France: Un phénomène nouveau au début du XXe siècle en France." *Déviance et société* 11, 1 (1987): 100–141.

————. *Le monde des polices en France, XIXe–XXe siècles.* Paris: Éditions Complexe, 1996.

————. "A Republican Political Police? Political Policing in France under the Third Republic, 1875–1940." In *The Policing of Politics in the Twentieth Century,* edited by Mark Mazower. Providence, RI, and Oxford: Berghahn Books, 1997.

Bernard, Philippe, and Henri Dubief. *The Decline of the Third Republic, 1914–1938.* Translated by Anthony Forster. The Cambridge History of Modern France. Cambridge and Paris: Cambridge University Press and Éditions de la Maison des Sciences de l'Homme, 1985.

Berstein, Serge. *Édouard Herriot ou la république en personne.* Paris: Presses de la Fondation Nationale des Sciences Politiques, 1985.

Bertaux, Sandrine. " 'Processus' et 'population' dans l'analyse démographique de l'immigration en France (1932–1996)." In *L'invention des populations: Biologie, idéologie et politique,* edited by Hervé Le Bras with Sandrine Bertaux. Paris: Éditions Odile Jacob, 2000.

Berthet, Claire. *Contribution à une histoire du logement social en France au XXe siècle: Des bâtisseurs aux habitants, les HBM des États-Unis de Lyon.* Paris: L'Harmattan, 1997.

Bienfait, Jean. "La population de Lyon à travers un quart de siècle de recensements douteux (1911–1936)." *Revue de géographie de Lyon* 1–2 (1968): 63–132.

Blanc-Chaléard, Marie-Claude. *Les Italiens dans l'est Parisien (années 1880–1960). Une histoire d'intégration.* Rome: École française de Rome, 2000.

Blanc-Chaléard, Marie-Claude, Caroline Douki, Nicole Dyonet, and Vincent Milliot, eds. *Police et migrants, France 1667–1939.* Rennes, France: Presses Universitaires de Rennes, 2001.

Blès, Adrien. *Dictionnaire historique des rues de Marseille. Mémoire de Marseille.* Paris: Éditions Jeanne Laffitte, 1989.

Blévis, Laure. "Les avatars de la citoyenneté en Algérie coloniale ou les paradoxes d'une catégorisation." *Droit et société* 48 (2001): 557–80.

————. "La citoyenneté française au miroir de la colonisation: Étude des demandes de naturalisation des 'sujets français' en Algérie coloniale." *Genèses* 53 (December 2003): 25–47.

Blum, Alain. "Comment décrire les immigrés—A propos de quelques recherches sur l'immigration." *Population* 3 (1998): 569–88.

Bonnet, Jean-Charles. "Étude des petits commerçants étrangers dans l'agglomération lyonnaise (1919–1939), à partir du régistre du commerce." *Bulletin du Centre d'Histoire Économique et Sociale de la Région Lyonnaise* 1 (April 1975): 1–40.

————. *Les pouvoirs publics français et l'immigration dans l'entre-deux-guerres.* Lyon: Centre d'Histoire Économique et Sociale de la Région Lyonnaise, n.d. [1976].

————. "Naturalisations et révisions de naturalisations de 1927 à 1944: L'exemple du Rhône." *Le mouvement social* 98 (January–March 1977): 43–75.

Bonneville, Marc. *Naissance et métamorphose d'une banlieue ouvrière, Villeurbanne: Processus et formes d'urbanisation.* Lyon: Presses Universitaires de Lyon, n.d. [1978].

Borruey, René. "Ville et infrastructure." In *Atlas historique des villes de France,* edited by Jean-Luc Pinol. Paris: Hachette, 1996.

Bosniak, Linda. "The Citizenship of Aliens." *Social Text* 56, 16, 3 (Fall 1998): 29–35.

———. *The Citizen and the Alien: Dilemmas of Contemporary Membership.* Princeton, NJ: Princeton University Press, 2006.

Bourdieu, Pierre. "The Forms of Capital." Translated by Richard Nice. In *Handbook of Theory and Research for the Sociology of Education,* edited by John Richardson. New York: Greenwood Press, 1986.

———. *Acts of Resistance. Against the Tyranny of the Market.* Translated by Richard Nice. New York: New Press, 1998.

Boushaba, Zouhir. *Étre Algérien hier aujourd'hui et demain.* Alger: Editions Mimouni, 1992.

Brett, Michael. "Legislating for Inequality in Algeria: The Senatus Consulte of 14 July 1865." *Bulletin of the School of Oriental and African Studies* 51, 3 (1988): 440–61.

Broche, François, ed. *Assassinat de Alexandre Ier et Louis Barthou, Marseille le 9 Octobre 1934.* Paris: Éditions Balland, 1977.

Brown, Keith. "The King Is Dead, Long Live the Balkans! Watching the Marseilles Murders of 1934." Paper delivered at Sixth Annual World Convention of the Association for the Study of Nationalities, Columbia University, 5–7 April 2001. Watson Institute for International Studies, Brown University. http://www .watsoninstitute.org/pub_detail.cfm?id=132. Accessed 1 August 2000.

Brubaker, Rogers. *Citizenship and Nationhood in France and Germany.* Cambridge, MA: Harvard University Press, 1992.

———. "Ethnicity without Groups." *Archives européennes de sociologie* (May 2002): 163–89.

Brubaker, William Rogers, ed. *Immigration and the Politics of Citizenship in Europe and North America.* Lanham, MD: University Press of America for the German Marshall Fund of the United States, 1989.

———. "Membership without Citizenship: The Economic and Social Rights of Noncitizens." In *Immigration and the Politics of Citizenship in Europe and North America,* edited by William Rogers Brubaker. Lanham, MD: University Press of America for the German Marshall Fund of the United States, 1989, 145–62.

Bruschi, Christian, and Myrto Bruschi. "Le pouvoir des guichets." *Les temps modernes* 42 (1984): 2019–30.

Burrin, Philippe. *France à l'heure allemande.* Paris: Seuil, 1995.

Calavita, Kitty. *Immigrants at the Margins: Law, Race, and Exclusion in Southern Europe.* Cambridge and New York: Cambridge University Press, 2005.

Calvès, Gwénaële. " 'Il n'y a pas de race ici': Le modèle Français à l'épreuve de l'intégration européenne." *Critique internationale* 17 (October 2002): 173–86.

Camiscioli, Elisa. "Intermarriage, Independent Nationality, and the Individual Rights of French Women: The Law of 10 August 1927." In *Race in France: Interdisciplinary Perspectives on the Politics of Difference,* edited by Herrick Chapman and Laura Frader. New York and London: Berghahn Books, 2004.

Caron, Vicki. "Loyalties in Conflict: French Jewry and the Refugee Crisis, 1933–1935." *Leo Baeck Institute Year Book* 36 (1991): 305–37.

———. "The Antisemitic Revival in France in the 1930s: The Socioeconomic Dimension Reconsidered." *Journal of Modern History* 70, 1 (March 1998): 24–73.

———. *Uneasy Asylum: France and the Jewish Refugee Crisis.* Stanford, CA: Stanford University Press, 1999.

Carrot, Georges. "L'étatisation des polices urbaines." *Revue de la police nationale* 121 (September 1984): 40–48.

———. *Histoire de la police française. Tableaux, chronologie, iconographie.* Paris: Librairie Jules Tallandier, 1992.

Castles, Stephen. "The Guestworker in Western Europe—An Obituary." *International Migration Review* 20, 4 (Winter 1986): 761–78.

Castles, Stephen, and Alistair Davidson. *Citizenship and Migration: Globalization and the Politics of Belonging.* New York: Routledge, 2000.

Castles, Stephen, and Godula Kosack. *Immigrant Workers and Class Structure in Western Europe.* London and New York: Oxford University Press, 1973.

Chapman, Herrick. *State Capitalism and Working-Class Radicalism in the French Aircraft Industry.* Berkeley and Los Angeles: University of California Press, 1991.

———. "French Democracy and the Welfare State." In *The Social Construction of Democracy, 1870–1990,* edited by George Reid Andrews and Herrick Chapman. New York: New York University Press, 1995.

Chatelain, Abel. *Les migrants temporaires en France de 1800 à 1914: Histoire économique et sociale des migrants temporaires des campagnes françaises au XIXe siècle et au début du XXe siècle.* 2 vols. Villeneuve-d'Ascq, France: Université de Lille III, n.d. [1976].

Chevalier, Louis. *La formation de la population parisienne aux XIXe siècle.* Paris: Presses Universitaires de France, 1950.

———. *Laboring Classes and Dangerous Classes in Paris during the First Half of the Nineteenth Century.* Translated by Frank Jellinek. New York: Howard Fertig, 1973.

Childers, Kristen Stromberg. *Fathers, Families and the State in France 1914–1945.* Ithaca, NY: Cornell University Press, 2003.

Claverie, Élisabeth. "Les dockers à Marseille de 1864 à 1941. De leur apparition au statut de 1941." PhD diss., Université d'Aix en Provence, 1996.

Cohen, William B. "The Colonial Policy of the Popular Front." *French Historical Studies* 7, 3 (Spring 1972): 368–93.

Cole, Joshua. "Discipline and Punish or Preserve and Protect? The 'Action social pour les Français Musulmans d'Algérie,' 1959–1962." Paper delivered at the Society for French Historical Studies, Chapel Hill, NC, March 2001.

Collomp, Catherine. "Immigrants, Labor Markets, and the State, a Comparative Approach: France and the United States, 1880–1930." *Journal of American History* 86, 1 (June 1999): 41–66.

Collot, Claude. *Les institutions de l'Algérie durant la période coloniale*

(1830–1962). Paris and Algiers: Centre National de la Recherche Scientifique and Office des Publications Universitaires, 1987.

Colton, Joel. *Compulsory Labor Arbitration in France, 1936–1939.* New York: King's Crown Press of Columbia University, 1951.

———. "The Formation of the French Popular Front, 1934–6." In *The French and Spanish Popular Fronts: Comparative Perspectives,* edited by Martin S. Alexander and Helen Graham. Cambridge and New York: Cambridge University Press, 1989.

Conklin, Alice. *A Mission to Civilize: The Republican Idea of Empire in France and West Africa.* Stanford, CA: Stanford University Press, 1995.

———. "Colonialism and Human Rights, A Contradiction in Terms? The Case of France and West Africa, 1895–1914." *American Historical Review* 103, 2 (April 1998): 419–42.

Cooper, Frederick. *Decolonization and African Society: The Labor Question in French and British Africa.* Cambridge and New York: Cambridge University Press, 1996.

Cooper, Frederick, and Ann Laura Stoler, eds. *Tensions of Empire: Colonial Cultures in a Bourgeois World.* Berkeley and Los Angeles: University of California Press, 1997.

Corbel, Maurice. *Vénissieux la rebelle.* Paris: Éditions Cercle d'Art, 1997.

Cornelius, Wayne A., Philip L. Martin, and James F. Hollifield, eds. *Controlling Immigration: A Global Perspective.* Stanford, CA: Stanford University Press, 1994.

Cottereau, Alain. "The Distinctiveness of Working-Class Cultures in France, 1848–1900." In *Working Class Formation,* edited by Ira Katznelson. Princeton, NJ: Princeton University Press, 1986.

Courault, Bruno. "Les étrangers 'catégories' du marché dual ou 'vecteur' de la flexibilité du travail?" In *L'immigration au tournant: Actes du colloque du GRECO 13 sur les mutations économiques et les travailleurs immigrés dans les pays industriels,* under the direction of G. Abou-Sada, B. Courault, and Z. Zeroulou. Paris: CIEMI/L'Harmattan, 1990.

Courdurie, Marcel, and Jean-Louis Miege, eds. *Marseille colonial face à la crise de 1929.* Marseille: Chambre de Commerce et d'Industrie de Marseille-Provence, 1991.

Craig, Gordon. *Germany, 1866–1945.* Oxford History of Modern Europe. New York and Oxford: Oxford University Press, 1980.

Crémieux-Brilhac, Jean-Louis. *Les Français de l'an 40.* 2 vols. Paris: Gallimard, 1990.

Cristofol, Jacqueline. *Batailles pour Marseille: Jean Cristofol, Gaston Deferre, Raymond Aubrac.* Preface by Raymond Jean. Paris: Flammarion, 1997.

Cross, Gary S. "The Structure of Labor Immigration into France between the Wars." PhD diss., University of Wisconsin-Madison, 1977.

———. *Immigrant Workers in Industrial France: The Making of a New Laboring Class.* Philadelphia, PA: Temple University Press, 1983.

Crozier, Michel. *The Bureaucratic Phenomenon.* Translated by the author. Chicago: University of Chicago Press, 1964.

————. *La société blocquée*. Reprint, Paris: Éditions du Seuil, 1994.

Dahbour, Omar, and Micheline R. Ishay, eds. *The Nationalism Reader*. Atlantic Highlands, NJ: Humanities Press International, 1995.

Daniel, Christine, and Carole Tuchszirer. *L'état face aux chômeurs: L'indemnisation du chômage de 1884 à nos jours*. Paris: Flammarion, 1999.

Daumalin, Xavier, Nicole Girard, and Olivier Raveaux, eds. *Du savon à la puce: L'industrie marseillaise du XVIIe siècle à nos jours*. Marseille: Editions Jeanne Laffitte, 2003.

Davis, Natalie Zemon. *Fiction in the Archives: Pardon Tales and Their Tellers in Sixteenth-Century France*. Stanford, CA: Stanford University Press, 1987.

De Baecque, Francis, ed. *Les directeurs de ministère en France (XIXe–XXe siècles)*. Geneva: Librairie Droz, 1976.

Denéchère, Yves. *La politique espagnole de la France de 1931 à 1936: Une pratique française de rapports inégaux*. Paris: L'Harmattan, 1999.

Deschodt, Pierre-Jean, and François Huguenin. *La république xénophobe*. Paris: JC Lattès, 2001.

Dewitte, Philippe. *Les mouvements nègres en France 1919–1939*. Paris: L'Harmattan, 1988.

Donzel, André. *Marseille, L'expérience de la cité*. Paris: Éditions Economica, 1998.

Dornel, Laurent. "Les usages du racialisme. Le cas de la main-d'oeuvre coloniale en France pendant la première guerre mondiale." *Genèses* 20 (September 1995): 24–47.

————. *La France hostile: Socio-histoire de la xénophobie (1870–1914)*. Preface by Gérard Noiriel. Paris: Hachette Littéraires, 2004.

Downs, Laura Lee. *Manufacturing Inequality: Gender Division in the French and British Metalworking Industries, 1914–1939*. Ithaca, NY: Cornell University Press, 1995.

Dreyfus-Armand, Geneviève. *L'exil des républicains espagnols en France. De la guerre civile à la mort de Franco*. Paris: Albin Michel, 1999.

Dubois, Laurent. "La République Métissée: Citizenship, Colonialism, and the Border of French History." *Cultural Studies* 14, 1 (January 2000): 15–34.

Dudziak, Mary L. *Cold War Civil Rights: Race and the Image of American Democracy*. Princeton, NJ: Princeton University Press, 2000.

Dupaquier, Jacques, ed. *Histoire de la population française*. Vols. 3 and 4. Paris: Presses Universitaires de France, 1988.

Dutton, Paul. V. *Origins of the French Welfare State: The Struggle for Social Reform in France, 1914–1947*. Cambridge: Cambridge University Press, 2002.

Échinard, Pierre, and Émile Temime. *Migrance: Histoire des migrations a Marseille*. Vol. 1, *La préhistoire de la migration (1482–1830)*. La Calade, Aix-en-Provence, France: Edisud, 1989–1991.

Eden, Anthony. *Facing the Dictators: The Memoirs of Anthony Eden*. Boston: Houghton Mifflin, 1962.

El-Mechat, Samia. "Le gouvernement du Front Populaire et la poussée nationaliste au Maghreb (1936–1937)." *Revue d'histoire maghrébine* 11, 33–34 (June 1984): 85–91.

Englander, David. *Poverty and Poor Law Reform in 19th Century Britain,*

1834–1914. From Chadwick to Booth. Seminar Studies in History. London and New York: Longman, 1998.

Esping-Andersen, Gøsta. *The Three Worlds of Welfare Capitalism.* Princeton, NJ: Princeton University Press, 1990.

(Les) étrangers à Marseille (1880–1939). Marseille: Conseil Général des Bouches-du-Rhône, 1988.

Evans, Patricia Russell. "Likely to Become a Public Charge: Immigration in the Backwaters of Administrative Law, 1882–1933." PhD diss., George Washington University, 1987.

Ewald, François. *L'état providence.* Paris: Éditions Grasset et Fasquelle, 1986.

Faidutti-Rudolph, Anne-Marie. *L'immigration italienne dans le sud-est de la France.* Études et Travaux de "Méditerranée." Revue géographique des pays méditerranéens. Gap, Hautes-Alpes, France: Éditions Ophrys, n.d.

Fassin, Didier. "La supplique: Stratégies rhétoriques et constructions identitaires dans les demandes d'aide d'urgence." *Annales: Histoire, sciences sociales* 55, 5 (2000): 955–81.

Fassin, Éric. " 'Good to Think': The American Reference in French Discourses of Immigration and Ethnicity." In *Multicultural Questions,* edited by Christian Joppke and Steven Lukes. Oxford: Oxford University Press, 1999.

Favell, Adrian. *Philosophies of Integration: Immigration and the Idea of Citizenship in France and Britain.* Basingstoke, UK: Macmillan; New York: St. Martin's Press, 1998.

Feldblum, Miriam. "Reconsidering the 'Republican' Model." In *Controlling Immigration: A Global Perspective,* edited by Wayne A. Cornelius, Philip L. Martin, and James F. Hollifield. Stanford, CA: Stanford University Press, 1994.

———. *Reconstructing Citizenship: The Politics of Nationality Reform and Immigration in Contemporary France.* Albany: State University of New York Press, 1999.

Fette, Julie. "Xenophobia and Exclusion in the Professions in Interwar France." PhD diss., New York University, 2001.

Fletcher, Yaël Simpson. "Towards 'A More Perfect Equality'?: Colonial Workers and French Communists in Marseilles, 1936–1938." *Proceedings of the Western Society for French History: Selected Papers of the Annual Meeting.* Vol. 24. N.p.: University Press of Colorado, 1997.

———. "City, Nation and Empire in Marseilles." PhD diss., Emory University, 1999.

Ford, Caroline. *Creating the Nation in Provincial France: Religion and Political Identity in Brittany.* Princeton, NJ: Princeton University Press, 1993.

Fraisse, Geneviève. *Reason's Muse: Sexual Difference and the Birth of Democracy.* Translated by Jane Todd. Chicago: University of Chicago Press, 1994.

Fraser, Nancy, and Linda Gordon. "Civil Citizenship against Social Citizenship? On the Ideology of Contract-Versus-Charity." In *The Condition of Citizenship,* edited by Bart van Steenbergen. London: Sage Publishers, 1994.

Freeman, Gary. *Immigrant Labor and Racial Conflict in Industrial Societies: The French and British Experiences, 1945–1975.* Princeton, NJ: Princeton University Press, 1979.

———. "Migration and the Political Economy of the Welfare State." *Annals of the American Academy of Political and Social Science* 485 (May 1986): 51–63.

Gallissot, René, Nadir Boumaza, and Ghislaine Clement. *Ces migrants qui font le prolétariat*. Paris: Méridiens-Klincksieck, 1994.

Gani, Léon. *Syndicats et travailleurs immigrés*. Paris: Éditions Sociales, 1972.

Gauthier, Ursula. "La guerre des démographes." *Le nouvel observateur,* no. 1776 (1998).

Gildea, Robert. *Marianne in Chains: In Search of the German Occupation*. London: Macmillan, 2002.

Gorboff, Marina. *La Russie fantôme: L'émigration russe de 1920 à 1950*. Lausanne: Éditions l'Age de l'Homme, 1995.

Gordon, Daniel A. "The Back Door of the Nation State: Expulsions of Foreigners and Continuity in Twentieth-Century France." *Past and Present* 186 (February 2005): 201–32.

Green, Nancy L. *The Pletzl of Paris: Jewish Immigrant Workers in the Belle Époque*. New York and London: Holmes and Meier, 1986.

———. "L'immigration en France et aux Etats-Unis, Historiographie comparée." *Vingtième siècle* 29 (January–March 1991): 67–82.

———. *Ready-to-Wear and Ready-to-Work: A Century of Industry and Immigrants in Paris and New York*. Durham, NC: Duke University Press, 1997.

———. *Repenser les migrations*. Paris: Presses Universitaires de France, 2002.

Gribauldi, Maurizio. "Itinéraires personnels et stratégies familiales: Les ouvriers de Renault dans l'entre-deux-guerres." *Population* 44, 6 (November–December 1989): 1213–32.

Guerry, Linda. "Le genre de la naturalisation: L'exemple des Bouches-du-Rhône (1918–1939)." Paper presented at colloquium Histoire/Genre/Migration. École Normale Supérieure, March 2006.

Guichard, Éric, and Gérard Noiriel, eds. *Construction des nationalités et immigration dans la France contemporaine*. Paris: Presses de l'École Normale Supérieure, 1997.

Guichard, Éric, Gérard Noiriel, Olivier Le Guillou, and Nicolas Manitakis. "Les étrangers et les naturalisés dans la société française. Commentaire des recensements de 1931 et 1936." In *Construction des nationalités et immigration dans la France contemporaine,* edited by Éric Guichard and Gérard Noiriel. Paris: Presses de l'École Normale Supérieure, 1997.

Guillen, Pierre. "L'antifascisme, facteur d'intégration des Italiens en France." In *L'emigrazione socialista nella lotta contro il fascismo (1926–1939)*. Florence, Italy: Sansoni, 1982.

Guiral, Pierre. "Ombres et lumières sur Marseille entre 1919 et 1939." *Marseille, revue municipale* 153 (March 1989): 84–87.

Hammar, Tomas. *Democracy and the Nation State: Aliens, Denizens and Citizens in a World of International Migration*. Aldershot, England, and Brookfield, VT: Gower Publishing, 1990.

Harouni, Rahma. "Le débat autour du statut des étrangers dans les années 1930." *Le mouvement social* 188 (July–September 1999): 61–75.

Haus, Leah A. "Labor Unions and Immigration Policy in France." *International Migration Review* 33, 3 (Fall 1999): 683–716.

——. *Unions, Immigration, and Internationalization: New Challenges and Changing Coalitions in the United States and France.* Europe in Transition: The NYU European Studies Series. Foreword by Martin A. Schain. New York: Palgrave Macmillan, 2002.

Hay, Douglas, Edward Thompson, and Peter Linebaugh, eds. *Albion's Fatal Tree: Crime and Society in Eighteenth-Century England.* London: Allen Lane, 1975.

Herbert, Ulrich. *A History of Foreign Labor in Germany, 1880–1990: Seasonal Workers, Forced Laborers, Guest Workers.* Translated by William Templer. Ann Arbor: University of Michigan Press, 1990.

Herriot, Édouard. *Jadis.* Vol. 2, *D'une guerre à l'autre, 1914–1936.* Paris: Flammarion, 1952.

Hobsbawm, Eric. *Primitive Rebels: Studies in Archaic Forms of Social Movement during the Nineteenth and Twentieth Centuries.* Manchester: Manchester University Press, 1959.

——. *Bandits.* Harmondsworth: Penguin, 1969.

——. "Social Criminality: Distinctions Between Socio-Political and Other Forms of Crime." *Bulletin of the Society for the Study of Labour History* 25 (1972): 5–6.

——. *Age of Extremes: The Short Twentieth-Century, 1914–1991.* New York: Viking Penguin, 1994.

Hoffmann, Stanley. "Paradoxes of the French Political Community." In *In Search of France: The Economy, Society and Political System in the Twentieth Century,* edited by Jean-Baptiste Duroselle, François Goguel, Stanley Hoffmann, Charles R. Kindleberger, Jesse R. Pitts, and Laurence Wylie. New York: Harper and Row, 1963.

——. *Decline or Renewal? France since the 1930s.* New York: Viking, 1974.

——. Foreword to *Prison Journal 1940–1945,* by Édouard Daladier. Compiled and annotated by Jean Daladier with Jean Daridan. Translated by Arthur D. Greenspan. Boulder, CO: Westview Press, 1995.

Hollifield, James. *Immigrants, Markets and States: The Political Economy of Postwar Europe.* Cambridge, MA: Harvard University Press, 1992.

——. "Immigration and Republicanism in France: The Hidden Consensus." In *Controlling Immigration: A Global Perspective,* edited by Wayne A. Cornelius, Philip L. Martin, and James F. Hollifield. Stanford, CA: Stanford University Press, 1994.

Holston, James, ed. *Cities and Citizenship.* Durham, NC and London: Duke University Press, 1999.

Horne, John. "Immigrant Workers in France during World War I." *French Historical Studies* 14, 1 (Spring 1985): 57–88.

——. *Labour at War: France and Britain, 1914–1918.* Oxford: Clarendon Press; New York: Oxford University Press, 1991.

Hovanessian, Martine. *Le lien communautaire: Trois générations d'Arméniens.* Paris: Armand Colin, 1992.

Hugo, Victor. *Les misérables.* Paris: Pagnerre, 1862.

Humphries, Stephen. *Hooligans or Rebels? An Oral History of Working Class Childhood and Youth 1889–1939.* Oxford: Blackwell, 1981.

Huntington, Samuel P. *Clash of Civilizations and the Remaking of World Order.* New York: Simon and Schuster, 1998.

———. *Who Are We? The Challenges to America's National Identity.* New York: Simon and Schuster, 2004.

Hyman, Paula E. *The Jews of Modern France.* Berkeley: University of California Press, 1998.

Jackson, Gabriel. *The Spanish Republic and the Civil War, 1931–1939.* Princeton, NJ: Princeton University Press, 1965.

Jackson, Julian. *The Politics of Depression in France, 1932–1936.* Cambridge: Cambridge University Press, 1985.

———. *The Popular Front in France: Defending Democracy, 1934–38.* New York and Cambridge: Cambridge University Press, 1988.

———. *France: The Dark Years, 1940–1944.* Oxford: Oxford University Press, 2001.

Jacobson, David. *Rights across Borders: Immigration and the Decline of Citizenship.* Baltimore, MD: Johns Hopkins University Press, 1996.

Jankowski, Paul. *Communism and Collaboration: Simon Sabiani and Politics in Marseille, 1919–1944.* New Haven, CT, and London: Yale University Press, 1989.

———. *Stavisky: A Confidence Man in the Republic of Virtue.* Ithaca, NY: Cornell University Press, 2002.

Jolly, Jean, ed. *Dictionnaire des parlementaires Français: Notices biographiques sur les ministres, sénateurs et députés Français de 1889 à 1940.* Paris: Presses Universitaires de France, 1960–77.

Joppke, Christian, ed. *Challenge to the Nation-State: Immigration in Western Europe and the United States.* New York and Oxford: Oxford University Press, 1998.

———. *Immigration and the Nation-State: The United States, Germany, and Great Britain.* Oxford: Oxford University Press, 1999.

———. "Citizenship between De- and Re-ethnicization." *Archives Européennes de Sociologie* 44, 3 (2003): 429–57.

———. *Selecting by Origin: Ethnic Migration in the Liberal State.* Cambridge, MA: Harvard University Press, 2005.

Joppke, Christian, and Steven Lukes, eds. *Multicultural Questions.* Oxford: Oxford University Press, 1999.

Joppke, Christian, and Elia Marzal. "Courts, the New Constitutionalism and Immigrant Rights: The Case of the French *Conseil Constitutionnel.*" *European Journal of Political Research* 43, 6 (October 2004): 823–44.

Joppke, Christian, and Ewa Morawska, eds. *Toward Assimilation and Citizenship: Immigrants in Liberal Nation-States.* London and New York: Palgrave Macmillan, 2003.

Julien, Charles-André. *Histoire de l'Algérie contemporaine.* Vol. 1, *La conquête et les débuts de la colonisation (1827–1871).* Paris: Presses Universitaires de France, 1964.

Kaplan, Marion A. *Between Dignity and Despair: Jewish Life in Nazi Germany.* New York and Oxford: Oxford University Press, 1998.

Kemp, Tom. *The French Economy, 1913–39: The History of a Decline.* London: Longman, 1972.

Kerber, Linda. "The Meanings of Citizenship." *Journal of American History* 84 (December 1997): 833–54.

Kessler-Harris, Alice. *In Pursuit of Equity: Women, Men and the Quest for Economic Citizenship in 20th-Century America.* Oxford and New York: Oxford University Press, 2001.

Kévonian, Dzovinar. "Les réfugiés de la paix. La question des réfugiés au début du XXe siècle." *Matériaux pour l'histoire de notre temps* 36 (October–December 1994): 2–10.

Keynes, John Maynard. *General Theory of Employment, Interest and Money.* New York: Harcourt, Brace, 1936.

Khagram, Sanjeev, and Peggy Levitt. "Constructing Transnational Studies." John F. Kennedy School of Government, Hauser Center for Nonprofit Organizations Working Paper No. 24, April 2004. http://ssrn.com/abstract=556993.

Kingsley, J. Donald. "The Execution of Policy." In *Reader in Bureaucracy,* edited by Robert K. Merton, Ailsa P. Gray, Barbara Hockey, and Hanan C. Selvin. New York: Free Press; London: Collier-Macmillan, 1952.

Kitson, Simon Keith Andrew. "The Marseille Police in Their Context, from Popular Front to Liberation." DPhil thesis, Sussex University, 1995.

Knibiehler, Yvonne, Catherine Marand-Fouquet, Régine Goutalier, and Éliane Richard, eds. *Marseillaises: Les femmes et la ville.* Paris: Côté-Femmes, 1993.

Kriegel, Annie. *La croissance de la C.G.T., 1918–1921: Essai statistique.* Paris: Mouton, 1966.

———. *La grève des cheminots 1920.* Paris: Armand Colin, 1988.

Kuisel, Richard. *Capitalism and the State in Modern France: Renovation and Economic Management in the Twentieth Century.* Cambridge and New York: Cambridge University Press, 1981.

Kymlica, Will, and Wayne Norton. "Return of the Citizen: Recent Work on Citizenship Theory." *Ethics* 104, 2 (January 1994): 352–81.

Lacouture, Jean. *Léon Blum.* 1977. Paris: Éditions du Seuil, 2000.

Laferrère, Michel. *Lyon, ville industrielle.* Paris: Presses Universitaires de France, 1960.

Lambert, Olivier. *Marseille entre tradition et modernité: Les expériences déçues (1919–1939).* Marseille: Chambre de Commerce et d'Industrie Marseille-Provence, 1995.

Larmour, Peter J. *The French Radical Party in the 1930's.* Stanford, CA: Stanford University Press, 1964.

Lebovics, Herman. *True France: The Wars over Cultural Identity, 1900–1945.* Ithaca, NY, and London: Cornell University Press, 1992.

——. *Bringing the Empire Back Home: France in the Global Age.* Durham, NC: Duke University Press, 2004.

Le Bras, Hervé. *Marianne et les lapins: L'obsession démographique.* Paris: Olivier Orban, 1991.

Le Bras, Hervé, ed., with Sandrine Bertaux. *L'invention des populations: Biologie, idéologie et politique.* Paris: Odile Jacob, 2000.

Le Clère, Marcel. "La direction de la Sûreté Générale sous la IIIe République." In *Les directeurs de ministère en France (XIXe–XXe siècles),* edited by Francis de Baecque. Geneva: Librairie Droz, 1976.

Lees, Lynn Hollen. *The Solidarities of Strangers: The English Poor Laws and the People, 1700–1948.* Cambridge and New York: Cambridge University Press, 1998.

Lefebvre, Henri. *The Production of Space.* 1974. Translated by Donald Nicholson-Smith. Oxford: Oxford Univeristy Press, 1991.

Legrand, Christian. *Le logement populaire et social en Lyonnais, 1848–2000.* Lyon: Editions aux Arts, 2002.

Le Guillou, Olivier. "L'émigration russe en France, Boulogne-Billancourt et les usines Renault: Lieux d'habitation et emplois des émigrés russes dans l'entre-deux-guerres." In *Construction des nationalités et immigration dans la France contemporaine,* edited by Gérard Noiriel and Éric Guichard. Paris: Presses de l'École Normale Supérieure, 1997.

Lemire, Vincent, and Stéphanie Samson, eds. *Baraques: L'album photographique du dispensaire la Mouche-Gerland, 1929–1936.* Lyon and Cognac: ENS-Éditions Le temps qu'il fait, 2003.

Lepetit, Bernard, ed. *Les formes de l'expérience: Une autre histoire sociale.* Albin Michel, 1995.

Lequin, Yves. *Les ouvriers de la région lyonnaise (1848–1914).* Lyon: Presses Universitaires de Lyon, n.d. [1977].

——. "Compte rendu de fin d'étude d'une recherche sur structures sociales et représentations collectives: Quatre communautés ouvrières de la second industrialisation." *Bulletin du Centre d'Histoire Économique et Sociale de la Région Lyonnaise* 4 (1980): 1–28.

——. "Social Structures and Shared Beliefs: Four Worker Communities in the 'Second Industrialization.'" *International Labor and Working-Class History* 22 (Fall 1982): 1–17.

——, ed. *La mosaïque France: Histoire des étrangers et de l'immigration.* Preface by Pierre Goubert. Paris: Larousse, 1988.

——. "Une grande ville industrielle." In *Atlas historique des villes de France,* edited by Jean-Luc Pinol. Paris: Hachette, 1996.

Levy, David A. L. "The Marseilles Working-Class Movement, 1936–1938." DPhil thesis, Oxford University, 1982.

——. "From Clientelism to Communism: The Marseille Working Class and the Popular Front." In *The French and Spanish Popular Fronts: Comparative Perspectives,* edited by Martin S. Alexander and Helen Graham. Cambridge and New York: Cambridge University Press, 1989.

Lewis, Martin Deming. "One Hundred Million Frenchmen: The Assimilationist

Theory in French Colonial Policy." *Comparative Studies in Society and History* 4, 2 (1962): 129–53.

Lewis, Mary Dewhurst. "The Company of Strangers: Immigration and Citizenship in Interwar Lyon and Marseille." PhD diss., New York University, 2000.

———. "Une théorie raciale des valeurs? Démobilisation des travailleurs immigrés et mobilisation des steréotypes à la fin de la Grande Guerre." Translated by Sandrine Bertaux. In *L'invention des populations: Biologie, idéologie et politique*, edited by Hervé Le Bras with Sandrine Bertaux. Paris: Odile Jacob, 2000.

———. "The Strangeness of Foreigners: Policing Migration and Nation in Interwar Marseille." In *Race in France: Interdisciplinary Perspectives on the Politics of Difference*, edited by Herrick Chapman and Laura Frader. New York and London: Berghahn Books, 2004.

———. "Les pratiques d'expulsion dans le Rhône durant la crise." In *Le bon grain et l'ivraie: La sélection des migrants en occident, 1880–1939*, edited by Philippe Rygiel. 2d Ed. Paris: Éditions Aux lieux d'être, 2006.

Linebaugh, Peter. *The London Hanged: Crime and Civil Society in the 18th Century*. London: Allen Lane, 1991.

Lipsky, Michael. *Street-Level Bureaucracy: Dilemmas of the Individual in Public Services*. New York: Russell Sage Foundation, 1980.

Livian, Marcel. *Le parti socialiste et l'immigration. Le gouvernement Léon Blum, la main-d'oeuvre et les refugiés politiques (1920–1940)*. Preface by Jules Moch. Postface by Édouard Depreux. Paris: Éditions Anthropos, 1982.

Lochak, Danièle. *Étrangers, de quel droit?* Paris: Presses Universitaires de France, 1985.

Lopez, Renée, and Émile Temime. *Migrance: Histoire des Migrations à Marseille*. Vol. 2, *L'expansion marseillaise et l'invasion italienne (1830–1918)*. La Calade, France: Édisud, 1990.

Lyons, Amelia. "Invisible Immigrants: Algerian Families and the French Welfare State in the Era of Decolonization (1947–1974)." PhD diss., UC Irvine, 2004.

MacMaster, Neil. *Colonial Migrants and Racism. Algerians in France, 1900–1962*. New York: St. Martin's Press, 1997.

Maga, Timothy P. "Closing the Door: The French Government and Refugee Policy, 1933–1939." *French Historical Studies* 12, 3 (Spring 1982): 424–42.

———. *America, France and the European Refugee Problem*. New York and London: Garland Publishing, 1985.

Maitron, Jean, ed. *Dictionnaire biographique du mouvement ouvrier français*. Quatrième Période, Vols. 16–43, *De la première à la seconde guerre mondiale, 1914–1939*. Paris: Les Éditions Ouvrières, 1964–97.

Mandel, Maud S. *In the Aftermath of Genocide: Armenians and Jews in Twentieth-Century France*. Durham, NC: Duke University Press, 2003.

Manela, Erez. "Wilsonian Moment: Self Determination and the International Origins of Anticolonial Nationalism, 1917–1920." PhD diss., Yale University, 2003.

Marrus, Michael. "Vichy avant Vichy." *H-Histoire*. Special issue no. 3, "Les Juifs en France" (November 1979): 77–92.

————. *The Unwanted: European Refugees in the Twentieth Century.* New York: Oxford University Press, 1985.

Marrus, Michael R., and Anna C. Bramwell, eds. *Refugees in the Age of Total War.* London: Unwin Hyman, 1988.

Marrus, Michael R., and Robert O. Paxton. *Vichy France and the Jews.* New York: Basic Books, 1981.

Marshall, T. H. "Citizenship and Social Class." Lecture given in honor of Alfred Marshall, Cambridge, England, 1949. In T. H. Marshall and Tom Bottomore, *Citizenship and Social Class.* London: Pluto Press, 1992.

Martin, Philip L. "Germany: Reluctant Land of Immigration." In *Controlling Immigration: A Global Perspective,* edited by Wayne A. Cornelius, Philip L. Martin, and James F. Hollifield. Stanford, CA: Stanford University Press, 1994.

Massard-Guilbaud, Geneviève. *Des Algériens à Lyon, de la Grande Guerre au Front Populaire.* Paris: L'Harmattan, 1995.

Math, Antoine. "Les allocations familiales et l'Algérie coloniale: A l'origine du FAS et de son financement par les regimes de prestations familiales." *Recherches et prévisions* 53 (1998): 35–44.

Matsuda, Matt K. "Doctor, Judge, Vagabond: Identity, Identification, and Other Memories of the State." *History and Memory* 6, 1 (1994): 73–94.

Mazower, Mark, ed. *The Policing of Politics in the Twentieth Century.* Providence, RI, and Oxford: Berghahn Books, 1997.

————. *Dark Continent: Europe's Twentieth Century.* New York: Knopf, 1999.

Memmi, Albert. *The Colonizer and the Colonized.* Introduction by Jean-Paul Sartre. Translated by Howard Greenfeld. N.p.: Orion Press, 1965; reprint, Boston: Beacon Press, 1967.

Meniri, Hocine. "Les immigrés dans la commune de Vénissieux." Mémoire de maîtrise, Université de Lyon II, 1978–79.

Merriman, John. *The Margins of City Life: Explorations on the French Urban Frontier.* New York: Oxford University Press, 1991.

Meynier, Gilbert. *L'Algérie révélée: La guerre de 1914–1918 et le premier quart du XXe siècle.* Preface by Pierre Vidal-Naquet. Geneva: Librairie Droz, 1981.

Miller, Michael B. *Shanghai on the Metro: Spies, Intrigue, and the French between the Wars.* Berkeley: University of California Press, 1994.

Milza, Pierre, ed. *Les Italiens en France de 1914 à 1940.* N.p.: Collection de l'École Française de Rome 94, 1986.

————. *Voyage en Ritalie.* Paris: Librairie Plon, 1993.

Milza, Pierre, and Denis Peschanski, eds. *Exils et migration: Italiens et Espagnols en France, 1938–1946.* Paris: L'Harmattan, 1994.

Ministère de la Justice. *La nationalité Française: Recueil des textes législatifs et réglementaires, des conventions internationales et autres documents.* Paris: La Documentation Française, 2002.

Mioche, Philippe. *L'alumnie à Gardanne de 1893 à nos jours: Une traversée industrielle en Provence.* Grenoble: Presses Universitaires de Grenoble, 1994.

Moch, Leslie Page. *Paths to the City: Regional Migration in 19th C. France.* Beverly Hills, CA: Sage Publications, 1983.

Montand, Yves, with Hervé Hamon and Patrick Rotman. *You See, I Haven't Forgotten.* Translated by Jeremy Leggatt. London: Chatto and Windus, 1992.

Morris, Lydia. *Managing Migration: Civic Stratification and Migrants' Rights.* London and New York: Routledge, 2002.

Murracciole, L. *L'émigration algérienne: Aspects économiques, sociaux et juridiques.* Bibliothèque de la Faculté de Droit de l'Université d'Alger. Vol. 6. Algiers: Librairie Ferraris, 1950.

Navel, Georges. *Travaux.* Paris: Plon, 1945.

———. *Passages.* Paris: Le Sycamore, 1982.

Ngai, Mae. *Impossible Subjects: Illegal Aliens and the Making of Modern America.* Princeton, NJ: Princeton University Press, 2004.

Noiriel, Gérard. *Longwy: Immigrés et prolétaires: 1880–1980.* Paris: Presses Universitaires de France, 1984.

———. *Les ouvriers dans la société française XIXe–XXe siècle.* Paris: Éditions du Seuil, 1986.

———. *Le creuset français: Histoire de l'immigration XIXe–XXe siècle.* Paris: Éditions du Seuil, 1988.

———. *La tyrannie du national: Le droit d'asile en Europe, 1793–1993.* Paris: Calmann-Lévy, 1991.

———. "Immigration: Amnesia and Memory." *French Historical Studies* 19, 2 (1995): 367–80.

———. *The French Melting Pot: Immigration, Citizenship and National Identity.* Translation of *Creuset Français* by Geoffroy de Laforcade. With a foreword by Charles Tilly. Minneapolis: University of Minnesota Press, 1996.

———. *Les origines républicaines de Vichy.* Paris: Hachettes Litératures, 1999.

Nora, Pierre. *Les lieux de mémoire.* 3 vols. Paris: Gallimard, 1984–92.

Nord, Philip. *Paris Shopkeepers and the Politics of Resentment.* Princeton, NJ: Princeton University Press, 1986.

———. *The Republican Moment: The Struggle for Democracy in 19th-Century France.* Cambridge, MA: Harvard University Press, 1995.

Nouschi, André. "La politique coloniale du Front Populaire: Le Maghreb." *Les cahiers de Tunisie* 27, 109–10 (1979): 143–60.

Offen, Karen. "Depopulation, Nationalism and Feminism in Fin-de-Siècle France." *American Historical Review* 89, 3 (June 1984): 648–76.

Ogden, Philip E., and Marie-Monique Huss. "Demography and Pronatalism in France in the Nineteenth and Twentieth Centuries." *Journal of Historical Geography* 8, 3 (1982): 283–98.

Pacini, Alfred, and Dominique Pons. *Docker à Marseille.* Paris: Éditions Payot & Rivages, 1996.

Papy, Michel, ed. *Barthou, un homme, une époque. Actes du colloque de Pau 9 et 10 Nov 1984.* Pau: J&D Editions, 1986.

Passmore, Kevin. *From Liberalism to Fascism: The Right in a French Province, 1928–1939.* New York: Cambridge University Press, 1997.

Paul, Kathleen. *Whitewashing Britain: Race and Citizenship in the Postwar Era.* Ithaca, NY, and London: Cornell University Press, 1997.

Paxton, Robert O. *Vichy France: Old Guard and New Order 1940–1944*. New York: Knopf, 1972.

———. *Europe in the Twentieth Century*. 3rd ed. New York: Harcourt Brace College Publishers, 1997.

———. "Gérard Noiriel's Third Republic." *French Politics, Culture and Society* 18, 2 (Summer 2000): 99–103.

Pedersen, Susan. *Family, Dependence, and the Origins of the Welfare State: Britain and France 1914–1945*. Cambridge: Cambridge University Press, 1993.

Peer, Shanny. *France on Display: Peasants, Provincials and Folklore in the 1937 Paris World's Fair*. SUNY Series in National Identities. Albany: State University of New York Press, 1998.

Perrot, Michelle. "Les rapports des ouvriers français et des ouvriers étrangers, 1871–93." *Société d'histoire moderne et contemporaine* 58, 12 (1960): 4–9.

———. *Les ombres de l'histoire: Crime et châtiment au XIXe siècle*. Paris: Flammarion, 2001.

Persell, Stuart Michael. *The French Colonial Lobby, 1889–1938*. Stanford, CA: Hoover Institution Press, 1983.

Peschanski, Denis. *La France des camps: L'internement, 1938–1946*. Paris: Gallimard, 2002.

Peyrenet, Marcel. *La dynastie des Gillet: Les maîtres de Rhône-Poulenc*. Paris: Le Sycomore, 1978.

Pierrein, L. *Industries traditionnelles du port de Marseille. Le cycle des sucres et des oléagineux, 1870–1958*. Marseille: Institut Historique de Provence, 1975.

Pinol, Jean-Luc. *Espace social et espace politique: Lyon à l'époque du Front Populaire*. Lyon: Presses Universitaires de Lyon, 1980.

———. *Les mobilités de la grande ville. Lyon fin XIXe–début XXe*. Paris: Presses de la Fondation Nationale des Sciences Politiques, 1991.

———, ed. *Atlas historique des villes de France*. Paris: Hachette, 1996.

Piore, Michael. "Dualism in the Labor Market: A Response to Uncertainty and Flux—The Case of France." *Revue économique* 1 (January 1978): 26–48.

———. *Birds of Passage: Migrant Labor and Industrial Societies*. New York and Cambridge: Cambridge University Press, 1979.

Polanyi, Karl. *The Great Transformation*. 1944. Boston: Beacon Press, 1960.

Ponty, Janine. *Polonais méconnus: Histoire des travailleurs immigrés en France dans l'entre-deux-guerres*. Paris: Publications de la Sorbonne, 1988.

Prost, Antoine. "L'immigration en France depuis cent ans." *Esprit* 34e année, 348 (April 1966): 532–45.

———. "Les manifestations du 12 février 1934 en province." *Le mouvement social* 54 (1966): 7–28.

———. "Les grèves de Mai–Juin 1936 revisitées." *Le mouvement social* 200 (2002): 33–54.

Radcliff, Pamela Beth. *From Mobilization to Civil War: The Politics of Polarization in the Spanish City of Gijón, 1900–1937*. Cambridge: Cambridge University Press, 1996.

Renaut, Marie-Hélène. "Vagabondage et mendicité: Délits périmés, réalité quotidienne." *Revue historique* 606 (April–June 1998): 287–322.

Rist, Ray C. "Migration and Marginality: Guestworkers in Germany and France." *Daedalus* (1979): 95–108.

Rivet, Daniel. *Le Maghreb à l'épreuve de la colonisation.* Paris: Hachette Litéra-tures, 2002.

Roberts, Mary Louise. *Civilization without Sexes: Reconstructing Gender in Postwar France, 1917–1927.* Chicago and London: University of Chicago Press, 1994.

Rogers, Susan Carol. *Shaping Modern Times in Rural France: The Transforma-tion and Reproduction of an Aveyronnais Community.* Princeton, NJ: Prince-ton University Press, 1991.

Roncayolo, Marcel. *Les grammaires d'une ville: Essai sur la genèse des structures urbaines à Marseille.* Collection Civilisations et Sociétés 92. Paris: Éditions de l'École des Hautes Études en Sciences Sociales, 1996.

Roncayolo, Marcel, and Antoine Olivesi. "Pouvoirs et politiques." In *Atlas his-torique des villes de France,* edited by Jean-Luc Pinol. Paris: Hachette, 1996.

Rosenberg, Clifford. "The Colonial Politics of Healthcare Provision in Interwar Paris." *French Historical Studies* 27, 3 (Summer 2004): 637–68.

———. *Policing Paris: The Origins of Modern Immigration Control between the Wars.* Ithaca, NY, and London: Cornell University Press, 2006.

Rosental, Paul-André. "Maintien/rupture: Un nouveau couple pour l'analyse des migrations." *Annales* 45, 6 (November–December 1990): 1403–31.

———. *Les sentiers invisibles: Espace, familles et migrations dans la France du 19e siècle.* Paris: Editions de l'École des Hautes Études en Sciences Sociales, 1999.

Rossiter, Adrian. "Popular Front Economic Policy and the Matignon Negotia-tions." *Historical Journal* 30, 3 (1987): 663–84.

Rousso, Henry. *The Vichy Syndrome: History and Memory in France since 1944.* Translated by Arthur Goldhammer. Cambridge, MA: Harvard University Press, 1991.

Ruedy, John. *Modern Algeria: The Origins and Development of a Nation.* Bloomington: Indiana University Press, 1992.

Ryan, Donna F. *The Holocaust and the Jews of Marseille.* Urbana and Chicago: University of Illinois Press, 1996.

Rygiel, Philippe. *Destins immigrés, Cher 1920–1980: Trajéctoires d'immigrés d'Europe.* Besançon: Annales Littéraires de l'Université de Franche-Comté, 2001.

———, ed. *Le bon grain et l'ivraie: La sélection des migrants en occident, 1880–1939.* 2d Ed. Paris: Éditions Aux lieux d'être, 2006.

Saada, Emmanuelle. "La 'question des métis' dans les colonies françaises. Socio-histoire d'une catégorie juridique (Indochine et autres territoires de l'empire français; années 1890–années 1950)." PhD diss., École des Hautes Études en Sciences Sociales, 2001.

———. "The Empire of Law: Dignity, Prestige and Domination in the 'Colonial Situation.'" *French Politics, Culture and Society* 20, 2 (Summer 2002): 98–120.

———. "Citoyens et sujets de l'empire français. Les usages du droit en situation coloniale." *Genèses* 53 (December 2003): 4–24.

Sahlins, Peter. *Boundaries: The Making of France and Spain in the Pyrenees.* Berkeley: University of California Press, 1989.

———. *Unnaturally French: Foreign Citizens in the Old Regime and After.* Ithaca, NY, and London: Cornell University Press, 2004.

Saint-Exupéry, Antoine de. *The Little Prince.* Translated by Richard Howard. New York: Harvest Books of Harcourt, 2000.

Salais, Robert, Nicolas Baverez, and Bénédicte Reynaud. *L'invention du chômage: Histoire et transformations d'une catégorie en France des années 1890 aux années 1980.* Paris: Presses Universitaires de France, 1986.

Sassen, Saskia. *Guests and Aliens.* New York: New Press, 1999.

Sauvy, Alfred. *Histoire économique de la France entre les deux guerres.* 3 vols. Paris: Economica, 1984.

Sayad, Abdelmalek. "Les trois 'âges' de l'immigration algérienne." *Actes de la recherche en sciences sociales* 15 (June 1977): 59–79.

———. "Qu'est-ce qu'un immigré?" *Peuples Méditerranéens/Mediterranean Peoples* 7 (April–June 1979): 3–23.

———. "Immigration et conventions internationales." *Peuples Méditerranéens/ Mediterranean Peoples* 9 (October–December 1979): 29–49.

———. "Immigration et naturalisation." In *La citoyenneté et les changements de structures sociale et nationale de la population française,* compiled by Catherine Wihtol de Wenden. Paris: Edilig/Fondation Diderot, 1988.

———. "Naturels et naturalisés." *Actes de la recherche en sciences sociales* 99 (September 1993): 26–35.

———. *The Suffering of the Immigrant.* Translated by David Macey. Malden and Cambridge, MA: Polity Press, 2004.

Schain, Martin A. "Immigrants and Politics in France." In *The French Socialist Experiment,* edited by John S. Ambler. Philadelphia, PA: Institute for the Study of Human Issues, 1985.

———. "Immigration and Trade Unions in France: A Problem and an Opportunity." In *A Century of Organized Labor in France,* edited by Herrick Chapman, Mark Kesselman, and Martin Schain. New York: St. Martin's Press, 1998.

———. "Minorities and Immigrant Incorporation in France: The State and the Dynamics of Multiculturalism." In *Multicultural Questions,* edited by Christian Joppke and Steven Lukes. Oxford: Oxford University Press, 1999.

Schnapper, Dominique. *La France de l'intégration: Sociologie de la nation en 1990.* Paris: Éditions Gallimard, 1991.

Schneider, William. *Quality and Quantity: The Quest for Biological Regeneration in Twentieth-Century France.* Cambridge: Cambridge University Press, 1990.

Schor, Ralph. *L'opinion française et les étrangers, 1919–1939.* Paris: Publications de la Sorbonne, 1985.

———. *Histoire de l'immigration en France de la fin du XIXe siècle à nos jours.* Paris: Armand Colin/Masson, 1996.

Scott, James. *Seeing Like a State. How Certain Schemes to Improve the Human Condition Have Failed.* New Haven, CT, and London: Yale University Press, 1998.

Scott, Joan Wallach. "The Evidence of Experience." *Critical Inquiry* 17, 4 (Summer 1991): 773–97.
———. *Only Paradoxes to Offer: French Feminists and the Rights of Man.* Cambridge, MA: Harvard University Press, 1996.
———. *Parité! Sexual Equality and the Crisis of French Universalism.* Chicago: University of Chicago Press, 2005.
Sewell, William H., Jr. *Structure and Mobility: The Men and Women of Marseille, 1820–1870.* Cambridge: Cambridge University Press, 1985.
———. "A Theory of Structure: Duality, Agency, and Transformation." *American Journal of Sociology* 98, 1 (July 1992): 1–29.
Shepard, Todd. *The Invention of Decolonization: The Algerian War and the Remaking of France.* Ithaca, NY: Cornell University Press, 2006.
Shorrock, William. "The Tunisian Question in French Policy toward Italy, 1881–1940." *International Journal of African Historical Studies* 16, 4 (1983): 631–51.
Silberman, Bernard S. *Cages of Reason: The Rise of the Rational State in France, Japan, the United States and Great Britain.* Chicago and London: University of Chicago Press, 1993.
Silverman, Maxim. *Deconstructing the Nation: Immigration, Racism and Citizenship in Modern France.* London and New York: Routledge, 1992.
Sirot, Stéphane. "Les conditions de travail et les grèves des ouvriers coloniaux à Paris des lendemains de la première guerre mondiale à la veille du Front Populaire." *Revue française d'histoire d'outre-mer* 83, 2 (1996): 65–92.
Skran, Claudena M. *Refugees in Inter-war Europe: The Emergence of a Regime.* New York: Oxford University Press, 1995.
Slaby, Philip. "Industry, the State, and Immigrant Poles in Industrial France, 1919–1939." PhD diss., Brandeis University, 2005.
Smail, Daniel Lord. "Introduction." In *Imaginary Cartographies: Possession and Identity in Late Medieval Marseille.* Ithaca, NY, and London: Cornell University Press, 1999.
Smith, Paul. *Feminism and the Third Republic: Women's Political and Civil Rights in France, 1918–1945.* Oxford: Clarendon Press, 1996.
Smith, Timothy. "Assistance and Repression: Rural Exodus, Vagabondage and Social Crisis in France, 1880–1914." *Journal of Social History* 32, 4 (1999): 821–46.
———. *Creating the Welfare State in France, 1880–1940.* Montreal and Kingston: McGill-Queen's University Press, 2003.
Soucy, Robert. "Centrist Fascism: The Jeunesses Patriotes." *Journal of Contemporary History* 16, 2 (April 1981): 349–68.
Soysal, Yasemin Nuhoğlu. *Limits of Citizenship: Migrants and Postnational Membership in Europe.* Chicago and London: University of Chicago Press, 1994.
Spire, Aléxis. "Semblables et pourtant différents. La citoyenneté paradoxale des 'Français musulmans d'Algérie' en métropole." *Genèses* 53 (December 2003): 48–68.
———. *Étrangers à la carte: L'administration de l'immigration en France (1945–1975).* Paris: Grasset, 2005.

Stein, Louis. *Beyond Death and Exile. The Spanish Republicans in France, 1939–1955.* Cambridge, MA, and London: Harvard University Press, 1979.

Stoler, Ann Laura. "Sexual Affronts and Racial Frontiers: European Identities and the Cultural Politics of Exclusion in Colonial Southeast Asia." *Comparative Studies in Society and History* 34, 3 (1992): 514–51.

Stora, Benjamin. "Avant la deuxième génération: Le militantisme algérien en France (1926–1954)." *Revue européenne des migrations internationales* 1, 2 (1985): 69–91.

———. *Messali Hadj: Pionner du nationalisme algérien (1898–1974).* Paris: Éditions L'Harmattan, 1986.

———. *Ils venaient d'Algérie: L'immigration algérienne en France (1912–1992).* Paris: Fayard, 1992.

———. *Histoire de l'Algérie coloniale (1830–1954).* Paris: Éditions La Découverte, 1994.

Stovall, Tyler. *The Rise of the Paris Red Belt.* Berkeley: University of California Press, 1990.

———. "Colour-blind France? Colonial Workers during the First World War." *Race and Class* 35, 2 (1993): 35–55.

———. "The Color Line behind the Lines: Racial Violence in France during the Great War." *American Historical Review* 103, 3 (June 1998): 737–69.

Sugier, Fabrice. "Les mines du Gard, 1938–1940." In *Exils et migration: Italiens et Espagnols en France,* edited by Pierre Milza and Denis Peschanski. Paris: L'Harmattan, 1994.

Suleiman, Ezra. *Private Power and Centralization in France: The Notaires and the State.* Princeton, NJ: Princeton University Press, 1987.

Tabili, Laura. *"We Ask for British Justice": Workers and Racial Difference in Late Imperial Britain.* Ithaca, NY: Cornell University Press, 1994.

Taguieff, Pierre-André. "The Doctrine of the National Front in France (1972–1989)." *New Political Science* 16/17 (Fall/Winter 1989): 29–70.

———. "Face a l'immigration: Mixophobie, xenophobie ou sélection. Un débat Français dans l'entre-deux-guerres." *Vingtieme siècle* 47 (July–September 1995): 103–31.

Talha, Larbi. "Espace migratoire et espace national: Opposition et convergence." In *Les Algériens en France (Genèse et devenir d'une migration).* Jacqueline Costa-Lascoux et Émile Temime, coordonnateurs. N.p.: Publisud, 1985.

———. *Le salariat immigré dans la crise: La main-d'oeuvre magrhébine en France (1921–1987).* Paris: Éditions du Centre National de la Recherche Scientifique, 1989.

———, ed. "Maghrébins en France. Emigrés ou immigrés?" In *L'annuaire de l'Afrique du Nord.* 1981. Paris: Éditions du Centre National de la Recherche Scientifique, 1983.

Tapinos, Georges. "Questioning the Hidden Consensus." In *Controlling Immigration: A Global Perspective,* edited by Wayne A. Cornelius, Philip L. Martin, and James F. Hollifield. Stanford, CA: Stanford University Press, 1994.

Tartakowsky, Danielle. "Stratégies de la rue, 1934–1936." *Le mouvement social* 135 (April–June 1986): 31–62.

Temime, Émile. "L'évolution du tissu industriel marseillais." *Marseille, revue municipale* 164 (August 1992): 70–73.

———. *Marseille transit: Les passagers de Belsunce.* Paris: Éditions Autrement, 1995.

———. *France, terre d'immigration.* Paris: Gallimard, 1999.

———. *Histoire de Marseille de la Révolution à nos jours.* Paris: Librairie Académique Perrin, 1999.

Temime, Émile, and Marie-Francoise Attard-Maraninchi. *Migrance: Histoire des migrations à Marseille.* Vol. 3, *Le cosmopolitisme de l'entre-deux-guerres (1919–1945).* Aix-en-Provence, France: Edisud, 1990.

Tévanian, Pierre. *Le voile médiatique: Un faux débat, l'affaire du foulard islamique.* Paris: Raisons d'Agir, 2005.

Thalmann, Rita. "L'immigration allemande et l'opinion publique en France de 1933 à 1936." In *La France et l'Allemagne: 1932–1936: Communications présentées au colloque franco-allemand tenu à Paris du 10 au 12 mars 1977.* Paris: Éditions du Centre National de la Recherche Scientifique, 1980.

———. "L'émigration allemande et l'opinion publique française de 1936 à 1939." In *Deustchland und Frankreich, 1936–1939: Deutsch-Französisches Historikerkolloquim des Deutschen Historischen Instituts Paris (Bonn, 26–29. September 1979.* Munich: Artemis, 1981.

———. "Jewish Women Exiled in France after 1933." In *Between Sorrow and Strength: Women Refugees of the Nazi Period,* edited by Sibylle Quack. Washington, DC, and Cambridge: German Historical Institute and Cambridge University Press, 1995.

Thompson, E. P. *Whigs and Hunters: The Origins of the Black Act.* Harmondsworth: Penguin, 1977.

Thompson, Elizabeth. *Colonial Citizens: Republican Rights, Paternal Privilege and Gender in French Syria and Lebanon.* New York: Columbia University Press, 2000.

Tilly, Charles. "Citizenship, Identity and Social History." *International Review of Social History* 40, Suppl. no. 3 (1995): 1–17.

———. "A Primer on Citizenship." *Theory and Society* 26, 4 (August 1997): 599–602.

———. "Where Do Rights Come From?" In *Democracy, Revolution, and History,* edited by Theda Skocpol. Ithaca and London: Cornell University Press, 1998.

Tocqueville, Alexis de. *Democracy in America (1835–1840).* Translated by Arthur Goldhammer. New York: Library of America, 2004.

Todd, Emmanuel. *Le destin des immigrés: Assimilation et ségrégation dans les démocraties occidentales.* Series L'histoire immédiate. Paris: Éditions du Seuil, 1994.

Topalov, Christian. *Naissance du chômeur: 1880–1910.* Paris: Albin Michel, 1994.

Topalov, Christian, and Susanna Magri, eds. *Villes ouvrières: 1900–1950.* Paris: L'Harmattan, 1989.

Torpey, John. *The Invention of the Passport: Surveillance, Citizenship and the State.* Cambridge Studies in Law and Society. Cambridge: Cambridge University Press, 2000.

Tribalat, Michèle. *Faire France: Une grande enquête sur les immigrés et leurs enfants*. Preface by Marceau Long. Paris: Éditions la Découverte, 1995.

Tripier, Maryse. "Les conséquences sociales de la crise: La France au carrefour de plusieurs modèles." In *L'immigration au tournant: Actes du colloque du GRECO 13 sur les mutations économiques et les travailleurs immigrés dans les pays industriels,* under the direction of G. Abou-Sada, B. Courault, and Z. Zeroulou. Paris: CIEMI/L'Harmattan, 1990.

Valette, Jacques. *La France et l'Afrique. L'Afrique française du nord 1914–1962*. Paris: Sedes, 1993.

Veillon, Dominique. *Vivre et survivre en France 1939–1947*. Paris: Payot & Rivages, 1995.

Viala, Bernard. "Immigration algérienne en France et associations: Variations de sens, d'acteurs et de rapports sociaux." In *Les Algériens en France (Genèse et devenir d'une migration),* Jacqueline Costa-Lascoux et Émile Temime, coordonnateurs. N.p.: Publisud, 1985.

Viala, Bernard, and Bernard Panza. "L'immigration Nord-Africaine à Marseille." Memoire de maîtrise, Aix-en-Provence, France, 1976–77.

Videlier, Philippe. "Banlieue sud. Vénissieux entre les deux guerres." Thèse de 3e cycle. Universite de Lyon II, 1982.

———. "Les Italiens de la région lyonnaise." In *Les Italiens en France de 1914 à 1940,* edited by Pierre Milza. N.p.: Collection de l'École Française de Rome 94, 1986.

———. "Espace et temps de l'intégration des immigrés dans la région lyonnaise." In *Les étrangers dans la ville: Le regard des sciences sociales,* edited by Ida Simon-Barouh and Pierre-Jean Simon. Paris: L'Harmattan, 1990.

———. *Décines: Une ville, des vies*. Vénissieux, Rhône, France: Editions Paroles d'Aube, 1996.

Videlier, Philippe, and Bernard Bouhet. *Vénissieux de A à V, une banlieue à travers le miroir de l'informatique*. Lyon: Presses Universitaires de Lyon, 1983.

Viet, Vincent. *La France immigrée: Construction d'une politique 1914–1997*. Paris: Librairie Arthème Fayard, 1998.

"(Le) vieux port de Marseille à l'heure allemande." *L'histoire* 16 (October 1979): 115–22.

Vogel, Marie. "Politiques policières et systèmes locaux. Les polices des villes dans l'entre-deux-guerres." *Revue française de sociologie* 35, 3 (July–September 1994): 413–34.

Vormeier, Barbara. "La situation des réfugiés en provenance d'Allemagne (Septembre 1939–Juillet 1942). In *Zones d'ombres 1933–1944: Exil et internement d'Allemands et d'Autrichiens dans le sud-est de la France,* edited by Jacques Grandjonc and Theresia Grundtner. Aix-en-Provence, France: Éditions Alinea, 1990.

Wagniart, Jean-François. *Le vagabond à la fin du XIXe siècle*. Paris: Belin, 1999.

Walzer, Michael. *Spheres of Justice: A Defense of Pluralism and Equality*. Reprint, New York: Basic Books, 1984.

Weber, Eugen. *Peasants into Frenchmen: The Modernization of Rural France, 1870–1914*. Stanford, CA: Stanford University Press, 1976.

———. *The Hollow Years: France in the 1930s.* New York and London: Norton, 1994.

Weber, Max. *Economy and Society.* Vols. 1 and 2. Edited by Guenther Roth and Claus Wittich. Translated by Ephraim Fischoff et al. Berkeley: University of California Press, 1978.

Weil, Patrick. *La France et ses étrangers: L'aventure d'une politique de l'immigration, 1938–1991.* Paris: Calmann-Lévy, 1991.

———. "From Hidden Consensus to Hidden Divergence." In *Controlling Immigration: A Global Perspective,* edited by Wayne A. Cornelius, Philip L. Martin, and James F. Hollifield. Stanford, CA: Stanford University Press, 1994.

———. "Racisme et discrimination dans la politique française de l'immigration 1938–1945/1974–1995." *Vingtième siècle* 47 (1995): 77–102.

———. *Qu'est-ce qu'un Français? Histoire de la nationalité française depuis la Révolution.* Paris: Éditions Grasset & Fasquelle, 2002.

Weil, Patrick, and John Crowley. "Integration in Theory and Practice: A Comparison of France and Britain." *West European Politics* 17, 2 (April 1994): 110–17.

Wiener, Antje. "Making Sense of the New Geography of Citizenship: Fragmented Citizenship in the European Union." *Theory and Society* 26, 4 (August 1997): 529–60.

Wihtol de Wenden, Catherine. "Immigrants as Political Actors in France." *West European Politics* 17, 2 (April 1994): 91109.

Wilder, Gary. *The French Imperial Nation-State: Negritude and Colonial Humanism between the Two World Wars.* Chicago: University of Chicago Press, 2005.

Woloch, Isser. *The New Regime: Transformations of the French Civic Order, 1789–1820s.* New York and London: Norton, 1994.

Wright, Gordon. *Between the Guillotine and Liberty: Two Centuries of the Crime Problem in France.* New York and Oxford: Oxford University Press, 1983.

Zola, Émile. *Germinal.* 1885. Paris: Charpentier, 1888.

Index